Revolutionary Soldiers Buried In Indiana
(1949)

With Supplement
(1954)

Compiled by

Margaret R. Waters

WITH AN ADDED TABLE OF CONTENTS

Two Volumes in One

CLEARFIELD

Originally Published
Indianapolis, 1949, 1954

Reprinted with permission and an added Table of Contents
Genealogical Publishing Company
Baltimore, 1970

Reprinted for
Clearfield Company, Inc. by
Genealogical Publishing Co., Inc.
Baltimore, Maryland
1992, 1999

Library of Congress Catalogue Card Number 72-107084
International Standard Book Number: 0-8063-0385-9

Made in the United States of America

NOTICE

This work was reproduced by the photo-offset process from the original mimeographed edition. A characteristic of mimeographed copy—from which the offset printer must work—is that the copy is often very light and uneven, while at the same time over-inking may be present, such as, for example, when individual letters appear as a smear. Every effort has been made by our photo-offset printer to produce as fine a reprint of the original mimeographed edition as possible.

GENEALOGICAL PUBLISHING COMPANY

Table of Contents

Revolutionary Soldiers Buried in Indiana _____ 3

    Contents _____ vii

    Index _____ 41

Revolutionary Soldiers Buried in Indiana: A Supplement _____ 5

    Contents _____ iii

    Index _____ 155

NOTE: This is not intended to be a complete guide to the Contents of this work. The reader is advised to consult the Contents pages of each volume for more specific information.

REVOLUTIONARY SOLDIERS

BURIED IN INDIANA

300 Names Not Listed in the Roster of Soldiers and Patriots of the American Revolution Buried in Indiana

Margaret R. Waters

Indianapolis
1949

CONTENTS

Foreword   1

Alphabetical List of Soldiers   3

Soldiers Listed by Counties   39

Index   41

FOREWORD

In 1938 the Indiana Daughters of the American Revolution published the "Roster of Soldiers and Patriots of the American Revolution Buried in Indiana", edited by Mrs. Roscoe C. O'Byrne.

Since that time, I have been collecting names of Revolutionary soldiers who died, or were buried, in Indiana and whose names were not listed in the above book. This compilation is in no way intended as a supplement to the "Roster", which was sponsored by the State D.A.R. and entries in which are considered authentic proof for membership in the D.A.R.

The sole purpose of this compilation is to provide for descendants some helpful hints for their genealogical research. I do not guarantee the service of any soldier in my list, the burial place, nor the genealogical data. I have no doubt but that many of the data can be verified. Aside from the pension research mentioned below, I have made no effort to check the information given in the references. I do guarantee the accuracy of the references indicated and the pension abstracts which I have personally copied. All of my material has been gathered from public records open to anyone.

There are 300 names in this list. This summer, through the courtesy of Mr. Leavitt and the help of Mrs. Orrison, both of the National Archives in Washington, D.C., 984 pension files for these names were made available to me. For some names on my list, there were no files; for others, there were several for men of the same name. I think there were 27 John Williamses! For men whose given name I did not have, all the files for that surname were pulled for me to check. In abstracting the service records, I have given only one pair of officers (to provide a clue as to the locality in the state) as the service records are often very long. Full data can be obtained from the National Archives.

The main source of the names was the Veterans' Graves Registration --- an Indiana American Legion project which attempted to list the burial place of every veteran in Indiana from the Revolutionary War through World War I up to deaths in 1940. Of the 92 counties in Indiana, they completed 48. In my list of 300 names, 108 were taken from this source. The Legion information was obtained from field trips, soldiers' burial claims, sextons' lists, cemetery record books, county rosters, undertakers' records, flags, flag holders, government markers, stones inscribed "A Soldier", descendants, old residents, and present owners of farm cemeteries. They made plats for each cemetery; and where this had not been done before (as in the case of private burying grounds), they made an arbitrary plat.

The records are typed on thousands of 3 x 5 cards and are preserved in 90 file drawers in the Archives Division of the Indiana State Library along with the cemetery plats. Where the war was not given on the card, I did not include anyone born after 1765. Many cards bear the notation that government markers or flags were on the graves; but since no dates were given and no war was filled in, I did not copy these names --- some of whom were probably Revolutionary War soldiers.

Another source was a series of articles called "Builders of the Nation", written about Delaware Co., Ind., Revolutionary soldiers by A. L. Kerwood in the "Muncie Star" for about two months from May to July 1910. Some of these clippings (in the Genealogy Division of the Indiana State Library) have the date at the end; on others it has been cut off.

Other sources which I have used are the 50 volumes of the National Society, D.A.R., yearly reports to the Senate; county histories; and manuscripts and typescripts on file in the State Library, Genealogy Division. Personal friends have furnished several names, about six of which were received after my pension research in Washington this summer.

Of the 300 names, there is some uncertainty as to whether about 20 of them died in Indiana; but I have included them to provide a clue to further research.

Abbreviations (other than b., d., m., chn., etc.) are:

ae.	aged	loc.	located
affid.	affidavit	pens.	pension
Am. Leg.	American Legion	poss.	possibly
ante	before	post	after
appl.	application, applied	prob.	probably
Blk.	block	R.	rejected pension
BLW	bounty land warrant	S.	soldier's pension
ca.	about	Sec.	section
dis.	discharged	sold.	soldier
enl.	enlisted	SV	Sons of Veterans
gr.	grave	tr.	transfer(red)
ISL	Ind. State Library	ts	typescript
liv.	lived, living	W.	widow's pension

My gratitude for their assistance is expressed to Mr. Leavitt and Mrs. Orrison of the National Archives; Janye Pruitt, Fairfax, Va.; Margaret Pearson (Archives Division), Margarete Butz (Genealogy Division), Hazel Hopper and Edna Whetsell (Indiana Division), Caroline Dunn (Pioneer Society), and Dorothy Riker (Historical Society), all of the Indiana State Library; Thelma Murphy, Wallace Weatherholt, and Lewis Jones, all of Indianapolis; and to Katherine Wakefield Gilliatt, Franklin, Ind.

Margaret R. Waters
20 N. Bosart Avenue
November 15, 1949　　　　　　　　　　　　　Indianapolis 1, Ind.

ADDINGTON, JOHN Randolph Co.
d. 1819; bur. Ridgeville Cem. REF-DAR 28, p. 156.

AKERS, JOSEPH Floyd Co.
bur. Heil Cem., Floyd Knobs, Ind.; Gr. 2, Lot 2, Blk. 1, Sec.1.
Wife, Annie. Pvt. in Rev. REF-Am. Leg.

ALEXANDER, SAMUEL Owen Co.
bur. Old Union Cem., 2 mi. W of Gosport, Ind.; gr. loc. by
Spencer Chap., DAR. REF- DAR 2, p. 120.

AISMAN, ANDREW Sullivan Co.
b. 1748; d. 1858; bur. Paxton Cem. REF-"Rev. Sold. Bur. in
Sullivan Co."(State DAR ts in ISL.)

ANDERSON, PETER Posey Co.
b. 1748; d. 8-5-1845; bur. Mt. Pleasant Cem.; Gr. 3, Lot 39,
Row 8. REF-Am. Leg.

ANGEVIN, JAMES Dearborn Co.
bur. York Twp. REF-DAR 28, p. 156.

APPLEGATE, JOHN Clinton Co.
b. 1758(?); bur. Kirklin Cem., Frankfort, Ind. REF-DAR 28,p.156.

ARMSTRONG, AMBROSE Johnson Co.
b. 1759-1760; bur. Adams farm, Blue River Twp. Pens. appl. on
9-24-1832, ae. 72, Fayette Co., Ky., where had liv. more than 30
yr. Enl. Essex Co., Va., Capt. O.P. Davenport, Col. Porterfield.
REF-Pens. S.14921 Va.

ARMSTRONG, THOMAS Clark Co.
bur. at Springville. Capt. in Rev. REF-"Rev. Sold. Bur. in
Clark Co." (State DAR ts in ISL.)

BAKER, HENRY Monroe Co.
b. 1756; d. 5-22-1838; bur. Burch Cem.; Gr. 8, Lot 5, Row 7.
REF-Am. Leg.; Monroe Co. CAR Book, 1886, p. 51.

BARBER, PHILIP Harrison Co.
b. 1768-1769, Orange Co., Va.; d. 10-17-1818, in 49th yr.; bur.
in cem. at Corydon, Ind. Stone:"Sacred to the memory of Briga.
General Philip Barbour a native of Henderson County K who was
born in Orange County State of Virginia and departed this life
Oct the 17th 1818 at Corydon State of Indiana in the 49th year
of his age." Gr. loc. by Piankeshaw Chap., DAR, New Albany, Ind.
REF-DAR 4, p. 223; DAR 6, p. 158.

BARLOW, JOSEPH Dearborn Co.
d. ante 1835; bur. Dearb. Co. Pens. appl. 9-4-1820, ae. 60,
Boone Co., Ky.; no fam.; lives with bro. Enl. 1779, Va., Capt.
Young, Col. Crockett; dis. 1781 at Falls of the Ohio River in
Ky. On 4-17-1827, affid. of Thomas Curry, ae. 66, Franklin, Ind.
(see "Roster", p. 111) that he well remembers his friend Barlow

in the Rev., that Barlow was a pvt. ca. 2 yr. in Capt. Young's Comp. (Since Curry enl. from Loudoun Co., Va., poss. Barlow did too. MRW.) Also affid. of Thomas Davis of Greene Co., O. REF-Pens. S.35773 Va.; Bowen's "Hist. of Dearborn Co., Ind." (1915), p. 284; "Hist. of Dearborn & Switzerland Cos., Ind." (1885), p.199.

BARNES, JAMES   Vigo Co.
b. 12-14-1748, Northumberland Co., Va., on the Potomac River; bur. Otter Creek Union Cem., Otter Creek Twp., Gr. 2, Lot 281. Pens. appl. 11-19-1832, ae. 83, near Terre Haute, Ind.; pd. there to 3-4-1837; on 9-25-1838 asked for tr. to Morgantown, Blount Co., Tenn., where had gone to live with chn.; mentions James Barnes, Jr. (son? MRW.) Enl. 1776 or 1777, Mecklenburg Co., Va., Capt. John Burton, Col. Munford; later Col. Lew Burrell, Capt. Rellis Jeffries, Lt. James Brown. After War, migr. to Charlotte Co., Va.; Burke Co., N.C.; Ky.; Vigo Co., Ind. (Can find no mention that he retd. from Tenn. to Ind., but such a definite grave location would seem to indicate proof that he did or at least was brought back for burial. There is no James Barnes in 1840 Pens. List for Blount Co., Tenn. REF-Am. Leg.; Pens. S.1894 Va.; 1835 Pens. List, v. 3, p. 73; "Terre Haute Tribune", 7-6-1947.

BARNETT, HUMPHREY   Vanderburgh Co.
(Uncertain but probable.) m. Nancy; chn.-Hannah, b. 1800, d. 11-2-1862, m. John Fickas, b. 1795, d. 8-4-1862, Knight Twp. States that Humphrey was Rev. sold.; is in 1820 Cens. for Vanderb. Co. but not 1830. REF-Brant & Fuller's "Hist. of Vanderburgh Co., Ind." (1889), p. 634; Thelma Murphy.

BARNETT, JAMES OTIS   Putnam Co.
(Uncertain but probable.) b. Va.; migr. to Harrison Co., Ky.; in 1820 Cens. for Harrison Co., Ind.; ca. 1826 to Putnam Co., Ind.; m. Betsy Heller; chn.-Lewis m. Cynthia Harper; Solomon; Edward m.(1) --- Wilson, (2) --- Rariden, (3) Elizabeth E. Lane; Isaac; dau. m. John Killion; Elizabeth m. Franklin Abraham Baughman; dau. m. --- Diel (Deal); dau. m. Jim Thomas; David; Peter. REF-Thelma Murphy.

BARNETT, JOHN   Harrison Co.
d. 1816 (will wr. 3-22-1815; pr. 10-25-1816); m. --- O'Connell (liv. 1815); chn.-James P., b. 1762, Amherst Co., Va., (liv, 1832 Lincoln Co., Ky.), d. 3-31-1834; John; Jesse; Alexander m. Mary Faith; Jennie m. William Lawrence (& had chn.-Rachel & Samuel); Rachel m. Samuel Lawrence; Mary ("Polly") m. Elisha Hall; Ann m. Joseph Hall. Fam. moved to Guilford Co., N.C., when son James was young; there during Rev. John Barnett qualifies as a Patriot because his son James P. served as a substitute for him. REF-Pens. S.12963 N.C. & Va. (son James); "Ind. Mag. of Hist.", v. 37, p. 93; Thelma Murphy.

BARNGROVER, ---   Howard Co.
bur. in field just off New London Road, ca. 2 mi. SW of Kokomo, Ind. Trad. says he was Rev. sold. REF-Morrow's "Hist. of Howard Co., Ind." (1910?), p. 125.

-4-

BARTEE, JOHN — Putnam Co.
d. Feb. 1848; bur. in cem. on Yeats farm near his home. Lived near Rev. sold., Samuel Denny. Had 2nd wife & dau. At 16 was in Siege of Yorktown. Name on bronze tablet placed in Ct. Hse. by SV. REF-DAR 19, p. 86; Weik's "Hist. of Putnam Co., Ind." (1910), p. 216; "Putnam Co., Ind., Hist. & Gen.", Washburn Chap. DAR, Greencastle, Ind. (ts in ISL), v. 1, p. 193.

BARTLETT, JOHN — Cass Co.
d. 8-8-1791; killed in action with Indians at Battle of Olde Towne, N.W. Terr. (region now Cass Co.); bur. Olde Towne Cem., Gr. 2, Lot 1. Sgt. in Va. Cav.; Ky. Vol. REF-Am. Leg.

BAXTER, THOMAS — Morgan Co.
b. 1764; d. 1835; bur. West White Lick Cem., Gr. 3, Lot 107. REF-Am. Leg.

BENNETT, TIMOTHY — Crawford Co.
(Uncertain if he d. in Ind. Recd. too late to add data or check for pens.) REF-Crawford Co. Civil Order Book A, pp. 326-327; Dorothy Riker.

BINGHAM, FREDERICK — Greene Co.
b. 2-22-1792 (typo. error by Am. Leg. typist as card plainly says Rev. War); d. Feb. 1859; bur. Bingham Cem., Center Twp., Gr. 1, Lot 44. Next of kin: Granville Bingham, gr-son. Was a Fife Major in Rev. War. REF-Am. Leg.

BLAINE, ROBERT — Monroe Co.
bur. in Monroe Co.; gr. loc. by Sarah McCalla Chap., DAR, Bloomington, Ind. REF-DAR 3, p. 147.

BLAIR, DAVID — Allen Co.
bur. in Allen Co. Name on Memorial Inscription: "Dedicated to the memory of the following Revolutionary Soldiers Buried in Allen Co.", erected 1928 by Mary Penrose Wayne Chap., DAR, at the Swinney homestead, Ft. Wayne, Ind. REF- "Cem. Inscr. of Allen Co.", Mary Penrose Chap., DAR, Ft. Wayne, Ind., p. 1, (ts in ISL.)

BLOOMHART, DANIEL — Fayette Co.
d. 1837; bur. Orange Twp. Cem., gr. loc. by Connersville Chap., DAR, Connersville, Ind. REF-DAR 15, p. 85; DAR 18, p. 168; Bowen's "Hist. of Fayette Co., Ind." (1917), p. 320.

BLUNT (BLOUNT), WILLIAM — Delaware Co.
b. 1756-1757, Tenn.; will wr. 5-26-1831, pr. 5-3-1833; bur. at Muncie, Ind.; gr. loc. by Paul Revere Chap., DAR,' Muncie, Ind.; m. Mary McCoy, b. Tenn.; chn.-Rachel, Andrew, Margaret, Hannah, John, William, Mary, Elizabeth, Amos, Richard, Thomas, Joseph, Aaron; gr-son Thomas Blount Jones. Pens. appl. 5-1-1818, in 62nd yr., Muskingum Co., O. Pvt. in Col. Parker's Regt., Va.Line, 7 yr. After War; liv. in Tenn., Ky., Muskingum Co., O.; Wayne Co., Ind., 2 mi. below Richmond; Henry Co., Ind.; in 1820 to Perry Twp., Delaware Co., Ind., 7 mi. above Muncie; ent. land

-5-

12-9-1822, Liberty Twp., Delaware Co., Ind.   REF-Pens. S.42088;
DAR 15, p. 87; A. L. Kerwood, "Muncie Star", 5-16-1910.

        BODENSTADT, HENRY   Harrison Co.
bur. in Mauckport Cem.; gr. loc. by Piankeshaw Chap., DAR, New
Albany, Ind. REF-DAR 6, p. 158.

        BRANHAM, ---   Greene Co.
listed as Rev. sold. bur. there. REF-Bowen's "Biog. Mem. of
Greene Co., Ind." (1908), v. 1, p. 17.

        BRANT, CHRISTOPHER   Montgomery Co.
bur. Wesley Cem., Wayne Twp. REF-Am. Leg.

        BREWER, ZION   Greene Co.
bur. Bland Cem., Highland Twp., Gr. 1, Lot 81. In F.C. Vol.
REF-Am. Leg.; Bowen's "Biog. Mem. of Greene Co., Ind." (1908),
v. 1, p. 17.

        BROWN, JACOB   Henry Co.
b. 1-14-1755; d. 1832; bur. Flatrock Cem.; son of Thomas &
Ruth Large. Enl. 8-10-1780, N.C. Mil. REF-DAR 48, p. 184.

        BROWN, MARION   Howard Co.
bur. Russiaville Cem. REF-Am. Leg.; "Kokomo Dispatch", 5-30-
1915; "Kokomo Daily Tribune", 5-30-1922.

        BROWN, SAMUEL   Decatur Co.
bur. Wesley Chapel Cem.; stone (illeg.); gr. loc. by Lone Tree
Chap., DAR, Greensburg, Ind. REF-DAR 14, p. 73; DAR 15, p.86;
Harding's "Hist. of Decatur Co., Ind." (1915), p. 408.

        BROWN, WILLIAM   Owen Co.
b. 1750; d. 1830; bur. Whitehall Cem.; REF-DAR 28, p. 157.

        BROWN, WILLIAM   Putnam Co.
bur. in Putnam Co.; name on monument to Rev. dead, erected by
Washburn Chap., DAR, Greencastle, Ind.; also on bronze tablet
in Ct. Hse., erected by SV, Greencastle, Ind. REF-DAR 19,
p. 86; Weik's "Hist. of Putnam Co., Ind." (1910), p. 216;
"Putnam Co. Hist. & Gen.", v. 1, p. 194, Washburn Chap., DAR,
Greencastle, Ind. (ts in ISL.)

        BRUNNER, ---   Morgan Co.
bur. in Shiloh Cem. REF-Am. Leg.

        BRYANT, WILLIAM G.   Greene Co.
(Uncertain if he d. in Ind.) b. 1760-1761; may have d. in
Greene Co., Ind. (see Bowen below). Pens. appl. 5-31-1830, ae.
69, Versailles, Ripley Co., Ind.; formerly of Marion Co., Ind.;
in 1837 went to visit sis. in Smith Co., Tenn.; became ill &
stayed; pens. tr. there 1-21-1840 (not in 1840 Pens. List);
may have d. there; or may have retd. to Ind.; or may have been
brought back for burial. REF-Pens. S.3049 Va.; Bowen's "Biog.
Mem. of Greene Co., Ind. (1908), v.1; p.17; 1835 Pens. List,
v. 3, p. 50.

-6-

BUCKLIN, DAVID Gibson Co.
d. 10-19-1815; bur. Warnock Cem., Gr. 8, Lot 70 E½; metal marker. REF-Am. Leg.

BUCKNER, DANIEL Jackson Co.
b. 1761; d. 1840; bur. near Medora; gr. loc. by Christopher Harrison Chap., DAR. REF-DAR 26, p. 115.

BURCH, WILLIAM Monroe Co.
b. 5-10-1764; d. 9-18-1848; bur. Burch Cem., Gr. 7, Lot 4, Row 4. Enl. 1776. REF-Am. Leg.; Monroe Co. GAR Book (1886),p.51

BURLINGAME, CLARK La Porte Co.
b. 10-17-1757, R.I.; d. 1-13-1843; bur. Door Village Cem., Scipio Twp., Gr. 3, Lot 45, Blk. 2. Pvt. in Herrick's Regt., Vt. Mil. Govt. stone. REF-Am. Leg.

BURNHAM, JOHN Floyd Co.
(Uncertain if he d. in Ind.; recd. too late too add data or to check for pens.) Enl. 26th Mass. Regt.; ae. 75 in 1820. REF-Floyd Co. Civil Order Book A, pp. 141-142; Dorothy Riker.

BURROUGH, --- Dearborn Co.
listed as Rev. sold. bur. there. REF-"Hist. of Dearborn, Ohio, & Switzerland Cos., Ind." (1885), p. 199.

BURTON, GEORGE Jefferson Co.
bur. Halls Ridge Cem.; gr. loc. by John Paul Chap., DAR, Madison, Ind. REF-DAR 15, p. 86; DAR 28, p. 157; 1835 Pens. List,v.3,p.5.

BUSH, LIFHET Vigo Co.
d. 6-29-1829, Honey Creek Prairie; left wid. & relatives. Was a Capt. REF-"Terre Haute Western Register", 7-2-1829.

BYRD, JONATHAN Putnam Co.
d. 1827; bur. 10 mi. NE of Greencastle, Ind., farm of Elijah Walls; bur. on knoll; gr. loc. by 83 yr. old man (in 1922). Name on DAR monument to Rev. dead, erected by Washburn Chap., DAR, Greencastle, Ind.; also on bronze tablet in Ct. Hse., erected by SV, Greencastle, Ind. REF-DAR 19, p. 86; "How Sleep the Brave?", addr. by C. F. Posson, State SAR, 2-25-1922 (ISL); Weik's "Hist. of Putnam Co., Ind." (1910), p. 216; "Putnam Co., Ind., Hist. & Gen.", v. 1, p. 193, Washburn Chap., DAR, Greencastle, Ind., (ts in ISL.)

CANET, REUPP Knox Co.
bur. Knox Co.; gr. marked by Francis Vigo Chap., DAR, Vincennes, Ind. REF-DAR 12, p. 74.

CARPENTER, SOLOMON Greene Co.
listed as Rev. sold. bur. there. REF-Bowen's "Biog. Mem. of Greene Co., Ind." (1908), v. 1, p. 17.

CASEBOLT (CASHBOLT), ROBERT Gibson Co.
d. 4-9-1840; bur. Lawrence Cem., Gr. 32, Row 1. REF-Am. Leg.

CHAMBERS, BENJAMIN   Ohio Co.
b. ca. 1764; bur. in Ohio Co. Commissioned by Cont. Cong. as ensign in 1st Pa. Regt., 1778, when 14 yr. old; made lieut. next year. REF-"Hist. of Dearborn, Ohio, & Switzerland Cos., Ind." (1885), p. 200.

CHANDLER, JOSEPH   Randolph Co.
(Uncertain but probable.) b. ca. 1753; ae. 87 in 1840; prob. d. soon after; liv. in Jackson Twp. in 1840. REF-Smith and Driver's "Past & Pres. of Randolph Co., Ind." (1914), p. 412; 1840 Pens. List, p. 185.

CHENEY, FRANCIS   Greene Co.
bur. Grandview Cem., Bloomfield, Ind., Gr. 1, Lot 400, Sec. X (according to Am. Leg.); bur. 1 mi. S of Newark on Philpott farm (according to DAR). REF-Am. Leg.; DAR 27, p. 118.

CLARK, ABNER   Howard Co.
b. 7-7-1763; d. 10-5-1847, ae. 84-3-8; bur. Oak Mound Cem., Gr. 1, Lot 38, Row 10 (Am. Leg.); bur. Brown Cem., Ervin Twp. ("Tribune"); marble slab: "Born July 7, 1763, and came to Deer Creek township, Cass county in 1846". Served under Washington. REF-Am. Leg.; "Kokomo Daily Tribune", 5-30-1922; Morrow's "Hist. of Howard Co., Ind." (1910), v. 1, p. 468.

CLARKE, ---   Dearborn Co.
d. ca. 1831; bur. on the banks of Hogan; m. at beginning of Rev. War; wife d. 4-13-1846, in 88th yr., prob. Dearborn Co., Ind.; chn.-at least a dau. & son, the Rev. Samuel Clarke of Ft. Madison. Fam. once liv. in Winchester, Va. Sold. was in Stinson's Regt. REF-"Western Christian Advocate", vol. XIII, 6-5-1846, p. 31.

CLOUD, BAYLIS   Dearborn Co.
d. ante 1835; bur. there. REF-Bowen's "Hist. of Dearborn Co., Ind." (1915), p. 284; "Hist. of Dearborn, Ohio, & Switzerland Cos., Ind." (1885), p. 199.

COLE, ABRAHAM   La Grange Co.
liv. near Lima, Ind.; prob. bur. there. REF-Battey's "Cos. of La Grange & Noble, Ind." (1882), p. 110.

COLTRAN, JOHN   Vigo Co.
listed as Rev. sold. bur. there. Clue to further res. in an Am. Leg. card for John Coltrin (son?), b. 1793; d. 3-28-1848; bur. Rogers Cem., Harrison Twp.; War of 1812. REF-Am. Leg.; "Terre Haute Tribune", 7-6-1947.

CONWAY, WILLIAM   Greene Co.
bur. Grandview Cem., Bloomfield, Ind., Gr. 3, Lot 400, Sec. X (Am. Leg.); bur. 2 mi. SE of Newark in Ovley Cem. (DAR). REF-Am. Leg.; DAR 27, p. 118; Bowen's "Biog. Mem. of Greene Co., Ind. (1908), v. 1, p. 17.

COOL, ISAAC Marion Co.
d. 6-5/6-1828; bur. on his own farm, Indianapolis, Ind.; m. Mary Corle; chn.-Elizabeth m. --- Johnson; Daniel; Sophia m. --- Cox; Dr. Jonathan S.; William. Sgt. in Capt. James Moore's Comp., 2nd Battn., Somerset Co., N.J., Mil. Proof: "Off. Reg. of Off. & Men of N.J.", p. 463 (Adj. Gen., Wash., D.C.) REF-Thelma Murphy.

COOPER, --- Decatur Co.
bur. in Milford Cem. near his friends James Crawford & George King (DAR 14, p. 73); bur. in Kingston Cem. (DAR 15, p. 86); gr. loc. by Lone Tree Chap., DAR, Greensburg, Ind. REF-as given.

COOPER, ELIJAH Marion Co.
b. 1746; d. 4-17-1833; m. 10-28-1792, Northfield, Mass., by Bapt. Elder, Bunker Gay, to Sarah Giles, b. 8-8-1772; chn.-3 older than Joshua, b. 8-28-1804. Pens. appl. 12-20-1832, ae. 86; wid. pens. pd. in Indianapolis, Ind., 1846; in Bloomington, Ill., 1847-1848, where son Joshua liv.; tr. back to Indianapolis 3-7-1849 because Joshua moved back. Enl. from Hindsdale, Cheshire Co., N.H., Capt. Mind, Col. Read, 7 yr. 20 da. REF-Pens. W.9802.

COVERT, PETER Clark Co.
bur. in cem. at New Washington, Ind.; gr. loc. by Ann Rogers Clark Chap., DAR, Jeffersonville, Ind. REF-DAR 7, p. 193.

COX, THOMAS Posey Co.
bur. Old County Cem. REF-Am Leg.

CRAWFORD, JAMES Decatur Co.
b. 1756-1757; d. Feb. 1836, ae. 79 yr.; bur. in Milford Cem. near his friends George King & Mr. Cooper; gr. loc. by Lone Tree Chap., DAR, Greensburg, Ind. REF-DAR 14, p. 73.

CRAWFORD, WILLIAM Wayne Co.
b. 1768; d. 1834; bur. Bryant's Chapel Cem. (A different man from the one in the "Roster", p. 400.) REF-DAR 27, p. 118.

CROCKS, MICHAEL Clay Co.
b. 1760, near Philadelphia, Pa.; bur. Cottage Hill Cem., Brazil, Ind. Pens. appl. 9-13-1838, ae. 78, Knox Co., Ind.; rej. as did not serve 6 mo. As a boy, mov. with parents to Loudoun Co., Va., & Berkeley Co., Va. Enl. Jan. 1781, Shepherdstown, Berkeley Co., Va.; Capt. Henry Bedinger, Va. Line; Capt. Kirkpatrick. After War, liv. Berkeley Co., Va.; Ky.; Ind.; liv. 1840, ae. 80, Jackson Twp., Clay Co., Ind., with James Harland. REF-Pens. R.2504; Am. Leg.; 1840 Pens. List, p. 181.

CROUSORE, CHRISTIAN Howard Co.
bur. Chandler Cem., Gr. 3, Lot 39, Row 9. REF-Am. Leg.

CRUMB, CHRISTOPHER Tippecanoe Co.
b. 1762; d. 1830-1831; mar.; wife ae. 54, 12-7-1820 when sold. was ae. 58 & had a ch. ae. 14; wife d. 2 yr. after he d.; chn.-3 surv.: Benjamin of Western Texas, ca. 1846; Chandler of Southern Ind., ca. 1846; Isaac D. of Scioto Co., O., 1852. Enl. 12-1-

1778, Minnisink, N.Y., 2nd N.Y. Regt., Capt. Charles Newkirk,
Col. Philip Courtland; Capt. Timbrook; Gen. Sullivan; dis. 6-7-
1783, Newburgh, Capt. Jacob. Wright, N.Y. Pens. appl. 4-30-
1819, Scioto Co., O.; tr. to Tippecanoe Co., Ind. Sold & fam.
also went under surname of Schoonover. REF-Pens. S.43421; "Ohio
Rev. Sold.", v. 2, p. 109.

CUMMINGS, THOMAS   Perry Co.
d. prob. ante 1815. Entered land 1807, Perry Co. Served in 2nd
Va. State Regt., Col. Gregory Smith. REF-Wallace Weatherholt.

CUNNINGHAM, ELIZABETH   Putnam Co.
b. 1769; d. 1840; bur. Greencastle Cem.; liv. 1840, ae. 69,
Greencastle, with Benjamin S. Cunningham. REF-DAR 27, p. 118;
1840 Pens. List, p. 184.

CURRANT, JAMES   Harrison Co.
bur. Green Valley Cem.; gr. loc. by Piankeshaw Chap., DAR, New
Albany, Ind. REF-DAR 12, p. 74.

DAILY, EPHRAIM   Orange Co.
bur. on Ben Purlee farm cem.; Gr. 5, Lot 6, Row 3. REF-Am. Leg.

DAMPLE, THOMAS   Vigo Co.
b. 1745-1746; ae. 87 in 1833. Listed as Rev. sold. bur. there.
Served in S.C. Line. REF-"Terre Haute Tribune", 7-6-1947;
1835 Pens. List, v. 3, p. 34.

DAVIDSON, ISAAC   Johnson Co.
This sold. did not die in nor was he bur. in Ind. although an
Am. Leg. card says so as well as DAR Chap. below. He definite-
ly. d. 10-17-1842, South Charlestown, O.; bur. Green Lawn Cem.
Asked for tr. of pens. 2-25-1841 to Clark Co., O., to live with
1 of his 2 sons there as no one in Ind. to care for him. REF-
Pens. S.2509 Va.; "Ohio Rev. Sold.", v. 1, p. 107; Am. Leg.;
"Cem. Rec. of Johnson Co., Ind.", Alexander Hamilton Chap.,
DAR, Franklin, Ind. (1932; ts in ISL).

DAVIDSON, JOSHUA   Johnson Co.
bur. Johnson Co.; name on bronze tablet in Franklin Cem., by
Alexander Hamilton Chap., DAR, Franklin, Ind. REF-Am. Leg.

DAVIS, JOSEPH   Randolph Co.
bur. New Pittsburg Cem. REF-DAR 28, p. 157.

DEAVER, WILLIAM   Wayne Co.
b. 1764, Harford Co., Md.; d. 2-9-1832; m. Mary ---, ae. 37-38
on 11-28-1820; chn.-(ages in 1820 pens. appl.)-William 17 (70
on 4-2-1873, Wayne Co., Ind., only surv. heir); Deborah 15;
Elizabeth 13; George 10; Rebecca 8; Micajah 7; Della 5; Mary-
Ann 2. Pens. first in Scioto Co., O.; tr. 1822 to Mason Co.,
Ky.; then Wayne Co., Ind. Enl. 7-1-1778, Md. Line, Col. Ramsey. REF-Pens. S.12754 Md.; "Ohio Rev. Sold.", v. 2, p. 118.

DEFORE, STEPHEN　　　　　　Owen Co.
bur. Defore Cem., ½ mi. N of Freedom, Ind.; liv. in Franklin
Twp. REF-Am. Leg.

DICKERSON, WAITSELL　　　　La Grange Co.
bur. there; liv. near Lima, Ind. REF-Battey's "Cos. of La
Grange & Noble, Ind." (1882), p. 110.

DILLMAN, JACOB　　　　　　Morgan Co.
bur. Shiloh Cem. REF-Am. Leg.

DOANE, JACOB　　　　　　　Washington Co.
bur. ca. 1 mi. from Hardinsburgh; rough stone, not marked. Was
from N.C.; scout in Fed. Army; gr. loc. by Piankeshaw Chap.,
DAR, New Albany, Ind. REF-DAR 7, p. 195.

DOVER, JEFFERSON　　　　　Greene Co.
listed as Rev. sold. bur. there. REF-Bowen's "Biog. Mem. of
Greene Co., Ind." (1908), v. 1, p. 17

DUDLEY, ---　　　　　　　　Randolph Co.
bur. at Windsor Cem. REF-Smith & Driver's "Past & Pres. of
Randolph Co., Ind." (1914), p. 413.

DUKES, ISAAC　　　　　　　Clinton Co.
b. 1760-1761; d. 4-17-1835; m. Apr. 1793, Worcester Co., Md.,
Elizabeth ---, b. 2-12-1772; chn.- Davis, b. 1-18-1794, Worcester Co., Md.; Mary, b. May 1796; James, b. May 1798; Isaac, b.
1800; Elizabeth, b. July 1802; Katharine, b. 1806; Spencer, b.
1808; Samuel, b. 1811. Pens. appl. 10-17-1832, ae. 70 or up-
ward, Concord Twp., Ross Co., O., where had liv. last 20 yr.;
in 1812 was 51 yr. old as given in Rec. of Indenture of apprenticeship; parents d. when he was a ch. Wid.'s pens. appl. 2-11-
1840, ae. 68 on next Feb. 12, Clinton Co., Ind. Enl. Worcester
Co., Md., Capt. Bennett, Col. Shield, Md. Mil., 14 mo. 8 da.
Liv. Worcester Co., Md., till 1812; then Ross Co., O.; then
Clinton Co., Ind. REF-Pens. R.3111 Md. Privateer; "Ohio Rev.
Sold.", v. 2, p. 126.

DUNBAR, JOHN　　　　　　　Posey Co.
bur. Bethany (Old Beech) Cem., Gr. 6, Lot 1, Row 33. REF-Am. Leg.

DUNCAN, JOHN　　　　　　　Parke Co.
bur. Rockville Cem. REF-"Parke Co. Memorial" (1916), p. 127.

DUNSEN, SAMUEL　　　　　　Knox Co.
b. 1756; d. 1847; bur. Upper Indiana Cem., Gr. 1, Row 11, Sec. 1.
REF-Am. Leg.

DURAND, ANDREW　　　　　　Indiana
(Uncertain.) b. 1758, Cheshire, Conn.; d. ca. 1836-1839; son of
Andrew & Eunice (Hotchkiss) Durand. Enl. 1777, Cheshire, Conn.;
Conn. Mil. 1 yr. 8 mo., Capt. Hotchkiss, Col. Cooke. From Conn.
to Burton, O., 1806; pens. appl. 8-10-1832, ae. 74, Burton Twp.,
Geauga Co., O., where had liv. past 23 yr. Affid. of Merriman

Cook, a Rev. sold. in same Comp., now liv. in Geauga Co., O. Sold. in 1835 Pens. List, v. 3, p. 123, Geauga Co., O. Moved to Ind. Prob. d. soon after as not in 1840 Pens. List. REF-Pens. S.2528 Conn.; "Ohio Rev. Sold.", v. 1, p. 444, v. 2,p.297.

DUTTEROE, JACOB   Clark Co.
d. 11-24-1824,*in 63rd yr.; bur. with Honors of War by Maj. Coldren. Obit says "an affectionate parent". Served 3 yr.; prisoner at Ft. Niagara; to Montreal till end of War. REF-"Charlestown Intelligencer", 12-4-1824; Dorothy Riker. at Utica, Ind.*

DYER, CHARLES   Harrison Co.
b. 1754-1755; d. 9-3-1831, ae. 76; bur. Bethlehem Cem., 1 mi. NW of Crandall; gr. marked; loc. by Piankeshaw Chap., DAR, New Albany, Ind.; m. (wid. d. ante 1855); chn.- Elizabeth Vaughn, decd.; William; Mary Hubbird, decd.; John, decd.; James, decd.; Charles; Hugh; Nancy Hurst; Elizabeth; Jonathan; Hettie (sp?); Hackly, decd.---all as given 3-12-1855 in affid. of Bennet & Austin Jacobs, Neosha, Iowa. Pens. appl. made out by Gov. Jennings of Ind. Orig. dis. signed by Capt. William Thee, Ft. Randolph. 9-25-1778, shows 12th Va. Regt., service upwards of 2 yr. REF-Pens. R.3176 Va.; DAR 7, p. 195.

EDMONDSON, WILLIAM   Putnam Co.
bur. in Greencastle Cem.; name on monument to Rev. dead, erected by Washburn Chap., DAR, Greencastle, Ind.; also on bronze tablet in Ct. Hse., by SV, Greencastle. REF-DAR 19, p. 86; 27, p. 118.

ELKINS, SHADRACH   Posey Co.
(Uncertain.) Resident of Posey Co. 1827, ae. 78, when proved elig. for pens. in Vanderburgh Co. Circuit Court. Prob. d. in Posey Co. REF-Brant & Fuller's "Hist. of Vanderburgh Co., Ind." (1889), p. 337.

EPHLIN (EPHLAND), JACOB   Parke Co.
d. 1840-1841; bur. Kennedy & Sowers Cem., Gr. 6, Lot 1, Orig. Sec. German fam. orig. Effland; first records in N.C.; migr. to Tenn.; then Liberty Twp., Parke Co., Ind., when sold. was elderly. As very young man in N.C., served in Cont. Army under Washington. Name on tablet in Ct. Hse., erected by Parke Co. Hist. Soc. REF-Am. Leg. "Rev. Sold. Bur. in Parke Co." (ts in ISL).

EVANS, EDWARD (REV.)   La Grange Co.
(Uncertain but probable.) b. 5-5-1767, Amenia, Dutchess Co., N.Y.; was liv. in Lima, La Grange Co., Ind., May 1848; prob. d. there soon after; mar.; chn.- at least a son, liv. 5-26-1835, Brockport, N.Y. Sold. liv. with parents in Mt. Washington, Berkshire Co., Mass.; after War, retd. there till 1798; to Grafton Co., N.H., 25 yr.; Woodstock, Windsor Co., Vt., 3 yr.; Orleans Co., N.Y., 3 yr.; Onondaga Co., N.Y., 1 yr.; Schoharie Co., N.Y., 1 yr., 1832 to at least 6-18-1833; on 10-10-1834, ae. 67, was in Brockport, Monroe Co., N.Y.; on 5-25-1835, in Vernon, Trumbull Co., O.; on 5-14-1848 had liv. in Lima, Ind., ca. 2½ yr. Enl. Apr. 1782, Mt. Washington, Berkshire Co., Mass., Capt.

Jonathan Perry, Col. Willit; Col. Morehouse; dis. 1784, 16 mo.
3 da. Presbyterian minister. REF-Pens. S.8437 N.Y.; "Ohio
Rev. Sold.", v. 2, p. 134.

   FAIRFIELD, ASA   Allen Co.
gr. loc. by Mary Penrose Wayne Chap., DAR, Ft. Wayne, Ind. Capt.
in Navy; captured by British at Dartmoutn, Eng., 6 mo. REF-
DAR 15, p. 87.

   FAIRFIELD, OLIVER   Allen Co.
gr. loc. by Mary Penrose Chap., DAR, Ft. Wayne, Ind. Capt. in
Navy; captured & imprisoned at Halifax, 16 mo. REF-DAR 15,p.87.

   FARBER, DANIEL   Jay Co.
(This sold. did not d. in Ind.; but because he was liv. here at
the time of his death, he is being listed here.) b. 3-4-1765,
Morris Co., N.J.; d. 2-21-1847 (1849?), Preble Co., O.; bur.
New Paris Cem.; m. Nancy ---, (liv. 12-3-1852, Portland, Jay Co.,
Ind.); chn.- Sally Ann m. David Goorman; Margaret m. John G.
Spade; Lewis S.; John; Lucinda; Philip; Nancy Jane Brice (or
Nancy; and Jane m. Brice); Catharine m. --- Connor; Vinny.
Entered land Jay Co. 1834; Died on trip home from Wash., D.C.
Drft. 3-15-1781, Morristown, N.J., Capt. John Howell, Col.
Seely; dis. 3-4-1784. REF-Pens. R.3432; "Ohio Rev. Sold.",
v. 2, p. 135.

   FARIS (PARIS?), ISAAC   Harrison Co.
bur. Funk #1 Cem., Gr. 4, Row 2, Lot 1; govt. marker; (Am. Leg.);
bur. in provate cem. on banks of Big Indian Creek near the Ohio
River; gr. loc. by Piankeshaw Chap., DAR, Now Albany, Ind. (DAR);
served under Geo. Rogers Clark. (I think this may be Faris, as
there are many land entries in S & SW Ind. by Faris families.)
REF-Am. Leg.; DAR 4, p. 223; DAR 7, p. 194.

   FELLOWS, WILLIS   Greene Co.
b. 10-5-1757, Mass., ca. 30 mi. from Boston; prob. d. in Ind.
(see Bowen below); m. (wife ae. ca. 49 on 11-8-1825); chn.-
(all of age in 1825): Willis, Jr.; Levi, ae. 32 in 1825, with
whom sold. lives. Pens. appl. 10-20-1824, ae. 67, Greene Co.,
Ind.; affid. 3-15-1825 of William Fellows, Jefferson Co., N.Y.,
that sold. now lives in Bloomfield, Ind.; affid. 4-16-1825 of
sold.'s bro. John Fellows, Shelburn (sp?) Co., Mass. Sold.
asked for tr. to Palestine, Crawford Co., Ill., 12-8-1828, old &
infirm & has friends & relations there; wid. liv. in Ill. 5-25-
1841. Enl. 1775, Mass. Cont. Line, Capt. Bryant, Col. Crane;
Capt. Taylor; 3 yr.; William Fellows in same Comp. (Can find no
mention that he retd. to Ind., but may well have done so, or may
have been bur. here.) REF-Pens. S.35303 Cont. Mass.; Bowen's
"Biog. Mem. of Greene Co., Ind." (1908), v. 1, p. 17.

   FERBY, E. B.   Randolph Co.
bur. New Pittsburg Cem. REF-DAR 28, p. 157.

   FERNALD, BENJAMIN   Clinton Co.
bur. in Jefferson Cem., Ind.; gr. loc. by Capt. Harmon Aughe
Chap., DAR, Frankfort, Clinton Co., Ind. REF-DAR 26, p. 124.

FINLEY, DAVID　　　　　　　　Orange Co.
b. 1755; d. 4-19-1848; bur. Finley Cem., Gr. 1, Row 3, Lot 15. REF-Am. Leg.

FLEENER, DAVID　　　　　　　Rush Co.
bur. in Hannegan Cem. REF-Alexander's "Sketches of Rush Co., Ind." (1915), p. 36.

FLINN, GEORGE　　　　　　　　Lawrence Co.
bur. Flinn-Guthrie Cem. REF-Am. Leg.

FOSTER, EDWARD　　　　　　　Owen Co.
bur. Owen Co.; 1835 Pens. List (I do not find.MRW); DAR; Spencer Libr., Spencer, Ind. REF-Am. Leg.

FOSTER, TIMOTHY　　　　　　　Jefferson Co.
b. 1734, Southampton, L.I.; d. ae. 85; bur. on Foster farm near Pisgah; m. 1758, Bethia Howell; chn.-Asa, b. 1759; Luke, b. 1764; Gabriel, b. 1774, Southampton, L.I., d. 1848, Jefferson Co., Ind., m. 1796, Pamelia M. Campbell, dau. of Rev. sold., William Campbell of Columbia, Hamilton Co., O.; Zebulon m. --- Wingate. Sold. & fam. migr. to Springdale, Hamilton Co., O., 1788; 1813 to Pisgah, Jefferson Co., Ind. Enl. 4-24-1775; Capt. Nathaniel Healey, Col. Leonard, 3 mo. 2 wk.; no pens. Long acct. of desc. in source below. (Pisgah is a M.E. Church near Graham between Deputy & Madison. The Foster farm is the sold.'s grandson's.) REF-"Jefferson Co. Fam. Records", v. 3, p. 44, John Paul Chap., DAR, Madison, Ind. (ts in ISL); Caroline Dunn.

FOWLER, NATHAN　　　　　　　La Grange Co.
bur. near Lima, Ind. REF-Battey's "Cos. of La Grange & Noble, Ind." (1882), p. 110.

FRAZIER, JONAS　　　　　　　　Dearborn Co.
d. ante 1835; bur. there. REF-Bowen's "Hist. of Dearborn Co., Ind." (1915), p. 284; "Hist. of Dearborn, Ohio, & Switzerland Cos., Ind." (1885), p. 199.

GEORGE, ROBERT　　　　　　　Clark Co.
d. 5-31-1804 (DAR below); d. 3-15-1804 (pens. files); at Woods Ferry (now Utica), Ind.; bur. Utica Cem.; will wr. Apr. 1803, names heirs (bros. & sisters & their desc.); unmarried. Capt. in Rev. War & early Indian Wars; Capt. in Ill. Regt., Va. Trps.; served in Geo. Rogers Clark's Regt.; long acct. of service in Brumbaugh below. REF-Pens. R.14396 Va.; "Rev. Sold. Bur. in Clark Co.", State DAR (ts in ISL); Brumbaugh's "Rev. War Rec. of Va.", pp. 546-548.; Thelma Murphy.

GILLILAND, JOHN　　　　　　　Decatur Co.
bur. in cem. on Gilmore farm; stone illeg.; gr. loc. by Lone Tree Chap., DAR, Greensburg, Ind. REF-DAR 14, p. 73; DAR 15, p. 86; Harding's "Hist. of Decatur Co., Ind." (1915), p. 408.

GLOYD, ASA　　　　　　　　　　Dearborn Co.
b. 1756-1757, prob. Mass.; mar.; wife d. ante Aug. 1820; prob. chn.; bur. Moores Hill Cem. Name on Dearborn Co. Auditor's

-14-

Rec., Bk. 29, p. 250. Pens. appl. 5-14-1818, ae. 61, Bath, Steuben Co., N.Y.; tr. 8-29-1820, ae. 63, to Hamilton Co., O.; wife then dead & no fam. liv. with him; farmer. Enl. 3-17-1777, Bridgewater, Mass., Capt. John Porter, 2nd Mass., 3 yr.; Col. Wigglesworth, 13th Mass.; dis. 3-17-1780. REF-Pens. S.42748 Mass.; DAR 28, p. 157; Court House.

GOBIN, DANIEL   Clark Co.
bur. Charlestown Cem.; gr. loc. by Ann Rogers Clark Chap., DAR, Jeffersonville, Ind. REF-DAR 7, p. 193.

GOTT, ROBERT   Montgomery Co.
d. 8-1-1840; gr. loc. & marked by Dorothy Quincy Chap., DAR, Crawfordsville, Ind.; name on DAR tablet to Rev. dead in P.O., Crawfordsville; m. twice; both wives d. ante sold.; chn.- son John Cott, Sr., whose affid. 4-9-1852, ae. 86, Greenville, Darke Co., O., says that his father d. the Sat. ante the pres. elec. of Gen. Harrison in 1840 (which elec. in Ind. was held the 1st Mon. in Aug., i.e. Aug. 3, that year. MRW). Enl. 3-15-1780 in Orange Co., N.C., Capt. William Galbreth, Col. Daniel Morgan; dis. 10-25-1781, Yorktown. REF-Pens. R.4150 N.C.; Am. Leg.; DAR 15, p. 85; Bowen's "Hist. of Montgomery Co., Ind." (1913), v. 1, p. 180; Mills' "Early Days in a College Town" (1924),p.126.

GRIDER, JACOB   Putnam Co.
b. 1762; bur. Skillman Cem., ca. 2½ mi. N of Fincastle on Road 43, then W 1 mi. at 2nd road after leaving Fincastle; name on monument to Rev. dead, erected by Washburn Chap., DAR, Greencastle, Ind.; also on bronze tablet in Ct. Hse., erected by SV. Pens. appl. 10-25-1855, ae. 93, Putnam Co. Militia rifleman, Capt. Michael Coger, Col. Andrew Lewis; mus. in Sept. 1781, Rockingham Co., Va.; dis. Nov. 1781; 2 mo. REF-Pens. R.4302 Va.; DAR 19, p. 86; Weik's "Hist. of Putnam Co., Ind." (1910), p. 217; "Putnam Co., Ind., Hist. & Gen.", v. 1, p. 194, Washburn Chap., DAR, Greencastle, Ind. (ts in ISL).

GRIFFITH, JOSEPH   Marion Co.
d. 1823; the first Rev. sold. bur. in Indianapolis, Ind.; m. Mary Thornton, an Englishwoman; chn.- Abraham, b. 1774; Sarah, b. 1777; John, b. 1778; Joseph, b. 1780; Elizabeth, b. 1783; Amos, b. 1786; their mother was lost while making a visit across the Allegheny Mts.; no trace found. (I could find no pens. for this sold. The source mentions a letter concerning amounts due the heirs. A search in Washington, D.C., and several letters as yet unanswered have not proved this statement. If an answer should come in time, I shall add it at the end of this booklet. MRW). REF-Dunn's "Indiana and Indianians" (1919) v. 3, pp. 1326-1327.

GRIFFITH, SAMUEL   Henry Co.
b. 6-13-1755, Dartmouth, Mass.; d. 12-25-1835 (or 12-25-1838); wife dead; surv. son, Judah. Enl. 1777, Canaan, N.Y., Capt. Nathan Herrick, Col. Van Dyke; orderly sgt. in Capt. John Smith's Comp.; dis. 11-15-1779; in 1780, pvt. in Capt. Jonathan Warner's Comp. After War, liv. in Delaware Co., Dela. (sic) ---prob. was N.Y. or Pa. (MRW) --- for 6 yr.; then 3 yr. in Shenango Co. on

Susquehanna River; 3 yr. in Montgomery Co. north of Albany; ca.
7 yr. Ontario, N.Y.; Berry, Orleans Co., N.Y. 6-7 yr.; Cuyahoga
Co., O,.3 yr.. Pens. granted 3-27-1833, Amhurst, Lorain Co., O.
Then to Henry Co., Ind. REF-Pens. S.3427 N.Y.; "Ohio Rev.
Sold."; v. 2, p. 159.

    GUDGEL, ANDREW   Gibson Co.
b. 1727; d. 8-16-1815; bur. Gudgel Cem., Gr. 13, Row 3. REF-Am.Leg.

    GULLION, JACKSON   Howard Co.
bur. Twin Springs Cem., 5 mi. SW of Kokomo, Ind. REF-Morrow's
"Hist. of Howard Co., Ind. (1910?), v. 1, p. 468; "Kokomo
Tribune", 12-14-1908.

    GULLIVER, JOHN   Howard Co.
bur. Twin Springs Cem.; gr. loc. by Gen. James Cox Chap., DAR,
Kokomo, Ind. REF-DAR 23, p. 125.

    GUTHRIE, DANIEL   Lawrence Co.
bur. Flinn-Guthrie Cem. REF-Am. Leg.

    HAMER, JAMES   Fayette Co.
d. 1837; bur. Union Cem., Jackson Twp.; gr. loc. by Connersville Chap., DAR. REF-DAR 15, p. 85; DAR 18, p. 205: Bowen's
"Hist. of Fayette Co., Ind." (1917), p. 320.

    HAMLIN, ISAAC   Greene Co.
listed as Rev. sold. bur. there. REF-Bowen's "Biog. Mem. of
Greene Co., Ind." (1908), v. 1, p. 17.

    HANDLIN, MATTHIAS   Montgomery Co.
b. 8-26-1751; d. 11-2-1840, Pleasant Hill (now Wingate), Coal
Creek Twp.; m. 9-10-1787, near Goshen, N.Y., Anna Head, b.
11-10-1765, d. 12-3-1854, Butler Co., O.; chn.-Britain, m. ante
1812, d. ca. 1830, Springfield Twp., Franklin Co., Ind., ae. ca.
40, his oldest dau. then ca. 17 yr. old (Britain's sis. Jerusha
says he d. 1824, Butler Co., O.); Phebe; Margaret, ca. 3 yr.
younger than Britain (who was 2-2½ yr. younger than Phebe; note
discrepancies), m. (1) ca. 1806, Wayne Co., N.Y., ae. 15 yr. &
8 mo., to Isaac Smith & had 6 chn. (had 2 in 1808, 1 dau. was
8-9 in 1832 & there were 4 older chn., the 3rd ch. was Chloe
Smith, ca. 12 in 1832), m. (2) --- Hock who d. ante 1855;
William; Isaac; Jerusha, ca. 5 yr. younger than Margaret, m.
ca. 1816, Joseph (or Job) Cooper or Cottrell & had chn.; Mary
m. Archibald Gladman & had 4-5 chn., had just moved from Hamilton Co., O., to Ind. (in 1855?); John; Rachel m. ca. 1824,
Reily Twp., Butler Co., O., Jonas Jones, "infare" held at home
of Nicholas Jones, Jonas d. ante 1855, & had at least David,
b. 12-4-1826, Matthew, b. 9-3-1828, George, b. 6-13-1831, &
Minerva, b. 11-14-1842; Viletta m. & div. Joel Jones (nephew
of Jonathan Jones) & had 2 chn., oldest ca. 1820 in 1855;
Orin; and a son who d. 1824 & who had mar. chn. in 1825 (this
son may be one of those above. iRW). Affid. of William Atwater
of Wayne Co., N.Y., that the Handlins liv. Wayne Co., N.Y.

prior to 1812 at which time they had large fam. of chn., some already married; they moved West 1817; to N.J. & then West. Affid. 5-22-1855, Rush Co., Ind., of Samuel S. Durbon, ae. 66, that his mother was a cousin of Anna (who recently liv. Butler Co., O.). Affid. of David Jones, ae. 29, Butler Co., O., admr. of Anna. Affid. June 1855, Butler Co., O., of Jonathan Jones, ae. 66, a res. of Union Twp., Montgomery Co., Ind., that he knew Matthias 35 yr. ago on Indian Creek, Reily Twp., Butler Co., O., & that after a few yrs. there, Matthias mov. near where Jonathan now lives in Montgomery Co., Ind. (he having moved there 1832) & that Jonathan's bro. m. Rachel Mandlin. More data on chn.- Margaret b. Feb. 10, ca. 3 yr. younger than Britain, in affid. 4-7-1854 from Montgomery Co., Ind., m. (1), 10-16-ca. 1806, ae. 15 yr. 8 mo., Wayne Co., N.Y., Isaac Smith; m. (2), --- Hock, & had in all 12 chn.-7 b. N.Y., 3 Ohio, 2 Ind. (6 liv. 1854), 4th ch. was Chloe Smith, ae. ca. 12 in 1832, 7th ch. was Isaac Smith b. 8 wks. ante they mov. from N.Y. to Ohio (Isaac now liv. ae. ca. 32-33, Crawfordsville, Ind., 1 dau. was 8-9in 1832; 3rd ch. was Lucinda who d. shortly after Battle of Port Neville in which husb. Isaac Smith was; her fam. mov. from Ohio to Montgomery Co., Ind., where Margaret's husb.(Smith or Hock?) d. ca. 1836, she now (1854) a wid. Jerusha, ca. 5 yr. younger than Margaret and ae. ca. 10 yr. younger than her parents' oldest ch., ae. 66-67 in affid. of 4-20-1854, Montgomery Co., Ind., m. ca. 1816, ae. ca. 18-19; she did not name her husb. herself; other affids. give him as Joseph or Job Cottrell; liv. ca. 3 yr. after mar. in N.Y.; then 1 yr. in Cincinnati, O., where oldest ch., a son, was b. & d. in a few days; 2nd ch., Britton Cottrell, b. ca. 3 yr. later in Cincinnati, now liv. Tippecanoe Co., Ind.; 3rd. ch. Jesse, b. 2 yr. 8 mo. after Britton, now liv. Montgomery Co., Ind. & was 35 on 12-22-1853; 4th ch. b. 4½ yr. after Jesse & is d.; 5th ch. Nicholas, b. 3½ yr. after Mary Ann & now liv. Montgomery Co., Ind. (compiler realizes discrepancies here but this was the most complicated of pension files); 6th ch. Rachel b. 3 yr. after Nicholas, is mar. & has 2 chn.; 7th ch. Anna, b. 3 yr. after Rachel & ae. 19 on 12-5-1853. Pens. appl. 10-27-1825, ae. ca. 68, Reily Twp., Butler Co., O.; wife Anna ca. 57, dau. ca. 16, son ca. 11; on 10-16-1832, ae. ca. 74, had liv. Butler Co., O., ca. 10 yr.; still there 6-21-1833; in 1840, ae. 89, in Cole Creek Twp., Montgomery Co., Ind. Enl. ae. ca. 15, 1775, Monmouth Co., N.Y., Mil., Capt. Benjamin Van Cleve, 1 yr.; Capt. Butler, Col. Ray, N.J. Line (above may be Monmouth Co., N.J.). REF-Pens. W.4218 N.J.; "Ohio Rev Sold.", v. 2, p. 165; 1840 Pens. List, p. 183.

HARDY, DAVID   see David Harley

HARFORD, JOHN   Jay Co.
b. Northumberland Co., Va.; d. 8-4-1843; m. 1790, Culpeper Co., Va., Rachel Compton; at death, had 11 chn., 50 gr-chn., 12 gt-gr-chn. When very young, took place of father who was due to go to Rev. War. Mov. with parents to Culpeper Co., Va.; in 1815 to Harrison Co., Va.; in 1825 to Warren Co., O.; 1837 to Jay Co., Ind. REF-"Western Christian Advocate", v. X, p. 192, 3-15-1844.

HARLEY (HARDY?), DAVID Perry Co.
b. 1744; bur. Tobinsport Cem. Enl. at Philadelphia under Capt.
Shay; captured at Ft. Washington; paroled; re-enl.; on L.I.;
dis. at Williamsburg, Va. REF-DAW 36, p. 79; De La Hunt's
"Hist. of Perry Co., Ind." (1916), p. 50; Wallace Weatherholt.

HARMON, ABRAHAM Harrison Co.
b. 1767, Shenandoah Co., Va.; d. 3-31-1837, ae. 70 yr.; bur.
Thompson's Chapel Cem. near Moberly, Ind., Gr. 3, Row 18, Lot 3.
Served under Capt. Sinkley (Sinkle?); much of service was in
fighting Indians. Bur. beside older bro. Joseph (see below).
REF-Am. Leg.; DAR 7, p. 195; DAR 8, p. 98.

HARMON, JOSEPH Harrison Co.
d. ante 1837; bur. Thompson's Chapel Cem. near Moberly, Ind.
beside younger bro. Abraham (see above). Served longer than
Abraham. REF-DAR 7, p. 195; DAR 8, p. 98.

HARVEY, SIPPLE Greene Co.
Listed as Rev. sold. bur. there. REF-Bowen's "Biog. Mem. of
Greene Co., Ind." (1908), v. 1, p. 17.

HAWLEY, SAMUEL Floyd Co.
(Uncertain.) ae. 65 in 1824; dau. Nancy McGowan, ae. 36, has
5 chn. (names & ages given). Enl. 1781 in Mass. (Recd. too
late to add data or check for pension.) REF-Floyd Co. Civil
Order Bk. A, pp. 447-448; Bk. B, p. 17; Dorothy Riker.

HAYES, JOHN Pike Co.
bur. Flat Creek Cem., Marion Twp., Gr. 3, Row 25, Lot 5.
Served in Sumpter's Brig., S.C. Mil. REF-Am. Leg.

HEILMAN, JOHN Monroe Co.
gr. loc. by Sarah McCalla Chap., DAR, Bloomington, Ind.
REF-DAR 3, p. 147.

HEITMAN, GARRETT Greene Co.
bur. Fairview Cem., Stockton Twp., Gr. 3, Lot W½ 794, Sec. B;
trans. from an unknown cem. to start the Fairview. REF-Am.Leg.

HELT, JOHN Vermillion Co.
b. 1762-1763; d. 8-17-1833, ae. 70; bur. Helt's Prairie Cem.,
Helt Twp., Gr. 1, Lot 100, Sec. 1 (War not filled in on card,
but would have been of Rev. service age.) REF-Am. Leg.

HERRING, EPHRAIM Posey Co.
(Uncertain.) b. 1761 on Muse River, N.C.; ae. ca. 72 on
11-14-1832, pens. appl.; has a bro. in Ill. Enl. 1778, 96th
Dist., S.C., Capt. Jeremiah Williams, Maj. Frederick Gray,
Col. David Glenn, Gen. Andrew Pickens. After War, liv. 96th
Dist., S.C., till ca. 1804; Christian Co., Ky. ca. 5 yr.;
then Posey Co., Ind. (Recd. too late to check for pension.)
REF-Posey Co. Probate Order Bk., Feb. 1828-May 1854, p. 263.

HIGGS, SAMUEL   Floyd Co.
(Uncertain.) Enl. 1774 in Va.; also in 1775. No family; was
a cabinet maker. (Recd. too late to add data or check for
pens.) REF-Floyd Co. Civil Order Bk. A, p. 210; Dorothy Riker.

HOOLEN (HOOTEN), THOMAS   Decatur Co.
b. 4-30-1752; d. 7-26-1841, ae. 89-2-26; Lone Tree Chap., DAR,
Greensburg, Ind.; liv. 1840, ae. 88, Decatur Co., with Hiram
Hooten. REF-DAR 15, p. 86; 1840 Pens. List, p. 182 (as Hooten).

HOOPS, DAVID   Clark Co.
bur. Utica Cem.; liv. at Utica, Ind. Was a major in Rev. REF-
Am. Leg.; "Rev. Sold. Bur. in Clark Co.", State DAR (ts in ISL).

HOPKINS, SILAS   Putnam Co.
b. Baltimore, Md.; d. in late 1830's; bur. north end of old
Gorham farm; chn.-John Deroysha Hopkins; dau. m. Thomas Gorham.
Name on monument to Rev. dead, erected by Washburn Chap., DAR,
Greencastle, Ind.; also on bronze tablet in Ct. Hse., by SV.
REF-DAR 19, p. 86; Weik's "Hist. of Putnam Co., Ind." (1910),
pp. 217, 219-221.

HOPKINS, TWINS   Vigo Co.
bur. Prairieton Cem., Prairieton Twp. REF-Am. Leg.

HUFFMAN, HENRY   Greene Co.
Listed as Rev. sold. bur. there. REF-Bowen's "Biog. Mem. of
Greene Co., Ind." (1908), v. 1, p. 17.

HUMSTON, EDWARD   Lawrence Co.
(Perhaps not Rev. sold.) Grave marked with SAR bronze marker
by John Wallace Chap., DAR, Bedford, Ind. However, Am. Leg.
card says b. 1770; d. 11-8-1853; bur. Green Hill Cem., Bedford,
Ind., Gr. 4, Lot 131, Sec. 2; says War of 1812. (Is birth date
wrong?). REF-DAR 12, p. 74; Am. Leg.

IDE, REUBEN   Howard Co.
b. 1763-1764; d. 1846, ae. 82; bur. Friends Cem. REF-Am. Leg.;
"Kokomo Tribune", 5-30-1922.

IKERD, PETER   Lawrence Co.
bur. Ikerd Cem., on Metcham farm, 1 mi. E of Bedford, Ind.;
Gr. 1, Lot 55, Blk. 2. REF-Am. Leg.; DAR 28, p. 157.

IMEL, PETER   Shelby & Johnson Cos.
b. 1764, Hesse-Cassel, Germany; d. 6-3-1849, ae. 84-9-3; bur.
Rock Lane Cem., Gr. 2, Lot 13, Blk. 7, Johnson Co.; m. widow Mrs.
Susan Kirkwood; chn.-4 daus. & sons John, Henry, George, Thomas,
Samuel, Peter, Conrad, James; all chn. had fams. but John; son
Henry b. 1790, Greenbriar, (W.) Va.; son George b. there 1793.
Sold. to Amer.* with bro. Thomas. Was drummer boy in Rev.; after
dis., settled in Shenandoah Co. Va.; whole fam. to Wayne Co.,
Ind., ca. 1810; sold liv. with son George near Fairland, Shelby
Co., Ind., where he d.; bur. on farm there; 1940 body mov. to
* in 1776

Rock Lane Cem., Johnson Co., beside George's. Pic. of old stone shows correct dates; new stone errs in b. 1754 instead of 1764. REF-Am. Leg.; Lewis Jones (a descendant).

INGERSOL, PETER — Greene Co.
Listed as Rev. sold. bur. there. Pens. appl. 5-15-1828, Bloomfield, Greene Co., Ind.; latest date on correspondence in file 7-20-1830. Served under Capt. Asa Coburn; orig. dis. in file, from Utica, 7th Mass. Regt., Col. Brock, 1807. REF-Pens. R.20192 Mass.; Bowen's "Biog. Hem. of Greene Co., Ind." (1908), v. 1, p. 17.

JEBINE, --- — Dearborn Co.
bur. in Wright's Corner Cem. REF-DAR 27, p. 119.

JOHNSON, W. (Gen.) — Knox Co.
Listed as Rev. sold. bur. there. REF-"Hist. of Knox Co., Ind." (1886), p. 204.

JONES, GEORGE — Vigo Co.
(This sold. did not die in Ind.; but because he was living in Vigo Co. at the time of his death, he is being listed here.) d. 1834-1835; m. (2nd) 7-28-1833, Vigo Co., Ind., Mrs. Sicha Dawson, b. 1776-1777, wid. of Maj. Isaac Dawson; chn.-at least 1 son by 1st wife. Various affids. in 1828 that he liv. Terre Haute, Ind.; from John F. Jones, Livingston Co., N.Y., that he knew sold. bef. the War.; same by Horatio Jones, Genessee Co., N.Y.; of Jacob & John Creviston, Pickaway Co., O. Pens. pd. to 9-4-1834. Sold left Vigo Co. sometime in Nov. 1834 for visit to N.Y.; was unwell at the time; never retd.; it was reported that he d. in passing thru Ohio in Dec. 1834; another affid. that he d. somewhere in N.Y. ca. 3-11-1835. Son came from N.Y. to Vigo Co. to settle estate. Enl. 1781, Capt. John Boyd's Comp. of Bedford Rangers, commanded by Lt. Richard Johnston, Pa. Line. REF-Pens. R.5745 Pa.; 1835 Pens. List, v. 3, p. 78.; "Terre Haute Tribune", 7-6-1947.

JONES, JOSEPH — Porter Co.
d. Boone Grove, Ind., a few yrs. after migr. from Holmes Co., O., to Porter Co., Ind., in spring 1841; bur. in old Cornell Cem. REF-Lewis' "Hist. of Porter Co., Ind." (1912), v. 1, p. 99.

KENNEY, DANIEL — Knox Co.
Grave marked by Francis Vigo Chap., DAR, Vincennes, Ind. Pens. appl., ae. 71, 3-3-1819, Knox Co.; ae. 90 in 1833. Enl. June 1776, Sunbury, Pa.; Capt. John Doyle's Independent Comp., attached to 1st Pa. Regt., Col. Edward Ham (sp?); later Col. James Chambers, 2 yr.; dis. Richmond, Va.; pvt. in Col. Magaw's Regt., Pa. Line, 2 yr. REF-Pens. S.37126 Pa.; DAR 12, p. 74; 1835 Pens. List, v. 3, p. 22.

KERR, JAMES — Johnson Co.
ae. 84, 1840; bur. Greenwood, Ind., Cem.; name on bronze tablet to Rev. dead in Franklin, Ind., Cem., by DAR below. REF-Am. Leg.; "Cem.Rec.of Johnson Co.",Alex. Hamilton Chap.,DAR;1840Pens.,p.183.

KILES, JOHN   see KYLE

KIMBALL, JOHN   Gibson Co.
bur. Kimball Cem., Gr. 23, Row 2. REF-Am. Leg.

KIRBY, ---   Decatur Co.
bur. in Burk's Chapel Cem., 5 mi. S of Greensburg, Ind. Known to have served in 1776. REF-DAR 14, p. 73; DAR 15, p. 86; Harding's "Hist. of Decatur Co., Ind." (1915), p. 408.

KITLEY, JOHN   Rush Co.
(Uncertain.) b. ca. 1763, prob. Mass.; son of John Kitley of Needham, Mass.; d. ante 9-4-1850 (last pens. payment (no proof that he d. in Rush Co. but very likely); m. Anna ---, b. ca. 1770; d. 4-22-1845. To Ohio, N.W. Terr. 1791; on 9-20-1826, ae. 63, Hamilton Co., O., mentions wife Anne, ae. 56, and "a girl named Mary March, ae. 16"; Mar. 1839 mov. from Hamilton Co., O., to Pike Co., Ill., to live with chn.; 6-15-1840, Pike Co., Ill., "my wife's chn. & all my relatives here"; ae. 80 on 5-18-1846; pens. tr. from Ill. to Rush Co., Ind., 1-31-1846 as no relatives in Ill., wife dead, & is going to live with William B. Leech & wife of Rush Co., Ind.; he had raised the wife of Mr. Leech. Enl. Jan. 1780, fifer, Mass., Capt. John R. Miles, Col. Henry Jackson; tr. to 7th Regt., Col. John Brooks, Capt. Walker; dis. ae. 16 at end of War at New Windsor, N.Y.; his bro. William Kitley in same Brig. REF-Pens. S.35510 Mass.; BLW 2410.

KRON, GEORGE   Harrison Co.
bur. in private cem. near New Middletown, Ind.; gr. loc. & marked by Piankeshaw Chap., DAR, New Albany, Ind. DAR 7, p.195.

KYLE, JOHN   Dearborn Co.
bur. in Wright's Corner Cem.; in 1840, ae. 84, liv. with Thomas Kiles, Manchester Twp. Was a Capt.; name on Dearborn Co. Auditor's Record Bk. 29, p. 250. REF-DAR 27, p. 119; Court House; 1840 Pens. List, p. 181 (as Kiles).

LASHBROOK, JOHN   Orange Co.
d. 1820; bur. Lashbrook Cem., Gr. 3, Row 1, Lot 1. REF-Am. Leg.

LASHLEY, JAMES   Daviess Co.
grave loc. by White River Chap., DAR, Washington, Ind.; deeds reserve burial plot of 54 sq. rd.; will be conveyed to City of Washington, under care of DAR. REF-DAR 10, p. 154.

LASSELLE, HYACINTH   Allen Co.
b. 2-25-1777 (sic; typo error?); d. 1-23-1843; gr. loc. by Mary Penrose Wayne Chap., DAR, Ft. Wayne, Ind. Was a General. REF-DAR 15, p. 87.

LEAZENBY, WILLIAM, Sr.   Kosciusko Co.
d. 1878; bur. Leesburg Cem., Gr. 1, Row 13, Lot 13, Old Part. (Rather old for Rev. sold., but not impossible; definitely is given as Rev. War on file card. MRW). REF-Am. Leg.

LEMASTERS, ABRAHAM   Johnson Co.
d. 1837; bur. Lemasters Cem. on Edgar Brewer farm (Am. Leg. &
"Cem. Rec." below); came from Carolinas to Ky. & in 1838 to Johnson Co., Ind., where he d. 2 yr. later ("Misc. Rec." below).
Name on bronze tablet to Rev. dead in Franklin, Ind., Cem., by
DAR below. REF-Am. Leg.; "Cem. Rec. of Johnson Co." & "Misc.
Rec.", both from Alexander Hamilton Chap., DAR, Franklin, Ind.,
(ts in ISL).

LEWIS, WILLIAM   Clark Co.
b. 1750; d. 1854; bur. New Chapel Cem., Gr. 8, Lot 84, Sec. B.
Liv. in Utica Twp. REF-Am. Leg.

LITCHFIELD, ---   Madison Co.
bur. County Farm Cem. Was a Capt. in Rev.; listed as Rev. sold.
in C.A.R. book. REF-Am. Leg.; GAR Burial Book, Madison Co.

LOWE, WILLIAM   Monroe Co.
d. 9-23-1840; bur. Rose Hill Cem., Bloomington, Ind., Gr. 4,
Lot 18, Row 10, Old Part. Listed as Rev. sold. in G.A.R. book.
REF-Am. Leg.; GAR Burial Bk. (1886), p. 27.

McAFEE, JOHN   see McHAFFIE

McALISTER, ZACHARIAH   Washington Co.
bur. Rodman Cem., Gr. 1, Row 3, Lot 4; private stone. Liv. in
Franklin Twp. REF-Am. Leg.

McARTHUR, JAMES   Montgomery Co.
Grave loc. & marked by Dorothy Quincy Chap., DAR, Crawfordsville, Ind.; name on DAR tablet to Rev. dead in P.C., Crawfordsville. Am. Leg. has a card for a James McArthur, War of
1812, bur. in Old Town Cem., Crawfordsville, Gr. 3, Row 9,
Lot 6. REF-Am. Leg.; DAR 15, p. 85; Bowen's "Hist. of Montgomery Co., Ind." (1913), v. 1, p. 180.

McCLINTOCK, FINLEY   Johnson Co.
bur. in Nay (or Tremaine) Cem., Fineveh Twp.; name on bronze
tablet to Rev. dead in Franklin, Ind., Cem., by DAR below.
REF-Am. Leg.; "Cem. Rec. of Johnson Co.", Alexander Hamilton
Chap., DAR, Franklin, Ind., p. 242 (ts in ISL).

McCLINTOCK, JOHN   Johnson Co.
bur. Nay Cem.; DAR below has official proof. REF-Alexander
Hamilton Chap., DAR, Franklin, Ind.

McCOLLUM, DANIEL   Posey Co.
(Uncertain.) In 1827, ae. 83, a resident of Posey Co., he
proved his eligibility for pens. in Vanderburgh Co. Circuit
Court; prob. d. in Posey Co. REF-Brant & Fuller's "Hist.
of Vanderburgh Co., Ind." (1889), p. 337.

McCONNELL, JOHN — Delaware Co.
b. 1763-1764; d. 1-6-1847, ae. 83 yr.; bur. Beech Grove Cem., Gr. 2, Row 32, Blk. 6; m. Barbara Bowman, b. 1775 of German ancy., d. Dec. 1838, ae. 63 yr., Delaware Co., Ind.; chn.-7; son William, b. 4-10-1801, Ky., bur. by father; gt-grsons Abram & Bethuel McConnell. Sold. of Scotch-Irish ancy.; mov. to Tenn.; to Scioto Co., O.; to Ind. 1833. Trad. that he was for yrs. a wagoner in Cont. Army. REF-Am. Leg.; DAR 15, p. 87; A.L. Kerwood in "Muncie Star", 1910 (May-July,: "Builders of the Nation").

McCULLOUGH, JOHN — Ripley Co.
d. 6-15-1823; m. 12-10-1787, Mercer Co., Ky., Constant Jones, b. 1769-1770, dau. of John Jones; mar. bond iss. 11-28-1787; bondsmen James McColloh & Jeremiah Sallyers; wid. liv. Shelby Twp., Ripley Co. Enl. 2-4-1777, 4th Regt., N.C., Capt. Cole; 3 yr. REF-Pens. W.9558.

McHAFFIE, JOHN — Putnam Co.
Name on monument to Rev. dead, erected by Washburn Chap., DAR, Greencastle, Ind.; also on bronze tablet in Ct. Hse., by SV. REF-DAR 19, p. 86; Weik's "Hist. of Putnam Co., Ind." (1910),217.

McKINNEY, ROBERT — Washington Co.
d. 8-24-1823; bur. Livonia Cem., Gr. 5, Row 10, Lot 3, Sec. 1; Govt. marker; gr. loc. by Christopher Harrison Chap., DAR. Tr. from Va., Pa., & Ky.; liv. in Washington Twp., Washington Co., Ind. Was a lieut. in U.S. Artill. REF-Am. Leg.; DAR 26, p. 116; 1835 Pens. List, v. 3, p. 10.

McMANNUS, JOHN — Pike Co.
ae. 74 in 1833; listed as Rev. sold. bur. there. Was in Va. Mil. (This may be the same man as in "Roster", p. 274, of Boone Co.) REF-1835 Pens. List, v. 3, p. 63; "Rev. Sold. of Pike Co.", DAR (ts in ISL).

McNEIL, WILLIAM — La Grange Co.
bur. there; believed to have been a Rev. sold. REF-Battey's "Cos. of La Grange & Noble, Ind." (1882), p. 110.

McNULTY, JOHN — Montgomery Co.
grave loc. & marked by Dorothy Quincy Chap., DAR, Crawfordsville Ind.; name on DAR tablet to Rev. dead in P.O., Crawfordsville. REF-Am. Leg.; DAR 15, p. 85; Bowen's "Hist. of Montgomery Co., Ind." (1913), v. 1, p. 180; Mills' "Early Days in a College Town" (1924), p. 126.

MARBLE, NATHAN — Ohio Co.
bur. old Rising Sun Cem. REF-DAR 28, p. 158.

MARTIN, JOHN — Parke Co.
b. 1-20-1766, Spartansburg, S.C.; d. 4-13-1827; bur. Martin Cem., Gr. 1, Lot 105, Orig. Sec.; stone; m. Margaret Paris, b. 1776; d. 5-20-1855; chn.-8 sons & 4 daus., all b. in S.C. Whole fam. to Union Twp., Parke Co., Ind.; all d. Union Twp., except 1 just across the line in Jackson Twp.; all bur. in Martin Cem.

Served as subst. for his father; was at siege of Yorktown. Name on tablet in Ct. Hse., erected by Parke Co. Hist. Soc. REF-Am. Leg.; "Rev. Sold. Bur. in Parke Co." (ts in I3L).

    MARTIN, JOHN   Posey Co.
b. 1759, on Great Pedee River, S.C.; mar.; chn.-at least a dau. who m. Elder Benoni Stinson, Bapt. preacher. Pens. appl. 5-22-1826, ae. 66, and 7-17-1832, ae. 73, Henderson Co., Ky.; latter says "sometime resident of Henderson Co. & sometimes of Posey Co., Ind."; tr. Mar. 1833 to Posey Co. After War, liv. Wilkes Co., Ga.; Christian Co., Ky.; Henderson Co., Ky.; Posey Co., Ind. Affid. of his bro's wife, Ruth Martin, Christian Co., Ky.; letter from sold., Evansville, Ind., 9-18-1834. Enl. Newberry Co., S.C., Capt. McIntosh, Col. James Williams, lost dis. after 15-16 yr. when house burned in Christian Co., Ky. REF-Pens. S.16459 Ga., S.C.

    MASON, WILLIAM   Montgomery Co.
grave loc. by Dorothy Quincy Chap., DAR, Crawfordsville, Ind., & marked; name on DAR tablet to Rev. dead in P.C., Crawfordsville. REF-DAR 15, p. 85; Bowen's "Hist. of Montgomery Co., Ind." (1913), v. 1, p. 180.

    MAXWELL, J. B.   Monroe Co.
bur. Rose Hill Cem., Bloomington, Ind.; listed as Rev. sold. in G.A.R. Book. REF-Am. Leg.; GAR Book (1886), p. 29.

    MILLER, REUBEN   Madison Co.
bur. Robinette Cem., Gr. 2, Row 3. Lot 1; liv. in Jackson Twp. REF-Am. Leg.

    MILLER, WILLIAM   Marion Co.
b. 1757; bur. Crown Point Cem., Pike Twp., ¼ mi. W of Trader's Point, Ind., Lot 5, Row 3; mar.; chn.-at least a dau. On 11-3-1828, ae. 71, Fleming Co., Ky., had wife, ae. ca. 67 & a dau. who had fits. Enl. Aug. 1776, 8th Regt., Pa. Troops, Capt. Montgomery, Col. McCoy, Pa. Line; 3 yr.; later Va. REF-Pens. S.16203 Pa., Va.; Am. Leg.

    MITCHELL, JOSEPH   Vigo Co.
Listed as Rev. sold. bur. there. REF-"Terre Haute Tribune", 7-6-1947.

    MITCHELL, ZENAS, Sr.   Vigo Co.
Listed as Rev. sold. bur. there. REF-"Terre Haute Tribune", 7-6-1947.

    MODERELL, ANDREW   Owen Co.
(Uncertain.) Pens. file of John McCullough, Rev. sold. of Owen Co., includes affid. of Andrew Moderell, son of George Moderell who was in War with John McCullough. Wording not clear whether it was Andrew or George in War. REF-Pens. S.32404 (McCullou--)

    MODERELL, GEORGE   Owen Co.
(Uncertain.) See Andrew Moderell above.

MOFFETT, SAMUEL — Orange Co.
bur. in cem. on Ben Purlee farm; Gr. 1, Lot 11, Row 3; liv. in Orangeville Twp. REF-Am. Leg.

MOORE, JOSEPH — Monroe Co.
(Uncertain.) b. ca. 1751, Somerset Co., N.J.; d. prob. 1823 (final pens. payment); mar.; chn.-at least a dau. Pens. appl. 10-19-1818, Whitley Co., Ky.; later liv. Floyd's Fork, Jefferson Co., Ky.; 7-18-1821, ae. ca. 70, was liv. with wife, aged & infirm, and mar. dau. in Jefferson Co., Ky., ca. 12 mi. from Louisville. Final pens. payment 3-4-1823 from Lexington, Ky., Agy. altho the sold. on 4-26-1823 had been liv. in Monroe Co., Ind., for 1 yr.; prob. d. soon after. Was a waggon-maker. Enl. 1776 Somerset Co., N.J., Troops, Capt. Joseph Meeker, Col. Hinds. REF-Pens. S.36177 N.J.; Thelma Murphy.

MOORE, JOSEPH — Washington Co.
bur. Hicksite Cem., Gr. 3 Row 11, Lot 11; private stone; liv. in Washington Twp. REF-Am. Leg.

MORRIS, JOHN W. — Johnson Co.
bur. in Greenwood, Ind., Cem., Gr. 6s, Lot 16, Sec. 7. -Am. Leg.

MORRIS, JOSEPH see Joseph Norris

MORRISON, EPHRAIM — Dearborn Co.
d. ante 1835 & bur. there. REF-Bowen's "Hist. of Dearborn Co., Ind." (1915), p. 284; "Hist. of Dearborn, Ohio, & Switzerland Cos., Ind." (1885), p. 199.

MOSES, HENRY — Knox Co.
bur. in Old Cathedral Cem., Vincennes, Ind. Was in infantry in George Rogers Clark's Army. REF-Am. Leg.

NEWELL, SAMUEL (omitted; see page 28)

NORRIS, JOSEPH — Decatur Co.
b. 1761, Md.; d. Aug. 1849, ae. 88, Greensburg, Ind.; bur. in the old cem.; removed (unknown unless poss. the Sand Creek Cem.); wife was liv. when he d.; she d. Greensburg. Enl. ae. 16 (DAR) or ae. 19 (Harding); served till end of War. REF-DAR 14, p. 73; DAR 15, p. 86; 1850 Mortality Schedules, v. 1, p. 273 (ISL); Harding's "Hist. of Decatur Co., Ind." (1915), p. 409.

OAKLEY, FIELDING — Greene Co.
Listed as Rev. sold. bur. there. REF-Bowen's "Biog. Mem. of Greene Co., Ind." (1908), v. 1, p. 17.

O'DELL, JAMES — Carroll Co.
b. 3-19-1765; d. 4-17-1845; bur. Delphi, Ind. Enl. in S.C. late in War; mov. to Ohio 1802; to Wayne Co., Ind., 1809; to Carroll Co., Ind. & liv. on the Angel farm till death. REF-DAR 18, p.235.

OGDEN, STEPHEN — Floyd Co.
(Uncertain.) ae. 76 in 1825; 7 chn. (names & ages given). Enl. in N.J., 1777. (Recd. too late to add data or check for pens.) REF-Floyd Co. Civil Order Bk. B, pp.24-25; Dorothy Riker.

OLIVER, JOHN   Johnson Co.
d. 8-7-1833; bur. Miller Cem., White River Twp., Gr. 4, Lot 5, Blk. 9; grave loc. near Peter Doty & fam. REF-Am. Leg.; "Cem. Rec. of Johnson Co.", Alexander Hamilton Chap., DAR, Franklin, Ind., p. 243 (ts in ISL).

OLMSTED, JERRY   Clark Co.
bur. in Bethlehem Cem. REF-Am. Leg.; DAR 15, p. 85; DAR 18,p.235.

PALMER (PARMER), NATHANIEL C.   Carroll Co.
b. 1754; d. 12-11-1838; ae. 85; first bur. on James Cornell farm, ½ mi. E of Brethren Church on Michigan Rd.; on 7-4-1847 was rem. to E pt. of Deer Creek Cem., Delphi, Ind. Was in many battles under Washington. REF-DAR 18, pp. 236-237.

PARIS, ISAAC   see Isaac Faris

PARKE, BENJAMIN   Knox Co.
Listed as Rev. sold. bur. there. REF-"Hist. of Knox Co., Ind." (1886), p. 204.

PARKER, ICHABOD   Decatur Co.
bur. Sand Creek Cem.; gr. loc. by Lone Tree Chap., DAR, Greensburg, Ind.; stone says Sold. of Rev. & gives date of death, etc. (but neither source below copied it. MRW). REF-DAR 14, p. 73; DAR 15, p. 86; Harding's "Hist. of Decatur Co., Ind."(1915),410.

PARMER, NATHANIEL C.   see Nathaniel C. Palmer

PARR, JAMES   Johnson Co.
d. ae. 93; name on bronze tablet to Rev. dead in Franklin Cem., erected by DAR below, which has official proof on this sold. REF-Am. Leg.; "Cem. Rec. of Johnson Co.", Alexander Hamilton Chap., DAR, Franklin, Ind., p. 243 (ts in ISL).

PETERS, DAVID   Rush Co.
bur. in Goddard Cem. REF-Alexander's "Sketches of Rush Co., Ind." (1915), p. 36.

PHILLIPS, J. P.   Greene Co.
bur. on Fillinger farm, Richland Twp., Gr. 1, Lot 1. Was in N.C. Inf. REF-Am. Leg.; Bowen's "Biog. Mem. of Greene Co., Ind." (1908), v. 1, p. 17.

PIERCE, JAMES   Fayette Co.
bur. Orange Twp. Cem., Connersville, Ind., gr. loc. by Connersville Chap., DAR. REF-DAR 15, p. 85; DAR 18, p. 240; Bowen's Hist. of Fayette Co., Ind." (1917), p. 520.

PLACE, ---   La Grange Co.
Rev. sold. who liv. near Lima, Ind. REF-Battey's "Cos. of La Grange . Noble, Ind." (1882), p. 110.

POLIN, CHARLES   Harrison Co.
bur. in Green Valley Cem., gr. loc. by Piankeshaw Chap., DAR,
New Albany, Ind. REF-DAR 12, p. 74.

POTONGER, ROBERT   Montgomery Co.
bur. Potonger Cem., Brown Twp.; liv. in New Market, Ind.; son
Samuel, b. 1807. REF-Am. Leg.

PRINCE, WILLIAM   Gibson Co.
b. 1769; d. 9-4-1821; bur. Warnock Cem., Gr. 4, Lot 34 E½.
REF-Am. Leg.

QUINN, JOHN   Delaware Co.
b. 1759, Scotland; d. 1840, in 81st yr., Yorktown, Ind.;
at time of 1840 Census., was 82; bur. Yorktown Cem., Gr. 2,
Row 8, Lot 13, Sec. O.P. "AB"; m: in Scotland, Sarah Tapper;
chn.-Harrison, Harvey, John T., Joseph, 4 daus., gr-dau. Mrs.
Cynthia A. Randal (dau. of John T.); gr. loc. by Paul Revere
Chap., DAR, Muncie, Ind. In Delaware Co., Ind., by 11-24-1832
when he entered land in Sec. 2, Delaware Twp. REF-Am. Leg.;
DAR 15, p. 87; A. L. Kerwood in "Muncie Star", 1910; 1840
Pens. List, p. 182.

RAGER, LEONARD   Tippecanoe Co.
b. 1746; d. 4-20-1833; m. 10-25-1781, Catharine Hays, b. ca.
1749-1750, d. 10-1-1831; chn.- at least son Burket (in Louisville, Ky., 2-29-1856, ae. 72); grchn.-Daniel Boyer, b. 1808-
1809 & Jonathan Potter, b. ca. 1819. Enl. fall 1775, Sheperds-
town, Berkeley Co., (W.) Va., in Va. Cont. Line, Col. Muhlen-
berg; pvt.; dis. Valley Forge, fall 1777. Liv. Lemon Twp.,
Butler Co., O., 8-20-1818 & in 1820. REF-Pens. S.40315 Va.

RAY, SAMUEL see Samuel Reigh

REECE, JEHU ("Daddy")   Washington Co.
bur. Posey Twp. Cem., Gr. 3, Row 10, Lot 10; private marker.
Liv. in Madison Twp. REF-Am. Leg.

REIGH, SAMUEL   Harrison Co.
bur. in Rehoboth Presby. Church Cem. REF-DAR 7, p. 195.

RHOADS, DANIEL   Vigo Co.
(Uncertain; see discrepancy below). b. 10-5-1755; d. 4-26-1839;
bur. Pisgah Cem., Sugar Creek Twp., Gr. 1, Lot 114; m. (1st),
2-10-1777, Eve Foust, ae. 15 yr. 3 mo., d. 1-15-1792, ae. 30 plus;
m. (2nd), 3-15-1794, Nelson Co., Ky., Elizabeth Newman, b. 3-20-
1773, d. post 1849, Edgar Co., Ill.; chn.-David, b. 11-20-1778;
Elizabeth, b. Feb. 1779, m. 12-10-1807, --- Black; Jacob, b. 8-10-
1786; Rachel, b. 11-25-1780; child, b. ,-10-1783; Catharine, b.
4-6-1789; Sarah, b. 4-6-1789; Hannah, b. 11-15-1791, d. 5-8-?;
Thomas, b. 7-13-1794(?); Jonathan, b. 9-3-1798; Isaac, b. 2-2-
1803; Joseph, b. 1-17-1804(?); John, b. 2-7-1809; Newman, b.
10-3-1811 (of Edgar Co., Ill., 1848); George, b. 12-11-1814.
Pens. appl. 8-1-1818, Knox Co., Ind., in 63rd yr., 5 chn. with
him, only 1 ch. old enough to work; on Ind. Pens. Roll, 5-3-1830,

liv. in Vigo Co., Ind.; in 1833, ae. 79, Vigo Co.; wid. in
Edgar Co., Ill., 1848-1849. (None of the affids. in file indicate anything but that the sold. d. in Ind. However, an affid.
from a man in Richmond, Ray Co., Mo., says sold. d. in Edgar
Co., Ill., within 5 mi. of Paris, Ill. It is possible that he
has confused the sold. & the wid., as pens. file says sold. was
pd. in Ind. up to time of death, and grave location seems positive. He might, however, have d. in Edgar Co., Ill., just over
the State Line & been bur. in Vigo Co., Ind. In contradiction,
the sold. is said to have d. in Edgar Co., Ill., & bur. in
Ogden Cem. This man is said to have been from Mass. & served
in Mass., Capt. Samuel Payson, Col. John Graton; later Col.
Joseph Read. This disagrees completely with the service record below, which I found in the pens. file. I think that there
were likely two men of the same name. MRW.). Enl. June 1775,
Bedford Co., Pa., Comp. of Riflemen, Capt. Cluggage (sp?), Col.
Thompson; 1 yr. REF-Pens. W.1485 Pa.; Am. Leg.; 1835 Pens. List,
v. 3, p. 34; "Ill. Rev. Sold.", p. 35.

NEWELL, SAMUEL   Owen & Montgomery Cos.
(omitted from page 25.) b. 11-4-1754; d. 9-21-1841, ae. 87-10-17, Owen Co., Ind.; m. 9-30-1782, Jane Montgomery, b. Sept.
1763, d. 2-11-1843, ae. 81 yr. 5 mo., Owen Co.; chn.-Esther M.,
b. 9-30-1783, m. 1-28-1812, Jesse Evans, of Owen Co., 1844;
Samuel, Jr., b. 3-24-1786, m. 4-4-1809, Nancy Owens; Margaret E.,
b. 6-3-1788, m. 3-9-1815, William Owens; John M., b. 9-20-1790,
m. 2-1-1820, Peggy Beatie; Susannah, b. 11-4-1792, m. 9-9-1819,
Andr. Evans; Dorcas, b. 3-7-1795, d. 9-7-1824; Elizabeth C., b.
8-24-1797, d. 8-7-1831; Joseph B., b. 7-28-1800, m. 1-24-1824(?)
Jane Hinant? Winant? Winread?; William, b. 5-7-1803, m. 9-9-1830, Peline (sp?) Ja-- (sp?); Jane, b. 3-13-1806, m. 4-20-1837,
James Evans, of Boone Co., Ky. Orig. Bible pages on file but
faded in spots. Affid. 10-1-1844, Owen Co., Ind., of son William,
ae. 41, admr. of mother's est., that chn. liv. now as follows:
Samuel, John M., Joseph B., Margaret E., all in Pulaski Co., Ky.;
Jane, in or near Miami Reserve, Ind.; Susannah, in Northern Ind.
Sold. was on Tenn. Pens. Roll, 3-2-1810; tr. 9-4-1816 from Tenn.
to Ky.; on 6-17-1833, ae. 78, liv. Pulaski Co., Ky.; tr. Sept.
1837 to Owen Co., Ind., to live with son William. After War,
to Green Co., N.C., on River (?) French Broad (?) till 1797;
to Ky. to Pulaski Co., orig. Lincoln Co., later called Wayne
Co., now called Pulaski Co.; to Owen Co., Ind. Enl. Apr. 1776,
Washington Co., Va., Capt. John Shelby; sgt. & lieut. in Capt.
Montgomery's Comp., Col. Campbell, Va. Mil., 1776. In 1840, ae.
86, liv. Montgomery Twp., Owen Co., Ind. Altho he prob. d. in
Owen Co., name is on DAR tablet to Rev. dead in P.O., Crawfordsville, Montgomery Co., Ind., erected by Dorothy Quincy Chap.,
DAR, Crawfordsville, Ind. REF-Pens. R.7617 Va.; Bowen's "Hist.
of Montgomery Co., Ind." (1913), v. 1, p. 180; Mills' "Early
Days in a College Town" (1924), p. 126; 1840 Pens. List, p.184.

RHODES, THOMAS   Perry Co.
bur. in plot on Riley farm set aside for free burying ground.
Served under Gen. Gates in Ulster Co., N.Y. A homeless man when
he came to Perry Co., Ind., he liv. with James Riley of Oil Twp.

REF-De la Hunt's "Hist. of Perry Co., Ind." (1916), p. 50;
Wallace Weatherholt.

        RICE, BEN.   Monroe Co.
bur. in Monroe Co.; gr. loc. by Sarah McCalla Chap., DAR,
Bloomington, Ind. REF-DAR 3, p. 147.

        RICKETTS, WILLIAM   Ohio Co.
DAR reference below is in error; listed here to disprove.
Pens. file definitely states NOT Rev. War.; N.W. Indian Wars,
1791; on Invalid Indian Roll, 1835, Dearborn Co., Ind. File
mentions Rising Sun, Ind. REF-O.W. Inv. File 26367 Va.;
DAR 28, p. 158; 1835 Pens. List, v. 3, p. 3.

        ROBERTS, WILLIAM   Crawford Co.
(Uncertain.) m. Elizabeth ---, ae. 57 in 1823; chn.- 13,
names given. Enl. N.C. (Recd. too late to add data or check
for pens.) REF-Crawford Co. Civil Order Bk. A, pp. 250-252;
Dorothy Riker.

        ROBINETTE, CLEMUEL   Madison Co.
bur. Robinette Cem., Gr. 4, Row 3, Lot 2. REF-Am. Leg.

        ROBINSON, BENJAMIN   Knox Co.
bur. Indiana Church Cem., Gr. 42, Blk. 18. REF-Am. Leg.

        ROGER, LEONARD see Rager

        ROMINE, JESSE   Grant Co.
b. 1-10-1794 (typo error as card in file definitely says Rev.
War.); d. 2-16-1855; bur. Union Chapel Cem., Gr. 5, Lot 56.
REF-Am. Leg.

        ROSE, ELISHA   Clark Co.
bur. in Bluelick Cem.; gr. loc. by Ann Rogers Clark Chap., DAR,
Jeffersonville, Ind. REF-DAR 7, p. 193.

        ROSE, WILLIAM   Floyd Co.
(Uncertain.) wife & dau. Mary (ae. 25). Enl. 15th Va. Regt.
(Recd. too late to add data or check for pens.) REF-Floyd Co.
Civil Order Bk. A, p. 140; Dorothy Riker.

        ROSECRANS, BENJAMIN   Perry Co.
b. 1746; bur. Tobinsport, Ind. Enl. N.Y.; served with Va. Troops,
with Col. Morgan at Short Hills, Red Banks, Trenton; was at
Princeton & White Plains. To Perry Co., Ind., ante 1820. REF-
DAR 36, p. 79; De la Hunt's "Hist. of Perry Co., Ind." (1916),
p. 50; Wallace Weatherholt.

        RUSSELL, DAVID   Vigo & Vermillion Cos.
b. 1759, Shenandoah Valley, Va.; d. fall 1835; bur. first in
cem. near Dana, Ind.; rem. 1942 to Rose Lawn Cem. N of Terre
Haute, Vigo Co. Enl. 11-5-1779; from Va. rec. of men recruited
from Shenandoah Co., Va.; pvt. in Capt. Abraham Heller's Comp.,
Col. Montgomery; in Illinois Dept. under Gen. George Rogers
Clark. REF-DAR 46, p. 169.

RUST, DAVID   Greene Co.
Listed as Rev. sold. bur there. REF-Bowen's "Biog. Mem. of
Greene Co., Ind." (1908), v. 1, p. 17.

SAGE, JOHN   Scott Co.
d. 9-15-1872, near Lexington, Scott Co. Newspaper, 9-20-1872
says "an old citizen of this (Jefferson Co., Ind.) county and
a Rev. sold." (May have had a son, George Washington Sage,
b. 1831, Smyrna Twp., Jefferson Co. MRW). REF-"Items From
Early Newspapers of Jefferson Co., Ind., 1817-1886", copied by
Mary Hill, DAR, Madison, Ind.; Thelma Murphy.

SAFFER, JOHN   Harrison Co.
d. 1843; bur. in a pioneer Baptist cem., Little Flock Baptist
Church, 3-4 mi. S of Elizabeth, Ind.; last burial there. REF-
"How Sleep the Brave?", address by C.F. Possen, Ind. Soc. SAR,
2-25-1922 (copy in ISL).

SANDERS, JOHN   Monroe Co.
b. 10-11-1792 (typo error as card in file definitely says Rev.
War), at Charleston, S.C.; d. 1847; bur. Mayfield Cem., Gr. 4,
Lot 8, Row 3. Enl. 1776; dis. 1776. REF-Am. Leg.; "Biog.
Sketches", Monroe Co.

SANDS, JACOB   Montgomery Co.
Listed as Rev. sold. bur. there. REF-Am. Leg.

SAVARNS, JOHN   see John Severns

SCHOCNOVER, CHRISTOPHER   see Christopher Crumb

SCOTT, JAMES   Knox Co.
b. 1755; d. 10-23-1842; bur. Upper Indiana Cem., near Vincen-
nes, Ind.; m. Jane McClure, b. 1759, d. 8-18-1845; bur. Upper
Indiana Cem. (sis. of Rev. soldiers Daniel, George, John &
William McClure, all bur. in Knox Co., Ind.). Pvt. 3rd cl.,
Capt. James McFarline, 2nd Batt., Cumberland Mil., 9-8-1781.
REF-"Pa. Arch.", 5th Ser., v. VI, p. 193; DAR 48, p. 184.

SCOTT, SAMUEL   Posey Co.
d. 1849; bur. Templeton Cem. Pvt., Mounted Volunteers; tr.
from Western Tenn. REF-DAR 28, p. 158; 1835 Pens. List,
v. 3, p. 8.

SEA, JOHN   Henry Co.
b. 1757; ae. 73 in 1833; bur. Knightstown Cem., gr. loc. by
Maj. Hugh Dinwiddie Chap., DAR, Knightstown, Ind. Va. Mil.
REF-DAR 26, p. 116; 1835 Pens. List, v. 3, p. 53.

SELCH, MICHAEL   Johnson Co.
bur. there; name on bronze tablet to Rev. dead in Franklin Cem.,
erected by DAR below. REF-Am. Leg.; "Com. Rec. of Johnson Co.",
by Alexander Hamilton Chap., DAR, Franklin, Ind., p. 243 (ISL).

SEVERNS, JOHN — Gibson Co.
Listed as Rev. sold. bur. there. REF-Bowen's "Hist. of Gibson Co., Ind." (1914), p. 208.

SHAFFER, WILLIAM — Clinton Co.
bur. in Old Tennessee Cem., Ind.; gr. loc. by Capt. Harmon Aughe Chap., DAR, Frankfort, Ind. REF-DAR 23, p. 131.

SHARP, BEN — Gibson Co.
bur. Sharp Cem. REF-Am. Leg.

SHAVER, JACOB — Perry Co.
(This sold. did not die in Ind.; but because he was liv. here at the time of his death and because he was bur. here, he is being listed.) d. 8-9-1814, Hardin Co., Ky. bur. Oil Creek Cem., Perry Co., Ind., ca. 1 mi. NW of Asbury Mtg. Hse.; m. Sept. 1779 or 1780, Fayette Co., Pa., Nancy Allen, b. ca. 1764, dau. of Benjamin Allen of Fayette Co., Pa.; chn.-1 ch. d. in infancy; Benjamin, b. May 1783, nearly 3 yr. after their mar.; Adam Allen, b. ca. 50 yr. ago (affid. of 1852?), liv. near Georgetown, Scott Co., Ky., & soon Mov. to Ohio; Sarah m. Jonathan D. Esarey. Wid. liv. near Rome City, Ind., 3-2-1852, ae. ca. 88; 5-16-1853 she had a bro. Adam Allen in Fayette Co., O., 4-18-1851; and a bro. Benjamin Allen in Edgar Co., Ill.; she said to be an "own cousin" of Gen. Ethan Allen. Sold. to Oil Twp., Perry Co., Ind., ca. 12 mi. from mouth of Little Blue River with Esarey fam. in 1810. He went to Louisville, Ky., to attend a meeting of Rev. soldiers about to petition Congress; d. 8-9-1814, Hardin Co., Ky. (no indication as to whether while on this trip or on another; seems likely that he visited Hardin Co. while down at Louisville). Enl. 9-20-1775 near Forks of Youghiogheny River, Pa. (poss. in the disputed region now W. Va. MRW); dis. 11-20-1778, Ft. Pitt. REF-Pens. W.9648 Pa.; De la Hunt's "Hist. of Perry Co., Ind." (1916), p. 50; Wallace Weatherholt.

SHAW, JAMES — Carroll Co.
(Uncertain.) b. 1741-1743. Pens. 8-24-1819, ae. 77; tr. from Gallatin Co., Ky., to Ind.; in 1833, ae. 91; prob. d. soon after as is not in 1840 Pens. List. Pvt. in Va. Line. REF-1835 Pens. List., v. 3, p. 11; "Hist. of Carroll Co., Ind." (1882), p. 169.

SHAW, JOHN — Clark Co.
(Uncertain.) ae. 75 in 1825; wife Sarah. Enl. 1775 in N.Y. (Recd. too late to add data or check for pens.) REF-Clark Co. Civil Order Bk. 1, pp. 354-356; Dorothy Riker.

SHROYER, JOHN — Greene Co.
Listed as Rev. sold. bur. there. (May be error for John Shyer below.) REF-Bowen's "Biog. Mem. of Greene Co., Ind." (1908), v. 1, p. 17.

SHYER, JOHN — Greene Co.
b. 5-14-1753, York Co., Pa.; bur. Grandview Cem., Bloomfield, Ind., Gr. 1, Lot 413 Sec. X. Enl. Dec. 1776, Md. Mil., Capt. George Hawkins; dis. 1-1-1788 (typo error for 1778?). (This may be the John Shroyer above.) REF-Am. Leg.

SILLIMAN, WILLIAM   Floyd Co.
b. 1756; d. 10-6-1816; bur. 10-8-1816, Fairview Cem., New
Albany, Ind., Gr. 3, Lot 6, Blk. 12, Sec. 1. Was a Major.
REF-Am. Leg.

SIPES, GEORGE   Lawrence Co.
b. 3-17-1760; d. 7-3-1853; bur. Sipes Cem., Gr. 3, Lot 4. In
1840, ae. 81. REF-Am. Leg.; 1840 Pens. List, p. 183.

SKEETS, JAMES   Dearborn Co.
(Uncertain.) d. ante 1835 (Bowen below) and bur. there; liv.
1840, ae. 84, Kelso Twp., with William Row. REF-Bowen's "Hist.
of Dearborn Co. Ind." (1915), p. 284; "Hist. of Dearborn, Ohio,
& Switzerland Cos., Ind." (1885), p. 199; 1840 Pens. List,p.182.

SLAUGHTER, GEORGE   Clark Co.
d. 6-17-1818, Charlestown, Ind.; bur. there; gr. loc. by Ann
Rogers Clark Chap., DAR, Jeffersonville, Ind.; m. 2-10-1767,
Culpeper Co., Va., Mary Field, b. 1750-1751, liv. 8-17-1836, ae.
85, Warsaw, Gallatin Co., Ky. Affid. 9-13-1836, Owen Co., Ky.,
of William Roberts, ae. 40; affid. 8-30-1836, Shelby Co., Ky.,
of Capt. Benjamin Roberts, in 87th.yr., that he d. sold. were
in Col. Crockett's Regt.; sold. was Maj. & Lt.-Col. REF-Pens.
W.8729 Va.; Am. Leg.; DAR 7, p. 193; DAR 18, p. 253.

SMITH, ALDEN   Clark Co.
b. 1786 (typo error as card in file definitely says Rev. War);
d. 8-8-1827 (Am. Leg.); d. 1847 (DAR 18 below); bur. old cem.
at New Washington, Ind., Gr. 1, Row 18, Lot 7. Said to be a
desc. of John & Priscilla Alden. REF-Am. Leg.; DAR 18,p.253;
"Rev. Sold. Bur. in Clark Co.", State DAR (ts in ISL).

SMITH, EDWARD   Harrison Co.
d. 1828; bur. Mt. Zion #1 Cem., Gr. 4, Row 8, Lot 1; marker
"Soldier in 1774". (NOT the Lt. Edward Smith bur. in Cedar
Hill Cem., Corydon, Ind. MRW). REF-Am. Leg.

SMITH, JOHN   Harrison Co.
bur. in unmarked grave ½ mi. S of Corydon. Deserted English
Army to join colonists. REF-DAR 7, p. 195.

SOBIE, DAVID   Greene Co.
Listed as Rev. sold. bur. there. REF-Bowen's "Biog. Mem. of
Greene Co., Ind." (1908), v. 1, p. 17.

STALELY, JOHN   Greene Co.
Listed as Rev. sold. bur. there. Was a Colonel; served on
Washington's staff. REF-Bowen's "Biog. Mem. of Greene Co.,
Ind." (1908), v. 1, p. 17.

STEELE, MIFLIN   Owen Co.
b. 1-14-1763; d. 3-10-1831; bur. Surber Cem., 4½ mi. N of Gosport, Ind., Gr. 3, Lot 16; gr. loc. by Spencer Chap., DAR, Spencer, Ind. From N.C. to Benton Co., Ky., ca. 1800; to Owen Co.,
Montgomery Twp., 1819. REF-Am. Leg.; DAR 2, p. 120.

STEWART, JAMES   Ohio Co.
b. 1765-1766; d. 1833, ae. 78, near Rising Sun, Ind. REF-"Hist. of Dearborn, Ohio, & Switzerland Cos., Ind." (1885), p. 200.

STOBAUGH (STONEBAUGH), ABRAHAM   Putnam Co.
d. Sept. 1836; bur. with honors in cem. on old Gorham farm in Marion Twp. Came from Montgomery Co., Va., to Floyd Twp., Putnam Co., Ind.; son Jacob came with father. Name on bronze tablet to Rev. dead in Ct. Hse., Greencastle, Ind., erected by DAR below. REF-DAR 19, p. 86; "Putnam Co. Hist. & Genealogies", Washburn Chap., DAR, Greencastle, Ind., p. 198 (ts in ISL); Weik's "Hist. of Putnam Co., Ind." (1910), p. 218.

STONE, PHILIP   Harrison Co.
bur. on his farm, 2 mi. or more W of Corydon, Ind. REF-DAR 7,196.

STONER, GEORGE   Tippecanoe Co.
bur. Greenbush Cem.; on cemetery book; name on bronze tablet to Rev. dead, erected by Gen. de Lafayette Chap., DAR, Lafayette, Ind. REF-DAR 3, p. 146; DAR 6, p. 155.

STOUT, DEWEY   Delaware Co.
Listed as Rev. sold. bur. there. REF-Am. Leg.

STRAIGHT, HENRY   Daviess Co.
d. 2-11-1858; newspaper files. From Ohio. REF-Am. Leg.

STRICKER, WOLF   Clark Co.
b. 1755; d. 2-15-1835; bur. Salem Cem., Gr. 1, Row 7, Lot 7. REF-Am. Leg.

SUTTENFIELD, WILLIAM   Allen Co.
b. 1758; d. Dec. 1836; gr. loc. by Mary Penrose Wayne Chap., DAR, Ft. Wayne, Ind. REF-DAR 15, p. 87.

SWARTZELL, JOHN   Starke Co.
b. 1751, York Co., Pa.; d. 1855; bur. Swartzell Cem., Washington Twp., Gr. 1, Lot 1, Blk. 1. Liv. in Knox, Ind. Next of kin: John Swartzell. (File card says War of 1812, but would have been of Rev. service age. MRW). REF-Am. Leg.

SWINDELL, WILLIS   Madison Co.
b. 3-5-1763; d. 5-9-1851; bur. Vinson Cem., Gr. 3, Row 6, Lot 16. Flag on gr. Liv. in Van Buren Twp. (File card says War of 1812, but would have been of Rev. service age. MRW). REF-Am. Leg.

TACKETT, LEWIS   Henry Co.
bur. in Lewisville, Ind., Cem. REF-DAR 27, p. 119.

TAYLOR, SILAS   Perry Co.
b. 1753; bur. Perry Co. Enl. in Pa., Capt. Lenox, Col. Shee, Pa. Cont. Line; fought at Germantown, Chestnut Hill; Yorktown; dis. at Carlisle, Pa. To Perry Co., Ind., ante 1820. Was a stonemason. REF-De la Hunt's "Hist. of Perry Co., Ind." (1916), p.50; Wallace Weatherholt. (Continued in center of page 34.)

TERRELL, ENOCH　　　　　　　Dearborn Co.
Uncertain. Recd. too late to add data or check for pension.
REF-Mrs. Walter Kerr, Aurora, Ind.

THOM, MICHAEL　　　　　　　Knox Co.
Grave marked by Francis Vigo Chap., DAR, Vincennes, Ind. REF-DAR 12, p. 74.

TILFORD, JAMES　　　　　　Clark Co.
d. 5-10-1821, ae. 61; obit. in paper. REF-"Charlestown Intelligencer", 5-24-1821; Dorothy Riker.

TILLINGHAST, JOHN　　　　　Vermillion Co.
b. 1765-1766, Providence, R.I.; d. 5-31-1837; bur. Newport Cem., Newport, Ind., Gr. 4, Lot 54, Orig. Sec. (File card says "Campaign of 1794--Battle of Rapids of Maumee", but might have been of Rev. service age. MRW). REF-Am. Leg.

TOMBLINSON, JOHN　　　　　Knox Co.
b. 1755; d. 8-12-1844, ae. 89, Russelville, Ill.; bur. Greenlawn Cem., Knox Co.; left large fam. Often refused to ask for pens. Was at surrender of Cornwallis. Bur. with military honors. REF-DAR 48, p. 185; obit in "Western Sun & General Advertiser", Vincennes, Ind., 8-17-1844.

TAYLOR, SILAS (continued)　　　Perry Co.
(Continued from page 33. Following data from pens. file.)
b. 1753-1755, Ireland; d. 10-18-1821; m. 3-12-1811, Franklin Co., Ind., Susannah Chandler (she used given name Rebecca later; NOT 2 wives), b. 1793-1794 (she m. 2nd, 2-9-1830, Perry Co., Ind., Arthur Wheatley who d. 2-9-1841); chn-Ebenezer, b. 2-5-1813; Jeremiah, b. 2-1-1816; Silas, b. 7-14-1820; Jefferson; gr-son A. L. Taylor (son of Silas, Jr.). Pens. appl. 9-28-1819, ae. 64, Perry Co. Affid. of wid. Rebecca Wheatley, 2-28-1860, ae. 66, Perry Co. & 10-28-1861. Affid. 3-31-1892, Pittsburg, Kans., of gr-son A. L. Taylor that sold. an Irishman, deserted Brit. Army, was at Valley Forge. Enl. 4-3-1774 (error?), Northampton Co., Pa., Capt. Joseph Hopely (sp?), 3rd Pa. Regt.; Capt. Lennox, Col. Shee, Pa. Cont. Line; 3 yr. REF-Pens. R.10432 Pa.; other ref. on page 33.

TOOTHMAN, JACOB　　　　　　Dearborn Co.
d. ante 1835 & bur. there. REF-Bowen's "Hist. of Dearborn Co., Ind." (1915), p. 284; "Hist. of Dearborn, Ohio, & Switzerland Cos., Ind." (1885), p. 199.

TURMAN, BENJAMIN　　　　　Sullivan Co.
b. 1748, Va.; bur. Mann Cem., Turman Twp.; mar.; chn-at least Thomas, b. 8-18-1796, Bedford Co., Va., d. 6-30-1863, bur. Mann Cem., m. Lavina White, b. Tenn., dau. of William White. Fam. to Ohio; to Ind. 1810. REF-Am. Leg.; "Rev. Sold. Bur. in Sullivan Co.", State DAR (ts in ISL); Wolfe's "Hist. of Sullivan Co., Ind." (1909), v. 2, p. 245.

TUTTLE, GERSHOM   Vigo Co.
b. 1737-1738; d. 1818, ae. 80 (newspaper below); d. 1823; bur.
Otter Creek Union Cem., Gr. 2, Lot 377; gt-grson of Deacon Timothy Tuttle; mar.; chn-at least son Gershom, b. 1769, m. 1788, Pamelia Strong, b. 1770. After War, sold. brought fam. to Vigo Co. Much abt. decs. in newspaper ref. Col. in War of 1812. REF-Am. Leg.; "Terre Haute Tribune", 6-22-1947.

TUTTLE, SOLOMON   Clark Co.
Grave loc. by Piankeshaw Chap., DAR, New Albany, Ind. REF-DAR 10, p. 154.

UPSON, JESSE   La Grange Co.
b. 1754; d. 8-16-1838; bur. Riverside Cem., Gr. 2, Lot 112, NE Sec. (File card says War of 1812, but would have been of Rev. service age. MRW). REF-Am. Leg.

VENARD, CEPHAS   Cass Co.
bur. Vennard (sic) Cem.; Rev. War; authority: Middleton. REF-Am. Leg.

WAGGONER, SAMUEL   Parke Co.
bur. Moore Cem.; stone (Am. Leg. did not copy data. MRW). REF-Am. Leg.

WALKER, ---   Howard Co.
bur. Poplar Grove Cem.; proof: caretaker's rec. REF-Am. Leg.

WARTHEN, WILLIAM   Morgan Co.
bur. Warthen Cem., Gr. 1, Lot 6. Proof: Ankie Ratts, Ashland Twp., a desc. REF-Am. Leg.

WATKINS, ROBERT   Delaware Co.
b. 1754, Md.; bur. ca. ½ mi. S of the John Truitt homestead on Muncie-Selma Turnpike, on E side of rd. with wife; gr. loc. by Paul Revere Chap., DAR, Muncie, Ind. Long service rec. in pens. appl. (Could find none at Archives. MRW.). In 1780 liv. with father in Union Co., S.C.; taken prisoner in Aug.; enl. Oct. 1, 1780, Capt. George Avery, Col. Thomas Brandon; dis. 7-1-1782. Liv. 20 yr. in S.C., 4 yr. in Ky., 1 yr. in Ohio, last 2 yr. in Ind. (11-13-1832, ae. 78, in Delaware Co. (rec. in Delaware Co. Circuit Court). REF-DAR 15, p. 87; A. L. Kerwood in "Muncie Star", 1910.

WATSON, JAMES   Jennings Co.
bur. in Paris Cem. REF-DAR 28, p. 158.

WELLS, WILLIAM   Allen Co.
d. 8-15-1812, killed by Indians; gr. loc. by Mary Penrose Wayne Chap., DAR, Ft. Wayne, Ind.; bro-in-law of Ma-che-can-noch-qua (Little Turtle), b. 1751, d. 7-14-1812, bur. with military honors in Ft. Wayne. REF-DAR 15, p. 87.

-35-

WESTFALL, ABEL   Greene Co.
bur. Grandview Cem., Bloomfield, Ind., Gr. 2, Lot 531, Sec. X.
Served in 8th Va. Regt. (Poss. bro. of Cornelius Westfall in
"Roster", p. 377. MRW). REF-Am. Leg.; Bowen's "Biog. Mem. of
Greene Co., Ind." (1908), v. 1, p. 17.

WHEELER, ---   Decatur Co.
bur. Milford Cem. with his friends James Crawford & George King.
REF-Harding's "Hist. of Decatur Co., Ind." (1915), p. 409.

WHEELER, JOHN   La Porte Co.
bur. Low's Cem. near Waterford, Ind. REF-DAR 27, p. 119.

WHETZEL, JACOB   Morgan Co.
b. 1765; d. 1827; bur. McKenzie Cem., Gr. 4, Lot 120. (File
card says War of 1812, but might have been of Rev. service
age. MRW). REF-Am. Leg.

WHISENAND, JACOB   Monroe Co.
b. 1771 (sic; obvious typo error) in Penn.; d. 9-17-1813; bur.
Rose Hill Cem., Bloomington, Ind., Gr. 3, Lot 15, Row 3, Old
Part. Was a Rev. spy. File claims, etc., Court House, Monroe
Co. REF-Am. Leg.

WHISTLER, JOHN   Allen Co.
b. Ireland; d. Allen Co.; gr. loc. by Mary Penrose Wayne Chap.,
DAR, Ft. Wayne, Ind.; m. Ann Bishop; chn-at least son George
Washington, b. 5-19-1800 while father was Commandant at Ft.
Wayne. Sold. in Brit. Army under Gen. Burgoyne; after dis.,
retd. tosettle in Amer.; became officer (Major - DAR below) in
U.S. Army. Gr-father of James Abbott McNeill Whistler, the
artist. REF-DAR 15, p. 87; "Dict. of Amer. Biog.", Scribners,
v. XX, pp. 72-73.

WHITE, JAMES   Clay Co.
(Uncertain.) b. 9-8-1763, Culpeper Co., Va.; mar.; chn-Smith;
James; Nancy m. -- Cooperider; Peggy m. & wid. of Benjamin
White; Polly m. -- Cooperider; Betsy m. -- VanMeter; all 1855
in Clay Co. Pens. appl. 1837, ae. 74, Clay Co. When ca. 23,
to Madison Co., Ky.; then to Montgomery Co., Ky.; liv. for 27
yr. in these two; then to Orange Co., Ind.; to Clay Co. 14 yr.
ago. Enl. 1778, Culpeper Co., Va., Capt. John Slaughter, Maj.
John Roberts, Col. Thorn. REF-Pens. R.11417.

WHITE, JAMES   Montgomery Co.
d. 7-15-1865; bur. Alamo Cem., Ripley Twp., Gr. 4, Row 4, Lot
14. REF-Am. Leg.

WHITE, MATTHEW   Tippecanoe Co.
bur. Greenbush Cem.; on cem. books; name on bronze tablet to
Rev. dead, erected by Gen. de Lafayette Chap., DAR, Lafayette,
Ind. REF-DAR 3, p. 146; DAR 6, p. 155.

WHITGAR (WITCHER), WILLIAM   Delaware Co.
bur. Strong Cem., Albany, Ind., Gr. 1, Row 7, Lot 7, Old Part;
gr. loc. by Paul Revere Chap., DAR, Muncie, Ind. In N.C. Mil.
REF-Am. Leg.; DAR 15, p. 37.

         WILES, JOHN   Putnam Co.
Name on bronze tablet in Ct. Hse., Greencastle, Ind. REF-
DAR 19, p. 86.

         WILKERSON, SOLOMON   Greene Co.
Listed as Rev. sold. bur. there. REF-Bowen's "Biog. Mem. of
Greene Co., Ind." (1908), v. 1, p. 17.

         WILKERSON, WILLIAM   Greene Co.
Listed as Rev. sold. bur. there. REF-Bowen's "Biog. Mem. of
Greene Co., Ind." (1908), v. 1, p. 17.

         WILLIAM, PETER   Owen Co.
b. 12-25-1749, Wythe Co., Va.; d. 12-25-1847; bur. in the old
cem., Spencer, Ind.; gr. loc. by Spencer Chap., DAR; chn-at
least a son still liv. 1897-1898. Was in Battle of Cowpens;
had pens. (I was unable to identify it. MRW). REF-DAR 2, p.120.

         WILLIAMS, JOHN   Morgan Co.
bur. in Shiloh Cem. REF-Am. Leg.; SV records.

         WILLIS, BENJAMIN, Sr.   Montgomery Co.
b. 1764-1765; d. 7-19-1833, ae. 68; bur. Willis Cem., NW of
Alamo, Ripley Twp.; stone. REF-Am. Leg.

         WITCHER, WILLIAM see William Whitgar

         WOODRUFF, ELISHA   Clinton Co.
bur. Paris Cem.; gr. loc. by Capt. Harmon Aughe Chap., DAR,
Frankfort, Ind. REF-DAR 23, p. 135.

         WRIGHT, PHILBURD   Union Co.
b. 1750, Md.; d. 1831, near Brownsville, Ind.; m. Elizabeth Reagan; 11 chn; son Joel, b. 2-5-1793, Randolph Co., N.C., m. 9-10-
1812, Sarah Byerly (or Birley), b. 4-30-1789, near Beards Hatter
Shop, N.C., d. ca. 5-1-1828, Wayne Co., Ind. Immediately after
War, sold. went to Randolph Co., N.C.; was a J.P. there; after
ca. 30 yr there, came to Union Co., Ind., 1813. REF-Ind. Pion.
Soc. lineages in "Yearbook" (Johnson desc.).

         WYATT, JERE   Gibson Co.
Listed as Rev. sold. bur. there. REF-Bowen's "Hist. of Gibson
Co., Ind." (1914), p. 208.

         YOUNG, JAMES   Washington Co.
b. 1740; d. 1822; bur. Young Cem., now Claud Gibbon's farm.
REF-DAR 28, p. 159.

NOTE: an answer recd. by Ind. State Archivist from Natl. Archives
concerning Joseph Griffith says no payment record found.

STATE
Durand, Andrew
  ALLEN
Blair, David
Fairfield, Asa
Fairfield, Oliver
Lasselle, Hyacinth
Suttenfield, William
Wells, William
Whistler, John
  CARROLL
O'Dell, James
Palmer, Nathaniel C.
Shaw, James
  CASS
Bartlett, John
Venard, Cephas
  CLARK
Armstrong, Thomas
Covert, Peter
Dutteroe, Jacob
George, Robert
Gobin, Daniel
Hoops, David
Lewis, William
Clmsted, Jerry
Rose, Elisha
Shaw, John
Slaughter, George
Smith, Alden
Stricker, Wolf
Tilford, James
Tuttle, Solomon
  CLAY
Crooks, Michael
White, James
  CLINTON
Applegate, John
Dukes, Isaac
Fernald, Benjamin
Shaffer, William
Woodruff, Elisha
  CRAWFORD
Bennett, Timothy
Roberts, William
  DAVIESS
Lashley, James
Straight, Henry
  DEARBORN
Angevin, James
Barlow, Joseph
Burrough, ---
Clarke, ---

Cloud, Baylis
Daniel, William
Frazier, Jonas
Gloyd, Asa
Jebine, ---
Kyle, John
Morrison, Ephraim
Skeets, James
Terrell, Enoch
Toothman, Jacob
  DECATUR
Brown, Samuel
Cooper, ---
Crawford, James
Gilliland, John
Hoolen, Thomas
Kirby, ---
Norris, Joseph
Parker, Ichabod
Wheeler, ---
  DELAWARE
Blunt, William
McConnell, John
Quinn, John
Stout, Dewey
Watkins, Robert
Whitgar, William
  FAYETTE
Bloomhart, Daniel
Homer, James
Pierce, James
  FLOYD
Akers, Joseph
Burnham, John
Hawley, Samuel
Higgs, Samuel
Ogden, Stephen
Rose, William
Silliman, William
  GIBSON
Bucklin, David
Casebolt, Robert
Gudgel, Andrew
Kimball, John
Prince, William
Severns, John
Sharp, Ben
Wyatt, Jere
  GRANT
Romine, Jesse
  GREENE
Bingham, Frederick
Branham, ---

Brewer, Zion
Bryant, William G.
Carpenter, Solomon
Cheney, Francis
Conway, William
Dover, Jefferson
Fellows, Willis
Hamlin, Isaac
Harvey, Sipple
Heitman, Garrett
Huffman, Henry
Ingersol, Peter
Oakley, Fielding
Phillips, J. P.
Rust, David
Shroyer, John
Sobie, David
Stakely, John
Westfall, Abel
Wilkerson, Solomon
Wilkerson, William
  HARRISON
Barber, Philip
Barnett, John
Bodenstadt, Henry
Currant, James
Dyer, Charles
Faris, Isaac
Harmon, Abraham
Harmon, Joseph
Kron, George
Polin, Charles
Reigh, Samuel
Saffer, John
Smith, Edward
Smith, John
Stone, Philip
  HENRY
Brown, Jacob
Griffith, Samuel
Sea, John
Tackett, Lewis
  HOWARD
Barngrover, ---
Brown, Marion
Clark, Abner
Crousore, Christian
Gullion, Jackson
Gulliver, John
Ide, Reuben
Walker, ---
  JACKSON
Buckner, Daniel

JAY
Farber, Daniel
Harford, John

JEFFERSON
Burton, George
Foster, Timothy

JENNINGS
Watson, James

JOHNSON
Armstrong, Ambrose
Davidson, Isaac
Davidson, Joshua
Imel, Peter
Kerr, James
Lensters, Abraham
Morris, John W.
McClintock, Finley
McClintock, John
Oliver, John
Parr, James
Selch, Michael

KNOX
Canet, Rhupp
Dunnsen, Samuel
Johnson, W.
Kenney, Daniel
Moses, Henry
Parke, Benjamin
Robinson, Benjamin
Scott, James
Thom, Michael
Tomblinson, John

KOSCIUSKO
Leazenby, William

LA GRANGE
Cole, Abraham
Dickenson, Waitsell
Evans, Edward
Fowler, Nathan
McNeil, William
Place, ---
Upson, Jesse

LA PORTE
Burlingame, Clark
Wheeler, John

LAWRENCE
Flinn, George
Guthrie, Daniel
Hunston, Edward
Illerd, Peter
Sipes, George

MADISON
Litchfield, ---
Miller, Reuben

Robinette, Clemuel
Swindell, Willis

MARION
Cool, Isaac
Cooper, Elijah
Griffith, Joseph
Miller, William

MONROE
Baker, Henry
Blaine, Robert
Burch, William
Heilman, John
Lowe, William
Maxwell, J. B.
Moore, Joseph
Rice, Ben
Sanders, John
Whisenand, Jacob

MONTGOMERY
Brant, Christopher
Gott, Robert
Handlin, Matthias
Mason, William
McArthur, James
McNulty, John
Newell, Samuel
Potonger, Robert
Sands, Jacob
White, James
Willis, Benjamin

MORGAN
Baxter, Thomas
Brunnemer, ---
Dillman, Jacob
Warthen, William
Whetzel, Jacob
Williams, John

OHIO
Chambers, Benjamin
Marble, Nathan
Ricketts, William
Stewart, James

ORANGE
Daily, Ephraim
Finley, David
Lashbrook, John
Moffett, Samuel

OWEN
Alexander, Samuel
Brown, William
Defore, Stephen
Foster, Edward
Moderell, Andrew

Moderell, George
Newell, Samuel
Steele, Ninian
William, Peter

PARKE
Duncan, John
Ephlin, Jacob
Martin, John
Waggoner, Samuel

PERRY
Cummings, Thomas
Harley (Hardy), David
Rhodes, Thomas
Rosecrans, Benjamin
Shaver, Jacob
Taylor, Silas

PIKE
Hayes, John
McMannus, John

PORTER
Jones, Joseph

POSEY
Anderson, Peter
Cox, Thomas
Dunbar, John
Elkins, Shadrach
Herring, Ephraim
Martin, John
McCollum, Daniel
Scott, Samuel

PUTNAM
Barnett, James Otis
Bartee, John
Brown, William
Byrd, Jonathan
Cunningham, Elizabeth
Edmondson, William
Grider, Jacob
Hopkins, Silas
McHaffie, John
Stobaugh, Abraham
Wiles, John

RANDOLPH
Addington, John
Chandler, Joseph
Davis Joseph
Dudley, ---
Ferby, E. E.

RIPLEY
McCullough, John

RUSH
Fleener, David
Kitley, John
Peters, David

SCOTT
Sage, John
SHELBY
Imel, Peter
STARKE
Swartzell, John
SULLIVAN
Alsman, Andrew
Turman, Benjamin
TIPPECANOE
Crumb, Christopher
Rager, Leonard
Stoner, George
White, Matthew

UNION
Wright, Philburd
VANDERBURGH
Barnett, Humphrey
VERMILLION
Helt, John
Russell, David
Tillinghast, John
VIGO
Barnes, James
Bush, Japhet
Coltran, John
Dample, Thomas
Hopkins, Twins
Jones, George

Mitchell, Joseph
Mitchell, Zenas
Rhoads, Daniel
Russell, David
Tuttle, Gershom
WASHINGTON
Doane, Jacob
Moore, Joseph
McAlister, Zachariah
McKinney, Robert
Reece, Jehu
Young, James
WAYNE
Crawford, William
Deaver, William

INDEX

Names indexed: wives (if maiden name is known), husbands and wives of children, miscellaneous names.

Names not indexed: soldiers, their officers, their children, their wives (if maiden name is not known), places.

ADAMS 3
ALDEN John-32;Priscilla-32
ALLEN Adam-31;Benjamin-31(2);
  Ethan-31;Nancy-31
ATWATER William-16
BAUGHMAN Franklin Abraham-4
BEATIE Peggy-28
BINGHAM 5
BIRLEY Sarah-37
BISHOP Ann-36
BLACK 27
BLAND 6
BOWMAN Barbara-23
BOYER Daniel-27
BRICE 13
BROWN Thomas-6
BRYANT 9
BURCH 3-7
BURK 21
BYERLY Sarah-37
CAMPBELL Pamelia M.-14;William-14
CHANDLER 9;Rebecca-34;Susannah-34

CLARKE Samuel-8
COMPTON Rachel-17
COOK Herriman-11-12
COOPER Job-16-17;Joseph-16-17
COOPERIDER 36(2)
CORLE Mary-9
CORNELL 20;James-26
COTTRELL Anna-17;Britton-17;
  Jesse-17;Job-16-17;Joseph-16-17;Mary Ann-17;Nicholas-17;
  Rachel-17
COX 9
CRAWFORD James-9-36
CREVISTON Jacob-20;John-20
CURRY Thomas-3
DAVIS Thomas-4
DAWSON Isaac-20;Sicha-20
DEAL 4
DENNY Samuel-5
DIEL 4
DOTY Peter-26
DURBON Samuel B.-17
ESAREY Jonathan D.-31

EVANS Andrew-28;James-28;
    Jesse-28
FAITH Mary-4
FELLOWS John-13;William-13
FICHAS John-4
FIELD Mary-32
FINLEY 14
FLINN 16
FOUST Eve-27
GAY Bunker-9
GIBBONS Claud-37
GILES Sarah-9
GILMORE 14
GLADMAN Archibald-16
GODDARD 26
GOORMAN David-13
GORHAM 33;Thomas-19
GOWEN Nancy-18
GUTHRIE 14
HALL Elisha-4;Joseph-4
HANDLIN Rachel-17
HENNEGAN 14
HARLAND James-9
HARPER Cynthia-4
HAYS Catharine-27
HEAD Anna-16-17
HEIL 3
HELT 18
HINANT Jane-28
HOCK 16-17
HOTCHKISS Eunice-11
HOWELL Bethia-14
HUBBIRD 12
HURST 12
JACOBS Austin-12;Bennet-12
JOHNSON 9
JONES Constant-23;David-16-17;
    George-16;Horatio-20;Joel-16;
    John-20-23;Jonas-16;Jonathan-
    16-17;Matthew-16;Minerva-16;
    Nicholas-16;Thomas Blount-5
KELLER Betsy-4
KENNEDY 12
KETCHAM 19
KILLINGER 26
KILLION John-4
KING George-9-26
KIRKWOOD Susan-19
LANE Elizabeth E.-4
LARGE Ruth-6
LAWRENCE 7;Rachel-4;Samuel-4;
    William-4
LEECH William B.-21
LOW 36

McCLURE Daniel-30;George-30;
    Jane-30;William-30
McCONNELL Abram-23;Bethuel-23
McCOY Mary-5
McCULLOUGH James-23;John-24
McKENZIE 36
MANN 34
MARCH Mary-21
MARTIN-23;Ruth-24
MAYFIELD 30
MONTGOMERY Jane-28
MOORE 35
NAY 22
NEWMAN Elizabeth-27
O'CONNELL 4
OWENS Nancy-28;William-28
PARIS 37;Margaret-23
POTTER Jonathan-27
PURLEE Ben-10-25
RANDAL Cynthia-27
RARIDEN 4
RATTS Ankie-35
REAGAN Elizabeth-37
RILEY 28;James-28
ROBERTS Benjamin-32;William-32
ROBINETTE 24-29
RODMAN 22
ROW William-32
SALYERS Jeremiah-23
SKILLMAN 15
SMITH Chloe-16-17;Isaac-16;
    Lucinda-17
SOWERS 12
SPADE John G.-13
STINSON Benoni-24
STRONG 37
SURBER 32
TAPPER Sarah-27
TEMPLETON 30
THOMAS Jim-4
THOMPSON 18
THORNTON Mary-15
TREMAINE 22
TRUITT John-36
TUTTLE Timothy-35
VAN METER 36
VAUGHN 12
VINSON 33
WALLS Elijah-7
WARNOCK 7-27
WESTFALL Cornelius-36
WHEATLEY Arthur-34;Rebecca-
    34;Susannah-34
WHISTLER James A. McN.-36
WHITE Benj.-36;Lavina-34;Wm.-34

WILLIS 37
WILSON 4
WINANT Jane-28
WINGATE 14
WINREAD Jane-28
YEATS 5
YOUNG 37

REVOLUTIONARY SOLDIERS BURIED IN INDIANA

A SUPPLEMENT

485 Names Not Listed in the
Roster of Soldiers and Patriots
of the American Revolution
Buried in Indiana
(1938)

nor in
Revolutionary Soldiers
Buried in Indiana
(1949)

Margaret R. Waters

Indianapolis
1954

CONTENTS

Section I

Soldiers Alphabetically Arranged (464 including 264 with pension files)	5

Section II

Additional Soldiers Received Too Late for Alphabetical Order (21 including 13 with pension files)	115

Section III

Additional Notes to Soldiers in Section I	119

Section IV

County List of Soldiers in Sections I-II	120

Section V

Other Soldiers From Various Places (190 mentioned in above records)	124

Section VI

Soldiers Who Lived in Indiana but Moved to Other States Where They May Have Died (55 including 54 with pension files)	126

Section VII

Widows Who Lived in Indiana After Their Soldier Husbands Died in Other States (121 including 120 with pension files)	131

Section VIII

County List of Widows in Section VII	139

Section IX

Revolutionary Soldiers (Husbands of Above Widows) Who Died in Other States (107 listed by states in which they died)	141

Section X

Additions and Corrections to "Revolutionary Soldiers Buried in Indiana (pub. 1949)	142

Section XI

Index (except alphabetically arranged names in above sections; see explanatory note)	155

FOREWORD

It was with great difficulty that I restrained myself from editorial comment in my "Revolutionary Soldiers Buried in Indiana", published in 1949. I stated in the Foreword: "I do not guarantee the service of any soldier in my list, the burial place, nor the genealogical data. I have no doubt but that many of the data can be verified. Aside from the pension research mentioned below, I have made no effort to check the information given in the references. I do guarantee the accuracy of the references indicated and the pension abstracts which I have personally copied. All of my material has been gathered from public records open to anyone."

During the preparation of this Supplement, I have occasionally come across data which contradict, clarify, or add to the information given in the first compilation. These data should, I believe, be supplied here for purchasers of my first booklet. I have placed the data at the back of this Supplement so that the pages may be detached and inserted into the 1949 booklet.

Oddly, the Supplement is larger than the original. This compilation contains 485 soldiers not listed in the "Roster of Soldiers and Patriots of the American Revolution Buried in Indiana", published by the Indiana D.A.R. in 1938, nor in my own "Revolutionary Soldiers Buried in Indiana" (300 names not listed in the "Roster"), published in 1949. In searching for possible pensions for these 485 soldiers, it was necessary, because of duplication of names, to read 2,495 pension files; from these I have abstracted 277 records. There are undoubtedly more; but from the meager information given in some cases, I was unable to identify the men to my own satisfaction.

I am including a list of 190 soldiers from various places; these men I found mentioned in papers in the above pension files. I have a list of 55 soldiers who lived in Indiana but moved to other states where they may have died; these men are not given in the "Roster", pp. 404-405. I have also included a list of 121 widows who lived in Indiana after the deaths of their husbands in other states and a list of the states in which 107 of these men died.

Other than soldiers given me by friends or clients, there have been three main sources for the names in this Supplement; first, the lists of pensioners (soldiers and/or widows) on the Indiana Agency Rolls, published by Katie-Prince Ward Esker in the D.A.R. Magazine from July through December 1949; second, a list of Revolutionary soldiers buried in Indiana compiled by Mr. John L. Schrum and sent by him to the Indiana State Library on January 11, 1936 (of which more later); and third, the lists of rejected and suspended pensions published by the Government in 1831 and 1852 as House and Senate Documents, respectively.

Those familiar with the D.A.R. Magazine know of Mrs. Ward's fine genealogical work. I was delighted that she chose to print the Indiana Agency Rolls while she was editor of the Genealogical Department of the magazine.

Mr. John L. Schrum of Crawfordsville, Ind., now deceased, was a prominent S.A.R. who devoted years to compiling his list of over 900 names. The list is typed and furnished nothing but the name of the soldier and the Indiana county. Consequently, while it is valueless as proof, it provides valuable clues for further research. It includes most of the names which were published in 1938 in the D.A.R. "Roster" although Mr. Schrum's list was sent to the library two years earlier. I have tried to account for his list. At first, I thought he had taken every pensioner paid in Indiana on the 1820, 1835, and 1840 published lists; but that does not always prove to be the case. He has many errors; for instance, he has a man buried in Adams County whereas, with proof, the man lies in next-door Allen County. This can be explained, I think, by the fact that courthouse records show when a man applied for a pension; Mr. Schrum evidently assumed that the place of death was the same as the place of residence at the time of the application. He has errors in surnames and/or forenames. These can all be excused. What I cannot account for is where he obtained all his names, especially ones which have been on no published lists available to me, ones who never applied for a pension or ones who died years before pensions were general --- and yet ones which I have been able to prove from his clues. I have been told by S.A.R.'s who knew him that Mr. Schrum visited old communities old cemeteries, and old residents. In this way, I feel, he compiled his list. It should, therefore receive serious consideration even though it unfortunately lacks proof and does show minor errors.

Again, I do not guarantee any of the data in this Supplement except pension abstracts which I have personally copied. I have made no particular effort to add data to names except in certain cases which aroused my interest or in sources such as county histories where I found the information easily or accidentally.

I am indebted to Mrs. Leo Schultheis of Vincennes, Ind., for an idea which, however, I was unable to carry out. She suggested that I could obtain the death dates (and other data) of the French signers of the Oath of Fidelity at Vincennes from the church records there since, within reason, most of them would have died there. All would qualify as Patriots for D.A.R. My limited French, however, proved inadequate to cope with faded ink, old-style writing, and erratic spelling. I refer to the Oath of Inhabitants of Vincennes on July 20, 1778, as published (among other places) on pages 56-59 of the "Illinois Historical Collections". v. 8, George Rogers Clark Papers, Virginia Series, v. 3, (1912), about 200 names. These names would undoubtedly raise the total of Revolutionary soldiers or patriots buried in Indiana.

I wish to call the reader's attention to matters connected with the 1835 and 1840 published pension lists. The 1835 list includes some pensioners who died years before the list was printed and is not, therefore, as some people think, a list of pensioners _living_ in 1835. Also, the ages given in this list are, in most cases at least, the age at the time of the application for a pension --- for the majority of men, in 1832-1833. The 1840 list includes some men whose pensions were pending, rejected, or suspended but who reported themselves to the enumerator as pensioners, possibly misunderstanding (because of their advanced age) his questions and thinking he was listing soldiers.

In the Government's 1852 list of rejected and suspended pensions, I find errors. Not only are many names given incorrectly (possible typographical errors), but also some men listed as being rejected were later given pensions or their widows were. Reasons for rejection should be considered and, in some cases, discounted. Many are for "not six months' service"; the 1832 law required that long a tour. However, the 1832 law did not credit service as a guide, Indian spy, waggoner, cook, and similar non-combat services which are accepted for eligibility to the D.A.R. Also, "deserter" should not be viewed with too much alarm; many men took a voluntary "corn furlough", did the planting, and then voluntarily returned to their companies (with no questions asked) --- sometimes doing this for several years. Many pensions were refused because of two men of the same name having served from the same state. It was a case of the "fustest with the mostest"; the second man lost out. However, in the 100 years since this list was printed, I feel that many more muster rolls and lists of soldiers have been discovered and printed by the various states so that service can now be proved for many men whose pensions were once rejected. Widows' pensions were often rejected because they were unable tp prove their marriages; again, many such records have been found and made available now.

Abbreviations (other than b., d., m., chn., etc.) are:

ae.	aged	migr.	migrated
affid.	affidavit	pens.	pension
Am. Leg.	American Legion	poss.	possibly
ante	before	post	after
appl.	application, applied	prob.	probably
BLW	bounty land warrant	R.	rejected pension
ca	about	S.	soldier's pension
dis	discharged	sold.	soldier
enl	enlisted	tr.	transfer(red)
IAR	Ind. Agy Rolls	ts	typescript
ISL	Ind. State Library	W.	widow's pension
liv.	lived, living	wid.	widow

ACKNOWLEDGMENTS

I wish to thank Dr. Neil Franklin and Mr. Thad Page of the National Archives in Washington, D. C., for permitting 2,495 pension files to be made available for me during the summers of 1951 and 1952; Mr. Frank E. Bridgers for supervising the arrangements; and Miss Christine Stokes and especially Mrs. Bernice E. Orrison (the latter formerly of the Archives Staff) for servicing the records.

I also wish to thank the following librarians, friends, or clients for furnishing clues or names and data:

Indiana State Library Staff:
Miss Eleanor Peterson   Mrs. Hazel Hopper
Miss Caroline Dunn   Miss Gayle Thornbrough
Miss Margaret Pierson   Miss Dorothy Riker   Mr. Harold Burton

Residents of Indianapolis:
Miss Thelma Murphy   Mr. Willard Heiss
Mrs. Irene Strieby   Mr. G. William Eppley
                Mr. Norman Keister

Residents of Indiana:
Mrs. Claude E. Gilliatt, Seymour   Mr. Wallace Weatherholt, Tell
Mrs. Lewis Osterman, Seymour   Miss Mary Hill, Madison /City
Mrs. Ira Tranter, Franklin   Mrs. Mabel Shanklin, Crawfords-
Mrs. M. G. Talbert, Franklin   Mrs. Edna Joseph, Jasper /ville
Mrs. John Brevoort   Vincennes   Mrs. Hazel Overleese, Rushville
Mrs. Leo Schultheis Vincennes   Mrs. Herbert Brown, Ft. Wayne
Mrs. Glenn Wheeler, Vincennes   Miss Edna Nowland, Mooresville
Mrs. Eva B. Davenport Vincennes   Miss Gertrude McCain, Delphi
            Mrs. D. Joseph Cummings, Brownstown
            Miss Frances Emerson Plymouth
            Mrs. Theodore Craven, N. Madison
            Mrs. Forrest E. Kempton, Centerville

Out-of-state residents:
Mr. Harry Wright Newman, Washington, D. C.
Miss Mary Lucille Cook, Portland, Oregon
Mrs. R. W. Valin, Newberg, Oregon
Mrs. Gustave B. Appelman, Tacoma, Washington
Mrs. Alice Vance Robinson, Seattle, Washington
Mrs. Arthur Whitmore Smith, Ann Arbor, Michigan
Miss Rose Anne Howe, Chicago, Illinois
Miss Mary Whitehouse, Cathedral City, California
Mrs. Olive Bare, Youngstown, Ohio
Mrs. Henry A. Humphrey, Wichita, Kansas
Mrs. William H. DeButts, Sioux City, Iowa
Mrs. Ruth Ravenscroft, Colorado Springs, Colorado

D.A.R. Chapters:
Caroline Scott Harrison, Indianapolis; Fort Vallonia, Seymour, Ind. John Paul, Madison, Indiana; Dorothy Quincy, Crawfordsville, Ind.

Indianapolis, Indiana   Margaret R. Waters
September 1, 1954   20 N. Bosart Avenue

ADAMS, GAVIN   Bartholomew
b. 6-7-1763, Fauquier Co., Va.; d. 1842; mar.; chn. (at least):
William (liv. 1854, LaGrange, Oldham Co., Ky.); Martha ("Patsy")
Anderson (in Washington Co., Ind., 6-12-1854); Elizabeth Seely
(power of atty. 9-20-1855, Bartholomew Co., Ind. Pens. appl. on
11-13-1837, Oldham Co., Ky., altho a res. of Bartholomew Co.,
Ind., ae. 75. Moved with father to Culpeper Co., Va. After War,
mov. to Henry Co., Ky.; was in Henry Co. & Oldham Co., Ky., ca.
30 yr. until 1830 when mov. to Bartholomew Co., Ind. Affid. 11-
13-1837 of John Coons, Sr., that he knew sold. was in Capt.
Green's Comp. (A slight doubt as to whether sold. d, in Bartholomew Co., Ind., or Oldham Co., Ky. A letter in file, 1854, says
shortly previous to 1843, Adams of this, Oldham Co., Ky., had
appl. for pens. Service: a res. of Culpeper Co., Va., when enl.
in Va. Mil., 1779, Capt. Basey. Pens. rej. "for further proof &
specification". REF: Pens. R.31 Va.; Susp. Pens. List, p. 411.

ADAMS, JOHN   Perry
b. 4-1-1763 Somerset Co. N.J. After War, liv. Morris & Essex
Cos. N.J.; Greenup Co., Ky., 1813-1840; to Troy, Perry Co.,
Ind., 1841. Pens. appl. 2-20-1847, ae. 83 yr., 7 mo., Troy, Ind.
Service: enl at age 13, 1776 or 1777, Somerset Co., N.J., Mil.,
Capt. John Parker, Maj. William Davison, Col. Frelinghuysen,
Gen. Wines. REF: Pens. R.39 N.J.; Susp. Pens. List, p. 411--for
further proof & specification.

ALEXANDER, JOHN (Sr.)   Tippecanoe
bur. Sugar Grove Cemetery, Tippecanoe Co., Ind. REF: reference
for his being a Revolutionary soldier and place of burial lost.

ALEXANDER, JOSEPH   Montgomery
b. 1756, Co. Tyrone, Ire. Emigr. to Amer. at age 9. Pens. appl.
3-19-1833, ae. 77, Coal Creek Twp., Montgomery Co., Ind. After
War, liv. Northumberland Co., Pa.; Centre Co., Pa.; till 30 yr.
old; to Ross Co., O.; in Clark Co., Ind., till Sept. 1828 when
mov. to Montgomery Co., Ind. Affid. 10-8-1833, ae. 68, of Leslie
Malone from Warren Co., Ind., but liv. in Fountain Co., Ind.;
also of Francis Malone of Vermillion Co., Ind. ("Roster" p.244).
Service: enl. ca. Xmas 1777 while liv. 1 mi. from Northumberland,
Pa.; Capt. Hugh White, Pa. Mil.; Sunbury, Northumberland Co.,Pa.;
pvt., ens., & 1st Lieut.; Capt. of Susquehanna boat service and
raised 50 men Apr. 1779; dis. ca. Nov. 1779; capt.'s commission
burned in his father's home 1780. REF: Pens. S.32091 Pa.; 1835
Pens. List, v.3, p.41, Clark Co., Ind.; Am. Leg.; Dorothy Quincy
Chap., DAR, Crawfordsville, Ind.

ALEXANDER, THOMAS   Jackson
b. 1752, Ireland; d. 8-10-1849; bur. Mitchell Cem., Owen Twp.;
m.(1) Shippensburg, Pa., Mary Barr; m.(2) Tenn., prob. Blountsville or Blount Co., ca. 1790 or earlier, Sally King, d. ca. 20
yr. ante husb.; chn.: William (by 1st wife); James M. (in Washington Co., Ind., 1855); Granville C. (last in Lawrence Co.,
Ind.; John H. (ae. 52, 1855, Jackson Co., Ind.); Thomas (of Washington Co., Ind., 1855). After War, liv. Knox Co., Ky.; Sullivan

-5-

Co., Tenn.; Washington Co., Ind.; Jackson Co., Ind. Pens. appl. 1-29-1848, ae. 95, Jackson Co., Ind. Affid. 3-21-1856, Jackson Co., Ind., of Richard Gallemore, ae. 68, that he knew sold. ca. 25 yr. ago in Washington Co., Ind.; that sold. d. 6 yr. or more ago in Jackson Co., Ind., at res. of son John H. Alexander. Affid. of son John H. that father had bros., George & William (the latter of whom had never mar. & had d. many yrs. ago, Washington Co., Ind.; had liv. at Shippensburg, Pa.); that Uncles George & William both older than sold.; that Robert McWhorter, a pensioner (see this Suppl.) who d. in Washington Co., Ind., many yrs. ago, had mar. father's sis., Jane, who surv. him but all her chn. are now dead; that Jane was older than sold.; that father kept a public house in Shippensburg, Pa., while mar. to 1st wife; that father & 1st wife had only 1 ch. he (John H.) knows of: William, who came to father's house & d. there when John H. was a boy. Affid. 4-4-1856, Jackson Co., Ind., of Charles L. Wayman, ae. 50, that he knew sold. 30 yr. ago in Washington Co., Ind., & later in Jackson Co., Ind.; that he often heard sold. 7 his father Edmond Wayman (now decd.) talk abt. their resp. service in War. Service: drf. ae. ca. 23, in May or June 1775, while res. Lancaster Co., Pa., in Pa. Line, Capt. Henry, Aide-de-camp Benjamin Harrison. REF: Pens. R.90 Pa.; Susp. Pens. List, p.411--claims 2 yr. service in Pa. Line as artillery artificer; proof of identity required with the Pa. records od a sold. of the same name.

  ALISLA, COONROD   Parke
This is a typographical error for which we have been unable as yet to guess the right name. It appears as above on the Suspended Pension List published 1852, p.411--"for further proof and specification". Although Coonrod is an old surname in southern & south central Indiana, there is no pension file for a Coonrod with a forename resembling Alisla. We have tried variations of sound for Alisla as a surname. If a reader can identify the above man, please communicate with the compiler.

  ALLEN, JOHN   Franklin
(Not to be confused with John Allen, "Roster", p.37, nor the John Allen below.) b. Penn.; d. Blooming Grove Twp.; bur. Hays farm (then owned by son John Allen, Jr.); m. Rebecca ---, bur. in fam. bur. gr. on Price Hill, Brookville Twp., Franklin Co., Ind.; chn.: Solomon, b. 1784, d. 6-23-1852, ae. 68, m. Sarah ---, d. 4-11-1836, ae. 30; Josiah b. 1-10-1789, Washington Co., Pa., d. 9-13-1874, Union Co., Ind., m. 12-26-1816, Wayne Co., Ind., Sarah Harvey, b. 2-12-1795, N.C., d. 7-12-1863, dau. of Caleb Harvey of Wayne Co., Ind.; Margaretta m. Jacob Hetrick; Joseph; William; Debby m. Daniel Mason; Eliphalet m. Elizabeth Shepherd; Naomi m. John Croaks; John, Jr.; Sarah m. Robert Cassa; Samuel; Elizabeth m. Solomon Shepherd. John Allen was reared a Quaker; with sons Solomon & Josiah to Brookville Twp., Franklin Co., Ind., summer 1805; entered NE¼ of Sec. 29 on 7-6-1805; mill; in fall, 2 sons retd. to Penn.; retd. 1806 to Brookville; rest of fam. prob. came same time. John Allen founded all of SE part of Brookville; home on Price Hill; family burial ground; wife Rebecca dau. Naomi Croak, dau. Debby Mason, & several chn. bur. there.

Later Allen mov. to Blooming Grove Twp.; was appt. J.P. for
Franklin Co., Ind., 12-13-1810 (maybe 1st J.P. in Brookville.
A John Allen (son?) was comm. Lieut. in Rifle Comp., 7th Regt.
Ind. Terr. Mil. (Franklin Co.); military fine for non-attendance
at Comp. muster, 7th Regt., Capt. David Kilgore's Comp., remitted
for John Allen on 3-24-1828; John Allen, Jr., comm. J.P. for
Franklin Co. 6-2-1822; same 6-29-1829; same 8-1-1834. Service:
comm. 4-3-1780; a Commissioner of Purchases for Westmoreland Co.,
Pa., Mil.; Capt. in 2nd Battn., Westmoreland Co., Pa., Mil., 3-14-
1782, 7-15-1782. REF: C.A.R. 67700; Pa. Arch., 6th Ser., v.2, pp.
261, 275 276 341; Franklin Co., Ind., Atlas (1882) pp. 94-95;
"Biog. & Gen. Hist. of Wayne, Fayette, Union & Franklin Cos.,
Ind." (1899) v.2, pp. 818-819; "Exec. Journ. of Ind. Terr., 1800-
1816", pp. 166, 228; "Exec. Proc. of Ind., 1816-1838", pp. 337,
220,438,440.

ALLEN, JOHN   Hamilton
(Not to be confused with the man above or man in "Roster" p.37).
b. ca. 1760, Franklin Co., Pa.; d. Mar. 1849 (or 2-28-1847), Jackson Twp.; m. ca. 1821, when advanced in yrs., Delaware Co., O.,
Elizabeth Rodgers, d. spr. 1840, Hamilton Co., Ind.; ch.: Frederick A. Allen, b. 10-4-1823, Delaware Co., O. Pens. appl. 6-12-
1835, ae. 75, Delaware Co., O.; also 11-9-1846, ae. 90, Hamilton
Co., Ind. After War Liv. Franklin Co., Pa., till ca. 1821; Delaware Co., O.; to Hamilton Co., Ind., 1835. Power of atty. 4-13-
1853, Van Wirt, O., of Frederick A. Allen, son & only heir; same
4-3-1854, from Delaware Co., O., but now res. in Vinton Co., O.;
that parents liv. Delaware Co., O., till 1835 when mov. to Ind.;
after mother d., sold. & son mov. back to Delaware Co., O., till
ca. 1846 when mov. back to Hamilton Co., Ind., & father d. intestate Mar. 1849 (see discrepancy below). Affid. 4-3-1854, Delaware Co., O., of James Durfey (sp? Dursey?) re sold.'s mar., wife
& only 1 ch. Affid. 8-2-1854, Delaware Co., O., of Luther M.
Davis, Sr., that he had liv. Jackson Twp., Hamilton Co., Ind., &
knew sold. had d. last day of Feb. 1847 & he had attended funeral
on Mar. 1. (However, affiant had sold.'s wife d. ca. 1836; so
son Frederiak may be correct on father's death). Affid. 4-3-1854
Delaware Co., O. of Alexander Rodgers (rel. to sold.'s wife not
stated) that he knew sold. well; of Mar., etc.; that sold. d. Mar.
1849 Affid. 5-26-1854, Delaware Co., O., of Alexander McCutcheon
that he knew sold. in Franklin Co., Pa;, from 1815; that in Mar.
1820, sold. with bro. Samuel & sis. Martha mov. to Delaware Co.,
O. where sold. became tenant on lands McCutcheon owned there
Service: enl fall 1775 or 1776, Chambersburg, Bedford Co., Pa.,
in Pa. Line, Capt. Brown, Col. Campbell in (he thinks) 6th or 7th
Regt. REF: Pens. R.122 Pa.; Susp Pens. List, p.411--for proof
of 5 yr. alleged service in Pa. Line.

ALLISON, JOHN   Marion
b. 9-5-1765, Rockbridge Co., (Va., I assume) ca. 3 mi. from the
Natural Bridge. Pens. appl. 4-3-1834, Marion Co., Ind., ae. 69.
In fall 1783 to Lexington, Fayette Co., Ky., a few motnhs in
town; in county till spr. 1793; to Bourbon Co., Ky. (part which
later became Nicholas Co., Ky.) till Oct. 1821; then Marion Co.,

-7-

Ind. Service: enl. in Washington Co., N. C., near Jonesborough, now Tenn., Capt. James Gibson, Col. John Sevier. Pens.S.32090 N.C.

ALSUP, JOHN   Jackson
Rev. sold. who d. there. In courthouse is will dated 8-30-1824; names "my beloved wife Nancy"; no other names. (From a letter I think perhaps that this may be an intestate record, or if a will it was probated on 8-30-1824 instead of written then.) REF: Will Bk. 1, p. 12; Fort Vallonia Chap., DAR, Seymour, Ind.; Mrs. D. Joseph Cummings,Brownstown, Ind. (deceased).

ANDREWS, JAMES   Delaware
(Uncertain). d. Nov. 1816 (or Nov. 1813); mar. (wife d. 3-4 yr. post husb.); chn. (surv. in 1850):*William P. (liv. Jasper Co., Ill.); Mary m. James Mansfield (liv. Delaware Co., Ind.); Samuel D. (of Delaware Co., Ind.). Pens. appl. by son Samuel D. Andrews, 3-29-1850, Delaware Co., Ind.; chn. want bounty land. Affid. 4-17-1850, Jasper Co., Ill., of son William P. Andrews that bro. Samuel's info is correct except that father d. Nov. 1816 instead of Nov. 1813 (as Samuel said); that William is the older bro. & is now 56 yr.; that father was an orphan bound out in Bucks Co., Pa.; that father served as a subst. for his master on the promise of his freedom; that father later enlisted. Affid. 5-11-1850, Delaware Co., Ind., of William Lee that he knew sold. & fam. well when they liv. in same neighborhood in Ohio for several yrs. (Note: this sold. may have d. in Ohio altho he is not in DAR "Rev. Sold. Bur. in Ohio". The region around the present Delaware Co., Ind. was very sparsely settled as early as 1813-1816.) REF: Pens. R.213 Pa.; Rej. Pens. List, p.4-6--he died before the passage of the pension laws. (*Rachel m.John Crum(liv.Delaware Co.Ind.

ANGEVINE, JOHN   Dearborn
b. France; d. 1831, York Twp.; mar. (wife d. 1833); chn.: 11 daus. & 1 son (youngest ch.) James. b. ca. 1776; d. 7-10-1874, La Salle Co., Ill. where he had been taken by relatives in his 93rd yr.; reared in New York; sailor; m.(1) wife d. 11 yr later; no chn.; at ae. 36 m.(2) 11-9-1812, Susan Montfort (parents from Pa., anc. from Holland); 12 chn., incl. James A., b. 1814, N.Y. City. (For poss. help on Monfort line, see Warren Co., O., records, and Presbyterian Church records for Ohio & Ind. for 5 Monfort ministers). "John Angevine came to America prior to the Revolution, in which he participated as a soldier.---He was a shoe-maker--- in 1818 came to this county with his son James, with whom he resided until death". REF: Mr. Schrum; "Hist. of Dearborn, Ohio, & Switzerland Cos., Ind." (1885) p.611.

ANSLEY, JOHN   Dearborn
b. Apr. 1749. Original pens. appl. lost. Only paper in file is an affid. 2-15-1839, Dearborn Co., Ind., that he will be 90 yr. old this April. Service: enl. 1778, N.J. Line, 3rd Battn., Col. Ogden. No family data. REF: Pens. R.226 N.J.;,Susp. Pens. List p.411--for further proof of his 3 yr. enlistment in 1777 in Ogden's Regt., N. J. Line.

APPLEGATE, ROBERT   Harrison
b. 3-13-1759 within 1 mi. of Princeton, N.J. Pens. appl. 4-24-
1837, Alleghany Co., Pa.; pens. tr. from Pittsburgh Agy. 3-4-1841;
had liv. Alleghany Co., Pa. Declaration 5-15-1843, Harrison Co.,
Ind., ae. 86, that he had vol. under Capt. Heth at Pittsburgh,
Gen. Hand, Col. Gibson; later drf. at Walltower's (sp?) Station
in Westmoreland Co., Pa. One tour of service was as a subst. for
his father who gave him a good farm for doing it. During Rev.
liv. above Pittsburgh at Forks of Gough (sp?), now is Westmoreland Co., Pa., he thinks; ever since liv. Alleghany Co., Pa., till
came to Harrison Co., Ind., ca. 3 yr. ago. Affid. 5-16-1845, Harrison Co., Ind., of Irwin Applegate (rel. not stated). Affid.
3-7-1837 of William Alexander of Washington Co., Pa., that he &
sold. ent. service on 4-1- 1779 under Capt. Zadock Wright from
Youghiogheny Co., Va. Affid. 12-29-1836. Alleghany Co., Pa., of
2 men who say sold is 77 yr old. Sold. may have liv. Elizabeth
Twp., Alleghany Co., Pa. Decl. 3-25-1835, sold. ae. 76. Mention
of a Vincent Applegate (rel. not stated). Service: as given
above; and pvt. under Capt. Minton, Youghiogheny Co., Va. (Note:
this is now West Va.). REF: Pens. S.32097 Pa. & Va.

APPLEGATE, SAMUEL   Jackson
Rev. sold. bur. in Grassyfork Twp.; mar.; chn. (at least): Heze-
kiah, b. 1776, m. Eleanor Daily, b. Va.; Eli. REF: Probate Bk.
C, p. 132; Fort Vallonia Chap., DAR, Seymour, Ind.; Mrs. D.
Joseph Cummings, Brownstown, Ind. (deceased).

ARBUCKLE, DAVID JONES   Jefferson
Rev. sold. d. there. REF: Mr. Schrum.

ARMANTROUT, FREDERICK   Montgomery
Rev. sold. bur. Lutheran Cem., Union Twp. REF: lost.

ARMSTRONG, AMBROSE   Johnson
b. 1759, prob. Va.; d. 11-16-1841, ae. 82, Blue River Twp.; bur.
Armstrong Cem. on Adams farm; stone; m. Elizabeth ---; chn. (at
least): Ambrose Jr. m., Johnson Co., Ind., Harriet Roberts;
Mary m. Abraham Lay; John b. ca. 1790, killed 2-24-1847, Batt.
of Buena Vista, m. 4-7-1812, Lexington, Ky., Jane Stone (dau. of
Jane Stone & gr-dau. of William Stone). Pens. appl. 9-24-1832,
ae. past 72, Fayette Co., Ky.1 had liv. in Ky. over 30 yr.
Service: enl. while res. of Essex Co., Va., ca. 3 yr. before
Cornwallis' defeat; pvt. in Capt. Opie Davenport, Col. Porter-
field's Va. Regt. at Old Williamsburg, Va. REF: Pens. S.14921;
Mrs. Ira Tranter, Franklin, Ind.; Banta--"Hist. of Johnson Co.,
Ind." p. 728.

ARNOLD, RICHARD   Dearborn
b. ca 1757; d. 7-24-1843; m. 1-3-1783, Durham Twp., Bucks Co.,
Pa. Mary Blackmon; chn.: George b. 12-1-1785, Durham Twp.,
Bucks Co , Pa.; Mary; William; Catharine; Richard; Samuel; Charles; Elizabeth b. 1809; Jane. Liv. Bucks Co.,
Pa.. 1783-1800; Hunterdon Co., N.J.; 1800-1802; in 1802 or early
1803 to Hamilton Co., O.; 1831 to Dearborn Co., Ind. Affid. of

wid., Harrison Twp., Dearborn Co., Ind., ae. 87; same 2-23-1854, ae. 89; same 3-24-1855, ae. 91. Affid. 4-13-1852 of Rev. pensioner, Jonas Frazee, a 2nd cous. of sold. Affid 3-25-1851, Dearborn Co., Ind., of William Pursell. Sold.'s pens. appl. 11-14-1832 ae. ca. 75, Logan Twp., Dearborn Co., Ind. Service: in Pa. Mil., Col. Hiester, Capt. Brooks; later an artificer. REF: Pens. W.10289 N.J. & Pa.; BLW 28532-160-55; Rej. Pens. List, p.406--not military service.

BAKER, NICHOLAS   Lawrence
b. 1743, Va.; d. 11-2-1832, Indian Creek Twp.; m. (bond) 2-10-1792, m. 2-14-1791(note discrepancy), Culpeper Co., Va., Lucy Lampkin, dau. of Edward Lampkin of Culpeper Co., bondsmen Nicholas Baker & Edward Lampkin; she d. 12-28-1847. Lawrence Co., Ind.; Daniel; Susan m. Mr. Leatch; Anna m. Mr. Spear (all of Lawrence Co., Ind.; William; Philip; Armisted; Robert; Elizabeth m. Mr. Peyton (all of Martin Co., Ind.; Eliza m. Mr. Stephens of Washington Co., Ind. Pens. appl. 6-16-1818, ae. 74, Fayette Co., Ky., but a res. of Woodford Co., Ky.; 2-5-1821, ae. 78, Woodford Co., Ky., that wife near 60, Philip 16, Robert 12, Betsy 19, Anna 17, Susan 14. on 2-28-1832, :awrence Co., Ind., ae. 89. Pens.first in Woodford Co., Ky. Wid.'s pens. appl. 11-18-1842, ae. 75, Lawrence Co., Ind. Lewis J. Baker (rel. not stated) was appt. admr. for Lucy Baker. Service: enl. Mar. 1781 Culpeper Co., Va., 4th Regt., Capt. Crain, Col. Gaskins; pvt. REF: Pens. W.27812 Pa. & Va.

BALLARD, JOHN MURRAY   Jennings
b. ca 1758, Mass. or Conn.; d post 1833, Hopewell, Ind.; bur. on Steven Corya farm south of Vernon, Ind., on State Rd. 3; m. in Penn., Thankful M. Wheeler, d. post 1865; chn.: Olive b. N.Y., m. Isaac White; Horatio)an M.D.), unm. went South, poss. New Orleans; Joseph W. b. 7-4-1800, N.Y., m. Mary Beasley; Almoda Fellers b. 11-2-1802, N.Y., d. 2-20-1871, Jennings Co., Ind., m. 2-10-1820, Jennings Co., Ind., Elijah Bacon, b. N.Y. Sold. liv. Mass. or Conn.; Vt.; N.Y.; Ohio; Jennings Co., Ind. Service: ptv. in N.Y. Line, Col. Albert Pawling, Capt. Daniel Williams. REF: Fernow--"Men in the Rev.--Arch. of N.Y.", p. 300; Mrs. William H. DeButts, Sioux City, Iowa.

BANTA, CORNELIUS   Jefferson
b. ca. 1760, Bergen Co. or Somerset Co., N.J.; d. ca. 1835, prob. near Canaan, Ind.; son of Henry & 2nd wife Antie (Demarest) Banta; m.(1) Mary Magdalena (Shuck) Durie, wid. of Samuel Durie; m.(2) Agnes Shuck (sis-in-law)1 m.(3) Mrs. Nancy VanNise who surv. him; chn. (8-all by 1st wife): see Banta Gen. for full details. Sold. liv. York Co., Pa. (where prob. had Rev. service); near Pleasureville, Henry Co., Ky.; then Jefferson Co., Ky. (error for Ind.?); then Jefferson Co., Ind. Said to have been a Rev. sold. REF: "Frisian Family--Banta Genealogy" (1899) pp. 49,60,94, et al; Mrs. Herbert E. Brown, Ft. Wayne, Ind.

BARLOW, JOHN   Dearborn
Rev. sold. d. there. (Note: might be confused with the Joseph
Barlow of Dearborn Co., Ind., in my 1949 Rev. sold. & Mr. Schrum
might have erred in forenames. Or, more likely, the pension record of Joseph Barlow states that he lived with his brother. The
brother may be this John Barlow, and both men may have had service
although John had no pension. REF: Mr. Schrum; Pens. S.35773 Va.,
Joseph Barlow).

BARNES, JOHN   Delaware
b. ca. 1757; mar. (wid. in Muncie, Ind., 1854). Pens. appl. 8-
28-1838, ae. 81, Delaware Co., Ind. Service: enl. Nov. 1776,
Cecil Co., Md., Capt. Henderson, Col. Hollings, Lt. Thomas; later
drf. in Newcastle Co., Dela. REF: Pens. R.520 Del. & Md.; Susp.
Pens. List, p.406--did not serve 6 mos.

BEBOUT, DANIEL   Rush
b. 9-22-1764, N.J. Pens. appl. 10-6-1834, ae. 70 on Sept. 22,
Rush Co., Ind. After War liv. Washington Co., Pa.; Trumbull Co*,
O.; Rush Co., Ind. now for 7 yr. Service: drf. 1781 when ca.
16 yr old, Somerset Co., N.J., in N.J. Mil., Capt McCoy. REF:
Pens. R 689 N.J.; Rej Pens. List, p.406--did not serve 6 mos.
                                   (*9 yr.; 23 yr. in Ky.)
BECKES, BENJAMIN   Knox
b. 1753; d. 1823-1830; prob. bur. in Decker Cem., Decker Twp.
(loc. on banks on White River ca. 1 mi. S of railroad bridge;
many bodies washed away); m.(1) Mary (poss. Webb); she d. ante
8-31-1810; he m.(2) 9-16-1815, Mrs. Sarah Browning, b. ca. 1772;
chn. (all by 1st wife but poss. others by her): Parmenas Webb d.
1813, m. ante 1-21-1804, Eliza Clark (poss. wid. of Judge Clark);
Benjamin Vincennes b. 1786, Vincennes, Ind., d. 12-3-1859, m.(1)
2-13-1807, Sarah Harbin, m. (2) 5-25-1812, Elizabeth F. Pea b.
1783, d. 4-9-1856; Sarah d. 1-25-1820, m. 8-4-1804, William
Watson b. 3-29-1780, d. 7-26-1857; William Penn b. 3-10-1790,
d. 9-18-1858, m. 4-26-1814, Margaret Jordan b. 1793, d. 6-13-
1853. Sold.'s pens. appl. rejected because he had too much property. In 1822 he removed, prob. for a short time, to White Co.,
Ill.; perhaps liv. with some of his 2nd wife's chn. there. There
are no courthouse records of the Beckes family in White Co., Ill.;
so descendants believe that the sold. died in, or at least was
buried, in Knox Co., Ind. One son is bur. in City Catholic Cem.
in Vincennes; another in West Salem Cem. in Johnson Twp. Sold.'s
landbordered on both Luke & Moses Decker's lands. Sold.'s wid.
tried to get pens. in 1846; liv. Bloomington, Ind. REF: Pens.
R.695; Mrs. Glenn E. Wheeler, Vincennes, Ind.; "Exec. Journ. of
Ind. Terr.", p.94; "Hist. of Knox Co., Ind." p.312; Carter--
"Terr. Papers of the U.S.-- Ind. Terr.", v.7, p. 169; 1831 Rej.
                Pens. List, p.48. (See p. 119 later).
BELL, BENJAMIN   Clay
b. 1762. Berkeley Co. Va.; bur. in Calcutta Cem., Van Buren
Twp.; Grave 3, Lot 19 Block 1. Father mov. to Pa., when sold.
was small. Pens appl 10-18-1843, ae. 81, Clay Co., Ind. After
War mov. to Ohio; Putnam Co., Ind., for 20 yr.; last 5 yr. in
Clay Co, Ind., where sett. in NE pt. of Van Buren Twp. Affid. of

bro. Nathaniel Bell, 11-13-1843, Johnson Co., Ind. Service: enl. 1780, Washington Co., Pa., as a spy for Col. Crooks' Comp.; was in same Comp. as bro. Nathaniel Bell ("Roster" p.56). REF: Pens. R.718 Pa.; Susp. Pens. List, p.411; Am. Leg.; Mr. Schrum; "Hist. of Clay & Owen Cos., Ind." (1884) p.233; Travis--"Hist. of Clay Co., Ind." (1900) v.1, p.350; Posson--"Sold. of the War of the Rev. in Clay Co., Ind." (1929) pp. 2-3.

BENNET, ARCHIBALD   Decatur
b 1-12-1763 mouth of Antietam Creek, Md. Pens. appl. 11-13-1837, ae. 75 next Jan. 12, Salt Creek Twp., Decatur Co. Ind. When ca. 6 yr. old, mov. with father to Washington Co., Pa., ca. 14 yr.; 1793 to Mason Co., Ky, for ca. 50 yr.; 1834 to Salt Creek Twp., Decatur Co., Ind. Service: drf. Mar. 1778, Washington Co., Pa. Lt. Samuel Hardesty, Capt. William McFarland. REF: Pens. R 749 Pa.; Rej. Pens List, p.4-6--not under competent authority.

BETTS (BATES), JOSEPH   Montgomery
b. 1768, New Mills, Burlington Co., N.J. Liv. there with father till 1786 when mov. to the Monongahela in Pa. for 7 yr.; to Scott Co., Ky.; till 7 yr. ago to Montgomery Co., Ind. Pens. appl. 9-24-1834, ae. 66, Union Twp., Montgomery Co., Ind. Letter 9-26-1834, Crawford Co., Ind. from Alb. T. White that sold.'s father who d. this summer, ae. 90, served all thru War; that Joseph enl. in early youth & later served in Indian Wars & War of 1812. Service: enl. 7-4-1781, 1 mi. from New Mills, Burlington Co., N.J., as drummer, Capt. Samuel Gaskins, Lt. Thomas Budd, Col. John Lacy. REF: Pens. R.806 N.J.; Rej. Pens. List, p.406--under age & not 6 mos. service.

BILES, CHARLES   Clark
Affid. 11-12-1833, Clark Co., Ind., in pens. file of George Lewis (see this Suppl.) that he & Lewis were in service together. A fuller abstract of Lewis' entire service record in his pens. file might lead to Biles' service as I abstracted only Lewis' first tour. REF: Pens. R.21100 Md. (of George Lewis).

BIVINS, WILLIAM   Montgomery
b. 4-14-1748, Somerset Co., Md. Pens. appl. 9-22-1834, ae. 85 next April, Ripley Twp., Montgomery Co., Ind. After War liv. Del.; Md.; Va.; Ohio; Ind. Dis. burned in home in Lawrence Co., Ohio, ca. 13 yr. ago. Service: drf. the 4th or 5th yr. of War, Sussex Co., Del., in Del. Mil., Capt. Wingate. REF: Pens. R.876 Del.; Rej. Pens. List, p.406--no proof of service.

BLADS (BLADE), ELI   Scott
b 2-21-1764 Somerset Co., Md. When very young, mov. with father to Worcester Co., Md. In Apr. 1789 to Waters of the Elkhorn, Woodford Co., Ky., for ca. 10 yr.; to Clermont Co., O., ca. 3 yr.; to Clark Co., Ind., 1 yr.; to Lexington Twp., Svott Co., Ind. Pens. appl. 2-19-1841, ae. 77 on Feb. 21, Lexington Twp., Scott Co., Ind. Service: enlisted from Worcester Co., Md., the spring before Cornwallis' defeat, in the Maryland Troops, Capt.

James Patterson, First Lieutenant Joseph Stevenson. REF: Pens,
R.908 Md.; Rej. Pens. List, p.406--Not 6 mos. actual service.

    BLAINE, JOHN   Monroe
Said to have been a Rev. sold. bur. there. The "Roster", p. 62,
has a James Blaine of Monroe Co.; my 1949 compilation has a
Robert Blaine of Monroe Co. Possibly Mr. Schrum confused John
Blaine with one of these; or this may be a new man hitherto not
found elsewhere as yet. REF: Mr. Schrum.

    BLAKE, JOHN   Martin
b. 1761 or 1762, on Watesee (sp?) River, Fairfield Co., S.C.; m.
Sarah ---; chn. After War, mov. to Broad River; then mar. &
mov. back to Fairfield Co., S.C., ca. 2 yr.; mov. to N.C. (he
thinks Anson Co.) 3 yr.; to Chesire (sp?) 1 yr.; to Granger Co.,
Tenn., ca. 4 yr.; to Cumberland River in Ky., 3-4 yr.; to Hardin
Co., Ky., 20 yr.; to Martin Co., Ind., last 5 yr. Pens. appl.
10-17-1832. ae. 71, Monroe Co., Ind., but a res. of Martin Co.,
Ind. Later deposition 8-11-1834 by sold. that he has found old
Rev. sold., Reuben Demoss, who can vouch for his service. Affid.
8-11-1834, Martin Co., Ind., of Reuben Demoss, ae. ca. 84. that
he knows sold. well; was with him in War; that they have liv. in
same neighborhood for many yrs. Affid. 8-11-1834, Daviess Co.,
Ind. of John White that he knew sold. had entered War. (Possible
clue that White was a Rev. sold.) Letter 2-14-1850, Bloomington,
Ind., mentions wid. Sarah & chn., heirs of John Blake, decd., late
of Martin Co. Ind. Service: enl. ca. 1777-1778, S.C. Mil., while
res. Fairfield Co. S.C., Capt. Thomas Starks; later serv. as a
subst. for a man named Yarbry or Yarberry. REF: Pens. R.913 S.C.;
Susp. Pens. List., p.411--did not serve 6 mos.

    BLEVINS, DANIEL   Lawrence
b. ca. 1753, Botetourt Co., Va.; d. 9-5-1839 or d. 1840; mar. (she
d. ante 10-19-1853); chn., at least: Daniel 15; William.11;
John 8; Polly Eliza 2; Thomas 13 days (all ages in pens. appl.
of 10-29-1823, sold. ae. 63), and Nancy. Pens. appl. 3-1-1834,
Morgan Co., Tenn., ae. 81. After War, to Buncomb Co., N.C.; after
many yrs., to Sullivan Co., East Tenn.; after many yrs., to Harlan Co., Ky.; again to Morgan Co., E. Tenn. Pens. there; then
tr. to Bedford, Ind. (Agy.?) 12-19-1836. Affid. 10-19-1853 of
Polly Maden & Nancy Maden, of Rockcastle Co.; Ky., only surv.
chn. of sold.; no wid. Service: enl. 25 mi. from Lead Mines in
Va. near the N.C. line; pvt. in N.C. Mil., Capt. Noll. REF:
Pens. S.31555 N.C. & Va.

    BLISS, CHARLES   Harrison
Said to have died there. Name found inserted in copy of "Roster"
at Kentucky Historical Society. REF: Miss Thelma Murphy,
Indianapolis, Ind.

    BLISS, JAMES   Harrison
b. ca. 1763; d. 8-12-1831 (or 8-13-1831); m. 1790-1791, Middletown, Conn., Mehitable Johnston, b. ca. 1770; (dau. of Joseph &
Thankful Johnston); 11 chn., incl.: youngest, Charles W. Bliss,

ae. 35 in affid. 8-26-1843 Louisville, Ky.; Hannah m. Mr. Walker (she ae. 52-53 in affid. 3-16-1843, Harrison Co., Ind.); daughter 2 yr. older than Hannah; Bailey. Affid. of wid., Mehitable, 2-27-1849, ae. 79, and 3-17-1855, ae. 85, Harrison Co., Ind. Affid. of son Charles mentions "my Uncle Seth Johnston" & a quit claim deed between James & Mehitable Bliss of Thetford, Vt. to Seth Johnston of Middleton, Conn., in estate of father Joseph Johnston, Feb. 1790; Joseph Johnston's will, pr. 4-2-1787, names wid. Thankful & 4 sons & 5 daus. incl. Constant & Dorothy. Pens. appl. 3-18-1823, ae. 60, Harrison Co., Ind.; wife ae. 54: Polly 18; Baley 22. After War, from Conn. to Vt., 50 yr. ago; ca. 41 yr. ago to West Penna.; in 1814 to Ind. Service: enl. Mar. 1781, Conn., Capt. James Denny (sp?); pvt. REF: Pens. W.9728 Conn. BLW 814.

BLUE, CORNELIUS   Tippecanoe
Said to be Rev. sold. bur. there. REF: Mr. Schrum.

BLUE, DAVID   Parke
b. 6-9-1760, Bucks Co., Pa.; d. Jan. 1855; son of Uriah Blue. Pens. appl. 10-15-1838, Union Co., Ky., ae. 78. After War, to Ky., 1808; in Henderson Co., & Union Co., now Union Co. since it became a county in 1811. Affid. 10-15-1838, Union Co., Ky., of John Blue (rel. not stated) & George Johnson. Service: drf. fall 1779, Shepherdstown, Va., while a res. of Berkeley Co., Va.; hauled flour. Later his father hired John Lindsey as a subst. for son David. Later David served as a subst. for a relation, Jacob Blue (rel. not stated). Pens. rejected as "did not serve 6 mos. in a military capacity. While David Blue did not receive a pens. for Rev. service, he did have one for service in Gen. William Darke's Regt., 1791, of Shepherdstown, Va. "Roster", p.405, is correct; but he should be credited also for Rev. service as a patriot who rendered aid and as a substitute. REF: Pens. R.964 Va.; O. W. File 6670; 1835 Pens. List, v.3, p.8.

BLUNT, SAMUEL   Washington
Said to be Rev. sold. bur. there (1st Ref. below). Bur. in Little York Cem. Came from Germany (2nd Ref. below). Note: this is prob. the Samuel Blunt, will wr. 7-8-1842 pr. 9-20-1842; names wife Sally; sons: Isaac, David, Joseph; daus.: Sally, Polly, Nancy, Rachel, Elizabeth Ellen; and probable step-chn. (chn. of probable 2nd wife Sally): Barbara Ellen Henning & Angelo E. Henning (a minor). REF: Mr. Schrum; Stevens--"Hist. of Washington Co., Ind." (1916), p.634; "Abstr. of Wills of Washington Co., Ind., 1814-1900"--Christopher Harrison Chap., DAR, Salem, Ind., (1953), pp.34-35 (from Washington Co., Ind., Prob. Bk. D, pages 231-232).

BOGAN, SAMUEL   Marion
Said to be Rev. sold. bur. in Crown Hill Cem., Indianapolis, Ind. REF: Mrs. Herbert R. Hill, Indianapolis, Ind.

BOOTH, JOHN   Jefferson
(Uncertain). b. 1768, Booth's Creek, Harrison Co., Va.; d. ca.
Nov. 1845; m. 1793, Shelby Co., Ky., Sally Kinder (consent of
Peter Kinder on mar. bond). Pens. appl. 11-11-1834, ae. 66, Jefferson Co., Ind. Liv. in Harrison Co., Va.; to Madison Co., Ind.,
1810; tavern keeper. Letter 11-19-1834 from W. G. Singleton says
he has been informed by Jesse Martin that John Booth was b. 3-15-1775, the info. having been given by an aunt of Booth & had been
procured by Martin, with a view to be used in a threatened law
suit. Service: enl. 1782, Harrison Co., Va., at age 14; serv. 8
mos. in Va. Line, Capt. Louden, Lt. John Caine. REF: Pens.
R.1020 Va.; "Biog. α Hist. Souv. of Clark --- Jefferson --- and
Washington Cos., Ind.", Gresham (1889), p.167; Jefferson Co., Ind.
Probate Bk. F, p.540; Miss Mary Hill, Madison, Ind.; Rej. Pens.
List, p.406--under age, born in 1775. Note: 1782 is well within
the period for which Rev. service is accepted. The matter of the
law suit and the testimony of the aunt (who might be wrong, especially if of advanced age) as to John's birth must be weighed.
    BOREN, NICHOLAS--see p. 115.
    BORDERS, WILLIAM B.   Randolph
Said to be Rev. sold. bur. there. REF: Mr. Schrum.
    BOSTON, ELIJAH--see p. 115.
    BOWER, BENJAMIN   Indiana
d. 5-6-1835. Private. Placed on Ind. Agy. Rolls 7-11-1833,
certif. # 13,908. (Note: am unable to identify from several men
of same name as pens. files for them do not indicate a trans. to
Ind. Rolls. One had Mass. service; one N. H. Mil.; one Vt. (to
Maine). REF: I.A.R.; Natl. Archives pens. files.

    BOWMAN, WILLIAM   Washington
b 1760; d. 4-2-1843; will wr. 12-16-1842, pr. 4-19-1843; heirs
(rel. not stated but prob. are chn.): Samuel Bowman, Edward Bowman Elisha Bowman, Polly Giles, Sarah Hendricks, Nancy Burke,
Elizabeth Bowerman, John Bowman (decd.), William Bowman (decd.).
Pens appl. 4-5-1833 ae. 71, Washington Co. Ind. Service: enl.
Sept 1777, Amherst Co., Va., Capt. Nicholas Cabal (sp?); other
tours thru until 1780. Is in 1835 Pens. List ae. 72, pvt. in
Va. Mil.; in 1840 Pens. List, ae. 80, liv. with Isabella Stuart,
Monroe Twp. His bro. John Bowman & bro-in-law, Joseph Lane both
live in Tenn. (1832). REF: Pens. S.16328 Va.; 1835 Pens. List,
v.3, p.75; 1840 Pens. List, p.185; Mr. Schrum; "Abstr. of Wills
of Washington Co., Ind., 1814-1900", Christopher Harrison Chap.,
DAR, Salem, Ind. (1953), p.35 (from Washington Co., Ind., Prob.
Bk. D, pp.299-300; Sweeny--"Amherst Co., Va., in the Revolution"
(1951), p. 54.

    BOYER, JOHN   Rush
(Note: this is not the John Boyer of "Roster", p.68). b. 11-18-1759, Northumberland Co., Va.; d. by 7-4-1841 (poss. d. 7-5-1839);
no. surv. wife & chn. Admr. appt. was Elijah Thompson. Pens. app.
9-17-1832, ae. nearly 73, Hamilton Co., O.; 11-7-1837, ae. 78,
Noble Twp., Rush Co., Ind. Dur. Rev., liv. near Camden, Dist. 96,
S. C.; after War, in 1804 to Baltimore, Md.; in 1805 to Hamilton
Co., O., for last 20 yr., Cincinnati, then to Big Miami in Ohio;

to Noble Twp., Rush Co., Ind., 1830. Father's family Bible prob. still in Va. Service: enl. 1776, S. C. Mil., Capt. Isaac Cook. (Original commission as Lieutenant by Gen. Hathanael Greene is in pens. file). Comm. Capt. in Jan. 1779 by Gov. John Rutledge. REF: Pens. S.32125 S. C.

BRADY, JOSEPH   Vigo
b. 1760, Johnson Co. N.C.; d. 9-6-1838; m.; chn., at least: Isaac; John (admr. of sold.'s estate); Joseph (d. & left chn., James, Emeline, William, John); James; Rhoda m. William Anderson; Mary m. Christopher Acred; Nancy m. Mr. Blankenship (she d. & left chn., Joseph, Louisa). Pens. appl. 8-11-1834, ae. 73, Vigo Co., Ind., and 11-3-1834. ae. 73, Knox Co., Ind. formerly of near Vincennes, now of Vigo Co., Ind. Affid. 11-14-1845, Vigo Co., Ind., of son John Brady, admr., that sold. had liv. Vigo Co., Ind., 12 yr. ante death & before that in Knox Co., Ind. Sold. after War to Albert Co., Ga. for ca. 5 yr.; to Wilkes Co., Ga., for ca. 7 yr.; to Baldwin Co., Ga., for ca. 1 yr.; to Rutherford Co., Tenn., for ca. 12-15 yr.; to Vigo Co., Ind., where has liv. ca. 7 yr. (in pens. appl. of 8-11-1834). Service: enl. N.C. Mil., from Johnson Co., N.C., Capt. Bryant; then to Roan Co., N.C. & again served. REF: Pens. S.32143 N. C.

BRENTON, ADAM   Owen.
b. 5-8-1763, on the waters of the Potomac, Hampshire Co., Va. Pens. appl. 2-10-1834, ae. 70. After ca. 7 yr., to Cheat River, Va., a fork of the Monongahela River, for ca. 2 yr.; to Redstone Old Fort ca. 7 yr.; to Ky. (Va.) on Cain River near Harrodsburg 1 yr.;to Danville 2-3 yr.; to Millers Station, Garrett, Shelby; in 1798 to Clark's Grant, Ind., till 1816; to Owen Co., Ind., ever since. Service: was a subst. for James Lawson in a county which is now Fayette Co., Pa., Thomas Brown, Commander, stationed at Redstone Old Fort, 1778. Then subst. for John Purdy. Later enl. in what is now Ky. (was then Va.), summer 1781 in what is now Mercer Co., Ky., James Kincaid, Commander; in Oct. 1782 enl. again at Danville, Ky. (Non-Rev. service: enl. Sept. 1786, Garrett Co., Ky., as a subst. for Edmund Parker in Capt. John Downing's Comp.) REF: Pens. R.1178 Pa. & Va.; Rej. Pens. List, p.406--Only 4 mo. & 5 da. service. Also in Indian War 1794.

BRIDGES, JOHN--see p. 115.

BRIDGEWATER, SAMUEL   Scott
b 4-17-1747; d. 5-17-1827; m. 6-2-1771, Mecklinburgh Co., Va., Mary Ann Coughman, b. 10-25-1755; d. 3-21-1847; chn. (Bible leaves in pens file):Margaret b. 7-6-1772; Mary b. 1-17-1773; Anna b. 8-23-1775; Isaac b. 7-2-1777; Cisiah (prob. Keziah) b. 3-18-1779; Rebecca b. 11-30-1780; Levi b 1-31-1782; Rachel b. 2-5-1784; Sarah b. 12-17-1786; Samuel b. 8-7-1788; Christian b. 7-31-1790 (had large fam. of chn., some now liv., 1847); Elias b. 1-14-1792; Elizabeth b. 4-5-1794; Patience b. 7-6-1796; Ellenor b. 5-26-1798. Wid. pens. appl. 8-19-1844, ae. 89. Service: enl. 1776, Va., Capt. Springer. Also signed Oath of Alleg. & Fidel.; orig. certif. slip dated 10-15-1777 in pens. file. (Note: I think some of this family moved to Jackson Co., Ind.) REF: Pens. W.9371 Va.

BROADHEAD, WILLIAM HALL   Jefferson
Said to be Rev. sold. bur. there. REF: Mr. Schrum

     BROCK, GEORGE   Washington
b. Aug. 1762, Shenandoah Co., Va.; d. Jan. 1839; m.(1) mother of
his chn.; m.(2) 5-28-1824, Washington Co., Ind., Julia Ann Bruner
(evid. dead by 1828); chn. (from will & estate rec.): Molly m.
Abraham Lefevers;   Barbara m. Adam Barnett;   Caty m. Frederick
Nightever;   George, Jr., m. Polly --- (& had Elizabeth, George,
Martin, Henry);   Susan m.(1) 2-19-1824, Washington Co., Ind.,
John Ard (&had George W. Ard), m.(2) 2-8-1827, Washington Co.,
Ind., Henry Fitts (&had Jacob Fitts);   Elizabeth m. John Tindall
(&had Samuel); other gr-chn. mentioned are: Elizabeth, Sarah,
Abraham, & Susan Nightever. Will wr. 4-27-1828, pr. 2-13-1839;
guardianship rec. of the Nightever, Ard, Tindall, & George Brock,
Jr.'s chn. names them as minors. At time of will, Elizabeth &
John Tindall, John Ard, & Susy Ard Fitts were all dead. Sold. is
given as Sr. in will & in 2nd mar., too. Pens. appl. 10-14-1834,
ae. 72, Washington Co., Ind. After War, liv. Shenandoah Co., Va.,
6-7 yr.; to Waters of Holston in Va., 18 yr.; to Ky. 3-4 yr.; to
Washington Co., Ind. Amended appl. 6-13-1835; ae. 73, Washington
Co., Ind. Pens. appl. 7-16-1853, Washington Co., Ind., of dau.,
Barbara Barnett, heir of George Brock. Service: drf. Sept. 1779,
Shenandoah Co., Va., Col. Booth, Maj. Welch, Capt. Sharp. REF:
Pens. R.1231 Va.; Susp. Pens. List, p.411--for further proof and
specification; Washington Co., Ind., court rec., Prob. Rec.,
1831-1842, p.233 (et al); Prob. Bk. C, pp.93-96; Mar. Bk. A,
pp. 114, 110, 192.

     BROWN, JAMES   Orange
b. 11-9-1761, ca. 7 mi. above Redfield Ford on Haw River, Chatham
Co., N.C.; (son of Thomas Brown); d. 6-4-1850; m. Dubois Co.,
Ind. (by Richard Kirby), Mary ---; chn. (at least): Cynthia Ann.
Sold. liv. with father in Orange Co., N.C.; left his father there
ca. 3 wks. before enl. After War. liv. Newberry Co., S.C.; Green-
ville Co., S.C.; Pendleton Co., S.C.; Bunkum Co., N.C.; to Ind.
Terr. 1815; Washington Co., Ind.; Gibson Co., Ind.; Pike Co.,
Ind.; Dubois Co., Ind.; Orange Co., Ind. Pens. appl. 3-30-1842,
ae. 80 on 11-9-1841, Orange Co., Ind. Wid.'s pens. appl. 4-20-
1853, Orange Co., Ind. Power of atty. 12-17-1852, Orange Co.,
Ind., by Cynthia Ann Brown, dau. Service: enl. 4-14-1780 in 19th
yr., S.C. State Troops, Capt. John Williams; mus. in at Camden,
S.C. Was in service with his relatives (rel. not stated): Mark
Littleton, Savage Littleton, Charles Littleton. (Note: not the
James Brown, "Roster" p.73, Clark Co., Ind., d. 1837). REF:
Pens. R.1309 S.C.; Susp. Pens. List, p.411--for proof from S.C.

     BROWN, JOHN   Hendricks
Said to be Rev. sold. bur. there. REF: Mr. Schrum.

     BROOKS, WILLIAM--see p. 115.
     BROTHERTON, JOHN--see p. 115.

BROWN, SAMUEL   Switzerland
d. 1816 (estate rec.); m. Susan Bacon; chn.: Jemima d. 1873, bur.
Wesleyan Cem., 4003 Colrain Ave., Cincinnati, O., m. 10-19-1813
Greene Co., O., Isaac Shingledecker; Polly b. 6-17-1783, Harrodsburg, Ky., d. 9-4-1869, Vevay, Ind., bur. Florence, Switzerland Co., Ind., m. 6-17-1800, William Campbell, b. Aug. 1776, *
Rowan Co., N.C., d. 2-10-1832, Florence, Ind.; Elizabeth m. 12-
25-1812, Greene Co., O., Evan Brock; Samuel m. (wife d. Cincinnati, O.);   William b. Aug. 1776, Rowan Co., N.C., d. 2-10-1832,
Florence, Ind. (note discrepancy with Polly's husb. above*), m. &
had dau. Polly Campbell (*), b. 4-9-1809, Greene Co., O., d. 11-
13-1889, Vevay, Ind., m. 11-29-1826, William Protzman, b. 2-1-
1801, Danville, Ky., d. 11-5-1866, Vevay, Ind. (& had dau. Flora
Protzman Betts Morrison). Service: 3 yr. in Va. Cont. Line; with
Geo. Rogers Clark in Ky.; bounty land given. REF: Brumbaugh--
"Rev. War Rec. of Va.", v.1, pp.135, 187, 395; photostat of Capt.
James Downing's Comp. of Lincoln Co., Ky., Mil., 11-24-1782;
"Hist. of Dearborn, Ohio, & Switzerland Cos., Ind."; DAR # 293046;
Miss Mary Hill, Madison, Ind.

BRYANT, JOHN   Monroe
Said to be Rev. sold. bur. there. REF: Mr. Schrum.

BUCK, JOHN   Tippecanoe
b. Feb. 1760. Pens. appl. 5-13-1833, ae. 73 last Feb., Shelby
Twp., Tippecanoe Co., Ind. Service: enl. ca. 1777, Kent Co.,
Del., Capt. Joseph Alford or Capt. Waitman Sipple. (Note: this
is not the John Buck of "Roster" p.76, Pens. S.32155, Putnam Co.,
Ind.). REF: Pens. R.1396 Del.; Rej. Pens. List, p.406--service
as a pilot & express rider.

BUCKMAN, JAMES   Washington & Clark
d. in Washington Co., Ind.; bur. in cem. near the old Baptist
Church in Salem, Ind. (Washington Co.); remains removed by DAR
to Jeffersonville Clark Co., Ind. REF: Mr. Schrum; Stevens--
"Hist of Washington Co., Ind." (1916) p.633.

BULLOCK, WILLIAM T.   Clark
b. 10-4-1760, St. Mary's Co., Md.; d. 1-11-1844; m. Oct. 1778,
Sarah Ord, b. ca. 1765; d. 10-23-1846; chn. (at least): William;
Catharine m. Mr. Brenton; Susan m. Mr. Oard; Nancy m. Mr.
Griffin (these 4 surv. the wid.). Pens. appl. 4-26-1833, ae. ca.
73. After War liv. St. Mary's Co., Md., ca. 6 yr.; to Berkeley
Co., Va., ca. 11 yr. till 1799; to Jefferson Co., Ky., ca. 3 yr.;
to Clark Co., Ind., Dec. 1802. Wants mail sent to West Port,
Ky., since he lives nearer it than to Charlestown, Clark Co.,
Ind., seat. Affid. 8-15-1844, Clark Co., Ind., of William T.
Bullock, gr-son of sold., ae. 26; reared by sold. Wid. Sarah, ae.
79 in affid. 8-15-1844. Co. Hist.:" On the road leading from New
Market to the Ohio, four miles, air measure, from Grassy flats,
on Mr. William Bullock's old farm, a fort was erected in 1812.---
Bullock came from the East and settled one mile from Tunnel mill.
He changed his residence after a few years and located in Owen
township." William Bullock (father or son?) was appointed a

Justice of the Peace for Clark Co., Ind., 4-23-1829. REF: Pens.
W.9765 Md.; "Hist. of the Ohio Falls Cities & Their Cos." (1882)
v.2, p.378; "Exec. Proc. of Ind., 1816-1836", p.384. Service:
                 pvt. in Md. Mil., Capt. William Waters.
    BURCH, DANIEL   Franklin
b. ca. 1759. Pens. appl. 8-22-1837, ae. 78, Franklin Co., Ind.
Service: enl. 1 yr. ante Batt. of Brandywine; drummer in Pa..Line
Reading, Pa. Had bro., John Burch; Daniel & John were together
in Reading in 1779. Sold. liv. 11-4-1839. Was maybe in Scott
Co., Ind., 11-6-1820. REF: Pens. R.1441 Pa.; Rej. Pens. List,
p.4-6--did not serve 6 mos.; Miss Thelma Murphy, Indinnapolis,Ind.

    BURKE, JOHN   Clark
b. 7-15-1761, Shenandoah Co., Va. After War liv. Montgomery Co.,
Va., 10-12 yr., till ca. 29 yr old; to Big Pigeon River in Tenn.
for ca. 15-27 yr.; Shelby Co., Ky., ca. 3 yr.; Franklin Co., Ind.
ca. 2 yr.; Dearborn Co., Ind., ca. 15-20 yr.; to Monroe Twp.,
Clark Co., Ind. Pens. appl. 5-21-1834, ae. 74, Clark Co., Ind.
Amended appl. 2-8-1841, ae. 79 on 7-15-1840, Monroe Twp., Clark
Co., Ind. Service: enl. June ante 21 yr. old; res. on New River,
a branch of the Kanawha River, Montgomery Co., Va.; Mounted Rifle-
man, Va. Mil., Capt. John Draper. REF: Pens. R.1458.Va.; Rej.
Pens. Liat, p.406--did not serve 6 mos.

    BURNETT, JOHN   Greene
Said to be Rev. sold. bur. there. REF: Mr. Schrum.

    BURTON, ABSALOM   Decatur
b. 6-2-1750; d. 10-6-1836; m. 1774, Rowan Co., N.C., Ann Jones,
b. 2-11-1759, Pa.; chn.: Betty b. 8-22-1775; John b. 2-11-1777;
William b. 3-22-1779; James b. 6-16-1781; Mary b. 7-5-1783;
Page b. 5-18-1786; Rebia b. 1-11-1788; Samuel b. 8-24-1791;
Thomas b. 8-22-1793. Wid.'s pens. appl. 3-1-1839, Decatur Co.,
Ind., that she b. in Pa.; in early life mov. with parents to N.C.
Affid. 11-14-1838, Daviess Co., Ky., & same 9-3-1843, of James
Jones, ae. 83 (1843), Rev. sold.; bro. of Ann Jones; that she m.
as above; that he was with sold. for part of service; liv. ½ mi.
from him then. Service: enl. 1776, Capt. Robinson, N.C. After
War, to Henry Co., Va.; 1802 to Ky.; 1835 to Decatur Co., Ind.
REF: Pens. R.1515 N.C.; Susp. Pens. List, p.416--service princi-
pally in driving pack horses.

    BUSH, DANIEL   Washington
Said to be Rev. sold. bur. there. REF: Mr. Schrum.

    BUSH, GEORGE   Clark
b. 1750; d. 1840; bur. Ross Cem., Bethlehem Twp. Said to be
Rev. sold. but no proof of service. REF: Clark Co., Ind. Cem.
Rec., I.S.L.

    BUSHMAN, JACOB   Indiana

Papers withdrawn from file & sent to Hon. W. Woodridge 3-2-1846.
Maryland service. REF: Pens.R.1535 Md.; Sus. Pens. List,p.411--for
proof from Annapolis.

BUSKIRK, AARON   Monroe
Pens. file env. has no papers. Private; placed on Ind. Agy. Rolls 6-11-1834, certif. # 26,833. In 1835 Pens. List, ae. 80, pvt. in Va. State Troops. (Note: I think this man may be a bro. of John Buskirk, "Roster" p.80, and of Isaac VanBuskirk. Altho "Roster" has John Buskirk of Ripley Co., Ind., I found only Greene Co., Ind., papers in John's pens. file. Mr. Schrum lists John as of Owen Co. & Greene Co., and lists Aaron as of Owen Co. & Monroe Co.). REF: Pens. I.A.R. certif. # 26,833; Mr. Schrum; 1835 Pens List, v.3, p. 60.

BUTLER, JOEL   Jay
Said to be Rev. sold. bur. there. (Note: This man can hardly be the Joel Butler of Jennings Co., d. 1822, "Roster", p.81. At Natl. Archives I found a pens. file for another Joel Butler, different from the Jennings Co. man, but no indication of any connection with Jay Co. So there may have been three Joel Butlers. REF: Mr. Schrum; Natl. Archives pens. files.

BUTTEN, DANIEL   Indiana
A pens. file for this man has not yet been located. Undoubtedly Butten is a typographical error for which we have not as yet hit the right name. He was a private. His wid., Charlotte Butten, was placed on the Ind. Agy. Rolls 2-16-1842 (Act of 1838), cert. # 6,552. There is the possibility that this man did not die in Indiana and that his widow moved here after his death. There is also the possibility that Butten (or variation) is the surname of a second marriage for her. If any reader happens upon the right name, please notify the compiler).

CARRITHERS, WILLIAM   Sullivan
b. 1-1-1760, Co. Donegal, Ire.; m. 1783, Fayette Co., Pa. Pens. appl. 2-8-1836, ae. 76, Sullivan Co., Ind. Came to Amer. 1774; liv. Cecil Co., Md., till 1779; to near Brownsville, Fayette Co., Pa., till 1799; to Nelson Co., Ky., till 1820; to Sullivan Co., Ind. Service: drf. 1781 in Pa., Capt. Hickman, Col. Gattis. NOTE: He may have forgotten the date he left Ky. & may have sett. in Ind. earlier. The following William Carrithers would seem to be the same man: appt. J. P. for Knox Co., Ind., 6-26-1810; appt. Judge for Knox Co. Ind., 2-24-1817; (Sullivan Co. formed 1817 from Knox Co.); had mov. from Knox Co. by 6-22- 1818; appt. J. P. for Sullivan Co., 2-28-1828 & resigned by May 1829. REF: Pens R.1789 Pa.; Rej. Pens. List, p.406--did not serve 6 mos.; "Exec. Journ. of Ind. Terr.", p.163; "Exec. Proc. of Ind.", pp. 27, 74 note, 612, 612 note.

CARTER, HENRY   Washington
b. ca. 1765, Albemarle Co., Va.; m. Sarah ---. Will wr. 7-28-1845, pr. 1-10-1851, names wife Sarah & following nephews (sons of Benjamin Nicholson, decd.): Henry W., David D., Peter J., Benjamin F., William M. In autumn 1781 to Harrod's Station, Ky., for 5 yr. (where was also in Indian Wars); to Bowman's Sta., now in Mercer Co., Ky., ca. 1½ yr.; to Smith's Sta. in fork of Kentucky River & Dick's River, ca. 2 yr.; to Fayette Co., Ky. Pens.

appl. 11-15-1843 ae. 78, Washington Twp., Washington Co., Ind. Power of atty. 6-13-1854, Washington Co., Ind., of wid. Sarah. Service: enl. a yr. or more ante Cornwallis' defeat, near Charlottesville, Va.; Albemarle Co., Va., Mil., Capt. Benjamin Burgy (Bergee?). REF: Pens. R.1744 Va.; Susp. Pens. List, p.411--did not serve 6 mos.; Washington Co., Ind., Will Bk. 1, p. 630.

   CARY (CAREY), SAUL   Hamilton (?)
b. 5-17-1756, Worcester Co., Md. After War liv. Worcester Co., Md., till 25-26 yr ago, went to Piqua Co., O.; 12 yr. ago to Hamilton Co., Ind. (Note:may poss. have later mov. to Marion Co., Ind., as latter Co. is given as res. in Rej. Pens. List; however, residences given in same have been proved wrong, in some cases, especially when the applicant has engaged the services of an atty. whose residence elsewhere may be listed for the sold.). Affid. 10-12-1839, Hamilton Co., Ind., of Levi Holloway, ae. 104 (see "Roster" p.193) that he knew sold. well ante War & served several places with him in same Comp. Pens. appl. 10-12-1839, ae. 83, Hamilton Co., Ind. Service: enl. as a sea fencible or minute man, Worcester Co., Md., in summer 1778, Capt. Josiah Neal (Beal?Veal?) later Capts. Littleton R. Robins, James Laws, George Bell (Beall?), & James Faucett; first enlistment was as subst. for Alexander Warrenton; 2nd enl. as subst. for Johnson Greg; 3rd enl. as a subst. for Campbell Neal (Beal? Veal?). REF: Pens. R.1684 Md.; Rej. Pens. List, p.406--not under military organization or author.

   CASE, JOSEPH   Clay
Rev. sold. who sett. early in NE part of the Co., in VanBuren Twp. REF: Travis--"Hist. of Clay Co. Ind." (1909), v.1, p.350; Posson--"Sold. of the War of the Rev. in Clay Co., Ind." (1929), pp.2-3; Blanchard--"Hist. of Clay & Owen Cos., Ind." (1884), p. 232; Mr. Schrum.

   CASE, OBADIAH   Clay
Rev. sold. who sett. early in the NE part of the Co. in VanBuren Twp. REF: Travis--"Hist. of Clay Co.", Ind." (1909) v.1, p.350; Posson--"Sold. of the War of the Rev. in Clay Co., Ind." (1929), pp.2-3; Mr. Schrum.

   CASSELL, RALPH   Decatur
b. 10-4-1760, Va. Pens. appl. 9-4-1839, ae. 79 in Oct., Decatur Co., Ind.; again on 11-24-1840, ae. 80 yr., 1 mo., 10 da. Lived S.C., 8-10 yr.; then Ohio till spr. 1839; to Decatur Co., Ind.; Service: enl. Newberry Co., N.C., Capt. Joseph Hayes, Col. Williams, spr. or sum. 1776. REF: Pens. R.1791 N.C.; Susp. Pens. List, p.411--for further proof & traditionary reputation.
   CHAMBERS, JOHN THOMAS--see p. 116.
   CHANCE, SAMUEL   Wayne
b. 1748, Queen Anne Co., Md. Liv. there till ca. 14 yr. old; mov. with parents to N.C. for 6-7 yr.; to Between Neuse & Trent Rivers (now called Wayne Co., N.C.); there till ca. 1797; to Richmond Co.,N.C.,till fall 1831;Wayne Co.,Ind. Pens. appl.1-25-1834,Wayne Co.,Ind.,ae.86. Service:drf.fall 1779,Wayne Co.,N.C.,Mil.,Capt.John Canada,Lt.Jacob Hooks. REF:Pens.R.1846 N.C.;Rej.Pens.List,p.406-- only 5 mo. service.

CHAPMAN, WILLIAM, SR.   Jay
Said to be Rev. sold. bur. there. REF: Mr. Schrum.

CHEEK, FRANCIS   Dearborn
d. ca. Mar. 1826; mar.; chn. (at least): William V.; daughter m. John Buffington. His affid. is in Pens. file of Hezekiah Roberts (Pens. W.9631 Va.; see this Suppl.) that he has known Roberts over 40 yrs.; that he did not see Roberts enlist but that his (Cheek's) captain, Capt. William Fields, told him (Cheek) that he (Fields) had enlisted Roberts for 3 yrs.; that he (Cheek) saw Roberts in service under Capt. Fields. (Note: four Cheek bros.: Francis, Page, Nicholas, and Tavner, came to Dearborn Co., Ind., 1798. Francis & Nicholas bought land in 1812 in Sec. 19, Twp. 4, Range 1 West (Nicholas below Wilson Creek). At the March Term 1826, Dearborn Co., Ind., Court, real estate was ordered sold to settle Francis Cheek's insolvent estate; son William V. Cheek, admr.) Service: prob. the same as Hezekiah Roberts (whom see). There is also the possibility that some of the other brothers of Francis Cheek served in the same Company and might thus be included in this Supplement. REF: Pens. W.9631 Va. (of Hezekiah Roberts); "Hist. of Dearborn & Ohio Cos., Ind." (1885) pp. 100,426, 848; Shaw--"Hist. of Dearborn Co., Ind." (1915) pp. 155, 158; Dearborn Co., Ind., Prob. Rec., 1826-1830, p. 110.

CHENOWETH, JOHN   Vermillion
d. 3-3-1820. (Pens. file does not actually state place of death. By inference, it is Vermillion Co., Ind.; but there is the possibility that it might have been Ky., and poss. Shelby Co., KY.); m. 3-13-1793, Shelby Co., Ky., Mary Buskirk (dau. of Michael Buskirk; bondsmen John Chenoweth & Thomas Buskirk), b. 10-17-1766; liv. 6-21-1842, ae. 75, Vermillion Co., Ind.; chn. (at least): Isaac (ae. 48 in affid. 6-21-1842, Vermillion Co., Ind. Affid. 6-4-1842, Tippecanoe Co., Ind., of sold.'s bro., Richard Chenoweth, ae. 84. Service: enl. at ae. 16 in (now) Alleghany Co., Md., Aug. 1776; sgt. in Md. Line, Capt. Michael Cresep, Col. Rawling's Rifle Regt. REF: Pens. W.9787 Md.

CLARK, JOHN   Lagrange
Said to be Rev. sold. bur. there. Evidently not the John Clark of Scott Co. in "Roster" p. 97. REF: Mr. Schrum.

CLARK, WILLIAM   Jay
Said to be Rev. sold. bur. there. REF: Mr. Schrum.

CLEMENTS, BERNARD   Marion
b. 1757, prob. Va.; d. 7-22-1839 (1840 or 1838; varying dates in affids.; I.A.R. says 7-21-1838); m. (bond dated 3-22-1785) Charlotte Co., Va., Sally Gore (or Goare), b. ca. 1763; liv. 4-27-1850; chn. (at least): Allen, b. not quite 1 yr. after par.'s mar., m. Polly Triplett (dau. of Hedgman Triplett) & was in Franklin Co., Ky., 1808; Catharine m. William Stephens & was in Franklin Co., Ky., 1805; William (liv. in Owen & Henry Cos., Ky.; dead but would be ae. 52-53 (affid. of 10-28-1843); Jane; Sally m. Presley Arnold & was in Franklin Co., Ky., 1817; Oston;

-22-

Nancy (ae. 40 in affid. 10-28-1843) m. Mr. Thornton. Pens. appl. 6-15-1819, ae. ca. 64, Franklin Co., Ky.; asked for tr. 2-20-1835 as now liv. in Marion Co., Ind., with chn. Affid. of wid. Sally 10-28-1843. ae. nearly 80, Marion Co., Ind., and 9-20-1848, Wayne Twp., Marion Co., Ind. Service: enl. Charlotte Co., Va., 8-9-1778, Capt. Edmond Reed; was quartermaster & sgt. in Cont. Line. REF: Pens. W.9792 Cont. (Va.); Darnell--"Forks of Elkhorn Church" (1946) pp. 101, 270, 290.

COLLINS, JOHN   Rush
b. 10-27 (or 28)-1768; d. 1-21-1828 (some doubt if Rush Co., Ind. or Ky.; had liv. Fleming Co., Ky.); m. 3-17-1786, Westmoreland Co., Pa., Margaret ---, b. 10-27 (or 2)-1768; chn. (10; 7 liv. with him 9-15-1818, Fleming Co., Ky.): Sally b. 6-12-1803; Levi b. 8-15-1805; Margaret b. 11-22-1807; James, 8th ch., b. 5-7-1801 (has 6 older bros. & sists. & 1 d. ante he was b.); eldest dau. Elizabeth (ae. ca. 10 when John, 6th. ch. was b.); Polly m. Mr. Lawrence; Elizabeth b. 11-9-1788, m. George Lawrence (& liv. Ky. 1839); Elisha b. 2-8-1791 (& liv. Ky. 1639). Pens. appl. 8-22-1818, ae. ca. 60, Ky. (Co. not named); 10-6-1820, Fleming Co., Ky.; 11-6-1820, ae. 62 on last Aug. 28; wife Margaret ae. 52 on 2nd of last month. Wid.'s appl. 6-7-1839, ae. 72, Rush Co., Ind. Affid. 2-5-1840, Boone Co., Ky., of son Elisha Collins that his oldest living sis., Elizabeth Graham was 51 yr. old last Nov. 9; that his parents lost their oldest ch.; that Elisha is 49 on 2-8-1840. Affid. 2-5-1840, Boone Co., Ky., of Elizabeth Graham that she 51 yr. old on Nov. 9 last. Affid. of wid., ae. 76, Rush Co., Ind., 8-31-1843. (Note: I think this wid. may be incorrectly listed in the 1840 Pens. List, p. 185, as Mary (instead of Margaret) Collins, ae. 75, liv. Posey Twp., Rush Co., Ind., with Andrew McRoberts). Service: enl. 3rd Va. Regt. of Light Drag., Capt. John Swan, Col. George Baylor, 1776. REF: Pens. W.9813 Cont. (Va.).

CONNOR, ABNER   Shelby
b. 1754, Md.; d. 12-25-1833, Jackson Twp.; m. soon after close of War, Anna Russell, d. Jan. 1836 (dau. of John Russell, a native of Ireland); chn.: Massa; John; William; Eleanor; Sarah; Abner b. 1-27-1804, Dearborn Co., Ind., m. 2-28-1837, Mary A. Doughman, b. 11-6-1817, Center Co., Pa. (dau. of Jacob & Elizabeth (Thompson) Doughman) & had 10 chn. (names & b. dates in ref. below). Sold. migr. to Va. at ae. 20; shortly after mar., migr. to Tenn. for 3 yr.; then Dearborn Co., Ind., where was 3rd settler in the Co.; in a few yrs., sold out & remov. to Franklin Co., Ind., for 3 yrs.; then to Jackson Twp., Shelby Co., Ind., 3-5-1823. Was a Mason. Service: none given; prob. Md. or Va. REF: "Hist. of Shelby Co., Ind." (1887), pp. 669-670; Waters--"Ind. Land Entries" (1946), v. 1, p. 18.

COOK, ELIHU   Harrison
b. ca. 1761; d. 9-13-1840, Maucksport, Ind.; m. 9-21-1797, First Congr. Ch., Wallingsford, New Haven Co., Conn., Lois Thorp (or Tharp?) ae. 47 in affid. 5-15-1821; chn. (at least 4 liv. with him 5-15-1821): Sherlock 15; Catharine 13; Lucena 11; Abby 9.

Affid. 5-15-1821, Sheffield, Berkshire Co., Mass., ae. 60; and
10-14-1826 that he on pens. roll of Conn. & then mov. to Mass.;
back to Hartford Co., Conn., Mar. 1824; asked for tr. to Mass.,
7-28-1821. Affid. 3-1-1839, Harrison Co., Ind., that had relatives here; attested by Eliga A. Cook. Pens. tr. from Conn.,
8-12-1839. Letter 8-3-1845, Rock River Rapids, Whiteside Co.,
Ill., signed Elira (sp? Eliza? Maybe above Eliga?) A. Cooke.
Wid.'s appl. 2-18-1849, ae. 72, Carroll Co., Ky. Affid. 2-18-
1849, Carroll Co., Ky., Lucina Dennis (prob. above dau. Lucena)
mentions that Elihu Cook took his family record "to New London
as evidence to prove the age of Jeremiah H. Cook who was detained
there a prisoner for deserting from the Fort" and never obtained
the record again. Affid. 2 -18-1849, Carroll Co., Ky., Eliza (sp?)
Cook says Jeremiah H. Cook was his (sic) 2nd son, b. 2-1-1800.
Sold. asked for tr. 3-14-1826 from Mass. to Conn. Affid. 1-9-
1850, Tallahassee, Leon Co., Fla., of Thomas Douglas, in 60th yr.,
of Jacksonville, Fla., b. Wallingsford, Conn., mov. 1797 to Mer-
iden, Conn., that Lois Tharp was the youngest sis. of his mother;
that 2nd son of sold. was named Jeremiah Hallock Cook; that Elihu
Cook had mov. from Wallingsford by 1815; in 1817 deponent mov. to
Ind. till 1826 when mov. to Fla. Sold. asked for tr. to Ind.
(enclosed in letter dated 3-18-1839). Service: enl. spr. 1778,
Wallingsford, Conn., 4th Conn. Regt., Col. Meigs, Capt. Stephen
Potter Pens. appl. 7-14-1819, Hartford Co., Conn. REF: Pens.
W.2066 Conn.

COONROD, ----- Marion
bur. on John McVey farm cem., ca. 4 mi. SW of Cumberland, Ind.;
old interurban stop # 6; now Franklin Road; go south from U.S.
Road # 40 to just across the Penna. Ry. tracks. Gravestone, but
lot is impenetrable. Sold. may have been related to others bur.
nearby: Israel Shue, Letitia Shue m. William Gross; Fergusons; &
Buchanans. REF: Mrs. Theodore Craven, North Madison, Ind.; Mr.
Norman Keister, Indianapolis, Ind.

COONROD, ALISLA (see Alisla, Coonrod)
The correct forename and surname have not yet been discovered.

COOPER, VINCENT Hancock
b. 1756, Stafford Co., Va.; mar.; chn.; one ch. wandered away in
1832 & was frozen to death on bank of Sugar Creek in Brown Twp.,
Hancock Co., Ind. Liv. Frederick Co., Va., dur. latter part of
War & for a few yrs. after; to Mason Co., Ky.; to Hancock Co.,
Ind., where was a 1st settler of Green Twp. Pens. appl. Feb.
1836, ae. 80, Hancock Co., Ind. Service: enl. 1780, Frederick
Co., Va., 3rd Va. Regt., Capt. Alexander, Col. Morgan. REF: Pens.
R.2305 Va.; Susp. Pens. List, p.411--for further proof & explan-
ation; Binford--"Hist. of Hancock Co., Ind." (1882), pp.96, 210.

COTTON, J. A, Perry
Said to be Rev. sold. bur. there. REF: Mr. Schrum.

COTTON, RALPH   Switzerland
b. 1-10-1742, Pa.; d. 1817; bur. Cotton Cem. near Mt. Sterling,
Ind.; m. ca. 1761, Elizabeth Kitchen, b. 1747; d. 1832; chn.:
Henry Smith b. 1763, m. Mary Harrold; Susanna b. 1765; Peggy
b. 1767; Jemima b. 1769; Mary b. 1772; John b. 1774;
William b. 1776, m. Christina Froman; Sarah b. 1778; Nathaniel
b. 1783; Ralph b. 1786; Robert b. 1788. Service: pvt. 6th
class, Capt. Timothy Downing, 3rd Batt., Washington Co., Pa.,Mil.,
5-18-1782. (Note: A Ralph Cotton (son?) was appt. J. P. for Jefferson Co., Ind. (from which Switzerland Co. was formed in 1814)
on 12-14-1810; on 6-15-1814, Coroner for Switzerland Co.; on 10-6-
1814, J. P. for Switzerland Co; on 12-23-1819, Associate Judge
for Switzerland Co. (resigned 9-21-1821); on 8-28-1827, Sheriff;
dead by Aug. 1828). REF: "Pa. Arch.", 6th Ser., v.2, pp.104-5,
117-8; John Paul Chap., DAR, Madison, Ind.; "Exec. Journ. of Ind.
Terr., 1800-1816", pp.167, 220, 222; "Exec. Proc. of Ind, 1816-
1836", pp. 121, 193 note, 206, 617 (2).

COUCH, JOHN   Indiana
(Uncertain). Private placed on Ind. Agy. Rolls, certif. #27,636
(Act of 6-7-1832). Note says "See Jonesborough, Tenn." He is
not on the 1835 or 1840 Pens. Lists for either Ind. or Tenn. At
Natl. Archives I found pens. files for three men of this name:
John & wid. Prudence (Pens. R.2360 Conn.); John & wid. Jane (Pens.
W.23841 Cont., Mass.); & John & wid. Lois (Pens. W.17640 Conn.);
no papers in files indicate Ind. res. REF: Ind. Agy. Rolls;
Natl. Archives pens. files.

COVENHOVER, THOMAS   Fountain
b. May 1766 or 1767, Monmouth Co., N.J. In 1810 to Warren Co.,
O., till 1831, to Fountain Co., Ind. Pens. appl. 5-14-1833,
Fountain Co., Ind. Service: enl. May 1782, Minuteman, Capt. John
Walton, Col. Elisha Walton, Monmouth Co., N.J. He was 12 yr. old
on the day the Batt. of Monmouth was fought & a few days later
had his name enrolled in a Comp. for drilling, it being customary
there for boys of 12 to be placed on muster roll & drilled till
they were 16 yrs. old & sent into actual service: so he was in
his 17th yr. in May 1782. REF: Pens. R.2380 N.J.; Rej. Pens.
List, p.4-6--did not serve 6 mos.

COWHERD, -----   Orange
Said to be Rev. sold. bur. there   REF: Mr. Schrum.

COX, NATHANIEL   Tippecanoe
b. 10-25-1759; d. 11-27-1846, ae. 89, Tippecanoe Twp.; bur. Pretty
Prairie M.E. Ch. Cem.; stone. Pens. appl. 8-14-1838, Tippecanoe
Twp., Tippecanoe Co., Ind., ae. 78 last Oct. 25. Service: enl.
June 1777, Eastern Shore, Dorchester Co., Md., Capt. Ezekiel
Vickers. (Note: possibility of a connection with a Nathaniel Cox
who came to Chillicothe? O.; then Jeffersonville, Ind.; then to
Indianapolis, fall 1821 & d. ca. 1850-1851; b. Talbott Co., Md.).
REF: Pens. R.2411 Md.; Susp. Pens. List, p.411--has not estab-
lished 6 mos. service.

CRANE, EDMUND--see p. 116.
Cross, John --see p. 119.

CRUSE, ALISON   Vigo (?)
(Uncertain). His affid. in pens. file of John Colwell ("Roster",
p.82) that he knew Colwell was a Rev. sold. Exactly same affid.
for William Durham who appl. for pens. on Maryland service (see
this Suppl.); so Cruse may have served in same Comp. No proof,
except by inference, that Cruse was of Vigo Co., Ind.; several
identical affids. from different men are in Colwell's file. REF:
Pens. S.16344 (of John Colwell).

CUNNINGHAM, RICHARD   Clay
Could find no pens. file at Natl Archives. In in 1840 Pens. List,
ae. 84, liv. with Francis Cunningham, Posey Twp., Clay Co., Ind.
REF: 1840 Pens. List; Posson--"Sold. of the War of the Rev. in
Clay Co., Ind." (1929), pp. 2-3.

CURRY, JOHN   Knox
b. ca. 1757, Botetourt Co., Va.; d. Knox Co., Ind., will wr. 6-17-
1822, pr. 2-25-1823; son of William & --- (McAfee) Curry; m. (1)
9-25-1777, Botetourt Co., Va., Margaret Adams, b. ca. 1759, Botetourt Co., Va.; d. ante 1816, Mercer Co., Ky.; he m. (2) 12-24-
1816, Knox Co., Ind., Mrs. Sarah Ingle; chn. (all by 1st wife &
all b. in what became Mercer Co., Ky.):Mary m. 9-2-1799, John
McClure (bro. of Samuel below);   William b. 1780, m. Polly Hogg;
Ann b. 1781, m. 9-3-1800, Samuel Brodie;   Samuel b. 12-22-1789,
m. 3-18-1813, Sarah Watson;   Andrew;   James b. 1791, m. 4-8-
1813, Isabella Hogg;   Margaret Walker m. 1-4-1812, James Harper;
Sarah b. 1797, m. 12-6-1815, James Brodie;   John, unm., d. 1813;
Jane b. 8-25-1783. m. 9-12-1805, Samuel McClure (bro. of John
above). Sold. to Knox Co., Ind., ca. 1806; land adj. son-in-law,
Samuel McClure. Service: Lincoln Co., Ky., Mil., 1780-1781-
1782, Capt. William McAfee (rel to sold.'s mother not stated).
REF: DAR # 398,636; Mrs. John Brevoort. Vincennes, Ind.; Gwathmey-
"Va. in the Rev.", I.P.D. 46 & 165.

DALE, CAMPBELL   Delaware
b. ca. 1765; mar.; chn. Entered land in Delaware Co., Ind., 1827;
his sons platted the village of Daleville, Salem Twp. Pens. appl.
7-15-1835, ae. 79, Delaware Co., Ind. Service: enl. Worcester
Co., Md., Mil. REF: Pens. R.2630 Md.; Rej. Pens. List, p.407--
did not serve 6 mos.; Kemper-- "20th Cent. Hist. of Delaware Co.,
Ind." (1908) v.1, p.98; Haimbaugh--"Hist. of Delaware Co., Ind."
(1924) v.1, pp. 110, 403.

DAVIS, DANIEL   Carroll
(This sold. did not die in Ind.; but because he was a resident at
the time, he is being included).   b. 12-25-1746, Reading, Berks
Co., Pa.; d. Nov. 1846, Preble Co., O.; m. in Pa., prob. Berks
Co., Sarah Albright, d. ca. 1826, Columbiana Co., O.; chn. (17;
order unknown except 3 oldest & 2 youngest, twins; data as of
1852): Elizabeth m. & liv. Berks Co., Pa.;   John, Berks Co., Pa.;
Daniel, Berks Co., Pa.;   Christian liv. ca. 25 mi. N between
Mansfield & Cleveland, O., ca. 3 mi. from Sandusky Plains (the
youngest bro. Israel once liv. with Daniel when Israel was small);
Adam, Columbiana Co., O.;   Jacob, Columbiana Co., O.;   Peter of

Jackson Co., O.; Samuel, Williams Co., O.; Emanuel, Columbiana Co., O.; Henry, Jackson Co., O.; Jonathan, Williams Co., O.; Susanna m. Levi Shy & liv. Jackson Co., O.; Levi (twin), Mahoning Co., O.; Israel (twin), Carroll Co., Ind.; 3 other chn.: Benjamin, Michael, & Sarah, all d. without heirs. Pens. appl. 10-13-1845, ae. ca. 99 next Dec. 25, Clinton Co., Ind., but a res. of Carroll Co., Ind., just over the Clinton--Carroll line. Affid. 3-31-1852, Carroll Co., Ind., of Israel Davis, ae. 27, one of sons & heirs; all remaining data, incl. re chn., except sold.'s service, furnished by Israel: sold. a weaver & brick or stone mason; son of a Welchman; after War, fam. liv. Berks Co., Pa.; when fam. mov. to Columbiana Co., O., 3 oldest chn. were then grown & stayed in Pa.; mother, Sarah Albright (German but so-pronounced in Eng.) d. when Israel ca. 2 yr. old; sold. liv. Columbiana Co., O., till Israel ca 3 yr. old; to Montgomery Co.; O., ca. 12 yr.; Clinton Co., Ind.; res. alternately in Clinton & Carroll Cos., Ind., till fall 1846; sold. started on visit to Columbiana Co., O.; stopped with Daniel Miller, Dunkard preacher in Preble Co., O.; took sick; preacher's fam. sick, too; sold. taken to poorhouse to die. Service: enl. 7-4-1778 (?), Reading, Pa., Capt. Nagle, Col. Lutz. REF: Pens. R.2707 Pa.; Susp. Pens. List, p.412--did not serve 6 mo.

DAVIS, DAVID Monroe
b. 1761-1762, Washington Co., Md. When a boy, mov. with father to Wythe Co., Va.; after War, liv. Wythe Co., Va., 30 yr. or more; then 22 yr. in Lee Co., Va.; in Monroe Co., Ind., 4 yr. or more now. Has a bro., John Davis of Ga., a Rev. pensioner, who says David is 71 or 72, not 67, as David is 4 yr. younger than John, who is 75; that David Johnson, a Rev. pensioner of Va., will know of David Davis' service. Pens. appl. 11-15-1834, Monroe Co., Ind. Service: drf. Wythe Co., Va., the year Cornwallis was taken; Va. Mil., Capt. James Newell. (Note: this is not the David Davis of Switzerland Co., Ind., "Roster", p.114, Pens. S.35878, last payment 3-27-1829). REF: Pens. R.2711 Va.; Susp. Pens. List, p.412--for further & more direct proof.

DAVIS, LEVI. Jackson.
b. 7-5-1751, Hampshire Co., Va.; d. 3-6-1846 (or 3-8-1847 (both dates given in pens. file); bur. Mitchell Cem., Owen Twp.; m. Hannah.---- (surv. husb. but d. by 11-27-1851); chn.: Irena m. John Hendrix; Rachel m. Solomon Ritchey; Sarah m. Shelby Harney; Stephen; James (admr. of father, who d. in 95th yr.); Rebecca m. John Crider; Effee m. Aaron Gilstrap; Jane m. Samuel Starr (decd.); Nancy (decd.) m. John McNeeley (decd.) & had Isaac & Levi McNeeley. After War, from Md to Nicholas Co., Ky.; Clark Co., Ind.; back to Nicholas Co., Ky.; back to Clark Co., Ind.; to Washington Co., Ind.; to Lawrence Co., Ind.; to Jackson Co. Ind.; back to Lawrence Co., Ind.; to Vermilion Co. Ill.; to Fulton Co., Ill.; to Knox Co., Ill.; to Fulton Co., Ind. (error for Ill.?); to Wapello Co., Iowa; back to Jackson Co. Ind. His bro. Ebenezer Davis, if liv., would know of his Rev. service. Affid. of Ebenezer Davis, Pickaway Co. O., bro. of Levi; when Levi 5-6 yr old, parents to Frederick Co., Md.; deponent from Md. to Pickaway Co., O., 1813, where has been ever since except for

1817 in Alleghany Co., Md., 1 yr.; affid. certified by Ebenezer
S. Davis, J.P. (son of Ebenezer?). Service: enl. 1777-1778 in
Md. under Capt. Thomas Bell of Fort Cumberland; pvt. in Md.
Troops, Col. Rawling's Regt. REF: Pens. S.32210 Md.; Susp. Pens.
List, p.412--for proof of identity with the war's man of the
Md. Line.

DAVISON, SAMUEL   Franklin
b. ca. 1765, 4 mi. from Tawney River, Pa. After War liv. near
Lynchburg, Bedford Co., Va.; East Tenn.; West Tenn.; Franklin
Co., Ind. Pens. appl. 10-11-1836, ae. 70, Ray Twp., Franklin
Co., Ind. Service: enl. 1781 near Lynchburg, Va., ca. 2 mo.
ante Batt. of Guilford, as subst. for father, James Davison;
served with bro-in-law, Michael Gilbert; served under Capt.
Moon (Moor?), who was killed at Batt. of Guilford. REF: Pens.
R.2694 Va.; Rej. Pens. List, p.4-6--did not serve 6 mos.

DEMOSS, REUBEN   Martin
(Uncertain, but probable because of advanced age). His affid. on
8-11-1834, Martin Co., Ind., ae. ca. 84, in pens. file of John
Blake (see this Suppl.) that he & Blake were in War together &
that they had liv. in same neighborhood for many years. See
"Roster" p.119, Andrew Demoss, b. 1753 (who could be younger bro.
of Reuben, b. ca. 1750) for possible clue as to Reuben's service.
Reuben never appl. for pens. REF: Pens. R.913 S.C. (John Blake).

DENBO, -----   Harrison
(Uncertain). Mr. Schrum has Rachel Denbow. She is possibly the
widow of a Denbo soldier who may or may not have died in Ind.
Or, Denbo may be her surname by a second marriage. A Joseph
Denbo was appt. Lieut. of the Light Infantry, 5th Regt. (Harrison
Co.), Ind. Terr. Mil., 7-26-1811. A Robert Denbo was appt. Lieut.
in Ind. Terr. Mil., Clark Co. (from part of which Harrison Co.,
was formed Dec. 1808) 7-6-1808. REF: Mr. Schrum; "Exec. Journ.
of Ind. Terr., 1800-1816" pp.175, 147.

DEREMIAH, JOHN   Washington
b. ca. 1744; d. 12-30-1831; m. Mary Ann --- (ae. 68, 10-9-1820).
Pens. appl. 8-23-1819, ae. 75, Washington Co., Ind.; 10-9-1820,
ae. 76. In 1835 Pens. List, ae. 87; pvt. in Va. Line. Service:
enl. Jan. 1777, Fort Pitt, Pa., Capt. Andrew (?) Waggoner, Col.
James Wood, 12th Va. Regt. in Cont. Estab., or Col. John Neville.
(Note: a John Deremiah (son?) was commn. Capt. in 19th Regt.,
Ind. Mil., Washington Co., Ind., 5-16-1818. REF: Pens. S.36504
Va.; 1835 Pens. List, v.3, p.36; "Exec. Proc. of Ind., 1816-1836"
page 70.

DEVORE, ELIJAH   Decatur
b. 10-16-1758, Huntington Co., N.J. After War liv. 11 yr. in
Ohio; then Franklin Co., Ind. Pens. appl. 8-26-1842, ae. 83 last
Oct. 16, Decatur Co., Ind. Service: enl. 1778, Londonderry Twp.,
Bedford Co., Pa., Capt. Cornelius Devore (Devour). REF: Pens.
R.2907 Pa.; Rej. Pens. List, p.407--not under competent military
authority.

DICKINSON, JOHN — Vermillion
b. ca. 1753; d. 7-9-1833, Newport, Ind.; m. fall 1793, North Bend, O., Catharine Aleandorf, b. 1767; chn. (Bible leaves in file): Mary b. 9-28-1796; Hannah b. 12-1-1799; John b. 11-1-1801; Mary Ann b. 7-31-1803; Elizabeth b. 11-2-1805; Sarah b. 11-28-1806; Catharine b. 12-16-1810. Pens. appl. 9-21-1829, Franklin Co., Ind., ae. 75. Affid. 9-19-1829, Franklin Co., Ind., of Samuel Meredith ("Roster" p.251) that he & sold. served together under Col. Henry Lee, Capt. George Handy. Same affid. by Ebenezer Wood of Butler Co., O. (See "Ohio Rev. Sold.", v.1, p.408). Wid.'s appl. 2-2-1853, ae. 86, Muscatine Co., Iowa; also same on 7-6-1855, ae. 88. Service: enl. end of 1775 or first of 1776 in Inf. Comp., Capt. Adam McClean, Col. Patton's Dela. Blues. (Note: this is not John Dickerson of Jefferson Co., Ind., "Roster" p.122, N.J. service; nor John Dixon, Ohio Co., Ind., "Roster" p.124, Pa. service.) REF: Pens. W.7026 Cont., Dela.

DIXON, PETER — Fountain
b. 1760, Augusta Co., Va. Pens. appl., ae. 74 Fountain Co., Ind. Dur. War. liv. Greenbrier Co., Va.; later liv. in Ky. Affid. of bro. George Dixon ("Roster" p.124), Warren Co., Ind., that he & Peter served together. Affid. 12-22-1834, Montgomery Co., Ind., of Joseph Swope that he knew George & Peter Dixon more than 30 yr. ago in Ky. & Va. Affid. 12-22-1834, Warren Co., Ind., of Peter Dixon (son of George), ae. 50, that his uncle Peter Dixon was drafted, etc. Sold. had bro. George who "was sent on an express to Ky." & joined same Comp. Service: drf. Greenbrier Co., Va., to join Geo. Rogers Clark in Ky. REF: Pens. S.32694 Va.

DOCK, JOHN — Monroe
Said to be Rev. sold. bur. there. REF: Mr. Schrum.

DODDRIDGE, PHILIP — Wayne
b. 1737; d. 1822; bur. Doddridge Chapel Cem., Washington Twp. on land given by sold. & son John; m. Mary Merricle or Bickerstaff (perhaps a widow), b. 1740; d. 1825; chn.: 2 days. & 1 son stolen by Indians; and Hannah b. 1778, d. 1838, m. David Jenkins; Sabra b. 1781, d. 1818, m. John Spahr; John b. 1786, d. 1841, m. Avis Manchester; Rachel m. William Walters (liv. State of Washington); Nancy b. 1788, d. 1813, m. Benjamin Manchester. Before coming to Ind. in 1814, sold. lived at "Lexington", a farm in Independence Twp., Washington Co., Pa. Service: under Capt. William Scott, Co. 4 Bat., Washington Co., Pa., 1782. REF: Ranck--"Doddridge Chapel Community, Yesterday and Today" pp. 35, 60, 66; Mrs. Forrest E. Kempton, Centerville, Ind. (Note: service can prob. be found in "Pa. Arch."); 1884 "Hist.of Wayne Co.", v.2, p.736.

DONAHUE, JOHN — Washington
Said to be Rev. sold. bur. there. REF: Mr. Schrum.

DOUGHERTY, JOHN--see p. 117.

DOUTHITT, THOMAS — Clark
bur. at Utica, Ind.; m. Mollie Wright; chn.:12; 7 daus. & 5 sons, incl. John Douthitt, with whom sold. lived. Descendants are: Applegate, McKinney, Goldsmith, Weir, Thacher, Connelly, Reuble,

Allan, et al. Sold. was an orphan; apprenticed to a shoemaker; seized by a press gang & put on British ship; he the only one of six who jumped overboard to reach shore. Went to Philadelphia; served 7 yrs. in Rev.; was at Valley Forge. Migr. from Pittsburgh & settled on Pennsylvania Run in Ky., 1789. REF: "Madison (Ind.) Courier", 2-5-1885; Miss Mary Hill, Madison, Ind.

 DUKES, RICHARD   Washington
Rev. sold. bur. in Little York Cem. REF: Stevens--"Hist. of Washington Co., Ind." (1916), p. 633.

 DUNNIGAN, THOMAS   Owen
Rev. sold. bur. in Asher Cem.; liv. in Harrison Twp. Note: a Thomas Dunagan was commn. J. P. in Morgan Co., Ind. (adjoins Harrison Twp., Owen Co.) on 11-1-1835). REF:*Am. Leg.; Mr. Schrum.

 DURHAM, WILLIAM   Vigo (?)
(Uncertain). His affid. in pens. file of John Colwell ("Roster" p.82) that he knew Colwell was a Rev. sold. (See Alexander Eagelton & Alison Cruse, & Joseph Macon in this Suppl.). Letter in Durham's file says "Name on Muster Rolls to have enlisted for during the War; private in 6th Md. Regt., 4-28-1778 & 11-1-1780; letter dated 11-26-1832. File says service is same as that. claimed by Ann Durham, wid. of Durham, in Md. Troops, Pens. W.4186 Md.; whose husb. wounded on head & hand; wandered from home ca. 1814; heard from in 1817 & supposed to have d. in 1817; his fam. say in 1842 that they have not heard from him in 20 yr. or over. REF: Pens. R.3160 Md.; Susp. Pens. List, p.412--not properly authenticated; papers withdrawn 11-30-1832; Pens. S.16344 (of John Colwell).

 DWIGGINS, ROBERT   Randolph
Said to be Rev. sold. bur. there. REF: Mr. Schrum.

 EAGELTON, ALEXANDER   Vigo (?)
(Uncertain). His affid. in pens. file of John Colwell ("Roster" p.82) that he knew Colwell was a Rev. sold. (See Alison Cruse, William Durham, & Joseph Macom in this Suppl.). REF: Pens. S.16344 (of John Colwell).

 ELKINS (ALKINS), SHADRACH   Posey (?)
(Uncertain). b. ca. 1749. Vanderburgh Co., Ind., court records show his appl. for pens. (under Act of 1818) in 1827, ae. 78, a resident of Posey Co., Ind. (Note: just recently found this ref. Have sent for abstract of his pens. file. If data received in time, will add at the end after Daniel Zink.). REF: Pens. R.3285 N.C.; "Hist. of Vanderburgh Co., Ind." 91889.), p. 337.(See p.119 later).

 ELLIS, GEORGE   Greene
Said to be Rev. sold. bur. there. REF: Mr. Schrum.

(* "Exec. Proc. of Ind., 1816-1836", p. 539.)

ELLIS, ROBERT   Greene
b. 2-1-1759 or 1760, Buckingham Co., Va.; d. ae. 96 yrs.; mar.;
chn. (at least 1 dau. & 4 sons) incl.: William m. Martha Robinson (dau. of Stephen Robinson, b. & d. in Tenn.); they came from
Tenn. to Monroe Co., Ind. After War, sold. liv. Abbeville Dist.,
S.C., ca. 1 yr.; to Elbert Co., Ga. & other places in Ga., ca.
13 yr.; to Knox Co., Tenn., ca. 6 yr.; Campbell Co., Tenn., 30
yr.; Morgan Co., Tenn., 5 yr.; Greene Co., Ind., 11 yr. (in 1838);
back to Morgan Co., Tenn.; back to Greene Co., Ind. Pens. appl.
11-10-1838, Morgan Co., Tenn., ae. 78; his appl. papers were pre-
pared in Greene Co., Ind., from which he mov. to Morgan Co., Tenn.
last July to live with his dau. Can prove part of his service by
James Blevins of Greene Co., Ind. ("Roster" p.63). Affid. 4-8-
1839 ae. 79 or 80. Pens. tr. 3-15-1841 from Tenn. to Linton,
Ind., Greene Co.; moving to some of his chn. On 2-10-1847, petition of Thomas Butler & 200 other citizens of Greene Co., Ind.,
asking for increase in pens. of Robert Ellis, ae, 93 who has
liv. Greene Co., Ind., for 20 yr. (Note: Co. Hist. ref. says
sold. b. Ireland & emigr. to Amer. in early youth). Service:
enl. fall 1780, Abbeville Dist., S.C., under William Conaway,
also Capt. Joseph Pickens, Col. McCall. Co. Hist. ref. says he
enl. at age 16; served in a Ga. Regt.; mov. to Tenn.; then Greene
Co., Ind. REF: Pens. S.26084 S.C.; "Biog. Mem. of Greene Co.,
Ind." (1908) v.3, p. 984.

ELLIS, ROBERT   Switzerland
Said to be Rev. sold. bur. there. (Could not be the man above).
REF: Mr. Schrum.

ELMER, ELIJAH   La Grange
b. 1753, Huntington, Conn.; mar.; chn. (at least): David. Pens.
appl. 4-8-1836, ae. 83, Lima Twp., La Grange Co., Ind. Power of
atty. 9-27-1852, La Grange Co., Ind., of David Elmer, son & heir.
Service: enl. spr. 1775, Redding, Conn., a res. of Huntington,
Conn., Capt. Reed. REF: Pens. R.3328 Conn.; Susp. Pens. List,
p. 412--for further proof.

EMETT, WILLIAM   Shelby
b. 1760-1761, Mecklinburg Co., N.C. Pens. appl. 9-5-1833, ae. 72,
Liberty Twp., Shelby Co., Ind. After War liv. Richmond Co., Va.;
to Russell Co., Va., for 6-7 yr.; Scott Co., Ky., 2 yr.; Boone
Co., Ky., 32 yr.; Shelby Co, Ind. Service: drf. Sept. 1780 in
Richmond Co., Ga, in Ga.Mil., Capt. Frederick Stump. (Note: it
would seem that the two above mentioned Va. counties would be Ga.
counties. This may be an error on my part when I abstracted the
data). REF: Pens. S.32237 Ga.

ENSMINGER, JOSHUA   Shelby
b. 3-8-1760, near the Sugar Loaf in Md. After War liv. Augusta
Co., Va., ca. 2 yr. till Co. was divided & his res. then became
Bath Co., Va.; liv. there ca. 2 yr.; Botetourt Co., Va., ca. 5
yr.; Rockbridge Co., Va., ca. 13 yr.; Monroe Co., Va., ca. 6 yr.;
Kanawha Co., Va., ca. 20 yr.; in Shelby Co., Ind., for last 12
yr. Pens. appl. 8-10-1841, Liberty Twp., Shelby Co., Ind., ae.

-31-

81 last Mar. 8. Thought he had lost his discharge in Va. but just recently recd. it from William Hunter, son of "my bro-in-law, James Hunter who d. 4-1-1841, Monroe Co., Va." Service: drf. Oct. 1780, Augusta Co., Va., Mil., 10th Regt., Capt. John B. Bary, Lt. William Deen, Col. Samuel Vance, Ens. William Bowler. REF: Pens. R.3360 Va.; Rej. Pens. List, p.4-7--fraudulent. (Note: I know that some of these "fraudulent" rejected claims were later proved and pensions granted).

  EVANS, EDWARD   Lawrence
b. June 1758; d. 10-25-1838 (10-10-1838 or 10-25-1837); m. 2-26-1804 (or 2-21-1801) in either Lincoln Co., Ky.; or Knox Co., Ky.; or Mercer Co., Ky., Elizabeth Howard (or Elizabeth Edwards) who later says she was m. Feb. ca. 1804, Knox Co., Ky., in one affid. & m. ca. 54 yr. ago, Mercer Co., Ky., in another affid.); chn. At Rev., sold. liv. with father in Pittsylvania Co., Va. Had a younger bro., John Evans (liv. Rockcastle Co., Ky., 1832) who says he was ca. 15 yr. old when his older bro. Edward enl. Affid. 6-4-1832, Rockcastle Co., Ky., of Thomas Farriss, who was in same Comp. with sold. Affid. 6-2-1832 of bro. John Evans. Pens. appl. 8-29-1827, ae. 69 last June, Lawrence Co., Ind.; again 5-15-1828 Indian Creek Twp., Lawrence Co., Ind. Wid.'s appl. Apr. 1856, ae. 72; that she m. ca. 1804, Knox Co., Ky., by Isaac Renfro, minister.; again 4-12-1858, ae. 75, Lawrence Co., Ind.; she nee Elizabeth Howard (Query: was she Mrs. Elizabeth (Howard) Edwards, or was Edwards as given above an error?); that she m. ca. 54 yr. ago, Mercer Co., Ky.; that husb. d. 10-25-1838, Lawrence Co., Ind. Service: enl. Feb. 1778, Va. Line & Cont. Line, Capt. Thomas Dillard, Col. Morgan's Regt. (Note: not the Reverend Edward Evans of La Grange Co., Ind., Pens. S.8437 N.Y., in my 1949 compilation, p.12). REF: Pens. R.3382; Susp. Pens List, p. 412-- for further proof.

  EVANS, ROBERT   Harrison
b. 1761. Pens. appl. 11-10-1834, ae. 73, Franklin Twp., Harrison Co., Ind. After War liv. Bucks Co., Pa., till 1788; in Va. till 1795; in Ky. till 1824; to Harrison Co., Ind. Service: enl. Sept. 1777, Bucks Co., Pa., in Pa. Line, Capt. Jacob Bennett. REF: Pens. R.3391 Pa.; Rej. Pens. List, p.407--no proof of such service.

  EWEN, TIMOTHY   Fountain
d. 2-12-1828 (or 5-7-1828, or 6-12-1828); m. 10-7-1789 (or Oct. 1786) near Brownsville, Pa., Sarah ---; b. 1-23-1771; chn. Wid.'s pens. appl. 11-14-1838, Warren Co., Ind.; again 4-1-1840; that sold. had liv. Juliustown, Burlington Co., N.J.; was son of Julius Ewen, for whom town was named; Ewen fam. trad. that Julius Ewen b. Argyle, Scot., & m. Catharine Campbell, b. Edinburgh, Scot.; that Catharine had molded bullets in Rev. War. Affid. 6-27-1839, Montgomery Co., Ky., of Joseph Starnes that he was present at mar. on Oct. 1786, ca. 2 mi. from Redstone Old Fort, Pa. Service: wid. says husb. enl. in N.J. or N.Y. REF: Pens. R.3416 N.J. or N.Y.; Susp. Pens. List--for further proof & specification.
          p. 418

EWING, GEORGE   Dearborn
Said to be Rev. sold. bur. there. ("Roster" p.137 has one in
Perry Co., d. 1824. I feel that it could hardly be the same man
as a Perry Co.--Dearborn Co. migration would be very unusual and
a Perry Co.--Dearborn Co. confusion would be most unlikely, esp.
geographically.) REF: Mr. Schrum.

FALL, CHRISTIAN   Union
b. ca. 1740; d. ca. 1815; m. (1) 11-16-1762, prob. Orange Co.,
N.C., Juliana Finn (sp?) & had 9 chn., 3 of whom died; Juliana
b. 1731; d. 8-8-1777. He m. (2) 8-4-1778, Guilford Co., N.C.,
Magdalena ---, & had 6 chn. He m. (3) ca. 1790, Guilford Co.,
N.C., Catharine ---, d. post 1801, Cincinnati, O., & had 6 chn.
Chn. (order unknown & mothers unknown except as birth dates check
with marriages):Elizabeth b. 1784, m. John Daniel Witt;   Agnes
m. George W. Wood;   Mary m. Jesse Starr;   Esther b. 8-13-1793,
Guilford Co., N.C., d. 8-13-1866, Boone Co., Ind., m. 6-17-1813,
Wayne Co., Ind. (from which Union Co. was formed), James Loudon
Taylor, Sr., b. 10-3-1794, Ovid Twp., Seneca Co., N.Y., d. 12-2-
1875, Boone Co., Ind.;   Daniel;   Christian, Jr.;   William m.
Anna Gift;   George m. Mary Taylor (sis. of J.L.T.);   Susannah
b. 1798 m. William Abernathy;   Peter;   Thomas;   Justus b.
3-6-1801, m. Rebecca DuBois. Service: furnished supplies in
Guilford Co., N.C. (Accepted by D.A.R.). REF: Treasurer's
Papers, Voucher # 80, N.C. Archives; Mrs. M. G. Talbert,
Franklin, Ind.

FARMER, NATHANIEL   Fayette
b. ca. 1757; wife ae. 61 (1827); chn. Pens. appl. 9-10-1827, ae.
70, Fayette Co., Ind.; wife 61; chn. have now left him. Service:
pvt. in Md. Line; enl. spr. 1778, 3rd Md. Regt., Capt. Griffin,
Col. Anderson. REF: Pens. S.35917 Md. (is not on I.A.R. printed
list); Mr. Schrum.

FIELDS, SAMUEL   Montgomery
(This is the most fascinating record in this Supplement).
b. ca. 1740; d. post 1825, Crawfordsville, Ind.; mar.; chn. (at
least) a dau. who m. John Thompson. (The account of this man
should be read in full; I have abstracted as briefly as possible).
The old man was living with his son-in-law, John Thompson, in
Bath Twp., Franklin Co., Ind., ca. 1 mi. S and ¾ mi. E of the
Copeland schoolhouse. On complaint of a neighbor woman, Robert
Murphy, a young constable, was sent on Nov. 3, 1824, to arrest
Fields, who refused to accompany Murphy. The latter returned
home but was exhorted by his father to carry out his first job.
In the meantime, Fields hid a butcher knife by his door. When
Murphy returned, Fields stabbed him. He died ten days later, and
Fields was indicted by the Grand Jury for murder in the first
degree. He was sentenced on Mar. 24, 1825, to be hanged on Fri.,
May 27, 1825 Feeling in the neighborhood ran high, and many
people wished to see him pardoned because of his services in the
Revolutionary War and because of his advanced age. Petitions
were circulated in several regions. The original petitions are
among the Secretary of State's Papers in the Archives Division of

the Ind. State Library. In all, there are 13 petitions bearing a total of 730 signatures. They read like the ancestor list of the Indiana Pioneer Society. The first, bearing 22 signatures and dated May 14, 1825, Centreville, Ind., is in full as follows: "To his Excellency J. B. Ray Governor and Commander in Chief of the State of Indiana The undersigned of the County of Franklin Respectfully represent to your Excellency that at the March Term of 1825 of the Franklin Circuit Court Samuel Feilds (sic) was indicted and tried for the murder of Robert Murphy found guilty by the Jury and Sentence of death pronounced against him by the Court But notwithstanding the Jury from the nature of the evidence felt themselves bound to find a virdict (sic) of Guilty Yet we beleive (sic) there were many circumstances turned out in evidence during the Trial that ought to be considered in mitigation of the crime It was proven on the Trial that the said Samuel Feilds was then in the Eighty fifth year of his age consequently in second childhood, that he was an active officer in the Revolutionary war and has supported a uniform Good Character ever since untill (sic) the unfortunate occurrance (sic) refered (sic) to --- And your Petitioners as in duty bound will ever pray."
The remaining petitions are worded almost, if not, identically with the exception of the 5th. The 2nd has 21 signatures; the 3rd nine; 4th is by two of the Jurors, John Colwell & John Davis; 6th has 191; 7th has 15; 8th has 49; 9th has 66; 10th has 53; 11th has 44; 12th has 114; 13th has 51. The 5th petition is the most important. While it is essentially the same as the first, it adds that Samuel Fields was an officer in the Continental Army, that he served in the Battles of Brandywine & Trenton. Originating in Montgomery Co., Ind., it mentions that several of his family are in Montgomery Co.; and is signed by 82 residents of Montgomery Co.; 5 of Hendricks Co., Ind.; 4 of Marion Co., Ind.; and 2 of the State of Ohio. I wish that space permitted me to list all of the 730 signatures as they would be valuable in proving residence in Indiana at that time. The Montgomery Co. petition is particularly important. The 1820 Census is the first for Indiana. Since Montgomery Co. was not then erected, the 1830 Census is the first list of its residents. This petition in the spring 1825 might be said to be the first census of Montgomery Co. as surely there were not many more than 82 householders there at that time. Descendants of early Franklin Co. and Montgomery Co. ancestors might be able to have a photostat of their ancestors' signatures from these peptitions. To continue the story--- a gallows was erected on Main Street in Brookville, Franklin Co. seat; and a grave was dug a short distance away. The rope was being drawn up around Fields' neck when the crowd noticed a man on horseback tearing down the hill. It was Governor Ray who had ridden all the way from Indianapolis on horseback. Dressed in the uniform of a general of the Indiana Militia, he dashed up to the gallows, held out a paper, and said dramatically, "Here, I give you your life!" (There must have been a bit of the ham in Gov. Ray because he pulled the same stunt the preceding year in the White River murder case). Samuel Fields was taken away by friends to near Hamilton, O., where he lived for a short while. From there he removed to Crawfordsville, Ind., where he died. It seems rea-

sonable to assume from the petition that he had children living in Crawfordsville. There is a Stephen Fields (possible son) in the 1840 Census, Union Twp., Montgomery Co., Ind., ae. 30-39. Service: none indicated. Considering the fact that these petitions were written less than 45 years after the Rev. War, there were undoubtedly many signers who actually knew of Fields' services, perhaps even served under him as an officer. REF: Smith--"Early Ind. Trials & Sketches" (1857) p.23; Reifel--"Hist. of Franklin Co., Ind." (1915) pp. 538-542, inclusive; "Atlas of Franklin Co., Ind." (1882) p.16; Riker--"Executive Proceedings of the State of Indiana, 1816-1836" (1947) p. 321 & footnote; Secy. of State's Papers, Ind. Archives; Mrs. Irene Strieby, Indianapolis, Indiana.

FINDLEY, SAMUEL   Spencer
b. Apr. 1762, Guilford Co., N.C. A few yr. after War, migr. West & sett. near Cumberland River in family of Maj. Edward Douglas, ca. 18 mi. from Nashville for 3 yr.; in War of 1812; liv. in Ky. over 30 yr.; now Spencer Co., Ind., where appl. for pens. 11-19-1836, ae. 74 last Apr. Service: enl. while liv. with mother on home on Allemance Creek as guide in Lee's Troops; later drf. in Guilford Co., N.C., Mil., Capt. George Stewart, Maj. John Gillespie, Col. James Martin. REF: Pens. R.14183 N.C., Va.; Rej. Pens. List, p.407--did not serve 6 mo. in a military capacity.

FITZJARRALL, JAMES   Gibson
b. ca. 1745-1750, Orange Co., Va.; d. 3-21-1836; m. Orange Co., Va., or Albemarle Co., Va. (wife d. 9-13-1838); chn. (at least): Johnson. Pens. appl. 8-10-1835, ae. 85-90, Gibson Co., Ind. A few yr. after War, mov. to Ky., spr. 1811 to Gibson Co., Ind. Affid. 7-27-1832, Franklin Co., Ky., of bro., Daniel Fitz Garrell, now dead (by 1835, evidently). Power of atty. 6-30-1853, Gibson Co., Ind., of sold.'s son, Johnson Fitz Gerald. Service: enl. June-July 1779 or 1780, Stanton, Augusta Co., Va., in Cont. Army, Capt. James Findley. REF: Pens. R.3585 Va.; Rej. Pens. List, p. 407--did not serve in a military capacity.

FLECK, CHRISTOPHER   Orange
b. 3-28-1756, Pa.; mar. in Va.; chn. (at least); a son who is a minister. Pens. appl. 11-9-1835, Orange Co., Ind., ae. 79 on 3-28-1835. Mov. when very young to Albemarle Co., Va.; after War, he retd. to father in Va.; m. there in ca. 1 yr.; mov. to Redstone, Pa., ca. 7 yr.; Nelson Co., Ky., ca. 30 yr.; Shelby Co., Ky., ca. 11 yr.; Orange Co., Ind. (Note: this may be the man who was appt. Ensign in 13th Regt., Orange Co., Ind., Mil., on 6-20-1820, and who was commn. J. P. for Orange Co. on 7-5-1833). Service: enl. when ca. 19 yr old, Shenandoah Co., Va., Capt. James McCreery. REF: Pens. R.3603 Va.; Susp. Pens. List, p.412--no proof of service; "Exec. Proc. of Ind., 1816-1836", pp.139, 543.

FLINT, JOHN   Union
b. 10-6-1756, Worcester Co., Md.; d. 1841; bur. Flint farm cem.;
m. Elizabeth Johnson; chn.: William b. 12-8-1789; John b. 4-30-
1791;   Sarah b. 8-31-1793;   Benjamin b. 2-28-1795;   Nancy b.
11-29-1796, m. John Howell;   Thomas b. 1-18-1799;   Peter b. 11-
27-1800; Phyllis b. 2-1-1803; Elizabeth b. 10-28-1804; Leah
b. 2-11-1807; Hetty b. 1-3-1810; Joshua b. 8-7-1811. Pens.
appl., ae 70, Bath Twp., Franklin Co., Ind., 6-7-1832. Liv.
Worcester Co., Md., till ca. age 54; to Ohio for a few wks.; to
Franklin Co., Ind.; to Union Co., Ind. (A John Flint was commn.
Ensign in 1st Regt., Ind. Terr. Mil., 2-3-1814; on 8-26-1817,
commn. Capt. of Rifle Comp., 16th Regt., Franklin Co., Ind.).
John Flint entered land in Fairfield Twp., Franklin Co., Ind., in
1811. Service: enl. from home in Worcester Co., Md., 2 mi. from
Wicomico River, spr. 1776, Capt. Ebenezer Handy; Comp. 3, 1st
Batt., Capt. Barton Lucas. Both John Flint & his father signed
Oath of Alleg. & Fidel. REF: Pens. R.3614 Md.; Rej. Pens. List,
p.4-7--not under competent military authority or organization;
"Franklin Co., Ind., Atlas" (1882) p.100; "Exec. Journ. of Ind.
Terr., 1800-1816", p.209; "Exec. Proc. of Ind., 1816-1836",p.54;
DAR # 139,933, # 261,821; Miss Mary Lucille Cook, Portland, Ore.

FOOTE, GEORGE   Harrison
b. ca. 1762; d. 1-9-1828; m. 4-15-1784, Caswell Co., N.C.,
Lucretia Nann (sp?), b. ca. 1764; chn.: (at least 5, in 1822):
Martha m. Judge Lynn of Harrison Co., Ind.;   Kinchelo of Henry
Co., Ky.;   William of Harrison Co., Ind. Pens. appl. 5-22-
1822, ae. 60, Harrison Co., Ind. Has wife, ae. 60 odd, & 5 chn.,
none liv. with him. After War, several yrs. after mar., mov. to
Rockingham Co., N.C.; back to Caswell Co., N.C.; back to Rockingham Co., N.C.; ca. 1816 to Harrison Co., Ind. Wid.'s pens.
appl. 1-28-1843, ae. 79; her father's res. was 1 mi. from the
sold.'s father's res. Affid. 1-19-1843, Harrison Co., Ind., of
Polly Allen, ae. 86, wid. of John Allen ("Roster" p.38) who
served at same time as Foote.; that she knew fam. & liv. near
them in N.C.; that sold. served as subst. for his bro., Newton
Foote & also as subst. for neighbor, Daniel Triplett. Affid.
1-11-1843, Harrison Co., Ind., of Peter Charley, son of George
Charley, Sr.("Roster" p.95) that George Charley, Sr., d. 1833,
was a pensioner & had served with Foote. Affid. 1-21-1843, Harrison Co., Ind., of John Smith, ae. 82, that he was in War at
same time as sold.; that he knows Lucretia Foote is ca. 86, &
that George & Lucretia were m. 1784. Affid. 1-13-1843, Harrison
Co., Ind., of Craven Lynn, that Lucretia is ca. 87, was m. 1784;
that he liv. for yrs. as a neighbor to sold. in N.C. & later in
Harrison Co., Ind. Affid. 6-17-1843, Harrison Co., Ind., of
William Foote (rel. not stated) that he had known George & Lucretia Foote a long time. Affid. of wid. 6-3-1845, ae. 83. REF:
Pens. W.10032 N.C.; 1831 Rej. Pens. List, p.48--serv. in regt.
                          not on cont. establishment.
     FORD, JOHN   Switzerland
Said to be Rev. sold. bur. there. REF: Mr. Schrum.

FORT, BENJAMIN   Wayne
b. 11-15-1753. Pens. appl. 3-17-1838, ae. 85 next Nov., Centerville, Wayne Co., Ind. Service: enl. 1775, Somerset Co., N.J.,
Capt. John Polhamis, Col. William Wines (sp?). REF: Pens.
S.32257 N.J.

FOTT, JOHN   Indiana
(Uncertain). His wid., Sarah, is given on Ind. Agy. Rolls, cert.
9,289, on roll 5-9-1845 (Act of 1838. Natl. Archives finds no
pens. file & does not find this surname in their Ind. Agy. Book
there. I think this is prob. a mis-interpretation of the surname; but in our attempts of trying spelling variations, we have
not yet hit upon the right name. There is the possibility that
the sold. did not die in Ind. & that his wid. moved here later.
If anyone happens upon the right name, please notify the compiler.

FOX, ADAM   Ripley
b. 7-16-1764, Frederick Co., Md.; mar.; chn. (at least): Jacob.
Pens. appl. 8-12-1837. ae. 75, Ripley Co., Ind. After War liv.
Frederick Co., Md.; Augusta Co., Va., ca. 27 yr.; Knox Co., O.,
ca. 4 yr.; Ripley Co., Ind. Affid. of Ninian Beall ("Roster"
p.54). Letter 4-30-1887 from son, Jacob Fox, Cincinnati, O.;
mother dead. Service: enl. ae. 15-16 yr., while liv. with Col.
Joseph Wood in Frederick Co., Md., as subst. for Henry Reede
(sp?), Oct. 1779, Capt. Valentine Cregger (Cregor?). REF: Pens.
R.3721 Md.; Rej. Pens. List, p.407--did not serve 6 mos.

FRANKLIN, JOSEPH   Hancock
(Uncertain. Inference is that he d. here, but may have d. Ky.).
b. 1756; d. 12-30-1829; m. 12-27-1788. Stafford Co., Va., Elizabeth ---; b. 1772; chn. (at least): John W. b. 6-27-1791; and 4
liv. with sold. in 1820: William A., ae. ca. 12; Sarah 8; Benjamin; Julia 4. Pens. appl. 5-11-1818, Mason Co., Ky.; again
10-2-1820, Bracken Co., Ky., ae. 64. Wid.'s appl. 9-21-1838, ae.
66, res. of Greenfield, Hancock Co., Ind.; her husb. had been a
Rev. pensioner in Boone Co., Ky.; she again appl. 9-11-1843, ae.
71, Greenfield, Ind. Service: enl. 10-21-1776, Va. Line, 2nd
Regt., Capt. John Willis, Col. Spotswood. REF: Pens. W.10041 Va.

FRANKLIN, MORDECAI   Owen
b. 1757 near Old Richmond, N.C. After War liv. there till 1827
to Owen Co., Ind., where appl. for pens. 2-10-1834, ae. 76; again
3-26-1834. Supporting affid. by John Franklin (rel. not stated).
Service: drf. spr. 1781, Old Richmond, Stokes Co., N.C., Capt.
Hickman. REF: Pens. R.3759 N.C.; Rej. Pens. List, p. 407-- only
5 mos. service.

FREDERICK, SEBASTION   Pike
b. 1763, Va.; d. 10-9-1827; m. 8-22-1778, Mary Catt, b. ca. 1757:
chn.: Magnelean b. 9-12-1779; Elizabeth b. 5-1-1781; Philip
b. 2-26-1783; Susenna b. 4-17-1785; Barberry b. 8-3-1787;
Rebekkey b. 12-23-1789; Mary b. 3-14-1791; Mikel b. 4-24-1794;
Daniel b. 7-5-1796; Anna b. 8-5-1799; Sarah b. 2-20-1802.
Wid.'s pens. appl. 2-15-1839, ae. 82, Madison Twp., Pike Co.,Ind.;

they liv. near Pittsburgh, Pa., till 1784-1785 when mov. West. Affid. 2-14-1839, Knox Co., Ind., of Michael Thorn ("Roster" p. 355) that he knew sold. was in service & knew sold. & wife were mar.; liv. ca. 3 mi. from them in Pa. Affid. 1839, Knox Co.,Ind., of Philip Catt ("Roster" p.91) ae. 89 next May 25; is a bro. of Mary Frederick; knew sold. served; liv. ca. 8 mi. below Cheat River on Monongahela; sold. was with him in Gen. McIntosh's exped. against Indiana; knew they were mar.; another affid. 6-30-1842, Knox Co., Ind., by Philip Catt; that wid. Mary Frederick now liv. Knox Co., Ind.; had 11 chn.; that Michael Frederick has the fam. record; that Michael Thorn was present at the mar. Affid. 6-30-1842, Knox Co., Ind., of Michael Frederick who has the fam. rec. in Sebastian Frederick's writing. (Fam. rec. says Bastian Frederick). Service: in Pa. Mil., Capt. Minter, ae. 19, as a spy; 7 mi. above Pittsburgh, Pa., on the Monongahela. REF: Pens. R.3771 Pa.; Rej. Pens. List, p.415--not 6 mo. service.

FUNK, DANIEL   Harrison
Rev. sold. bur. on W side of Indian Creek, ca. 1 mi. W of New Amsterdam, Ind.; grave marked by Piankashaw Chap., D.A.R., New Albany, Ind. REF: Mr. Schrum; "Ind. Mag. of Hist." v.32, p.307.

GALLAMORE, JOHN   Washington
b. 1-9-1760, Granville Co., N.C.; d. 12-31-1841; m. (2nd) 11-19-1831, Washington Co., Ind., Rachel Hensley, b. 1791; chn. (at least 1, by 1st wife): daughter m. Arthur Curtiss & liv. 11-13-1833, Crawford Co., Ind., & has the fam. Bible. Pens. appl. 11-13-1833, ae. 73. After War liv. Granville Co., N.C.; Randolph Co., N.C.; Clark Co., Ind., for ca. 14 yr.; then ca. 2 yr. ago to Washington Co., Ind. (In 1840 liv. ae. 78, Jackson Twp., Washington Co., Ind.). Wid.'s appl. 4-19-1856, ae. 65. Affid. of John Hensley (1856) and joint affid. of John & Jane Hensley (1857) that they knew fam. (See Richardson Hensley, this Supp.) Service: enl. Granville Co., N.C., ca. 8-1-1780 as subst. for his father who was drf.; Capt. Ralph Banks. REF: Pens. W.10051 N.C.; BLW 61149; 1835 Pens. List, v.3, p.75; 1840 Pens. List, p.185.

GALLION, THOMAS   Wayne
b. ca. 1763; d. 1828; mar.; chn. (at least): William b. 1779, prob. N.C., d. 1864, bur. near Blountsville, Henry Co., Ind., m. 1817, Mahulda Lamb, b. 1800, Randolph Co., N.C., d. 3-4-1874, bur. Jackson's Station Cem., Tipton Co., Ind., dau. of Thomas & Hannah (Lewis) Lamb. Possible other chn. (from Wayne Co., Ind., Mar. Rec.) are: Jacob m. 1814, Polly Porter; Thomas m. 1814, Tabitha Warren; Sophia m. 1814, James Warren. Service: altho Thomas Gallion (or Galyean) was a Quaker of Welsh cesdent, according to family tradition, he served 4 yr. & 6 mo. in the Rev. REF: "Hist. of Brewer & Related Fams." (1937) p.16; Wayne Co., Ind., Mar. Rec.; Miss Caroline Dunn, Indianapolis, Ind.

GALLOWAY, PETER   Carroll
b. ca. 1757, Ire.; mar.; chn. Pens. appl. 10-14-1834, ae. ca. 77, Adams Twp., Carroll Co., Ind. After War liv. S.C. till ca. 13 yr. ago; to Mo.; 4 yr. ago to Ind. Power of atty. 5-18-1853,

Carroll Co., Ind., of Jonathan N. (V.?) Galloway, gr-son & heir, of Lockport, Ind. Service: drf. Lancaster Co., S.C., Mil., Capt. Dunlap. REF: Pens. R.3878 S.C.; Rej. Pens. List, p. 407--did not serve 6 mos.

GARRIOTT, AMBROSE   Washington
b. France (or b. Eng. & mov. to France as young man & changed sp. of name from Garrett to Garriott); d. ante 1840, bur. in unmarked grave on Garriott farm near Norris or Harristown; m. (Perhaps 2nd mar.) Mary Turpen, b. Holland; chn.: William b. 1783, Va., d. 1863, Washington Co., Ind., m.(1) Rebecca Vaughn, b. 1790, d. 1827; m.(2) 10-28-1828, Salem, Ind., Dicy Perkins, b. 1808, Ky., d. 1870;   Jacob of Washington Co., Ind.;   Simeon, b. 1792, Ky., d. Oct. 1868, Washington Co., Ind., bur. Mt. Hebron Cem. near Little York, Ind., m.(1) prob. Jefferson Co., Ky., Nancy Vaughn; m.(2) 6-8-1847, Floyd Co., Ind., Mary Roberts, b.1816, Pa., d. 1909, bur. Mt. Hebron;   Love (or Loving; male) of near Carrollton, Ky., m. 1809, Margaret Wilhoit (dau. of Rev. sold., Jesse Wilhoit);   Daniel of near Carrollton, Ky.;   Phebe;   Barbara;   Mary;   Elizabeth;   Rhoda;   Elijah L.;   Zerilda A.; John W. of near Carrollton, Ky.;   Ambrose N. Guardianship rec. of last four, minor heirs, 2-11-1840; guardian John Thompson, security William Garrett (Garriott). Sold. liv. Culpeper Co., Va.; to Carroll Co., Ky., 1792; to Ind. between 1813-1818; sett. on Spurgeon Hill near Harristown, Washington Co. Ind. Fam. trad. says liv. briefly in Ky. but left for Ind. as did not believe in slavery. Co. Hist. ref. says 3 sons stayed in Ky. & 3 came to Washington Co., Ind. Service: the name of Ambrose Garriott is on list of 71 on "List of Classes in Culpeper Co. (Va.) for Jan. 1781 for Recruiting this State's Quota of Troops to serve in the Continental Army". REF: "List of Classes, Culpeper Co., Va.", DAR Libr. File Cab., Washington, D.C.; Fothergill--"Va, Tax Payers, 1784" p.47; Stevens--"Hist. of Washington Co., Ind." (1916) p.633; Mr. Schrum; Mrs. Ruth Ravenscroft, Colorado Springs, Colo.

GARRISON, JAMES   Washington
b. ca. 1761, Rowan Co., N.C.; d. 2-3-1858. Pens. appl. 9-27-1832, Washington Co., Ind.; again 3-28-1855, ae. 95, Washington Co., Ind. In 1840, ae. 78, Franklin Twp., Washington Co., Ind. After War liv. Rowan Co., N.C., till Davidson Co. was cut off from it; there till 1827; to Washington Co., Ind. Service: enl. spr. 1781 Rowan Co., N.C., Mil., Capt. John Lopp, Lt. Joseph Cunningham. REF: Pens. S.16123 N.C., 1840 Pens. List, p.185.

GEE, PARKER   Henry
b. 6-10-1753, Md.; d. Jan. 1842; m. Pittsylvania Co., Va., soon after Rev. service; wf. d. June 1847, Henry Co., Ind.; chn. (several; 3 surv. 1851): incl. son Job. Pens. appl. 1-26-1839, ae. ca. 86, Henry Co., Ind. When very young, mov. to Pittsylvania Co., Va.; there till 1818 to Madison Co., Ky.; to Butler Co.,O.; to Henry Co., Ind., last 4-5 yr. Power of atty. 4-12-1851, Hamilton Co., O., of Job Gee, ae. 51, res. of Kenton Co., Ky., one of 3 surv. chn.; father d. ae. ca. 87; was 5 ft., 8-10 in. tall

-39-

had dark hair & blue eyes. Service: enl. 8-12-1780, Botetourt Court House, Va., but a res. of Pittsylvania Co., Va., Capt. Ballard Smith. REF: Pens. R.3964 Va.; Susp. Pens. List, p. 412-- for proof of service.

GEORGE, JAMES Marion
Said to be Rev. sold. bur. there. (The 1840 Pens. List, p. 183, has a John George of Perry Twp., Marion Co.; "Roster" p. 154). REF: Mr. Schrum.

GLOVER, URIAH Orange
b. 1740, Long Isl., N.Y.; d. 6-11-1830, ae. 89; bur. Trimble Cem., Northeast Twp.; prob. son of Uriah Glover of Morris Co., N.J.; m. Elizabeth Robinson (or Robeson), d. 10-4-1822, ae. 78; bur. Trimble Cem.; chn.: Hannah m. Nelson Combs; Rebecca m. William Case; Elizabeth m. Abram Lucas; Jonah m. Fanny Boyd; Susan; Charles; John m. Malinda Green; Stephen m. Sarah Kirkham; Ruth m. William Reed; Uriah, Jr., b. 10-21-1773, Elizabeth, N.J., d. 1856, Orange Co., Ind. (War of 1812), m. 2-14-1797, Uniontown, Pa., Priscilla Gaddis. b. 5-13-1779, d. 1836, dau. of Rev. sold. Col. Thomas Gaddis. Prior to Rev., fam. mov. from L. I.? N.Y., to Elizabeth, N.J.; later to Uniontown, Pa.; in 1797 to Ky.; landed at Louisville; may have liv. in Shelby Co., Ky.; in 1814 entire fam. to Orange Co., Ind. Uriah Glover, Jr., was the architect & stone mason for the mill at Spring Mill State Park, Lawrence Co., Ind. Service: fam. trad. strong that he served in either N.J. or Pa.; one descendant is said to have proof (unable to locate to date). REF: "N.J. Arch.", 1st Ser., v.33, p.162; "Orange Co., Ind., Cem. Rec." --Lost River Chap., DAR, Paoli, Ind. (1947) p.246; Miss Edna Glover Nowland, Mooresville, Ind.

GOODWIN, WILLIAM Indiana
b. Va.; d. 1833, in Indiana on the way to Illinois; mar., chn. (at least): George W., b. 1779, d. 1863, Coles Co., Ill., m. 1803 Margaret Bowen, b. 1787, d. 1867, Ill. Fam. from Va. to Ky.; then to Ind.; may have liv. in Monroe Co., ca. 1830. Service: said to have been a Rev. sold. REF: Mrs. Esther C. Goodwin, Charleston, Ill.

GOULD (GOOLD), JOHN Washington
b. ca. 1761. This is prob. the John Gould of Brown Twp., Washington Co., Ind., will pr. 6-6-1836; mentions wife (not named); sons: John (eldest), Adolphus, & Lyman; dau. Sally Walker. Son Lyman Gould of Middletown, will wr. 1-3-1837, pr. 6-15-1837, mentions wife Priscilla. Pens. appl. 11-15-1832, ae. 71, res. of Brown Twp., Washington Co., Ind. Service: enl. 1776, res. of Windham, Conn., Capt. Mosely; enl. again, Ashford, Conn., Capt. Carlisle, Col. Elliott. Is in 1835 Pens. List, ae. 85, pvt. in R.I. State Troops. REF: Pens. S.16128 Conn., R.I.; "Abstr. of Wills of Washington Co., Ind., 1814-1900"--Christopher Harrison Chap., DAR, Salem, Ind. (1953) p. 19 (from Washington Co., Ind., Prob. Bk. B, pp. 326, 385-386; 1835 Pens. List, v.3, p. 75.

GORRELL, JOHN   Putnam
b. ca. 1764; mar.; chn. (at least 7; ages in 1820): Betsy ca. 19;
John 16;   Sene 11;   Joseph 8;   Nancy 6;   James 2;   Polly 9
mos. Pens. appl. 6-17-1818, Bath Co., Ky.; again 9-18-1820 (has
7 chn. liv. with him). Affid of William McGahey ("Roster" p.271)
who was in same Comp. On 3-11-1837 sold. asks for tr. since now
liv. Putnam Co., Ind.; formerly pd. in Bath Co., Ky. Service:
enl. Sept 1779, 7th Pa. Regt.. 4th Comp., Capt. Pratt, Col. William Butler. REF: Pens. S.35970 Pa.

GORSAGE, JOHN   Shelby
b. ca 1742 (?). Pens. appl. 11-26-1832, ae. 90 (70? see below),
Sullivan Co., Tenn. Tr. from Jonesborough (Agy.), East Tenn.,
6-28-1831 (sic). Was a blacksmith. Had also liv. Baltimore Co.,
Md., & Monroe Co., Tenn. In 1835 Pens. List as pvt. in Va. Mil.,
ae. 70 (90? see above). Service: drf. late 1780, Sullivan Co.,
Tenn. (sic), Capt. Topp, Cols. Shelby & Fletcher. REF: Pens.
S.2579 N.C.; 1835 Pens. List, v. 3, p. 68, Shelby Co., Ind.

GRAHAM, THOMAS   Monroe
Said to be Rev. sold. bur. there. REF: Mr. Schrum.

GRANT, DANIEL   Rush
b. 1-2-1759; d. 2-21-1831; mar.; wife b. ca. 1760; d. post 1831;
chn. (several; most of them res. of Ind. in 1829). Pens. appl.
9-8-1818, ae. 59, Fleming Co., Ky.; again 9-9-1820, wife now ae.
ca. 60. Mov. to Rush Co., Ind., to be near chn. Affid. 1829,
Rush Co., Ind., of Smith Grant (rel. not stated). In letter 2-27-1844 from Hse. of Repr., sold.'s bro., William Grant, asks if any
back pay due bro. Daniel, decd. Wid. surv. sold. In 1835 Pens.
List, pvt. in Va. Line, ae. 71; tr. from Washington Co., Ky.
Service: enl. 1775, Fauquier Co., Va., Minuteman, Capt. William
Pickett. REF: Pens. S.35985 Va.; 1835 Pens. List, v.3, p. 30.

GRAY, BENJAMIN   Warrick
(Uncertain). In pens. file of Forrest Davis, Hardin Co., Ky., is
affid. of Benjamin Gray, 9-10-1832 that in 1780 he res. in Montgomery Co., Md. & knows that Forrest Gray served. (Davis' pens.
appl. 10-15-1832, Hardin Co., Ky., ae. 70 last Dec., that he enl.
1780 at Fort Frederick. Md. for 3 yrs.). Affid. of Lodowick
Davis ("Roster" p.115) rel. not stated; of Warrick Co., Ind., that
he (Lodowick) enl. 1781 & k ew that Forrest Davis also enl. in the
Independent Comp. under John Reed, Lt. N. B. Magrider, Ensign,
Gabriel Jacobs (punct. as given in affid.); another affid. 1834
by Lodowick Davis of Spencer Co., Ind., that he knows Forrest
Davis was in the Rev. (Note: from these clues, service for Benjamin Gray may be found in a detailed study of the complete pens.
files of Forrest & Lodowick Davis). REF: Bell--"Md. Sold. of the
Rev. War, War of 1812, or Indian Wars Who Drew Pensions While
Residing in Ky.", pp. 43-44.

GRAY, MOSES   Switzerland
married (wife ae. 53, 6-23-1823; chn. (at least): William, ae.
18 in 1823. (Note: a Moses Gray was commn. J.P. for Scott Co.,
Ind., 6-14-1820; commn. Capt. in 6th Regt., Ind. Mil., 8-19-1818
and commn. Col. in 29th Regt., 8-3-1820; the 6th Regt. was Switz-
erland, Jefferson, Clark, & Scott Co. men; the 29th was Scott Co.).
Service: enl. k yr., Mar. 1775, Bedford Co., Pa., Capt. John
McDaniel (sp? McDonald?), Col. John Piper, Pa. Cont. Line; in
Batt. of Trenton & Brunswick. REF: Manifest dated 6-23-1823,
Switzerland Co., Ind., courthouse; "Exec. Proc. of Ind., 1816-
1836" pp.139, 110, 143; Miss Mary Hill, Madison, Ind.; 1831 Rej.
Pens.List, p.48--serv. in regt. not on cont. establishment.
       GRIFFIN, THOMAS   Marion
In 1840 Pens. List, Warren Twp., Marion Co., Ind., ae. 84. There
were several pens. files for men of this name (papers missing in
one file); I could not identify an Indiana man from the data.
His name does not appear on the I.A.R. list. REF: Mr. Schrum;
1840 Pens. List, p.183; Natl. Archives Pens. files.
       GREEN, RICHARD--see p. 117.
       GRIFFIN, WILLIAM   Clark
b. ca. 1755; d. 8-6-1832; m. 1-26-1787, poss. Prices Settlement,
Va., or Fauquier Co., Va., Nancy Morgan, b. ca. 1768; d. 9-2-
1849, Clark Co. (prob. Ind.), poss. Clark Co., Ill.; chn.:
William; Polly; Sally; John; Elizabeth; others, incl.
the 4 youngest: Nancy (ae. 19 in 10-12-1820); Lydia 17; Morgan
13; Anderson 9. Pens. appl. 10-12-1820, Jefferson Co., Ky., ae.
65; has 4 chn. liv. with him (see above). After War liv. Rowan
Co., N.C.; Jefferson Co., Ky.; Clark Co., Ind. Affid. 8-17-1844
Clark Co., Ind., of Morgan Griffin, ae. 36; that sold. m. 1787
in Va.; sold. d. 8-6-1832; after War from Va. to N.C.; served in
Capt. Humphreys or Scott, Gen. Bluford (see later). Wid.'s appl.
8-15-1844, Clark Co., Ind., ae. 76; that he vol. in Va. Affid.
7-23-1846, Putnam Co., Ind. of Thomas Job, ae. over 75, and of
James Etchinson, ae. over 70; that they knew sold. & wife in Row-
an Co., N.C.; that Etchinson knew them before they were mar. in
Fauquier Co., Va., & knew their chn. Affid. 9-22-1846, Clark
Co., Ind., of George A. Canter, ae. over 46; that sold. d. here
ca. 1832 & had liv. here at least 15 yr. & before that liv. in
Jefferson Co., Ky. Affid. 9-22-1846, Clark Co., Ind., of Jacob
L. Stilwell, ae. over 58; that he knew sold. last 14 yr.; that
sold. d. 1832, at which time sold. said had wife for last 40 yr.
Same affid. by Alexander Mars. Affid. 9-16-1850, Clark Co., Ill.
(not Ind.) of Morgan Griffin, ae. 42, son of Nancy Griffin, decd.;
that father pens. at Louisville, Ky., Agy.; that mother liv.
Clark Co., Ind. & she d. 9-2-1849, Clark Co. (Ind. or Ill. not
stated) & left only 2 liv. chn.: Morgan & Anderson, both of Clark
Co., Ill. (not Ind.). Service: enl. Oct. 1780 as pvt. in Va.;
Capt. Thomas Hord, Col. Abraham Buford (see above). REF: Pens.
W.24313 Va.

       GRIFFIS, JOHN G.   Vanderburgh
b. Aug. 1752. Pens. appl. 3-25-1834, ae. 82 next Aug., Pigeon
Twp., Vanderburgh Co., Ind.; again 11-8-1834. Ziba Arnold, Rev.
pensioner in Ky., & William Meads, Rev. pensioner, knew him in

the Rev. Affid. of William Meads, Vanderburgh Co., Ind. ("Roster" p.404, tr. to Ill.) that he & sold. were in same Comp. & enl. the same week. Service: enl. 1775 or 1776, Morristown, N,J., Capt. Dickinson, Lt. William Gordon, Col. Dayton; Jersey Blues. Took sick in winter & went South; enl. May-June 1779, Monk's Corner, ca. 40 mi. from Charlestown, S.C., Capt. John Lewis. REF: Pens. R.4322 S.C.; Rej. Pens. List, p.407--not on the rolls; no proof of service.
GUDGELL, JOHN--see p. 117.
GRIMES, BEN   Grant
Said to be Rev. sold. bur. there. REF: Mr. Schrum.
GUMP, FREDERICK--see p. 117.
HAAS, MICHAEL   Scott
b. ca. 1761; d. post 1830 near Lexington, Ind.; m. Sophia Breich; chn.: John m. Sarah Kurtz; Ezra; Lydia m. Mr. Meck; Katherine m. Mr. Downey; Christina m. Mr. Lemon; Mary m. William M. Patterson; Harriet m. Mr. Reuter; Sophia m. Mr. Fravel; Margaret. Is in 1820 Census, Scott Co., Ind., with males: 1(45/), 1(26-45), 2(-10); females: 1(45/*, 1(26-45), 1(16-26), 1(10-16), 3(-10); in 1830 Cens. with 1 male (60-69); females: 1(50-59), 1(10-14). On adjoining line in 1820 Cens. is fam. of John Haas, ae. 26-45; Ezra Haas is also in both 1820-1830 Censuses. Sold. came to near Lexington, Scott Co., Ind., in 1819. Service: in Lancaster Co., Pa. (several ref. in "Pa. Arch., 5th Ser., v.7; see Index under Hass, Haus, Hause, Hosst). REF: "Pa. Arch."; 1820 Cens., v.2, p.249; 1830 Cens., v.13, p.556; Miss Mary Hill, Madison, Ind.; Miss Frances E. Emerson, Plymouth, Ind.

HADDON, JOHN   Sullivan
b. 4-26-1760, Randolph Co., Va. (formerly Harrison Co., Va.); d. 6-19-1819, Carlisle, Ind.; bur. on own farm; m. 4-28-1785, Randolph Co., Va., Isabella Elliott, b. 1770-1771, prob. Va.; d. 5-21-1822, ae. 51, Carlisle, Ind.; chn. (order unknown): John; Richard, unm.; William R., b. 7-17-1805, d. 1-27-1859, m. (1) Julia A. Cartwright, m. (2) ---; Isabella m. John Weidner; David b. 2-29-1800, d. 3-28-1838, m. Julia Silvers; Helen m. Jesse J. Benefiel; Rebecca b. 4-19-1791, m. 1810, Thomas Scott; Virginia b. 1816, d. 1910, m. Richard Pierce (Pearce); (James) Elliott, b. 1-1-1812, d. 8-24-1866; Eliza Ann b. 7-27-1807, m. (1) Henry Harper, m. (2) John Alexander McClure; Jesse b. 1792-1793, d. 4-18-1872, m.(1) Elizabeth Piety, d. 1856, m.(2) Mrs. America (or Virginia) (Nash) Benefiel. Sold. was son of David Haddon, d. 1791, Randolph Co., Va., & wife Esther; parents formerly of N.J. Sold. to Sullivan Co., Ind. (was then Knox Co.) in 1805. Service: Revolutionary claims--militia scout, Oct. 1779, Augusta Co., Va.; member of 1st Court, 1778, Randolph Co., Va.; member of Va. Legis., 5 terms; pvt. 4th class, 6th Comp., 1st Batt., Cumberland Co., Pa., Mil., Col. James Johnston, 7-25-1781, 8-24-1782. Res. dur. Rev. was Randolph Co., Va., & Cumberland Co., Pa. REF: "Pa. Arch.", 5th Ser., v.6, pp.114, 131; "Hist. & Fam. Trees of Haddon & McClure Fams."--Brevoort (Francis Vigo Ch. DAR, Vincennes, Ind., 1947, pp.2-4-20-34-35-37-38-45; DAR #216,850 # 369,747; Mrs. John Brevoort, Vincennes, Ind.

HALL, BENJAMIN   Ripley (?)
(Note: this man is not the one of Ripley Co., Ind., "Roster" p.
170, Pens. S.32295. However, this man's res. is uncertain; see
below). b. 1749. Pens. appl. 10-16-1819, ae. ca. 70, Switzerland Co., Ind.; again 2-28-1820, ae. 70. Letter 8-23-1832 from
William C. Keen, Printer's Retreat, Switzerland Co., Ind., says
that sold. may make another appl. from Ripley, Dearborn, or Jefferson Co., Ind. Service: enl. Apr.-May 1776 for 3 yr., Lexington,
Conn., Capt. Elijah Lewis, Col. John Angle, Conn. Line; disch. at
White Plains, N.Y.; again enl. Sept. 1780, Easton, Pa., Maj. Ebenezer Adams, Artillery, & serv. till end of War. REF: Pens.
R.5362½ R.I.; Rej. Pens. List, p.407--Caveat to this claim from
William C. Keen, Printer's Retreat, 8-28-1832.(See p.119 later).

HALL, GEORGE   Washington
b. 3-11-1760, Pittsylvania Co., Va.; d. 12-13-1834; m. 12-28-1814
Halifax Co., Va., Jane Young, b. 1773; liv. 1855, ae. 82. Pens.
appl. 5-7-1833, ae. 73. Wid.'s appl. 4-8-1853, ae. 80. After
War, sold. liv. Va., N.C.; Washington Co., Ind., last 7 yr. (in
1833 appl.). Service: enl. Mar. 1781, Pittsylvania Co., Va.,
Capt. Spencer Shelton; serv. 6 mo. as subst. for John Hall (rel.
not stated) in Halifax Co., Va. REF: Pens. W.7643 Va.; BLW36734;
1835 Pens. List, v.3, p.75.

HALLY, JOEL   Orange
Said to be Rev. sold. bur. there. REF: Mr. Schrum.

HAMER (HAMES?), JAMES   Fayette
bur. in Union Cem., Jackson Twp.; stone says: "James Hamer, died
7-5-1837, aged 73 yrs.; Soldier, rest, thy warfare's o'er."
Mr. Schrum's list says James Hames. (Note: a question of misreading a dim 1837 stone or typo error on Schrum's part). REF:
Mr. Schrum; Barrows--"Hist. of Fayette Co., Ind." (1917) p.320;
"Hist. of Fayette Co., Ind." (1885) p. 208.

HAMMOND, LEWIS   Switzerland
b. 10-14-1762. Pens. appl. 5-25-1843, Switzerland Co., Ind., ae.
80 last Oct. 14. Service: Va. Mil., 1781, Winchester, Va., Capt.
Reynolds, Col. Holmes. REF: Pens. R.4535 Va.; Rej. Pens. List,
p.407--only 5 mo. service.

HAMPTON, JOHN   Brown
b. ca 1758; d. 2-15-1851; m. Jemima ---, d. a few yr. ante husb.,
Bartholomew Co., Ind.; chn. (at least): John (d.s.p. since sold.);
Henry; Enoch; Mary m. Ezekiel McBride; Amy m. Mr. Hatton.
Affid. 10-3-1855, Bartholomew Co., Ind., of David Cody, ae. 58,
admr. of John Hampton, late of Brown Co., Ind. decd. but a res.
of Bartholomew Co., Ind., ae. ca. 93-94. Affid. 2-13-1856, Jackson Co., Ind., of John Audubon that he knew John Hampton, decd.,
& wife Jemima; said wife d. while visiting at home of her son-in-law, Ezekiel McBride & her dau. Mary in Bartholomew Co., Ind. &
was bur. in a nearby cem.; deponent helped bury her & sold. then
picked next space & wished to be bur. beside wife; after wife's
death, sold. liv. with the McBrides; but short time before his

-44-

death, he went to stay some time at home of son Henry in Brown Co., Ind., where he took sick, died, & was bur. near his son's res. Affid. 2-9-1856, Bartholomew Co.; Ind.; of Nelson Rogers that Jemima d. a few yrs. before husb. Affid. 9-25-1855, Bartholomew Co., Ind., of William H. Lucas that he is a step-gr-son of sold. Bartholomew Co., Ind., Court records show that son John was still alive 4-5-1853. (Note: a John Hampton was appt. J.P. for Bartholomew Co., Ind., 6-23-1834). Sold. filed ca. 1791 for bounty land; pens. certif. # 39,024 on Ind. Agy. Rolls (discrepancy with Rej. Pens. file No.). Service: enl. early 1779 or 1780 in Pa., Capt. Wylie's Comp. of Artillery Artificers, Col. Flowers. REF: Pens. R.4548 Cont. (Pa.); "Exec. Proc. of Ind., 1816-1836" p.377. Is not on Rej. Pens. List for Ind.

HANEY, CHARLES   Jennings
Said to be Rev. sold. bur. there. In in 1840 Pens. List, ae.81. No pens. file found at Natl. Archives. One for a Burke Co., N.C., man; but age does not agree, nor is there any indication of a tr. to Ind. Haney may be a typo error & correct spelling not yet guessed. If any reader can clarify, please notify the compiler. REF: Mr. Schrum; 1840 Pens. List, p. 183, Jennings Co., Ind.

HANNA, JOHN   Marion
b. ca. 1763, Laurens Dist., S.C.; d. 1838-1839, Indianapolis, Ind.; bur. Greenlawn Cem. (no longer there; built over); grave marked by Daughters of the Revolution (not D.A.R.), Miss Tarquinia Voss, State Regent (liv. Franklin, Ind.); undated newspaper clipping, quite lengthy, about ceremonies; letter in Caroline Scott Harrison Chap., DAR, Indianapolis, Ind., file from Crown Hill Cem., Indianapolis, dates 1900, that they would reinter sold. free in the soldier section of the cem.; no record at the cem. that this was ever done. John Hanna m. Sarah Jones; chn.: Robert Ervin m. Nancy Adams; John Jones m. Mary Petre; Elizabeth Ann b. ca. 1795, Franklin Co., Ind., d. Apr. 1870, Indianapolis, Ind., m. Aug. 1814, Franklin Co., Ind., Peter Winchell (see "Winchell Gen."); Jennie m. George Adams; Margaret m. Andrew Smith; Nancy m. Andrew Howard; Joseph, unm.; Ezekiel d. intestate, Indianapolis, Ind., m. Nancy Todd.; James Parks m. Lydia Heward; Susan m. Peter Newland. John Hanna was commn. Justice for Franklin Co., Ind., 11-8-1814; commn. Associate Judge for Franklin Co., Ind., 2-14-1817; same 9-1-1823; mov. from Franklin Co., Ind., by Apr. 1829 to Indianapolis, Ind. REF: Hanna--"House of Hanna", p. 123 et al; "Exec. Journ. of Ind. Terr., 1800-1816" p.225; "Exec. Proc. of Ind., 1816-1836", pp. 25, 261, 438; Mrs. Olive Bare, Youngstown, Ohio. Service: enl. at age 14, Laurens Dist., S.C., under his father, Capt. Robert Hanna ("Roster" p.175); in Batt. of Bennington, 8-15-1777.

HANNA, THOMAS   Marion
Said to be Rev. sold. bur. there. REF: Mr. Schrum.

HARBIN, JOSHUA   Knox
b. Md.; d. 1790-1797; m. Elizabeth ---; chn.: Joshua, d.s.p.;
John m. Diana ---;   Elizabeth m. William Scott;   Cassandra m.
Michael Thorn ("Roster" p.355);   Massa b. 1770. m. 10-11-1789,
Vincennes, Ind., Abraham Westfall (see this Suppl.);   Lucy m.
Thomas Nicholls;   Sarah Dawden (or m. Mr. Dawden?).   Service:
enl. 7-25-1776 Upper Dist. (prob. of Frederick Co., Md.?), Lt.
Clement Hollyday, Maj. Francis Deakens.   REF: "Md. Arch.---Md.
Troops in the Rev."; Terr. Papers, v.2, p.621; Pens. W.9883 Va.
(of Abraham & Massey Westfall); Mrs. Eva B. Davenport, Vincennes.

HARNER, JAMES   Fayette
Said to be Rev. sold. bur. there.   Possibility that this might
be the James Hames or Hamer, earlier this Suppl. REF: Mr. Schrum.

HARNEY, HIRAM   Johnson
Verbatim copy: "To His Excellency William Hendricks Governor of
The State of Indiana, Whereas: in Commemorating the Ever Memorable
Event of American Independence Hiram Harney A veteran who has
Risked his life in His Countrys Cause Did Inadvertantly Swear and
was Returned --- Therefore we the undersigned Humbly pray you to
Remit the fine Imposed on the said Hiram Harney Before Spencer
Barnet of Blue River Township Johnson County (Justice of the
peace). Said Return was Made on the third Day of July 1824 to
said Spencer Barnet, Justice of the peace Aforesaid. we your
Petitioners Entreat you to Remit said fine and to Exhonerate said
Harney, As he has Lost His wife By Death, and Has a numerous family Depending upon him for support. Therefore it will be an Act
of Humanity and Magnanimity to Remit said fine and your petitioners will Ever pray etc.   Johnson County January 8th 1825.
P.S. if your Excellency in your wisdom please to Remit the fine
aforesaid Send A Line as soon as convenient to Hiram Harney Care
of William R. Hensley post Master Edinburgh, and Oblige your
Obedient Servants, etc."   Petition has 49 signatures, including
that of Spencer Barnet, J.P. The fine was remitted 1-14-1825.
REF: "Exec. Proc. of Ind., 1816-1836" p.320; "Pardons and Remissions of Fines" (Ind. State Archives).

HARRISON, GEORGE   Putnam
Said to be Rev. sold. bur. there.   REF: Mr. Schrum.

HARRISON (HARRIS), ZEPHANIAH   Vanderburgh
b. ca. 1762. Pens. appl. 8-11-1835, ae. 73, Vanderburgh Co., Ind.
His name is Harrison; but in Virginia & alsewhere he has lived,
he has generally been known as Harris; so does not know which
name he enlisted under, but prob. Harris. Service: enl. fall of
year before Cornwallis' defeat, Montgomery Co., Va., Col. Davis,
Capt. William Bentley, Va. Line. Served with: Isaac & Peter
Stiffey (or Stephen) Andrew & Henry Lore, and Austin & Valentine
Acres, all from Montgomery Co., Va. REF: Pens. R.4690 Va.; Rej.
Pens. List, p.407--did not serve 6 mos.

HARTLEY, DANIEL   Clark
b. 1753-1754; d. 1837; m. (wife b. ca. 1766); chn. (at least):
1 dau. ae. ca. 14; 1 son ca. 12; 1 son ca. 6 (ages 1820). Pens.
appl. 6-25-1815, in 64th yr., Shelby Co., Ky.; 9-19-1820, wife
over 54, 3 chn. liv. with him (ages as above); affid. 12-27-1837,
Clark Co., Ind.; has lately remov. from Ky.; chn. liv. in Clark
Co., Ind.; he now liv. with son in Clark Co. but within a few mi.
of New Albany, Floyd Co., Ind. Pens. tr. from Ky. 1-8-1838.
Affid. 11-10-1819, Clark Co., Ind., of James Taff ("Roster" p.350)
that he & sold. were in same Regt., 1777, Morgan's Rifles. Affid.
of David Hartley (rel. not stated) that he knew sold.; affid. of
Hugh Hartley (rel. not stated). Service: enl. 8-9-1776, Berkeley
Co., Va., Capt. Gabriel Long, 11th Va. Regt.; tr. to Va. Rifle
Regt., Col. Daniel Morgan. REF: Pens. S.36571 Va.; 1835 Pens.
List, v.3, p.61.

HAYMOND, CALDER   Franklin
b. 1734 in what is now Rockville, Montgomery Co., Md.; d. 3-7-
1815; m.(1) 1750 or 1753, Eleanor Owen (prob. dau. of Edward
Owen), d. 1780's; m.(2) ca. 1790, Catharine ---, d. 3-9-1832;
chn. (by 1st wife): Edward (oldest son; Rev. sold.) b. 1-6-1755,
Md., d. 1824 on visit back to old home in (West) Va., m. 1-18-
1780, Sarah Woodfon (Woodson?);   Thomas (Rev. sold.) d. ca.
1800, East. Shore, Md.;   John (youngest son) b. 4-7-1773, Monongalia Co., (West) Va., d. 8-21-1831, Liberty Twp., Shelby Co.,
Ind., m.(1) 12-3-1793, Dorcas Holt, b. 5-10-1776, Va., d. 12-29-
1805, dau. of John Holt; he m.(2). 12-18-1806, Mary Hollenbeck, b.
1-9-1784, Va., d. 2-29-1836; both but. fam. cem. where a corner
of Waldron, Ind., now is;   dau. m. Raynier Hall; dau. m. Mr.
Holt;   prob. a son Owen (killed in Rev. War);   sold.'s chn. by
2nd wife: Milly b. 2-5-1793, d. 1-10-1863, m. 8-20-1815, Demarquis Mizner (fam. liv. Shelby Co., Ind., few yrs. & then mov. to
Ill.)   Haymond genealogies from emigrant, John, in ref. below.
Calder Haymond b. at "Constant Friendship ", pat. 1734, near
where Montgomery Co., Md., now stands at Rockville; formerly Frederick Co. & Prince Georges Co., to which father, John Haymond,
had emig. from Eng. ante 1730, wife Margaret. Calder liv. in
present Montgomery Co., Md., till ca. 1773 to West Augusta Dist.,
Va. (present Monongalia Co., West Va.) on E side of Monongahela
River ca. 3-4 mi. below Fairmount; strong Methodist; many M.E.
preachers visited his home; ca. 1812 joined son John, who had
mov. to Hamilton Co., O., ca. 1810; they later mov. across line
to Ind. Terr.; Calder eventually sett. in present Franklin Co.,
Ind., on Whitewater River, ca. 12 mi. E of Brookville. Service:
pvt. in West Augusta Dist., Va.; a Comp. of Va. Mil..;- paid off at
Fort Pitt. REF: T.L. Haymond--"Haymond Fam." (1906) pp.6-7-8-12-
15-18-22-25-60-65-66; C.J. Haymond--"Haymond Fam." (1919) ts in
ISL, pp.2-4-5-6-10-12; "William & Mary Quarterly". Ser. 2, v.3,
pp.47-48; 1790 Cens., Monongalia Co., Va., p.35; DAR # 289,532;
Mrs. Arthur Whitmore Smith, Ann Arbor, Mich.

HAYS, JOSHUA--see p. 117.

HEALEY, HUGH   Wayne
b. 1758; d. 8-31-1834. Pens. appl. 5-28-1818, Orange Co., N.C.,
but a res. of Guilford Co., N.C., ae. 60; name spelled Hilly &
Haley on appl. papers; appl. 10-24-1820, ae. 62, Wayne Co., Ind.,
as Healy; lately remov. from N.C. to Ind. Service: enl. Jan.
1776, Philadelphia, Pa., Capt. Jonathan Daton, 3rd Jersey Regt.,
Col. Barber. REF: Pens. S.36578 N.J.; 1835 Pens. List v.3, p.37.

HEATON, DANIEL   Howard
Said to be Rev. sold. bur. there. (Possibility that he may have
been War of 1812). REF: Mr. Schrum; Blanchard--"Hist. of Howard
& Tipton Cos., Ind." (1883) pp. 101-102.
HENDERSON, DAVID--see p. 118.

HENRY, JOHN   Indiana
(Uncertain that he died here). Is a Rev. sold. living in Indiana
in 1822. REF: "Pa. Arch.", 2nd Ser., v. 13, p. 99.

HENRY, JOSEPH   Orange
b. ca. 1758; d. 9-14 or 15-1814 (or 1815 or 1816; differing affids.); m. 3-1-1781, Lincoln Co., N.C., Mary Shearer, b. ca.
1759; chn. (from Bible rec. in file): Mathew b. 6-25-1783; Nancy
b. 8-21-1785;   Philip b. 12-6-1787;   Sally b. 6-6-1790; Hannah
b. 6-10-1792;   William b. 10-25-1794;   Hugh (1st) b. 1-5-1796;
Hugh (2nd) b. 2-1-1798;   Joseph b. 5-12-1801;   Polly b. 8-2-
1805;   Malcom b. 12-1-1810. Affid. 8-26-1845, Washington Co.,
Ind., of Philip Henry, ae. 58, that he b. 1787, Lincoln Co., N.C.;
that parents had 11 chn., 2 older & 8 younger than self; that
Mathew is dead & Nancy last heard from was liv. Johnson Co., Mo.
Affid. of wid. Mary, ae. 85, Carroll Co., Ark., 7-25-1844; again
2-7-1846, Washington Co., Ind.; again 7-4-1848, Taney Co., Wis.,
that husb. would be over 90 if alive; again 10-30-1849, Taney
Co., Wis., that she had lately remov. from Ind. as her sons had
mov.; again 8-6-1851, Taney Co., Mo. (not Wis.). Affid. 8-6-1851
Taney Co., Mo., of Malcom Henry; youngest of the 11 chn., ae. 40
on 12-1-1851; bro. Mathew would be at least 68 if alive. Affid.
3-28-1839, Wayne Co., Ky., of Hannah Hamilton. ae. 85, sis. of
sold. Sold. had 2 bros. killed at Batt. of King's Mt., John
Henry & Moses Henry. Wid.'s pens. tr. to Mo., 11-26-1849.
Service: (from wid.'s affid.): enl. ca. Aug. 1778, Lincoln Co.,
N.C., Capt. Malcom or Macon, Col. Hamilton. REF: Pens.W.10096N.C.

HENSLEY, RICHARDSON, SR.   Washington
b. Spotsylvania Co., Va.; d. 1823; son of George Hensley (son of
Samuel & Elizabeth Hensley) & Mrs. Sarah (Richardson Hutcherson;
m. Winifred ---; chn.: Edmund m.(1) Polly Garrett; m.(2) ---;
Jonathan of Washington Co., Ind., m. Nancy Garrett;   Gabriel of
Franklin (Co.?), Ind., m. Ann Priddy;   Berryman of Morgan Co.,
Ind., m.(1) Elizabeth Morgan; m.(2) Elizabeth Clark; Richardson,
Jr., b. 3-10-1779, Spotsylvania Co., Va., d. 10-26-1868, Johnson
Co., Ind., bur. Bethlehem Cem., m. 3-26-1800, Shelby Co., Ky.,
Elizabeth Cully, b. 7-15-1783, d. 4-15-1859. (Richardson Hensley,
Jr., was for a while in Jackson Co., Ind.; 1823 to Johnson Co.,
Ind., where a twp. was named for him; had a dau. Mahala who m.
John McNutt, gt-gr-pars. of Paul V. McNutt). Sold. bought land

in Mercer Co., Ky., 10-22-1793; sold it 3-22-1796 when he & wife
were of Shelby Co., Ky. Sold. & sons Edmund, Jonathan, & Richardson to Washington Co., Ind. Edmund died & father was appt.
guard. of Edmund's chn. Sold. d. 1823 & Richardson, Jr., was
appt. guard. in father's place. Gabriel sett. Franklin Co., Ind.;
Berryman in Morgan Co., Ind. (Note: see John Gallamore, this
Suppl.). Service: proof in DAR Mag., Jan. 1950, p.58, Spotsylvania Co., Va., Mil. REF: Washington Co., Ind., Court Order Bk.1;
Mrs. Ira Tranter, Franklin, Ind.; much data on descendants in
"Johnson Co., Ind., Records", v.2, pt.4, Alexander Hamilton Chap.,
DAR, Franklin, Ind. (in ISL & DAR Library).

  HENSON, JESSE   Martin
b. 6-10-1759 (or 3-15-1761; or 1765), Culpeper Co., Va. Pens.
appl. 8-12-1835, ae. ca. 76 last June 10, Harrison Co., Ind.; now
a res. of Crawford Co., Ind., but late of Harrison Co. Mov. as a
lad with father to Randolph Co., N.C.; there till ca. 21 yr. ago;
Harrison Co., Ind., ca. 5 yr.; to Ky. for two (ten?) yr.; back to
Harrison Co., Ind., 1 yr.; to Crawford Co., Ind. Again appl. 12-29-1849, ae. 88, Martin Co., Ind.; says b. 3-15-1761; fam. Bible
was given a few yr. ago to Sarah Burton (rel. not stated) who now
liv. Camden Co., Mo.; sold. has liv. Ind. last 30 yr., now in
Martin Co. Again appl. 10-22-1850, ae. 85, Martin Co., Ind.; says
b. 1765; was just 16 on day of Batt. of Guilford Ct. Hse., a short
time before he enl.; after War liv. Randolph Co., N.C., till Apr.
1812; Harrison Co., Ind., till 1833 when came to Martin Co., Ind.
Service can be proved by Joseph Henson & Jeremiah Henson, his
neighbors in Carolina & in Harrison Co., Ind.; affid. from these
two (rel. not stated; prob. bros.) 8-12-1835, Harrison Co., Ind.
Sold. is a bro. of William Henson (see this Suppl. below). REF:
Pens. R.4906 N.C.; Rej. Pens. List, p.407--did not serve 6 mos.;
Susp. Pens. List, p.412--for proof of service.

  HENSON, JOHN   Vanderburgh
(Uncertain; am waiting for pension abstract. If received in time,
will add data at end of this section after Daniel Zink).
b. ca. 1766-1767. Pens. appl. 1829, ae. 62, Vanderburgh Co.,
Ind. (Act of 1818); in court records there. REF: "Hist. of Vanderburgh Co., Ind." (1889) p.337. (See p. 119 later).

  HENSON, WILLIAM   Harrison
b. 1758-1759, Culpeper Co., Va. Pens. appl. 3-27-1838, ae. ca.
76, Mitcheltree Twp., Martin Co., Ind.; liv. Culpeper Co., Va.,
till ca. 18 yr. old; mov. to Randolph Co., N.C., where was liv.
with father, Joseph Henson (whose house was made headquarters)
when enl. ae. 18-19; age in prayer book now in possession of his
bro., Jesse Henson (see this Suppl. above) ae. ca. 1½ yr. younger
who knows of his service. After War liv. Randolph Co., N.C., till
ca. 24 yr. ago; Harrison Co., Ind., 4 yr.; Martin Co., Ind.
Again appl. 4-14-1840, ae. ca. 81, Harrison Co., Ind.; says mov.
to Randolph Co., N.C., when small boy; liv. there till ca. 1809;
to Ind., where has since liv. in Martin Co. & Harrison Co. William
Wright ("Roster" p.391) could testify to his services as he was in
same Comp. Also remembers these others in the Comp.: Thomas Garner,

John Hines, Evans Wright, John Stephens, Robert Stephens, Shubel
or Jerry York, Anthony Rains, Robert Duncan, Charles Duncan (or
Dungan). Affid. 3-27-1838, Martin Co., Ind., of Jesse Henson,
ae. ca. 74, that he is younger bro. of William & that sold. serv.
as stated. Service: enl. Sept. 1780, Randolph Co., N.C., Capt.
John Rains, Lt. Aquilla Jones, Col. Thomas Dugan, Comp. of Light
Horse. REF: Pens. R.4910 N.C.; Rej. Pens. List, p.407--not under
competent military authority or organization.

HEROD, WILLIAM--see p. 118.

HIATT, ASA — Parke
b. ca. 1752, 9 mi. from Frederick, Md. Pens. appl. 5-5-1833, ae.
81, Parke Co., Ind.; again 2-12-1835, ae. 81, Florida Twp., Parke
Co., Ind. When enl., liv. with father, Messick Hyatt (then ae.
ca. 50 yr.) ca. 9 mi. from Frederick, Md. After War liv. Wake
Co., N.C., till 8-9 yr. ago to Florida Twp., Parke Co., Ind.
Father d. over 20 yr. ago (1835). Power of atty. 6-21-1854, of
Samuel Hiatt (rel. not stated), Parke Co., Ind. Service: enl.
Frederick Co., Md., July 1780, Capt. Philip Griffin, Lt. Nathan
Maynard, Col. Michael Rogers. REF: Pens. R.4943 Md.; Susp. Pens.
List, p.412--for further proof & explanation.

HICKMAN, JACOB — Floyd
b. 1746, Kent Co., Del. Pens. appl. 3-20-1834, Franklin Twp.,
Floyd Co. Ind., ae. 87. Liv. Kent Co., Del., till 1799; Henry
Co., Va., till 1802; Lincoln Co., Ky., till 1814; then to Floyd
Co., Ind. Service: enl. Aug. 1776, Capt. Henry Bernard, Kent Co.,
Del., Col. Wheatley. REF: Pens. S.32318 Del.

HICKS, DEMPSEY — Indiana
Poss. liv. in or near Parke Co., Ind. No papers in file. Letter
dated 1-2-1834 from John J. Davis of Rockville, Ind., Clerk
(poss. the Parke County Clerk?). Papers sent 2-26-1834 by Commr.
of Pens. to Hon. E. A. Hannegan. REF: Pens. R.4960; Rej. Pens.
List, p. 407--was a deserter.

HILEY, GEORGE — Perry
Said to be Rev. sold. bur. there. REF: Mr. Schrum.

HINKLEY, SETH — Indiana
b. ca. 1758; d. 9-2-1822; mar.; chn. at least 6. Pens. appl.
5-31-1818, ae. 60, Hamilton Co., O.; 8-29-1820, ae. 62, Hamilton
Co., O.; wife & 6 chn. living; chn. all support themselves; among
creditors is W. C. Hinkley (rel. not stated). Pens. tr. from
Hamilton Co., O., to Ind., 11-23-1821, but no Ind. county given.
(Note: this is not pens. for Seth Hinckley & wid. Genet). Service:
enl. ca. Mar. 1776, Boston, Mass., in Mass Line, Capt. Silas Wild,
Col. Seth Thwing. REF: Pens. S.36579 Mass; 1835 Pens. List,
v. 3, p. 37.

HITCH, GILLIS — Montgomery
b. ca. 1758, Bridge Branch (now called Bridgeville, Sussex Co.,
Del.); d. 11-7-1847; mar. (wife d. ante husb.); chn. (surv. 1851):
William; Gillis; John. Orig. pens. appl. lost as letter 7-10-
1839, Pendleton Co., Ky., from sold. asks why has not recd. pens.

Again appl. 2-19-1847, ae. ca. 89, Montgomery Co., Ind.; father d. shortly after sold. was born; he has older bros.; after War, liv. Bridge Branch till 5-6 yr. ago when came to Crawfordsville, Ind. Soldiers in his Comp. were: Thomas Matney (sp?), Richard Starrs, Joshua Cliffen (sp?), Bartholomew Adams. Power of atty. 1--3-1851 from William Hitch, son, ae. ca. 42, Montgomery Co., Ind. Service: enl. Aug. 2 yr. after War began, Bridge Branch, Sussex Co., Del., 1st Lt. Charles Kid, Capt. (later Col.) Joseph Vaughn. REF: Pens. R.5049 Del.; Susp. Pens. List, p. 412--for further proof & specification.

HOBBS, JAMES   Decatur
b. 5-16-1759 or 1760; d. Mar. 1847; m. ca. 1780, Rachael Reynolds, d. ca. Sept. 1841, ae. ca. 78; chn. (at least): James, Jr., b. ca. 1782. Pens. appl. 6-11-1831, ae. 72 next May 16, Decatur Co., Ind.; liv. with him are wife & 1 gr-ch. Again appl. 12-15-1842, ae. 84 on 5-16-1843, Decatur Co., Ind. Affid. 6-11-1831, Decatur Co., Ind., of John Davis; says he saw sold. in Cont. uniform in 1777-1778 in Md.; same by Robert Hobbs (rel. not stated). Power of atty. 8-5-1853, Clarksburg, Fugit Twp., Decatur Co., Ind., of James Hobbs, Jr., son, ae. 71. Service: enl. in 18th yr., spr. 1777, 4th Md. Regt., Md. State Line, Capt. Edward Wright. REF: Pens. R.5072 Md.; Susp. Pens. List, p.412--for proof from the records at Annapolis.

HODGENS, ROBERT   Knox
Said to be Rev. sold. bur. there.   REF: Mr. Schrum.

HOGG (HOGGATT?) -----   Washington
Said to be Rev. sold. bur. there. Said to be bur. in Polk Twp. (Note: a Quaker, Moses Hoggatt, came to Washington Co., Ind., in 1810. A Moses Hoggatt was appt. J. P. for Harrison Co., Ind. (from part of which Washington Co. was formed in 1813.) on 1-16-1809; commn. 2nd Judge of the Circuit Court for Washington Co., 1-10-1814. There was also a William Hoggatt (several refs. in "Exec. Proc.") who d. 12-3-1830, Orange Co., Ind., formerly of Washington Co., Ind.). REF: Mr. Schrum; Stevens--"Hist. of Washington Co., Ind." (1916) p.634; Morris--"Arch. & Hist. Survey of Washington Co., Ind." (1925) p.507; "Exec. Journ. of Ind. Terr., 1800-1816" pp. 153,207; "Exec. Proc.", several refs.

HOLLER, JOHN   Washington
b. 11-9-1763, Bucks Co., Pa.; d. 1849; m. Margaret ---; chn.: John; Andrew; Zachariah; George m. 2-18-1823, Washington Co., Ind. Lucy Robertson; Isaac m. 9-3-1835, Washington Co., Ind. Pelina Cunningham; Absalom; Christeaner; Catharine; Elizabeth (m. & had chn.); Ann; Sarah m. Mr. Taylor (had son David). Will wr. 1-30-1849; pr. 3-19-1849. Pens. appl. 10-1-1841, ae. 77, Washington Co., Ind.; has a fam. rec. in the German lang. in a book & thinks there is his birth rec. in a Presby. Church in Bucks Co., Pa. After War liv. Northampton Co., Pa., 2 yr.; to N.C. in Rowan Co. & Lincoln Co. ca. 30 yr.; Hamilton Co., O., ca. 4 yr.; since then in Washington Co., Ind. Service: drf. fall 1780 in what was then Linn Twp., Northampton Co., Pa., Capt.

Adam Statler (sp?); later served as subst. for Philip Kisler & Jacob Saunder. REF: Pens. R.5146 Pa.; Rej. Pens. List, p. 407-- did not serve 6 mos.; Washington Co., Ind., Will Bk. 1, pp. 592-593; Marriage Bk. A, p. 80; Marriage Bk. C, p. 43.

HOLMAN, WILLIAM NYE   Monroe
Said to be Rev. sold. bur. there. REF: Mr. Schrum.

HOLT, ELISHA   Orange
(Uncertain). b. ca. 1747, S.C.; ae. 103 in 1850 Cens.; so could not have liv. much longer. No proof he was a Rev. sold. but so likely that it seems helpful to include him for possible benefit of descendants in future. From census: Henry Holt, 22, b. Ky.; Shuey (Nancy? writing bad; person is a female) Holt, 22, b. Ky.; Sarah E. Holt, 1, b. Ind.; ELISHA HOLT (census enumerator's caps.), 103, b. S.C., blind; Susan Holt, 65, b. N.C. REF: 1850 Cens., Northwest Twp., Orange Co., Ind., 11-5-1850, v. 17, page 484, family # 1055.

HOUSE, LEVI   Ripley
b. ca. 1754; d. 10-8-1846; mar. chn. (at least, surv.): Sally m. Mr. Brashear; Susan m. Mr. Philips; Rachel m. Mr. Bomingon (sp? or Comingore sp?); Elizabeth m. John Hall. Pens. appl. 2-13-1835, ae. 80, Jefferson Co., Ind. Affid. by William Hall ("Roster" p. 171; prob. rel. of John Hall above) that he saw sold. in Comp. stated; that he has known sold. since he (Hall) was 13-14 yr. old; that sold. is a little older than he; that they liv. in same neighborhood on Ten Mile Creek & later served in same Comp. Letter 10-11-1846, Napoleon, Ripley Co., Ind. from Aaron & Casander Culver (rel. not stated) to John Hall & wife of Canaan, Jefferson Co., Ind.: "Dear Brother & sister Hall; father House d. 10-8-1846; entered in my graveyard; Moses is sick." Power of atty. 4-7-1851 from John Hall, ae. 70 last Dec. 19, husb. of Elizabeth Hall, one of the chn. of Levi House. (Note: sold. may at one time have liv. Franklin Co., Ky., as it seems at least part of estate may have been admr. there). Service: enl. May 1777, Capt. James Hook's Calico Hunting Shirt Comp., Va. Line, Lt. Adam Row, Col. Broadhead, Washington Co., Va. (now Pa.) on Ten Mile Creek. REF: Pens. R.5265 Va.; Susp. Pens. List, p. 412--for proof of service by witnesses.

HOUSTON, PETER   Monroe
Son of Samuel Houston. All other papers in file sent 2-5-1848 to Hon. George G. Dunn. Service: enl. Iredell Co., N.C. REF: Rens. R.5268 N.C.(?); Susp. Pens. List, p. 412--for further proof; memorial to Congress in "Laws of Indiana, 1830-1831", p.176.

HOWELL, WILLIAM E.   Jennings
b. 11-4-1759, Pennytown, Huntington Co., N.J.; d. between 9-26-1845 and 1853; mar.; chn. (at least): David S. Pens. appl. 8-23-1834, ae. 75, Brown Co., O.; after War liv. N.J.; Ohio; in Brown Co., O., 22 yr. Again appl. 5-11-1838, ae. 79, Brown Co., O.; after War liv. N.J., Pa.; now Brown Co., O. Again appl. 9-21-1840, ae. 81, Jennings Co., Ind. Power of atty. 4-30-1853, Jen-

nings Co., Ind., of son David S. Howell. Service: enl. Nov. 1779, Huntington Co., N.J., Mil.; Capt. Christopher Johnson, Col. Job Beavers, Maj. Grooendyke; Flying Camp; later serv. as subst, for Henry Johnson & Joseph Hunt. REF: Pens. R.5302 N.J.; Rej. Pens. List (1852) p.407--did not serve 6 mo. by order of competent authority.

HUBBELL, HEZEKIAH B.   Cass
b. 1760, Woodbridge Raway (sp?), Middlesex Co., N.J.; mar.; chn. (at least): daughter in Ill., 1838, has father's fam. Bible. After War, liv. Wyoming, Pa.; Fairfield Co., O.; Shelby Co., O.; Cass Co., Ind. Pens. appl. 2-12-1838, ae. ca. 78, Cass Co., Ind.; again appl. 9-2-1837 & says shortly after War, to Wyoming, Pa.; 1803 to Ohio; 1835 to Ind. Service: enl. in 14th or 15th yr., Capt. Nathaniel Randall, Jersey Line; after serv. 1 yr., came home & found that father & mother had died; again enl. under Randall; at enl., liv. same place where born (see above). REF: Pens. R.5317 N.J.; Susp. Pens. List (1852) p.412--for further proof.

HUDDLESTON, WILLIAM   Rush
(Uncertain; papers in file do not make place of death clear; he may have d. in Ky.). Sold. d. 5-11-1823; m. 12-3-1783, Cumberland Co., Pa., cousin Ann Huddleston, c. ca. 1761; chn.: David b. 4-6-1786; James b. 5-25-1788; William b. 4-3-1791; Alexander b. 8-25-1793; Samuel b. 2-19-1795; Jane b. 4-14-1799; Ann b. 7-26-1802; Elizabeth b. 1-8-1805. Wid.'s pens. appl. 11-16-1839, ae. 78, Rush Co., Ind. Affid. 11-16-1839, Rush Co., Ind., of John M. Hudelson (bro. of Ann) that name sometimes spelled Hedelston; that Ann's father unwilling for her to marry a cousin; fam. were memb. of Presby. Ch. Similar affid. by Jane Elizabeth Johnson. Affid. 12-9-1839, Orange Co., Ind., of David Hudelson, son of William the sold. (Fam. may be from Middleton Twp., Bucks Co., Pa.). Service: enl. in N.J., "Jersey Blues". REF: Pens. R.5323 N.J.; Susp. Pens. List (1852) p.419--not on the N.J. or Pa. army records in this office.

HUNT, ISRAEL   Hendricks
b. 1762, 1 mi. from Flemington, Co. seat of Hunterdon Co., N.J.; d. 12-10-1846; m. (wife predeceased him); chn. (at least): Eleanor m. William C. Cline (M.E. preacher); Sarah m. John Kirkpatrick; Mary m. John Goodwin (or Gooding); prob. some sons. Pens. appl. 2-13-1844, ae. 81, Hendricks Co., Ind. After War, liv. N.J. till ae. ca. 25; then Pa. for 3 yr.; Ky. for 12 yr.; Cincinnati, O., 6 yr.; Ky. again for 8 yr.; Decatur Co., Ind.; finally shortly before pens. appl., Hendricks Co., Ind. Service: enl. at Pennytown (Pennington), then in Hunterdon Co., now Mercer Co., N.J., 9 mi. from Princeton, Sept. 1776, Col. Joseph Phillips, Capt. John Hunt, Lt. Ralph Lanning. REF: Pens. R.5393 N.J.; Susp. Pens. List (1852) p.412--not 6 mo. service: Mrs. Irene Strieby, Indianapolis, Ind.

HUNT, JAMES   Rush
b. May 1755; mar. Pens. appl. 10-17-1831, ae. 76 in May 1831,
Clark Co., O.; has wife ae. 52. On pens. roll to begin 3-3-
1832; certif. #20,420, Ohio, issued 3-30-1832. Letter 12-7-
1840 that James Hunt of Indiana, formerly of Ohio, asks for ar-
rearages of pension. On 1840 Pens. List, ae. 85, Jackson Twp.,
Rush Co., Ind. Service: enl. 5-20-1778, Md.; Capt. Hatch Dent,
Col. Gunby (sp?). REF: Pens. S.41663 Md.: 1840 Pens. List,p.185.

HUTCHINSON, THOMAS   Putnam
b. 7-26-1757, near Wright's Ferry on Susquehanna River, Lancaster Co., Pa.; mar.; chn.(at least): Maria m. Charles G. Lee.
Pens. appl. 2-14-1845, ae. 87 last July 26, Madison Twp., Putnam
Co., Ind. Liv. in Md. during War; after War, to the glades of
Stoney Creek in Pa., 4-5 yr.; to N.C.; to Tenn.; to Ky.; to Madison Twp., Putnam Co., Ind. P of A 12-16-1854, Putnam Co., Ind.
of dau. Maria Lee. Service: drf. & hired & paid subst. for 2
tours; later drf. & serv., prob. 1781, Tawneytown, Frederick
Co., Md.; Capt. Robert Beatty. REF: Pens. R.5454 Md.; Susp.
Pens. List (1852) p.412--for further proof.

JACKSON, ANDREW   Madison
b. 1742; d. 1848, ae. 106; bur. on Lick Creek; m. Elizabeth ---;
chn. (at least): Levi, b. 2-26-1797, N.C., d. 8-21-1856, bur.
Cook Cem., Hancock Co., Ind., m. Elizabeth Harden, b. 1799,
N.C., d. 12-9-1875; bur. Cook Cem. (& had 8 chn.; Mr. Heiss has
data). Sold. is ae. 90-99 in 1840 Cens., where Jr. follows his
name. (Note: an Andrew Jackson, son?, was. comm. Associate
Judge, Madison Co., Ind., 9-8-1830; resigned 10-10-1831; comm.
Sheriff 8-10-1833; same 8-11-1835). REF: Harden--"The Pioneer",
p. 329; 1840 Cens., Madison Co., Ind., v.7, p.211; "Exec. Proc.
of Ind., 1816-1836", pp.511-512-513; Mr. Willard Heiss, Indianapolis, Ind.

JACOB, JEREMIAH   Clark
b. 1745, prob. Anne Arundel Co., Md.; d. 12-30-1824; bur. New
Chapel Cem., near Utica, Ind. (2nd M.E. Ch. in Ind.; he, wife, &
Walter Prather gave ground prior to 1804); son of Jeremiah &
Rachel (Gaither) Jacob; m. ca. 1770, Frederick Co., Md., Rebecca
Dowden, b. 9-19-1748; d. 7-17-1813, Clark Co., Ind.; bur. New
Chapel Cem; dau. of John & Mary (Gore) Dowden; chn. E.B.(female)
m. Daniel Rutledge, N.C.;   Jeremiah m. Miss Pinchback & d. in
Floyd Co., Ind.;   Mary b. 3-6-1775, d. 6-25-1818, bur. New
Chapel Cem., m. William Patrick;   Martha b. 1-30-1777, m. 6-13-
1791, Rowan Co., N.C., Walter Prather (son of Rev. sold., Basil
Prather, see later, this book) & liv. Clark Co., Ind.;   Thomas
b. 12-26-1783, m. Mary Holman, d. 3-12-1837 (dau. of Rev. sold.,
Isaac Holman, see "Roster" p.194);   John Dowden b. 3-4-1786,
m.(1) Ruth Blizzard, m.(2) Lucinda Gilmore;   Eli b. 3-30-1788,
m.(1) Jane Blizzard, m.(2) Lucinda (Gilmore) Jacob, wid. of his
bro.;   Solomon b. 9-29-1790, m. 4-16-1812, Ind., Elizabeth
Swartz (dau. of John & Elizabeth Oldweiler Swartz;   Edward, liv.
Ft. Wayne, Ind. Sold. liv. dur. Rev. in Frederick Co., later
became Washington Co., Md.; to Rowan Co., N.C., ca. 1781 for ca.

20 yr., where his 5 youngest chn. born; in 1800-1801 to Clark Co., Ind. Terr.; bought 500 ac. in Clark's Grant, 6-8-1807 from Rev. sold. John Swan. (Note: a Jeremiah Jacob, son?, was. comm. Lieut. on 5-12-1814 in 2nd Regt., Ind. Terr. Mil., Clark Co., from part of which Floyd Co., Ind., was formed 1819). Service: signed Oath of Fidelity in Washington Co., Md. REF: Newman-- "Anne Arundel Gentry", pp. 437-439; "Exec. Journ. of Ind. Terr., 1800-1816" p.213; "Hist. of the Ohio Falls Cities & Their Cos." (1882) v.2, pp. 402, 409.

JAMES, JOSEPH ROGERS   Owen
b. ca. 1756. Pens. appl. 11-17-1836, ae. 80, Owen Co., Ind. After War liv. Carter Co., Tenn.; Clay Co., Ky.; Preble Co., O.; Monroe Co., Ind. (where house burned & lost disch. papers); Cole Co., Ill.; Cass Co., Ind.; White Co., Ind.; now Owen Co., Ind. Service: enl. Mar. 1780, Burks Co., N.C.; Capt. Gill Fauld, Col. McDowell. REF: Pens. S.32340 N.C.

JEFFRIES, JOHN   Tippecanoe
b. 2-7-1760. Pens. appl. 10-11-1832, ae. 72 last Feb. 7, Fairfield Twp., Tippecanoe Co., Ind. After War, liv. Va.; N.C.; O.; now Ind. Service: enl. ca. 1777, Essex Co., Va.; Capt. William Gatewood, Col. Holt Richardson. REF: Pens. S.16888 Va.

JOHNSON, JACOB   Elkhart
b. 1763. Pens. appl. 5-21-1833, ae. 70, Elkhart Co., Ind.; again 9-30-1834, Elkhart Co., Ind. Service: forgot when enl. but was disch. before Batt. of Springfield; was a 6 mo. man; was at Elizabethtown, N.J.; again says enl. Reading Twp., Hunterdon Co., N.J.; Capt. Adam Hope, Lt. Jacob Emmons. REF: Pens. R* N.J. (* is a check mark instead of a number); Susp. Pens. List (1852) p.412--for further proof.

JOHNSON, JAMES   Franklin
b. ca. 1748. Pens. appl. 10-16-1835, ae. 87, Bath Twp., Franklin Co., Ind. Lost disch. when house in Washington Co., Pa., burned in 1783. Service: enl. 10-1-1776, near Morristown, N.J., 2nd Regt., N.J. Line; Capt. John Wade, Col. Newcomb, Morris Co., N.J. REF: Pens. R.5629 N.J.; Rej. Pens. List (1852) p. 407-- says "desertion".

JOHNSON, JAMES   Harrison
Said to have died there. Cannot be the James Johnson of Knox Co., d. prob. ante 1817, "Roster" p.210; would not seem to be the James Johnson of Ripley Co.; d. post 1843, "Roster" p.210; unlikely could be the James Johnston of Carroll Co., d. 1838, "Roster" p.212. Is in 1840 Cens., Posey Twp., Harrison Co., Ind., ae. 82. REF: Mr. Schrum; 1840 Pens. List, p. 182.

JOHNSON, JOSEPH   Monroe
(Not to be confused with the Jackson--Washington Co. man following, some of whose papers were mis-filed in the pension envelope of the Monroe Co. man. I called this to their attention at the National Archives but naturally changed no papers myself. Careful study has separated the two men for identification).
b. 10-20-1755, Frederick Co., Va.; m. 5-18-1776. Had a bro., David Johnson ("Roster" p.209, who d. ca. 1848 in Washington Co., Ind., not Jackson Co., Ind., having moved to Washington Co. ca. 1842); and a sis., Elizabeth Munday (sp?) of Ky. Pens. appl. 4-12-1833, ae. 78 next Oct. 20, Monroe Co., Ind. At age 14, mov. with father to New River in Va. & sett. a few mi. from Englishes Ferry on said river for 6-7 yr.; at age 18 mov. to Clinch River in Va. in the spring; after War, liv. 4-5 yr. in Powell's Valley (see service rec.); to Knox Co., Ky., 14 yr. plus; to Hawkins Co., O., ca. 2 yr.; Jackson Co., Ind., ca. 5-6 yr.; short time in Owen Co., Ind.; now Monroe Co., Ind. Service: enl. July 1774 in a Comp. of foot; Capt. Walter Crockett, Va. Mil.; vol. in Apr. 1775 as Indian spy while liv. in Montgomery Co., Va.; after mar., was persuaded by father-in-law to go with them to New River; after reaching New River, was requested by an uncle living on Roanoke River so he & wife went there to stay the season; enl. again under Capt. Hugh Crockett (bro. of Capt. Walter Crockett); sold. was in Montgomery Co., Va., again in 1777-78-79-80; in 1781, mov. to Powells Valley, now Lee Co., leaving fam. behind in Va. till fall; enl. there again 1781 & once more in 1782; bro. David Johnson serv. with him in tour to Guilford, N.C.; David now lives in Jackson Co., Ind. REF: Pens. S 31782 Va.; in I.A.R. List as Joseph Johnston, #26,833.

JOHNSON, JOSEPH   Washington
(Not to be confused with the man above). b. 12-25-1760, N.J.; d. 5-11-1852; bur. Mounts Cem., south of Little York Gibson Twp., Gr. 3, Row 12, Lot 4, flag; m. 2-15-1778 or 1779, Washington Co., Pa., Mary Clark, d. 5-14-1828, Jackson Co., Ind.; chn. (at least):Aris., b. ca. 1788, m. Mr. Blair. Pens. appl. 3-10-1837, ae. 76 last Xmas Day, Jackson Co., Ind., West Fork Twp.; has a bro. 2 yr. younger in Fleming Co., Ky., 2 or 3 mo. ago if still alive. On 11-3-1843 sold. now lives Fleming Co., Ky., having moved there Oct. 1841; bro. Ebenezer Johnson, ae. 81, lives there. (In later letters, Ebenezer is 108, no date; and 92 in letter of 3-5-1850). Sold. retd. to Washington Co., Ind. On 10-15-1855, affid. of Aris Blair, ae. 67, Grassy Fork Twp., Jackson Co., Ind., that she only ch. & heir of Joseph, decd.; no wid.; only chn. (error?) surviving were Aris Blair & Delilah Blair, both of Jackson Co. (is Delilah a dau. of Aris?). (Note: error in dates in Co. Hist. & Am. Leg. card, respectively: "He was seen in 1851 by P. T. Munden, who furnished the data for the Rev. solds. bur. in Gibson Twp., and at that time was in his 101st year"; Joseph Johnson, Sr., b. 1745, d. 1844.). Service: enl. fall 1779, Westmoreland or Washington Co., Pa., now Alleghany Co., Pa.; Capt. Ross, Col. Filandergon (sp?); bro. Ebenezer Johnson serv. with him. REF: Pens. R.5639 Pa.;Susp.Pens.List,1852 p.413-Service for 6 mo.allowed but declined;Stevens-"Hist.of Wash. Co.,Ind." (1916) p.634; Am. Leg.; Mr. Schrum.

JOHNSON, JOSIAH   Washington
died there; bur. on Dawson Purkheiser farm, Sec. 2, Twp. 1,
Range 3, Howard Twp. REF: Stevens--"Hist. of Washington Co.,
Ind." (1916), p. 632.

JOHNSON, ZACHARIAH   Randolph
b. ca. 1757. Pens. appl. 5-18-1836, ae. 79, Randolph Co., Ind.
Service: as subst. for Elijah Pope in 2nd Carolina Regt., Capt.
Stuart, Maj. Murphy, in Northampton Co., N.C. Later enl. while
liv. in Loudoun Co., Va. (One service was as a Dragoon. I.A.R.).
REF: Pens. S.32344 N.C.
JOHNSTON, JOHN--see p. 118.
JONES, NICHOLAS   Bartholomew
b. 11-14-1762, Caroline Co., Va. Pens. appl. 7-26-1832, ae. 69,
Clarke Co., Ky. In fall 1784, mov. from Caroline Co., Va., to
Spotsylvania Co., Va., till 1811; then to Ky.; last 14 yr. in
Clarke Co., Ky. Had two younger bros. Affids. of Joseph Jones
& John Jones, bros. of sold., 7-26-1832, Clarke Co., Ky. On
5-18-1835, Bartholomew Co., Ind., sold. asks for pens. tr. from
Ky. where has lately remon. because chn. & gr-chn. have moved;
Sr. follows name; pens. tr. 6-20-1835. Service: enl. Caroline
Co., Va., Capt. James Johnson, Va. Mil., Col. Holt Richardson;
also serv. as subst. for his father, Griffin Jones, who had been
drafted. REF: Pens. S.16169 Va.; 1835 Pens. List, Clark Co.,
Ky., v. 3, p. 83.

JONES, THOMAS   Bartholomew
(Not to be confused with two men of same name: Thomas Jones of
Putnam Co., Ind., Pens. S.36656, and Thomas Jones of Spencer Co.,
Ind., d. 1832, wid. Ann; both in "Roster" p. 214.).
d. 6-12-1832 (year given in two places; see discrepancy below);
m. 8-1-1793 (mar. bond, Charlotte Co., Va.; see discrepancy below), Mary ("Polly") Clarkson, b. ca. 1766; d. 7-30-1851; chn.
(surv. 1851): Margaret m. Archibald Thomson; Leannah m. George
Baker; Godfrey; Thomas S.; Joseph; Smith D. Wid.'s pens.
appl. 9-1-1845, ae. 79, Bartholomew Co., Ind.; that she m. sold.
on 8-1-1785 (see bond above); that mar. bond was signed by her
mother, Elizabeth Clarkson, since her father was dead; that she
had bros. William, Joseph, Thomas, & Drury the youngest; that
Joneses present at her mar. were David, Lewis, Godfrey, Betsy, &
Cad; that she & husb. liv. ca. 3 yr. after mar. in Charlotte Co.,
Va.; then Gallatin Co., Ky.; that ca. 10 yr. ago, bro. Drury
Clarkson liv. Ky., maybe Mercer Co.; that Thomas & another bro.
may still be liv. there; that Davis (error for David?) Jones,
her husb.'s bro., liv. ca. 10 yr. ago near Nashville, Tenn.
Affid. 10-18-1852, Johnson Co., Ind., of Godfrey Jones, ae. 48,
son; that father d. 1833 (see above); that father serv. in same
Regt. as Job Hamblen ("Roster" p. 172); Rev. pensr. who d. ca.
10-12 yr. ago in Brown Co., Ind. Affid. 3-5-1846, Brown Co.,
Ind., of William Chase, ae. 70; that he often heard sold. talk
about his service; that sold. was ca. 16 yr. old when he enl. in
N.C.; that sold. also when ae. ca. 56 was in War of 1812 with
deponent. Service: N.C. Mil. REF: Pens. R.5735 N.C.; Susp. Pens.
List (1852) p.419-for proof of identity with sold. of same name
on N.C. records.

JONES, WILLIAM   Morgan
Rev. sold. who d. there. In 1835 Pens. List, v. 3, p. 61, ae.
74; pvt. in Va. Cont. Line. No identifiable pension file among
the many William Joneses at Natl. Arch. REF: Mr. Schrum.

    KEISINGER, ANDREW   Owen
b. 12-25-1756, Lancaster Co., Pa. Pens. appl. 5-30-1834, ae. 77,
Owen. Co., Ind. When ae. ca. 10 yr., fam. mov. to Greenbrier
Co., Va. After War, he liv. Giles Co., Va.; Montgomery Co., Va.;
left Va. ca. 1815; Knox Co., Tenn.; was in Tenn. ca. 10 yr.; then
Monroe Co., Ind.; now Owen Co., Ind.; has been in Ind. ca. 8 yr.
Service: enl. Sept. 1774, Greenbrier Co., Va.; Capt. John Lewis,
Col. Andrew Lewis; was in Batt. of Pt. Pleasant at mouth of Kanawha River on 10-10-1774 with Shawnee Indiana; again enl. fall
1776, Greenbrier Co., Va.; Capt. John Henderson, Col. William Arbuckle. REF: Pens. R.5818 Va.; Rej. Pens. List (1852) p. 408--
not 6 mo. Rev. service.

    KELLER, DANIEL   Floyd
b. 5-6-1753, Hampshire Co., (W.) Va.; youngest ch. of Charles
Keller (who was killed 1756 by Indiana at Ft. Ashby, now Mineral
Co., W. Va.); d. 11-5-1838 at home of dau.-in-law, Zerviah
(Starr) Keller; bur. ca. 2 mi. NE of Georgetown, Ind.; m.(1)
1-27-1783, 1st Ref. Ch., Lancaster Co., Pa., Margaret Weller of
Rapho Twp., Lancaster Co., Pa.; d. prob. ante 10-1-1795 (sig. not
on a deed); m.(2) ca. 1800, prob. Hampshire Co., (W.) Va., Margaret (Eckstine) Shipman, b. 1762-1763; d. 4-11-1847 in 85th yr.;
bur. beside husb.; wid. of Benjamin Shipman & poss. dau. of Leonard Eckstine (will pr. 1800, Hampshire Co., Va.); chn. (by 1st
wife & all prob. b. Huntington Co., Pa.): Barbara b. 5-28-1787,
d. 1-31-1846, bur. by father, m. 5-20-1807, Jefferson Co., Ky.,
Jacob Brookhart, d. ante 1830, Clark Co., Ind., son of Jacob &
Catharine (Keller) Brookhart, & had Julia & Lewis (both d. young)
& Charles who m. ca. 1847, Elizabeth Bowler, had chn., & liv.
Clark Co. & poss. Harrison Co., Ind.;   Martha Keller b. 5-20-
1789, d. 12-6-1861, bur. Lutheran Cem., Sinking Valley, Blair
Co., Pa., m. 1806 Frederick Ramey (see "Remy Fam. if Amer.");
Daniel Keller b. 3-17-1791, d. 12-3-1836 on business trip at Mo-
bile, Ala., m.(1) 4-20-1817, Jefferson Co., Ky., Sally Risinger,
b. 11-24-1798, d. 7-17-1822, prob. New Albany, Ind.; he m.(2)
5-8-1823, Zerviah Starr b. 5-11-1801, Hampshire Co., Va., dau. of
Jeremiah Starr & Barbara Brookhart (who was dau. of Jacob Brookhart & Catharine Keller); Daniel Keller, Jr., had chn. by both
wives;   Rosanna Keller (dau. of sold. & 2nd wife) b. by 1804,
m. ca. 1830, prob. Clark Co., Ind., John C. Hagan, were in Texas
by 1835, had chn. Sold.'s father, Charles Keller had chn.:
Daniel;   Esther m.(1) Alexander Stockslager, m.(2) Joel Rees;
Mary m. Mr. Bowman;   John;   Catharine m. Jacob Brookhart.
Sold. mov. from Hempfield Twp., Lancaster Co., Pa., to Huntington
Co., Pa., ca. 1786; to Hampshire Co., (W.) Va., ca. 1799; to
Jefferson Co., Ky., ca. 1805-6; to Ind. 3-4 yr. later. Was mill
builder & boat inventor; friend of Robert Fulton; had 2 U.S.
patents on boats, 1795, 1799; first paddlewheel boat (horses
moved in circle on deck) on Ohio & Mississippi Rivers. Service:

pvt., 2nd class, 8th Comp., 4th Battn., Lancaster Co., Pa., Mil,, 6-4-1782. REF: "Pa. Arch.", 3rd Ser., v. 17, p. 812; 5th Ser., v. 7, p. 434; Mrs. Henry A. Humphrey (Margaret Keller), Wichita, Kans. (Note: a Daniel Keller, son?, was comm. Coroner for Floyd Co., Ind., 8-15-1823; "Exec. Proc. of Ind., 1816-1836", p. 257.

KEPLER, JACOB   Perry
b. 4-29-1741, near Philadelphia, Pa.; d. 12-12-1845, near Rome, Ind. (the earliest resident of Perry Co. of record to live over 100 yrs.); m. Mary Jane Klepinger; chn. (at least): William b. 1779, d. 1817, mar.;   Mary Jane b. 10-14-1782, m. 1799, David Groves;   Margaret b. 1784, m. John Graybill. The Kepler fam. came to the twp. with the Groves & Barger fams., to whom they were related by marriage. They sett. in the Groves' Bottoms between Rome & Derby. Fam. trad. says he was a Rev. sold. under Gen. St. Clair; was at Valley Forge & saw Gen. Washington kneeling in the snow & praying for his soldiers; was captured and paroled from army in New York in Jan. 1781 & walked home. REF: Mr. Wallace Weatherholt, Tell City & Indianapolis, Ind. (This sold. may be one of 2 men in "Pa. Arch.": (1st) in 5th Ser., v. 8, p.94, 1st Battn., Northampton Co., Pa., Mil.; (2nd) in 6th Ser., v. 2, pp. 459, 585, Ensign in 6th Comp., 2nd Battn., York Co., Pa., Mil., 10-1-1777.

KEYSACKER, GEORGE   Crawford
b. ca. 1748-1750; d. 1851, ae. 103; left 3 heirs. Pens. appl. 4-29-1834, ae. 74 (84?), Union Twp., Crawford Co., Ind. Left his disch. with his bro., Aaron (now decd.) in Berkley Co., Va.; those who know of his service are his bro-in-law, Barney Miller of Breckinridge Co., Ky., but here now in court (mar. sold.'s sis., Mary); Frederick Claycomb of Vincennes, Ind. ("Roster" p.98) and George Paul of Ky. Affid. of Barney Miller that he liv. in Berkley Co., Va., in 1781 & was drf. in same Comp. as sold. (Note: altho sold.'s pens. appl. was rejected, he is included in 1840 Pens. List as a pensr., ae. 90, liv. with William Keesucker). Service: drf. fall 1781, Berkley Co., Va.; Capt. Jarrett, Maj. Scott, Col. Dark. REF: Pens. R.5899 Va.; Rej. Pens. List (1852) p.408--did not serve 6 mo.; Pleasant--"Hist. of Crawford Co., Ind." (1926) p. 99; 1840 Pens. List, p. 181.

KILANDER, PHILIP   Fayette
b. July 1763, Hunterdon Co., N.J.; mar. (wife d. ca. 1825); chn. (all mar. by 1833). Pens. appl. 7-1-1833, ae. 70, Pendleton Co., Ky. Soon after War, mov. to near Brownsville, Pa., ca. 20 yr.; to Bracken Co., Ky., until lately. Letter 9-2-1835, now liv. in Fayette Co., Ind.; asks for pens. tr. 9-26-1835 as 2 sons have liv. in Ind. for some time; pens. tr. 5-16-1835. In 1835 Pens. List, Harrison Co., Ky.; pvt. in N.J. Line. Service: drf. June 1781, Hunterdon Co., N.J.; Capt. John Prale, Maj. Cornelius. REF: Pens. S.32363 N.J.; 1835 Pens. List, v. 3, p. 101.

KILLION, JOHN   Orange
b. 6-20-1758 (or Jan. 1759), Lincoln Co., N.C.; mar.; chn. (at
least): Mary b. 1785. Pens. appl. 11-11-1833, ae. 75, Orange
Co., Ind. After War, liv. N.C. till 1821; Warren Co., Tenn., 8
yr.; in Orange Co., Ind., last 4 yr.; again appl. 2-11-1835; now
gives b. as Jan. 1759; fam. rec. in father's Bible kept in German
language; left Lincoln Co., N.C., 1820; Warren Co., Tenn., till
1828; then to Orange Co., Ind. (Note: at one time, seems to have
liv. for a while in Maysville, Ky.). Service: drf. 1780, Lincoln
Co., N.C.; Capt. John Hasselbarger (sp?). REF: Pens. R.5916 N.C.;
Rej. Pens. List (1852) p.408--only 3 mo. service.

KING, WILLIAM   Washington
b. ca. 1755, prob. Va.; son of Arra King; mar.; chn. Pens. appl.
1-7-1833, ae. 77-78, Montgomery Co., Va.; asks for pens. tr. on
9-1-1837, Washington Co., Ind., from Va. to Ind. because he
"wanted to get out of a slave state" & because some of his chn.
live in Ind. Affid. 9-2-1832, Bedford Co., Va., of William Holiday (wife Elizabeth) that his father had served with William King
& had given King a shirt. Pens. tr. from Va. 9-19-1837; in 1840
Pens. List, ae. 87, Vernon Twp., Washington Co., Ind. Service:
enl. Bedford Co., Va., ca. 2 yr. ante Gates' defeat; Col. Charles
Lynch, Capt. Robert Adams; later serv. as subst. for his father,
Arra King, Bedford Co., Va.; later as subst. for James Mays, Bedford Co., Va. REF: Pens. S.32364 Va.; 1840 Pens. List, p. 185.

KINKAID, ----- (Maj.)   Dearborn
b. 1756; d. Jan. 1864. "A Rev. soldier living near Lawrenceburg,
Ind. Major Kinkaid, age 108 born 1756; served thru entire war &
came to Northwest Terr. in 1794; still able to read without
glasses." REF: "Items From Early Newspapers, 1818-1886"--Jeffer-
son Co., Ind., Records (DAR), v.3, p.220; abstracted by Miss Mary
Hill, Madison, Ind.

KITCHEN, THOMAS   Gibson
b. 4-27-1764, Buckingham Co., Va.; mar. (& liv. in Campbell Co.,
Va., ca. 4 yr.). Pens. appl. 8-23-1847, ae. 83, Gibson Co.,Ind.
After War, to S.C. for 15-16 yr.; Ga. ca. 14 yr.; Posey Co.,Ind.,
ca. 2 yr.; now Gibson Co., Ind. Service: drf. when very young,
Buckingham Co., Va., Feb. ante Batt. of Guilford Ct. Hse. REF:
Pens. R.5998 Va.; Rej. Pens. List (1852) p.408--did not serve
6 mo.

KLINGENSMITH, JACOB   Marion
b. 1757-1758, Northampton Co., Pa.; d. by 1853; left heirs. Pens.
appl. 3-31-1835, ae. 77, Marion Co., Ind.; mov. with father from
Northampton Co., Pa., to Md.; after 4 yr. mov. to Westmoreland
Co., Pa.; there till ca. 2 yr. ago to Marion Co., Ind. Affid. of
Peter Anthony & Jacob Sourwine (latter knew sold. in Pa. & since).
Service: drf. Dec. 1777 when ae. 18-19, Westmoreland Co., Pa.;
Capt. George Baird, 1st Lt. George Gray, Col. Archibald Laughrey.
REF: Pens. R.6005 Pa.; Rej. Pens. List (1852) p.408-- did not
serve 6 mo.

KNIGHT, WILLIAM   Warrick
b. 1759; Orange Co., N.C.; mar. (wife d. in Ky., ante 1833); chn. (at least): son John. Pens. appl. 12-20-1833, ae. 74, Henry Co., Ky.; on 4-11-1835 asks for pens. tr. to Aurora, Dearborn Co., Ind., to live with son John; on 1-13-1838 asks for tr. from Dearborn Co. to Vanderburgh Co., Ind.; on 5-21-1838 asks for tr. to Warrick Co., Ind., because son John has now mov. to neighborhood of Sprinklesburg, Ind. Affid. 5-3-1834, Henry Co., Ky., of William Lorance (Lawrence?), ae. 71, who serv. with Knight; also 5-26-1834, Henry Co., Ky., of Thomas Smith, ae. 70, that he serv. with sold. In 1835 Pens. List, Henry Co., Ky.; pvt. in N.C. Mil.; pens. tr. to Ind. from Ky., 5-16-1835. Service: enl. Sept. 1 (year illegible), Orange Co., N.C., as subst. for George Carrenton, who had been drft.; Capt. William Jameson, Col. Alexander Mabin. REF: Pens. S.31800 N.C.; 1835 Pens. List, v. 3, p. 105.

KNOX, GEORGE   Knox
Rev. sold. who died there. REF: Mr. Schrum.

KNOX, JAMES   Knox
Rev. sold. who died there. REF: Mr. Schrum.
KNOX, JOHN--see p. 118.

LAMB, JOSEPH B.   Wayne
(Uncertain). b. 7-29-1758; d. 1-11-1831, ae. 72 yr., 5 mo., 13 da.; bur. in Elkhorn Cem., near Richmond, Ind. Is prob. a bro. of James Lamb ("Roster" p. 226) of Wayne Co. No proof of service, but would be of right age. REF: Mrs. Forrest E. Kempton, Centerville, Ind.

LAMBERT, JAMES   Dearborn
b. 3-25-1757, Md.; d. 5-13-1844; m. Jane ------. Pens. appl. on 11-18-1841, ae. 85 on 3-25-1842, Dearborn Co., Ind. After War, liv. Va.; Md.; Pa.; Ohio; Ind. Again appl. 5-13-1844, ae. 86 on 3-25-1844, Ripley Co., Ind., but a res. of Dearborn Co., Ind.; lives ca. 30 mi. from Lawrenceburg but only ca. 15 mi. from Versailles & it is a better road. Affid. 7-23- 1841, Hamilton Co., O., of Lemuel Hungerford, ae. 79 last May 14, res. of Ross Twp., Butler Co., O.; that he & Lambert were in service at same time in same places. P of A, 3-14-1854, Dearborn Co., Ind., of wid., Jane Lambert. Service: first enl. June 1774, Wilson's Station in Tiger Valley on Monongahela River, in his 17th yr.; retd. to father at Wilson's Sta.; again enl. first Sept. 1774 for 3 mo.; father mov. to N fork of Potomac in Rockingham Co., Va.; drf. in July 1775; Col. Hillyard, Capt. Spencer; in first appl. he says drf. ae. 19, Augusta Co., Va., Mil.; Capt. Spencer, Maj. Guy Hamilton. REF: Pens. R.6099 Va.; Susp. Pens. List (1852) p. 413-- not on any rolls--no proof of service.

LAMPHEAR, ABEL   Dearborn
b. Feb. 1761, Stoningtown Point, Conn.; mar.; chn. (at least): son Abel H. Pens. appl. 8-27-1832, ae. 71, Elkland (sp?) Twp., Tioga Co., Pa.; on 9-2-1834 asks for tr. from Pa. to Alleghany Co., N.Y., to live with a son; on 5-19-1838, Dearborn Co., Ind., asks for tr. from N.Y. because now lives with son Abel H. Lamph__ear__

who has lately rem. from N.Y. to Dearborn Co., Ind.; pens. tr. from Albany, N.Y., Agy., 7-26-1838. Service: enl. 1776, Stamford, Conn.; Capt. Shutes; pvt. & fifer. REF: Pens. S.16440 Conn.

LANDERS, JONATHAN   Morgan
d. there; mar., post Rev., in Va., Mrs. Withero (a wid. with chn.); chn. (most of them b. in Va.), incl.: William, b. 1788, Va.; d. 10-10-1851, ae. 63; m.(1) in Ky., Eva Stone (dau. of Nimrod H. & Sarah Craig Stone, natives of Va.; Nimrod Stone a Rev. sold.); she d. 1821, Morgan Co., Ind.; William m.(2) Delilah Stone, b. Ky. (sis. of Eva); more abt. his chn. in ref. below; James, sett. in Mo. & was Confed. sold. in Civ. War; John, farmer in Ind.; Lucy, d. Iowa, m. Mr. Priest. Jonathan Landers was Scotch-Irish; was 21 when came from Eng., having lost all of his relatives by Black Plague; to Ky. 1798; to Morgan Co., Ind., 1820. Service: "served in the Rev. war". REF: Beers--"Comm. Biog. Rec. of Indianapolis & Vicinity" (1908) pp.412-413, 624; Mrs. Irene Strieby, Indianapolis, Ind.

LANGDON, PHILIP   Jackson
Rev. sold. who d. there. Intestate rec. on file at Courthouse. REF: Ft. Vallonia Chap., DAR, Seymour, Ind.

LANHAM, HENRY   Switzerland
b. 5-28-1761, Prince Georges Co., Md.; d. 11-20-1849; bur. on McKay Cem., Braytown, Ind.; m. Eleanor -----, b. 1765; chn.: Shadrach; Thomas b. 2-23-1792, Prince Georges Co., Md.; d. 4-22-1864, Clinton Twp., Decatur Co., Ind.; m. 6-28-1818, Switzerland Co., Ind., Elizabeth Peters, b. 6-12-1802, Va.; d. 2-9-1892, Rush Co., Ind.; John; Chloe b. 1795, m. Mr. Sadler; Mary b. 1800, m. Abisha McKay; Sarah m. Zachariah McKay; Meshack b. 1811, m. Susanna Bray; Milley m. Mr. McKay; Nancy m. Mr. McCarthy. Service: enl. 2-3-1776, 2nd Co., Md. Troops; batt. of Long Island, 1776. REF: "Md. Arch.--Md. Troops in the Rev.", p. 8; "Md. Hist. Mag.", v.14, p.117; Miss Mary Hill, Madison,Ind.

LANKER, JACOB   Indiana
Uncertain if he d. in Ind. His wid., Mary Lanker, is on Ind. Agy. Roll Book; but Natl. Archives was unable to find his pens. file under this name or under Sanker. It is prob. a mis-spelling; if any reader knows what this name should be, please notify the compiler. REF: I.A.R.; Natl. Arch.

LARGENT, NELSON   Montgomery
b. 9-27-1763, Hampshire Co., Va., ca. 18 mi. from Romney. Pens. appl. 9-22-1834, ae. 71, Union Twp., Montgomery Co., Ind. Affid. from Randall Largent (his ½ bro.) & George B. Conrad, both of Montgomery Co., Ind., that they knew him in Hampshire Co., Va., & here. Depos. 3-1-1834, Jackson Twp., Champaign Co., O., of Catharine Largent (rel. not given) supports service. (Note: the 1850 Cens. of Montgomery Co., Ind., shows these poss. Largent sons: Samuel 40; Nelson 38; William 26; all b. Ohio. There are also Largent families in nearby Fountain & White Cos., Ind. Service: drf. summer 1781, Capt. Miller; was ae. 19 when Corn-

-62-

wallis was defeated. REF: Pens. R.6166 Va.; Rej. Pens. List (1852) p.408--did not serve 6 mo.; 1850 Cens., Montgomery Co., Ind., v.16, pp. 757, 767, 1042.

LAWRENCE, ISAAC   Boone
b. 1762, Camden Dist., S.C. Pens. appl. 11-11-1833, ae. 69, Washington Twp., Hendricks Co., Ind. After War, liv. Westmoreland Co., Pa.; to Forks of the Potomac in Va.; to Mason Co., Ky.; to Hendricks Co., Ind. In 11-11-1846, ae. 84, now in Boone Co., Ind. Service: enl. June 1780 (or Aug. 1779), Camden Dist., S.C.; Capt. William Goodwin, Col. Williams; then went to live near Hagerstown, Washington Co., Md., & 2 wks. later was drf. on Nov. 25. REF: Pens. S.32373 Md., N.C., S.C.; 1835 Pens. List, v.3, p.53, Hendricks Co., Ind., pvt. in S.C. State Troops.

LAYTON, THOMAS   Franklin
Uncertain. Name obtained after this Suppl. was started. A Thomas Layton of Indiana is on the 1831 list of rejected pens., the reason:"served in a regiment not on continental establishment". He is prob. the man who later recd. Pens. S.32371 Pa. (when the qualifications were broadened). There is a Thomas Layton in the 1830 Cens. of Franklin Co., Ind., v.4, p.588. This sold., however, may be the Thomas Layton given in "Rev. Sold. Bur. in Ill.", p.19, who d. post 1835 in Clark Co., Ill.; service in the Northumberland Co., Pa., Mil. REF: "Rej. Appl. for Pens."(1831) p.49 (see note at end after Daniel Zink).

LAYTON, WILLIAM   Decatur
b. ca. 1758. Pens. appl. 2-11-1833, ae. ca. 75, Washington Twp., Decatur Co., Ind. Service: while res. in Somerset Co., N.J., enl. in spring (year not given) at Menesinks (sp?) on Delaware River in N.Y.; Capt. T. Pell, Col. Courtland, Clinton's Brig., 3rd N.Y. Regt. REF: Pens. R.6218 N.Y.; Rej. Pens. List (1852) p. 408--was a deserter.

LEDGERWOOD, JAMES   Sullivan
b. 1753, Va.; d. 1809; bur. in fam. cem. 400 ft. from Treaty Elm Tree on Road 41 near Carlisle, Ind.; son of William (d. 1794) & Rebecca (Moody) Ledgerwood: m. 12-29-1781, Botetourt Co., Va., Elizabeth McCoun, b. 2-7-1761, Va. (dau. of James McCoun, Jr., who m. 1744, Margaret Walker); chn.: William b. 12-29-1786; d. 4-30-1850; m. 9-26-1810, Catharine Jenkins, b. 11-16-1792; d. 8-25-1875; Samuel d. 5-5-1875; m. 9-27-1810, Nancy Leman; Joseph m. (in May?) 1810, Nancy Gill; Margaret m. 10-8-1810, James Lisman; Nancy; John Wesley d. young; Elizabeth; Sarah b. 1804 (1st white ch. b. in Sullivan Co., Ind.); d. 8-16-1889; m. William Cartwright; Melinda. Ledgerwood fam. orig. of Augusta Co., Va.. Sold. liv. Botetourt Co., Va.; to Lincoln Co., Ky.; in early 1800's to Ind. & was 1st settler of Sullivan Co. where had Ledgerwood Fort near Carlisle. Service: pvt. in 14th Regt., Va. Cont. Line. REF: Gwathmey--"Va. in the Rev.", p. 464; Mrs. Glenn E. Wheeler, Vincennes, Ind. (See p. 119 later).

LEE, JOHN   Jefferson
(Not to be confused with John Lee, a.k.a.See, of Henry Co., Ind.,
"Roster" p.232, wid. Margaret, Pens. S.17538). b. 7-20-1760,
Flemington, N.J.; d. 9-17-1837; m. 3-15-1780, Morris Co., N.J.,
Margaret -----, b. ca. 1762; chn.: Gershom, b. 2-11-1781; m.
Elizabeth Ford (dau. of Rev. sold., Warner Ford); Mary, b. 12-
8-1783; Rebecca, b. 2-10-1787; Nathan, b. 10-15-1789; John
b. 4-15-1792; James b. 5-12-1796; Sarah b. 2-24-1799; Nancy
b. 8-4-1801; Nathaniel b. 5-16-1804. Wid.'s pens. appl. 6-26-
1845, ae. 83, Milton Twp., Switzerland Co., Ind. (error: Milton
Twp. is in Jefferson Co., Ind. MRW); her husb. res. in Morris
Co., N.J.; fellow solds. in his Comp. were: David Barnes, Enos
Campbell, Henry Dow, James Joy, Stephen Price, James Welch, William Wright, and sold.'s bro., Joseph Lee, decd. ("Roster" p.232)
whose wid., Eleanor Lee is now a pensr. in Decatur Co., Ind.
Affid. 6-26-1845, Switzerland Co., Ind., of Samuel Bellamy, M.E.
clergyman, res. of Craig Twp., Switzerland Co., Ind., and near
line dividing Switzerland Co. from Jefferson Co., Ind.; that he
knew John Lee & wife well in Jefferson Co., Ind., ca. 14 yr. before John died; liv. within 8 mi. of them for 26 yr. till they
mov. onto the waters of Indian-Kentucky (in Jefferson Co., MRW)
ca. 3 mi. from where deponent now lives. Affid. of Thomas Mounts
("Roster" p.262) ae. 82; that he knew John & Margaret Lee since
they res. at mouth of Kentucky River since 1790. Same from Robert Poindexter, ae. 78; that he knew them over 50 yr. ago in
Woodford Co., Ky.; Gallatin Co., Ky.; that all 9 chn. were b. in
Gallatin Co., Ky. (I question this; MRW); that wid. Margaret now
res. on waters of Indian-Kentucky in Jefferson Co., Ind. Service:
N.J. Mil., 1776-1781, incl.; Capt. John Maxwell, Hunterdon Co.;
Capt. Chambers, Essex Co. REF: Pens. R.6254 N.J.; Susp. Pens.
List (1852) p.419--not proved so far for 6 mo. service; Miss Mary
Hill, Madison, Ind.; Miss Rose Anne Howe, Chicago, Ill.

LEE, SAMUEL   Jackson
(Uncertain; see below). b. 1763, Richmond Co., Va. Pens. appl.
5-19-1834, ae. 71, Spencer Co., Ky. Liv. Hardy Co., Va., till
1790; to Ky.; now liv. Spencer Co., Ky. (The 1840 Pens. List
has a Samuel Lee, ae. 77, pensr. liv. in Jackson Co., Ind., with
John L. Young. I found no positive proof that this Samuel Lee
is the right one, but I think it very likely that he mov. to
Ind. and died before his pens. could be trans. There were six
other Samuel Lee pens. files which were definitely not Ind. A
letter concerning Jackson Co., Ind., in this man's file would
imply that this is the right man; also the age agrees.) Service:
drf. early in 1781, Hardy Co., Va.; in Sept. his father was drf.
& he subst. for father. REF: Pens. S.38138 Va.; 1840 List,p.183.

LEFTYEAR (LEFTTER), URIAH   Franklin
b. 1750. Pens. app. 10-8-1832, ae. 82, Franklin Co., Ind. Service: enl. 1777, res. of Hartford Co., N.C.; 7th Regt., N.C. Line,
Lt Baker, Col. Hogan, Capt. Dickson. Deserted 3-26-1779. REF:
Pens. R.6271 N.C.; Rej. Pens. List (1852) p.408--was a deserter.

LEMON, MOSES   Union
b. ca. 1759, Baltimore Co., Md.; d. 8-29-1852; son of Elias &
Martha Lemon; mar.; chn. (at least): Joshua, & perhaps Joseph.
Pens. appl. Nov. 1844, ae. ca. 85, Union Co., Ind. Liv. in Md.
till ca. 1824; then Ohio for ca. 14 yr.; then Union Co., Ind.
P of A 2-1-1854, Union Co., Ind., from Joshua Lemmon, son, for
any pens. due. 1850 Cens., Liberty Twp., Union Co., Ind.: John
Ferguson, 71, b. Md.; Elizabeth, 41, Md.; Sarah E., 4, Ind.;
Martha E., 1, Ind.; Mary E. Berry, 12, Ind.; Moses Lemon, 91,
Md., Revolutionary Soldier (in enumerator's writing). Following
family: Joseph Lemon, 65, Md.; Emeraine Floyd, 36, Va.; Mary
Floyd, 6, Ohio. Pens. file has a letter 4-22-1884 from Dept. of
Pub. Wks., Toronto, Can., in re "poor woman named Stevenson"
whose grandfather Moses Lemon was a Rev. sold. (I doubt if same
man is meant as letter says he lived in Watertown, N.Y.; letter
was prob. just placed in this file. MRW). Service: enl. 5th
Regt., Md. Mil., ae. ca. 16; Col. Thomas Guess, Capt. Nicholas
Merriman; pvt., 1st Sgt., ensign. REF: Pens. R,6283 Md.; Rej.
Pens. List (1852) p.413--not 6 mo. service; 1850 Cens., v. 23,
p. 288, fams. 105-106.

Le MOUNTAIN, (JOHN) HENRY   Knox
b. ca. 1762; d. 10-10-1834; mar.; chn. (at least): George. The
sold.'s full name was John Henry but evid. used Henry only.
Pens. appl. 8-25-1832, ae. ca. 70; has liv. in Ind. past 20 yr.
Affid. 8-19-1834, Knox Co., Ind., of son George Le Mountain (or
Lehberg as known in the German language) that father belonged to
Lee's Horse. Affid. 8-19-1834, Knox Co., Ind., of Daniel
Strother (negro?) that he also Rev. sold. & knew that Le Mountain
was; see Strother's record later in this Suppl. Service: enl.
Berkeley Co., Va.; Capt. Conway Oldham, Col. Richard Campbell.
REF: Pens. S.32376 Va.

Le PERRA, LATASCO   Clay
Rev. sold. bur. in Zenor Cem. near Bowling Green. Spelling of
this French name may not be correct. REF: Mr. Jacob Luther, for-
mer Clay Co. Commr.; "Sold. of the War of the Rev. in Clay Co.,
Ind." (1929) p. 4, by Posson.

LEWIS, GEORGE   Clark
b. ca. 1764; d. 11-13-1854, ae. 90. Pens. appl. 10-23-1832, ae.
67, Clark Co., Ind. Obit says recd. a discharge from Gen. Washington. Pens. rejected; reason given he would have been too
young to serve. (I know of ones born later for whom there is
positive proof of service. MRW). Letter 5-25-1846 from Thomas
Henley of Washington, D.C., says: "Were not youths admitted into
the service? I think it quite likely that Lewis did enter very
young as his father was in the same service." Letter says father
was in same service; sold.'s age may be forgotten. Affid. 11-12-
1833, Clark Co., Ind., of Charles Biles; that he was in service
with George Lewis. Service; enl. 8-3-1780, Prince Georges Co.,
Md., 1st Md. Regt.; Capt. George Alexander Touman (sp?), 3 yr.
REF: Pens. R.21100 Md.; also in N.W. Indian Wars; "Madison Courier" 12-14-1854, abstr. by Mary Hill, Madison, Ind., p. 110.

LEWIS, WILLIAM   Franklin
Rev. sold. who died there. (No indication that he was pensioned.
There were pens. files for 19 William Lewises; none readily iden-
tifiable). REF: Mr. Schrum.

LINGENFELTER, MICHAEL   Marion
b. 11-17-1762, Frederick, Frederick Co., Md.; mar.; chn. (at
least): 2 sons. Pens. appl. 12-10-1832, ae. 70 last Nov. 17,
Port William Gallatin Co., Ky. After War, liv. in Md.; Va.; &
last 20 yr. in Ky. On 5-26-1835 asks for pens. tr. from Ky. to
Marion Co., Ind., where has 2 sons liv. in Indianapolis; pens.
tr. 7-13-1835. In 1835 Pens. List, Oldham Co., Ky.; pvt. in Md.
Line. Service: enl. summer 1779, Frederick, Md.; Capt. John
Carey. Note: Michael Lingenfelter was prob. bro. of Caterena
(Catharine) Lingenfelter who m. 4-24-1782, Rev. sold., Abraham
Cassel (Cassell), b. 9-25-1755 (chn. listed in his pens. file) of
Jefferson Co., Ky. REF: Pens. S.32379 Md.; 1835 Pens. List, v.3,
p. 128; Pens. W.2916 Md. (of Abraham Cassel).

LITTLEJOHN, JOHN   Jefferson
b. 11-29-1760, Orange Co., N.C. Pens. appl. 8-11-1834, ae. 73
yr., 9 mo., Jefferson Co., Ind. To Burke Co., N.C., when 6-7 yr.
old; there till 1799; to Rutherford Co., N.C., till 1805; to
Scott Co., Ky., till 1805; then Jefferson Co., Ind., for last 33
yr. Last pens. payment 9-4-1837. Methodist preacher. Service:
pvt. 6 mo. Apr. 1781; Capt. Daniel Smith, Col. Charles McDowel,
Burke Co., N.C.; at King's Mt.; later Mounted Rifleman against
Cherokee Indians; various service 1780--1783. REF: Pens.
S.32380 N.C.; Miss Mary Hill, Madison, Ind.

LONG, GEORGE (or SAMUEL)   Washington
Rev. sold; who died there; bur. on Thomas Lockwood farm, 3 mi.
N of Kossuth, as is wife Elizabeth, who d. 1846, ae. 85. Lived
in Monroe Twp. Sold.'s stone destroyed. Name possibly was Sam-
uel, not George. REF: Mr. Schrum; Stevens--"Hist. of Washington
Co., Ind." (1916) p. 633.

LONG, JOSEPH   Washington
b. 10-24-1761; d. 7-9-1824 (pens. file looked like 1827); m. 10-
26-1784, Frederick, Md., Elizabeth -----, b. 2-23-1761; chn. (in
will & in Bible): John b. 7-24-1785; Jacob b. 3-31-1788; Elizabeth b. 9-3-1790; m. 12-4-1816, Washington Co., Ind., John Mallincoat; Sarah b. 2-12-1793; m. Mr. Alstott; Margaret b. 9-
12-1795; m. 1-4-1816, Washington Co., Ind., John Alstott; Susanna b. 7-24-1798; m. 9-25-1819, Washington Co., Ind., Epaheras
(sp?) Phelps; Nancy b. 5-21-1801; m. 12-6-1821, Washington Co.,
Ind., John Perry; Anna b. 1804; m. 6-8-1822, Washington Co.,
Ind., John Umbarger; the will, wr. 3-8-1824 & pr. 9-10-1824,
names dau. Mary Brown, too; wife of James Brown, also named in
record. Wid.'s pens. appl. 9-27-1843. ae. 82 last Feb. 23, Washington Co., Ind.; her husb. could not write in Eng.; so one Samuel Perry wrote the above names in the Bible; her husb. added the
last child Anna in German script: Anna Long, --, 8, 1804. Service:
enl. ca. 1776 while liv. Sharpsburg, Washington Co.,Md. REF: Pens.
W.10201 Md.;Wash. Co.,Ind.,1st Will Rec.,1821-30,p.67;Mar.Bk.A,pp.
5,6,17,54,70.

LOW, JOHN   Franklin
b. 4-15-1763, Ulster Co., N.Y.; son of Nelus Low (Capt. in N.Y.
Troops, fell at Batt. of Saratoga). Pens. appl. 1-7-1834, ae.
71 next Apr. 15, Franklin Co., Ind. After War, liv. Sussex Co.,
N.J.; Wyoming, Pa.; Columbus, O.; now Franklin Co., Ind. Service:
enl. while res. Ulster Co., N.Y., 12-30-1776, 2nd N.Y. Regt.;
Capt. Hornbarrie, Col. Philip Van Cortland. Deserted 1777. Note:
however, is in 1840 Pens. List, ae. 77, as a pensr. REF: Pens.
R.6485 N.Y.; Rej. Pens. List (1852) p.408--was a deserter; 1840
Pens. List, p. 182, Franklin Co., Ind.

LOYD, ROBIN   Jennings
(Also known as Indian Robin; negro).   b. 1760, Dinwiddie Co.,
Va. Pens. appl. 11-10-1834, ae. 74, Jennings Co., Ind., of
Indian Robin, alias Robin Loyd. After War, to N.C. for 21 yr.;
to Indiana Terr.; again appl. 2-12-1838, ae. 80, Jennings Co.,
Ind.; formerly res. in Clark Co., Ind.; in Ind. over 20 yr.
Affid. 9-26-1838, Ripley Co., Ind., of John Grimes; that his
father James Grimes, decd. ("Roster" p. 165) often spoke of Ind-
ian Robin as a Rev. sold. Service: enl. June 1778, Dinwiddie
Co., Va.; Col. Bannister, Lt.-Col. Gee, Maj. Hunt, Capts. John
Jones & Ned Powell. REF: Pens. R.6501 Va.; Susp. Pens. List
(1852) p. 413--for further proof of service.

LUCAS, THOMAS   Marion (?)
(Uncertain). Name obtained after this Suppl. was started. A
Thomas Lucas of Indiana is on the 1831 list of rejected pens.,
reason: "too much property". He had a pens. under the 1818 law;
it was suspended after the 1820 law was passed. There is a
Thomas Lucas in the 1820 Cens. of Monroe Co., Ind., v.4, p.182;
there are two Thomas Lucases in the 1830 Cens. of Marion Co.,
Ind., v.9, pp. 409, 413. (Monroe Co. to Marion Co. was a normal
move). REF: "Rej. Appl. for Pens."(1831) p.71 (see note at end
after Daniel Zink.

LUCAS, WILLIAM   Putnam
b. 12-31-1764, Randolph Co., Va. Pens. appl. 2-19-1845, ae. 81
on 12-31-1844, Cass Twp., Clay Co., Ind. After War, to Montgomery Co., N.C.; now Cass Twp., Clay Co., Ind. (Prob. had mov. to
Putnam Co., Ind., by 1852). Service: enl. late in War, prob. in
fall 1781, in 17th yr., res. of Randolph Co., Va.; Col. John Col-
lier, Lt.-Col. Tibby Belford, Capt. John Knight. REF: Pens.
R.6509 N.C.; Rej. Pens. List (1852) p.408--only 3 mo. service
alleged.

LUSHER, JOHN   Carroll
b. ca. 1750. Pens. appl. 10-18-1832, ae. 82, Carroll Co.,
Ind. Service: enl. Mar. 1779, at Port Tobacco, Md., 1st Regt.,
Md. Line; Maj. Winder (sp?), Capt. Smith. REF: Pens. R.6527 Md.;
Rej. Pens. List (1852) p. 408---was a deserter.

LUSK, WILLIAM   Washington
Rev. sold. who died there. Pens. file shows only that he was a
Capt.; had Penna. service; war issues BLW 1275 for 300 ac. on
7-16-1789. No other papers in file. Co. Hist. gives mid. init.
as R. REF: Natl. Archives; Mr. Schrum; Stevens--"Hist. of
Washington Co., Ind." (1916) p. 634.

LUTHER, JACOB   Clay
b. ca. 1757; m. 1791, Sarah -----, d. 1833; chn. (at least):
Barbara m. Mr. Kendall (she res. Clay Co., Ind., 1852, and said
her parents had liv. in Clay Co. for 4 yr.). Pens. appl. 10-30-
1832, ae. 75, Bowling Green, Clay Co., Ind. Service: enl. at
Frederick, Md., in Md. Mil.; Capt. William Duval, Col. Baker
Johnson. REF: Pens. R.6533 Md.; Rej. Pens. List (1852) p.408--
team service in militia.

LYTLE, FRANCIS   Bartholomew
Picture in Directory below has caption: "Capt. Francis Lytle,
1767-1854, Color Bearer, Penna. Line, War of Revolution." REF:
Bartholomew Co., Ind., Directory, 1903-1904 (pub. 1904), part 2,
p. 80; Mrs. Ira Tranter, Franklin, Ind.

McCALLISTER, ALEXANDER   Delaware
b. 4-22-1761, Chester Co., Pa. Pens. appl. 7-1-1835, Delaware
Co., Ind. Since War liv. Westmoreland Co., Pa.; near Lexington,
Fayette Co., Ky.; Fleming Co., Ky.; Warren Co., O. (where fam.
Bible now is); now Delaware Co., Ind. Service: drf. July 1777,
Westmoreland Co., Pa., near Conemaugh River; Col. John Pomeroy,
Capt. Robert Lower (sp?). REF: Pens. R.6601 Pa.; Rej. Pens.
List (1852) p.408--did not serve 6 mo.

McCARTY, BENJAMIN   Franklin
b. ca. 1759, Va.; d. 8-16-1837, ae. 78; bur. Brookville Twp.;
mar.; chn. (at least): Enoch; Jonathan b. 8-3-1795, Va.; d.
1852, Keokuk, Ia.; Monroe; Isaac m. Margaret Cooksey; Abner
b. 1-29-1797, Granger Co., Tenn.; m. 5-17-1821, Franklin Co.,
Ind., Jane Templeton. McCarty was formerly a local M.E. preacher in Tenn. & then in Franklin Co., Ind.; later became United
Brethren. Entered first land in Franklin Co., Ind., Sec. 32,
Twp. 8 N, Range 1 on 5-25-1803. One of the Judges at the first
Court of Common Pleas, 12-14-1810. REF: Reifel--"Hist. of
Franklin Co., Ind." (1915), pp. 85-89-91-93-232-234-276-280-638-
947; Franklin Co., Ind., Atlas, pp. 12-13-14-61; "Exec. Journ.
of Ind. Terr., 1800-1816", p.167; "Hist. of Fayette Co., Ind.",
p. 114; Smith--"Early Indiana Trials", p. 163.

McCOLLUM, DANIEL   Posey
(Uncertain). b. ca. 1744. Vanderburgh Co., Ind., court records
show his appl. for pens. (under Act of 1818) in 1827, ae. 83, a
res. of Posey Co., Ind. No pens. file found at Natl. Archives
found with papers mentioning Indiana. One for a man b. N.J.;
with N.C. service; later liv. Pendleton Co., S.C.; Habersham
Co., Ga., where seems to have died. REF: "Hist. of Vanderburgh
Co., Ind." (1889) p. 337.

McCOOL, WILLIAM   Johnson
b. June 1759, Co. Derry, Ire. Pens. appl. 11-16-1832, ae. ca.
73, Marion Co., Ind., but a res. of Johnson Co., Ind. Mov. with
his fam. to Washington Co., Pa., before Ohio was settled, close
to Wheeling, ca. 1 mi. from Redstone Old Fort or Brownsville, Pa.
Affid. 1-15- 1833, Marion Co., Ind., of John Eule (Eulez?) that
he has known McCool over 20 yr., mostly in Meneer Co., Ky.; that
McCool came from Ky. to Johnson Co., Ind., ca. 2 yr. ago. (Note:
Many McCools in Johnson Co., Ind., in White River Twp., border-
ing Marion Co., Ind. Possibility that he may be bur. with other
Rev. solds. in Mt. Pleasant Cem. One Marshall McCool, ae. ca.
95, d. ca. 4-5 yr. ago (1953) in Johnson Co., Ind.). Service:
a res. of Pa., he enl. 1775, Chester Co., Pa., ca. 2 yr. before
Brit. took Philadelphia; Capt. Abraham Marshall; later hired a
subst.; after mov. to near Brownsville, Pa., again enl. to protect frontier; Capt. Joseph Thornton. REF: Pens. R.6645 Pa.;
Rej. Pens. List (1852) p.408--only 2 mo. service during the
Revolution; Mrs. Ira Tranter, Franklin, Ind.

McCORMICK, ROBERT   Knox
Rev. sold. bur. in Fairview Cem., Gr. 18, Row 8, Sec. S.R.
REF: Am. Leg.; Mr. Schrum.

McCOY, JOHN   Hendricks
b. ca. 1764-1765; mar.; chn. (at least): George. Pens. appl.
5-13-1833, ae. 68, Hendricks Co., Ind. After War, liv. Tenn. 8
yr.; Ky. 25 yr.; 7 yr. in Ind., Hendricks Co. P of A, 6-26-
1854 of George McCoy, heir, Hendricks Co., Ind. Service: enl.
Mar. 1782, Frederick Co., Va., as subst. for Simon Adams; Maj.
Welch, Capt. William Balis. Later had Indian Wars service.
REF: Pens. R.6663 Va.; Rej. Pens. List (1852) p.408--not 6 mo.
service during the Revolution.

McGILL, JAMES   Washington
(There is still some doubt whether this man died in Ky. or in
Ind. The grave location, however, looks so positive that I am
inclined to think it is correct even if the American Legion did
err in calling him William instead of James; they have the date
correct, the same as James' date of death.). b. ca. 1752; d.
9-20-1834, Washington Co., Ind.; bur. Livonia Cem., Gr. 3, Row
7, Lot 6, Sec. 1; m. 12-20-1775, Sarah -----; chn. (12, incl.
(ages in 1820): Thomas (no age); Samuel 14; William 12;
Anthony 9; Israel 7. Pens. appl. 6-1-1818, Bracken Co., Ky.;
again 9-9-1820, ae. 68, Bracken Co., Ky.; wife ae. 58. On 8-13-
1829, Jefferson Co., Ind., he says he has lately mov. here from
Ky. because all his chn. live here. Wid.'s pens. appl. 1-29-
1838, Pendleton Co., Ky., ae. 79. Says husb. drew pens. in
Bracken Co., Ky., α later liv. in Pendleton Co., Ky., till 1828
"when he removed from said Pendleton Co., Ky.; to the State of
Indiana and settled in Jefferson County, Ind. And while he lived
in Indiana he drew his pension at Coradon (Corydon Agy. MRW) in
that state until shortly before his death, and after his death
she removed back from the state of Indiana to Pendleton County,
Kentucky in order to live with son Thomas McGill and that she

now resides in Pendleton County, Ky.", etc. (I think this means
that the soldier died in Indiana---Jefferson Co. or Washington
Co.---and received his last pension payment shortly before he
died here---not that he moved back to Pendleton Co., Ky., shortly
before he died. The widow definitely seems to have been living
here and not to have moved back to Ky. until after her husband's
death. They may have lived for a while in Harrison Co., Ind., as
this place of residence is given in "Pa. Arch." ref. below; or
since the Corydon Agency was in Harrison Co., Ind., the latter
may have been assumed as the place of residence). Service: enl.
in Pa., 8th Pa. Regt.; Col. Enos McCoy; was a Sgt. REF: Pens.
W.8428 Pa.; 1835 Pens. List, v.3, p.20, Jefferson Co., Ind.;
I.A.R. #7,773; Am. Leg.; "Pa. Arch.", Ser. 3, v.23, p. 595.

McINTOSH, FRANCIS   Decatur
b. 1764-1765, Prince William Co., Va. Pens. appl. 8-14-1837, ae.
74, Decatur Co., Ind. After War, ca. 35 yr. ago, sett. in N.C.;
to E. Tenn. for some yrs.; to Ky. 10-12 yr.; to Ala. 4 yr.; to
Ind. Affid. 10-16-1833 (query--is above date 1833 or 1837?),
Montgomery Co., Ky., of Robert Garrett, who serv. in same Comp.
Service: drf. summer 1781, ae. 17-18, Prince William Co., Va.;
Capt. Valentine Payton, Col. Armsted Churohill; Va. Mil. (Note:
this man is on Mr. Schrum's list as of Bartholomew Co., Ind.).
REF: Pens. R.6741½ Va.; Rej. Pens. List (1852) p. 408--did not
serve 6 mo.

McKNIGHT, DAVID   Dearborn
b. 8-25-1760, Silver Springs, Cumberland Co., Pa.; d. 5-13-1821;
son of John McKnight, Sr., & Jane McAlister; m. 11-18-1790, in
Franklin Co., Pa., Eleanor Maclay (or McClay), b. 2-20-1769; dau.
of John & Jane McClay; chn.: (see below). Wid.'s pens. appl.
8-28-1838, ae. 70, Rising Sun, Dearborn Co., Ind.; also 3-23-
1843, ae. 74. Affid. 8-28-1838, Dearborn Co., Ind., of John
McKnight & Mary Reeder (prob. both chn. of sold.). Affid. 3-9-
1839, Cumberland Co., Pa., of Samuel Maclay, ae. 72 (prob. wid.'s
bro.) who was present at mar. in house of Eleanor's father, John
McClay in Franklin Co., Pa.; same of John Maclay, Esq. (prob. a
bro.) of Boro of Shippensburg, Cumberland Co., Pa. Affid. 7-29-
1839, Montgomery Co., O., that the following leaves were cut out
of the fam. Bible by Dr. Job Haines in the presence of the J.P.:
MARRIAGES: David McKnight & Eleanor Maclay 11-18-1790; James
Bayly & Elizabeth McKnight 3-6-1816; Jesse Reeder & Mary McKnight
4-11-1816; Ralph Turner & Jane S. McKnight 12-11-1828; David
McKnight & Juliana Fenner (or Turner?) 10-15-1829; Job Harnes (or
Haines? see above) & Eliza P. Bayly 12-8-1831." BIRTHS: David
McKnight 8-25-1760; Eleanor Maclay 2-20-1769; Molly McKnight 4-
25-1793; Jane McKnight 4-12-1795; Elizabeth McKnight 3-14-1797;
John McKnight 4-19-1799; Catherine McKnight 11-24-1801; David
McKnight 4-3-1804; Ebenezer Finley (sp?) McKnight 4-9-1806;
Eleanor McKnight 3-17-1808; Charles Maclay McKnight 12-8-1810;
William McKnight 4-10-1814. (Space). John Maclay 5-17-1734,
died 10-7-1804, ae. 70 yr. 6 mo; Jane Maclay b. 12-20-1734, died
4-3-1812, ae. 77 yr. 4 mo.; Catherine Maclay b. 7-28-1760. (Space).
John McKnight, Senr., was born in Scotland and was married to

Jane McAlister and removed to Silver Springs in Cumberland Co.,
Pa., where John, David, Mary, and Jane were born. (Space).
DEATHS: Catherine McKnight 4-8-1803; Charles Maclay McKnight 4-
17-1811; Eleanor McKnight 1-17-1813; William McKnight 6-23-1814;
David McKnight 5-13-1821 in 61st yr. Service: lieut. in 5th Pa.
Regt. REF: Pens. W.10215; BLW 1439 (1789).

McNULTY, SAMUEL   Montgomery
Rev. sold. who died there. REF: Dorothy Quincy Chap., DAR,
Crawfordsville, Ind.

McWHORTER, ROBERT   Washington
b. 2-16-1747, Bucks Co., Pa; m. Jane Alexander, b. ante 1752,
Ire.; d. post husb.; Jane was sis. of Rev. sold., Thomas Alexander; see forward, this Suppl.).; chn.: several; all d. by ca.
1856. Pens. appl. 11-3-1832, ae. 85, Washington Co., Ind. After
War, liv. Bucks Co., Pa.; Lancaster Co., Pa.; 1809 to near Bar-
boursville, Ky., on Cumberland River till ca. 1827; then to Washington Co., Ind. Service: enl. 1777 Middleton, a little above
Lancaster, Pa. (query: is this Middletown, now Womelsdorf, Berks
Co., Pa.?; Capt. James Crouch, Col. Elder; later serv. as subst.
for his bro., William McWhorter, Lancaster Co., Pa. (Note: the
writing seems to be plainly Bucks Co., not Berks Co.; but the
possibility of the other is suggested here). REF: Pens. S.16195
Pa.; 1835 Pens. List, v. 3, p. 75.

MACOM, JOSEPH   Vigo (?)
Uncertain. His affid. in pens. file of John Colwell ("Roster",
p. 82) says that he knew John was a Rev. sold. (See Alison Cruse,
William Durham, Alexander Eagelton, this Suppl.). A Joseph Macon
was appt. Ensign of the 4th Regt., Ind. Terr. Mil. (included
Gibson, Warrick, & Pike Co. men) on 9-19-1811;. offered here as
a possible clue to his residence. REF: Pens. S.16344 (of John
Colwell); "Exec. Journ. of Ind. Terr., 1800-1816", p. 177.

MANESS, AMBROSE   Owen
b. 10-27-1763. Pens. appl. 11-12-1838, ae. 75 last Oct. 27,
Owen Co., Ind. After War, mov. to Montgomery Co., N.C.; to Owen
Co., Ind., ca. 2-1-1835. Service: enl. 10-25-1780, Cumberland
Co., N.C.; Capt. William York, Col. William Gray, Lt. Ralph Lome.
REF: Pens. R.6862 N.C.; Rej. Pens. List (1852) p. 408--did not
perform 6 mo. actual service.

MANN, JOHN   Warren (?)
b. 1751; d. 4-29-1849, Warren Co., Ind. (three affids. say so;
one says d. Hamilton Co., O.; Franklin Co., Ind., Hist. below
says d. 4-30-1848, ae. 99 & bur. Otwell Chapel, Whitewater Twp.,
Franklin Co., Ind.; m. May 1797, Pawlett, Rutland Co., Vt.,
Persia Stratton, b. ca. 1767; chn. (prob. several; see below).
Pens. appl. 10-13-1832, ae. 81, Whitewater Twp., Franklin Co.,
Ind.; on 1-28-1835, asks for pens. tr. from Ind. to Ohio as now
liv. Hamilton Co., O.; chn. there. Pens. was tr. as of 9-4-
1834. Wid.'s pens appl. 5-20-1853, ae. 86, Hamilton Co., O.
Supporting affids. by Ormon Mann (rel. not given) & Mary

VanBlaricum; that they were present at the funeral of John Mann who d. 4-29-1849, Warren Co., Ind. Wid. again appl. 5-24-1855, Hamilton Co., O.; was still there 6-3-1856. Service: enl. 7-28-1779, Newburyport, Mass.; Capt. Jeremiah Putnam, Col. Nathan Tayler (Tyler); later enl. 1781, Hampton, N.H., where liv. dur. War while not in service. REF: Pens. W.2400 Mass., N.H.; 1835 Pens. List, v.3, p.49; 1840 Pens. List, p.182, ae. 90; both in Franklin Co., Ind.; Reifel--"Hist. of Franklin Co., Ind." (1915), p. 280; Franklin Co., Ind., Atlas, p. 79.

MASSY, CHARLES   Monroe
b. 2-28-1760; d. 1-2-1839; m. 3-8-1789, Prince Edward Co., Va., Elizabeth Davis, b. ca. 1763-1769; chn. (on 11-27-1843): James, decd.;   Peter, decd.;   Sherrod (sp?), decd.;   Sevier, decd.; Charles 40;   John 37-38;   Samuel 35;   Enoch, decd.;   Kitty, decd.;   Dolly prob. liv., ca. 44;   Joanna, decd.;   Elizabeth ca. 42;   Patsy ca. 33. Pens. appl. 7-12-1834, ae. 74, Monroe Co., Ind. Sold.'s father d. in Prince Edward Co., Va., the yr. after Cornwallis' defeat at Yorktown. Sold. had 3 bros., 2 older & 1 younger; both older bros. serv. in War considerable part of the time. After War, sold. liv. over 2 yr. in Prince Edward Co., Va.; 1 yr. in Pamelia (Amelia?) Co., Va.; then Prince Edward Co., Va., again ca. 4 yr.; Campbell Co., Va.; then Knox, Jefferson, & Cocke Cos., Tenn.; ca. over 32 yr.; Orange Co., Ind., 4 yr.; to Monroe Co., Ind., over 2 yr. ago. Wid.'s pens. appl. 9-21-1839, ae. 70, Monroe Co., Ind.; 4-3-1843, Orange Co., Ind., liv. with a son; 11-27-1843, ae. 80 (names chn. above); 4-11-1844, still Orange Co., Ind. Service: enl. Prince Edward Co., Va., spring of Gates' defeat at Camden (1780?); Capt. Jesse Owen. Later serv. as subst. for his oldest bro., Thomas Massy, in Capt. Ragsdale's Comp. Service attested by Bazel Newton's widow, Mary Hall (see this Suppl.). REF: Pens. W.9536 Va.

MATLOCK, see Medlock

MAXWELL, THOMAS   Indiana
Papers in pens file withdrawn by Hon. J. W. Davis, 1-22-1836. Letter Nov. 1835 says enl. late in 1776; Capt. Lee, Col. Bland's Regt. of Dragoons   REF: Pens. R.7048; Susp. Pens. List (1852), p 413--not on the rolls -- no proof of service.

MAYBEE, PHILIP   Lagrange
Rev. sold. who died there. REF: Mr. Schrum.

MEDLOCK (MATLOCK?), RICHARD   Jackson
Rev. sold. bur. in Mitchell Cem., Owen Twp.   REF: Ft. Vallonia Chap., DAR, Seymour, Ind.

MIDCAP, JOHN   Jennings
b. 11-15-1763, Alexandria, Va. Pens. appl. 11-10-1835, ae. 69 or 70 this Nov. 15, Jefferson Co., Ind. Letter 9-5-1837 says now in Jennings Co., Ind. Again appl. 1-1-1838, ae. 74, Jennings Co., Ind. Since War, has liv. Ky. (1792 liv. Nelson Co., Ky.) & in Ind.; now liv. Jennings Co., Ind. (Note: a fine was

imposed, and was remitted,* on John Midcap, late a citizen of Jefferson Co., Ind., for selling spirituous liquors without a license by Samuel McKinley, J.P., of Jefferson Co., Ind.). Service: enl. 1780, Fauquier Co., Va.; Capt. Moorhead, Col. Elias Edmonds; enl. again at Prince William Co., Va. After War, was in Indian Wars, July 1790; enl. at Birdstown; Col. Whitty. REF: Pens. R.7155 Va.; Rej. Pens. List (1852) p. 408--service after the Revolution. * 10-29-1819

MILLER, BARNEY   Spencer
b. ca. 1764, near Josephtown, Pa.; mar.; chn.: at least 2 sons & 2 daus. Pens. appl. 9-17-1832, ae. ca. 68, Breckenridge Co., Ky. Mov. to Berkley Co., Va., when ca. 10 yr. old; there ca. 17 yr.; then to Breckenridge Co., Ky. Affid. 9-17-1832, Breckenridge Co., Ky., of George Paul, who serv. in same Comp. Sold. is in 1835 Pens. List, Breckenridge Co., Ky.; pvt. in Va. Mil. On 1-5-1836 asks for pens. tr. to near Rockport, Spencer Co., Ind.; has 2 daus. & 2 sons liv. in Ind.; attested by Nicholas Miller & Barney Miller (sons?); pens. tr. 9-6-1836. In 1840 Pens. List, which incorrectly gives sold. Nicholas liv. with Barney & should be vice versa. Service: enl. spring 1781, Berkeley Co., Va.; Capt. McIntire, Col. Darke, REF: Pens. S.16973 Va.; 1835 Pens. List, v.3, p.76; 1840 Pens. List, p. 185.

MILLER, BENJAMIN   Marion
Rev. sold. who died there. In 1840 Pens. List, ae. 90, Wayne Twp., liv. with James Miller. REF: Mr. Schrum; 1840 Pens.,p.183.

MILLER, JACOB   Wayne
b. ca. 1763-1764; d. 1827, ae. 64; bur. King Cem. on Charles Wilson farm, Wayne Twp., ca. 1 mi. NW of Richmond, Ind., along the Chicago Division, Pa. R.R.; flag in metal holder on grave; m. Mary Vinnedge (dau. of Adam Vinnedge; see later this Suppl.). (Note: this man would not be the one in "Roster", p.253, of Montgomery Co., Ind., died 1839). REF: Mrs. Forrest E. Kempton, Centerville, Ind., whose husband's aunt, Mrs. Clara Kempton, ae. 88, says Jacob Miller was a Rev. sold.

MILLER, NICHOLAS   Spencer
Rev. sold. who died there. REF: Mr. Schrum.

MILLS, HARDY   Putnam
b. 1763, Halifax Co., N.C.; d. 3-6-(or 5)-1841, Greencastle, Ind.; mar.; chn.: at least 2 sons, incl. Henry. Pens. appl. on 11-25-1833, ae. 70, Hawkins Co., Tenn. On 2-12-1838, Putnam Co., Ind., asks for pens. tr to live in Putnam Co. with son & another son abt to move to Ind. In 1835 Pens. List, Hawkins Co., Tenn.; pvt. in N.C. Line. Pens. tr. from Jonesboro, Tenn., Agy., 4-17-1838. Letter 5-21-1857, Greencastle, Ind., from son Henry Mills mentions heirs, Service: enl. late summer 1780, Wilkes Co., N.C.; Capt. Nawl (Noll?), Col. Elisha Isaacs. Pens. file envelope has forename Handy, but sold.'s Tenn. appl. & Ind. tr. papers both say Hardy. REF: Pens. S.33100 N.C.; 1835 Pens. List, v.3, p. 68.

MONICAL, MOSES   Washington
Rev. sold. bur. in Mt. Pleasant Cem. REF: Mr. Schrum; Stevens--
"Hist. of Washington Co., Ind." (1916) p.633; Morris--"Hist. &
Arch. Survey of Washington Co., Ind." (1925) p.379.

MOORE, ASA   Posey
b. ca. 1764; d. 9-20-1834; m. 3-7-1790, Prince Georges Co., Md.,
Elizabeth Thomas, b. ca. 1766; chn.: at least, Lucy. Pens. appl.
3-21-1831, ae. 67, Hardin Co., Ky.; has wife 63, dau. 32 & her
ch., ae. 2. He serv. in Rev. with Thomas Hammond, liv. spr. 1830
in Meade Co., Ky. (more data abt. Hammond & his fam.). Affid.
10-28-1830 of Thomas Hammond, ae. 67; that he serv. in same Comp.
with Asa Moore & Nicholas Farr. Affid. of Nicholas Farr, Dist.
of Col.; that he serv. with Moore. Sold. again appl. for pens.
9-27-1832, ae. 68, Edgar Co., Ill. Wid.'s appl. 10-18-1839, ae.
73, Hardin Co., Ky.; attested by Lucy Moore, dau., ae. 40, Hardin
Co., Ky.; also by Mrs. Elenor Peck, ae. 68, Hardin Co., Ky., sis.
of Elizabeth Moore. Affid. of Ann Wilson Selby, Washington Co.,
Ky., sis. of Elizabeth Moore & wife of Richard Selby. On 6-1-
1843, wid. ae. 72-73, Hardin Co., Ky.; also on 12-7-1848. Service:
enl. 1779, Md.; Col. Peter Adams, Capt. Thomas Boyd. REF: Pens.
W.3030 Md.; A.G. 50,119; Brumbaugh--"Rev. War Rec. of Va.", v.1,
p.557; Miss Thelma Murphy, Indianapolis, Ind.

MORGAN, DANIEL   Switzerland
Rev. sold. who d. 1839. REF: Mrs. Herbert R. Hill, Indianapolis.

MORRIS, THOMAS   Randolph
b. ca. 1749. Pens. appl. 8-13-1834, ae. ca. 85, Randolph Co.,
Ind. Letter 8-15-1834 from Centerville, Wayne Co., Ind. Service:
drf. Mar. ca. 1780, N.C. Mil., while a res. of Pasquotank Co.,
N.C.; Capt. Owen Williams, Lt. James Greaves. REF: Pens. R.7409
N.C.; Rej. Pens. List (1852) p.408--did not serve 6 mo.

MORROW, JOHN   Jefferson
(Not the one in "Roster", p.261, of Marion Co., Ind.).
b. 6-17-1761, 10 mi. from Carlisle, Cumberland Co., Pa.; mar.;
chn.: at least 5, incl. Mary, b. Mar. 1797; m. Mr. King. Pens.
appl. 6-27-1833, se. 78, Worthington, Richland Co., O. After
War, liv. Westmoreland Co., Pa.; Alleghany Co., Pa.; Butler Co.,
Pa.; Wayne Co., O.; Richland Co., O. On 10-8-1844, has been liv.
in Jefferson Co., Ind., for 1 yr.; attested by dau., Mary King--
that father nearly 90; that she b. Mar. 1797; that father had 4
chn. older than herself. Affid. 12-24-1844, Ripley Co., Ind.,
of Isaac Levi, Sr., ae. 100 ("Roster" p.235) that he serv. with
sold. Service: enl. 1776, Hannastown, Hempfield Twp., Westmoreland Co., Pa.; Capt. William Guttery (Query:Guthrie?). REF:
Pens. S.33121 Pa.

MULBERRY, JOHN   Scott
b. ca. 1755; d. 4-14-1838 (pens. file; I.A.R. errs in 11-13-1826)
at home of step-son, Thomas Spillers; m. 8-22-1792, Scott Co.,
Ky., Mrs. Elizabeth Spillers (wid. of Philip Spillers); she d.
11-25-1842, at son Thomas Spillers' home; chn.: at least, Fanny,

b. ca. 1794; m. Mr. Drain; Cela, b. ca. 1797; Mary, b. ca.
1800; m. Mr. Hopkins. Pens. appl. 6-17-1818, Bath Co., Ky.; &
10-21-1820, ae. 65, Bath Co., Ky.; wife & 3 daus. liv. with him,
1 mar. & 2 with him, Fanny ca. 26, Cela ca. 23, Mary 20. On
8-1-1834, ae. 81 in Oct., Bath Co., Ky. Affid. of son-in law,
Francis Hopkins; that sold. lives on his farm. In 1835 Pens. List
Bath Co., Ky.; pvt. in Va. Line. On 3-23-1837, Scott Co., Ind.,
asks for pens. tr. to Scott Co., Ind., as self & wife will live
with her son, Thomas Spiller, Esq., of Scott Co., Ind.; pens. tr.
4-23-1837. Affid. 8-12-1850, Scott Co., Ind., of William H. English; that sold. m. Elizabeth Spillers 8-22-1792, Scott Co., Ky.;
that she d. 11-25-1842, Scott Co., Ind., at home of Thomas Spiller; that she had chn. by sold.--Fanny Drain & Mary Hopkins.
Affid. 9-20-1850, Lawrence Co., Ill., of Thomas Spillars, son of
Elizabeth by her 1st husb. Service: enl. Sept. 1775, Stafford
Co., Va., near Falmouth, ca. 3 mi. from Williamsburg, Va., 2nd
Va. Regt.; Capt. William Talliaferrio; later was sent to Hunters
Factory (munitions); after term over, stayed there 10-12 yr.
REF: Pens. W.9584 Va.; 1835 Pens. List, v.3, p.20.

MULL, ----- Washington
Rev sold. who died there. REF: Mr. Schrum.

NEAL, BENJAMIN Shelby
b. ca. 1760; d. 4-15-1853, at home of Woodbeck Low; m. 1805 in
Ohio (having gone from Ky. across Ohio River to be mar.), Delilah
Barton, b. ca. 1761; chn. (ages in 1857): Joseph 51; Mary 47-
48; m. Mr. Bird; Mathew H., decd.; Richard B.; Matilda m.
Woodbeck Low; Thomas T., decd.; Joshua, decd.; John;
Mahala m. Mr. Thomas. In 1851, Mary Neal Bird's addr. was % of
William Bird, Washington, D.C. (rel. not given). Affid. 1854,
Shelby Co., Ind., of Woodbeck Lowe; that he knew sold. & wife for
2 yr. After War, sold. mov. to Ky.; in 1833, Butler Co., Ky.;
May 1852, to Marion Co., Ind.; then Shelby Co., Ind. In 1835
Pens. List, Logan Co., Ky.; pvt. in Va. Line; in 1840 Pens. List,
Muhlenburg Co., Ky., ae. 80; pens. tr. to Ind., 8-24-1852. Wid.
liv. Rush Co., Ind.; Shelby Co., Ind.; & much time in D.C.; her
pens. tr. to D.C., 4-24-1857. Service: enl. 1777, Fauquier Co.,
Va.; Capt. Francis Atwell, Col. Martin Pickett, Va. Mil.; serv.
several wks. as subst. for his father who liv. Fauquier Co., Va.,
1777; other service. REF: Pens. W.10220 Va.; 1835 Pens. List,
v.3, p.114; 1840 Pens. List, p.165; Mrs. Ira Tranter, Franklin,Ind.

NEAL, CHARLES Switzerland
b. 1762-1763; d. 8-27-1831; m. Aug. 1784, Orange Co., Va., Ann ---,
b. ca. 1768; d. 7-30-1854; chn. (from Bible): Libbert M., b. 7-4-
1786; Margaret M., b. 2-2-1788; Charles, b. 2-22-1790;
Fielding b. 8-24-1792; John b. 11-30-1794; Poley b. 6-13-
1797; Betsy b. 9-1-1799; plus (not in Bible; ages 8-7-1820):
Anny 18; William A. 16; Lucy 14; Pens; appl. 4-22-1818, ae.
55, Scott Co., Ky. After War, liv. Madison Co., Ky.; Scott Co.,
Ky.; then Switzerland Co., Ind.; again appl. 8-7-1820, ae. 58; 6
in fam., incl.: Anny 52, Betsy 20, Anny 18, William A. 16, Lucy
14. Wid.'s pens. appl., ae. 70, Switzerland Co., Ind.; 7-6-1844

Pleasant Twp., Switzerland Co., Ind., ae. 76; 9-18-1848, ae. 80. Affid. 12-31-1818, Scott Co., Ky., of John Jacobs; that he serv. in same Regt. Service: enl. ca. 1779-1780; Col. William Washington's Regt. of Light Dragoons, 3rd Va. Regt. REF: Pens. W.9587 Cont. (Va.).

NEWKIRK, BENJAMIN   Jackson
b. 12-25-1754; d. 5-17-1840; bur. Brown Cem., Carr Twp.; m. Elgie -----, b. 3-11-1777; d. Oct. 1857, ae. 80. REF: Fort Vallonia Chap., DAR, Seymour, Ind.; Mrs. Claude E. Gilliatt, Seymour.

NEWKIRK, HENRY CONCKRIGHT   Franklin
b. 1760 (pens. file); bap. 6-21-1767, prob. Walikell, N.Y.; son of Henry & Agnes Anna (White) Newkirk; d. 1839 (evidence points to Ind., but Brewer below says Hamilton Co., O.); m. Julia Anna Taylor, b. 9-20-1770; d. 9-25-1836, ae. 66 yr., 5 da.; both bur. Little Cedar Cem., SE of Brookville on Riley Woodworth Farm; chn.: Katurah b. 6-30-1789, N.Y.; d. 9-12-1862, Franklin Co., Ind.; m. 11-30-1805, prob. Seneca, Ontario Co., N.Y., Ryleigh Woodworth, b. 8-1-1782, Salisbury, Conn.; d. 2-24(25?)-1855, Laurel, Franklin Co., Ind. (both bur. Little Cedar Cem.); mov. 1814 from N.Y. to Franklin Co., Ind. (he a son of Dyer Woodworth; see "Roster" p.389; Temperance b. 3-28-1792; d. 12-1-1832; m. Henderson Haggerty; Abraham Taylor b. 3-16-1793; d. 10-6-1890; m. 12-16-1815, Pamelia Osborn, b. 8-21-1796; d. 5-10-1863; Absalom W. (liv. 1866, Edwardsville, O.), m.(1); m.(2) 1843, Lucretia Thurston; Malinda m. Zeala Yoast (liv. in Mo.); Charles G. b. 11-11-1800; d. 12-8-1850; m. 4-11-1826, Margaret Milholland, b. 5-14-1809; d. 9-20-1877; Cornelius S. b. 3-24-1803; d. 1-28-1885; m. 12-24-1824, Mary E. Lackey, b. 4-16-1807; d. 2-16-1866; Artemedoris W. b. 5-31-1805; d. 4-19-1872; m.(1) Julia Ann Montgomery, d. 1833; he m.(2) 8-6-1843, Brookville, Ind., Lucretia Ann Thurston (note discrepancy above), b. 1821; d. 7-31-1890; Mary Ann b. 8-9-1807; m. John Bell (liv. in Mo.); Sarah V. m.(1) Andrew Smith; m.(2) Mr. Garrett; Elizabeth d. 1872; m. John Weller. Pens. appl. 10-14-1835, ae. 75, Brookville Twp., Franklin Co., Ind. Liv. Seneca, Ontario Co., N.Y.; in ca. 1819-1820, ae. ca. 60, liv. on hill near Brookville near Woodworth farm. Service: enl. 9-1-1778 at Newburgh on the North River, a res of Ulster Co., N.Y., in 1st Regt., N.Y. Line; Capt. John Newkirk, Col. William Falkner (pens. file); data wrong (prob. accts. for rejected pens.); official data: pvt. in 2nd Regt. (Capt. Faulkner) & 3rd Regt. (Capt. William Faulkner & Capt. John Newkirk), both Ulster Co., N.Y., Mil. REF: Pens. R.7622 N.Y.; Susp. Pens. List (1852)p.413--not on the rolls--no proof of service; Reifel--"Hist. of Franklin Co., Ind." (1915) p.278; Brewer--"Hist. of Brewer Fam. & Related Fams." (n.d.) pp.45,52-56; Roberts--"N.Y. in the Rev." (1898, 2nd ed.) pp.191,193,195,197.

NEWNAM, JOSHUA   Hendricks
b. ca. 1756. Pens. appl. 2-10-1834, ae. 78, Marion Co., Ind., but a res. of Brown Twp., Hendricks Co., Ind. Service: enl. ante Batt. of Saratoga, while res. of Queen Anne Co., Md., in Md. Line or Dela. Line; Capt. William Faulkener. REF: Pens. R.7631 Md.; Susp. Pens. List (1852) p.413--for proof of actual service.

NEWTON, JOHN Decatur
b. 1-17-1755, Montague, Hampshire Co., Mass.; d. 9-29-1839, St. Omer, Ind.; m. 1-29-1789, Deerfield, Mass., Abigail Parker, b. ca. 1768; chn.: others besides Calvin. Pens. appl. 8-11-1835, ae. 80 last Jan., Decatur Co., Ind. Liv. Deerfield, Mass., till ca. 40 yr. old; then Bristol, Ontario Co., N.Y., 14-15 yr.; Ky.; Ohio; Decatur Co., Ind., ca. 1826. Liv. with son Calvin. Wid.'s pens. appl. 12-13-1850, ae. 82, Rush Co., Ind.; other chn. besides Calvin. Affid. May 1851, Rush Co., Ind., of Mary P. Newton (rel. not given). Service: enl. Mar. 1775; Capt. Joseph Stebbins, Deerfield, Mass. REF: Pens. W.9589 Mass.; A.G. 50,125; Brumbaugh--Rev. War Rec. of Va., v.1, p. 558; Miss Thelma Murphy, Indianapls.
NIGHSWONGER, SOLOMON--see p. 118.

NOBLE, JONATHAN Madison
Rev. sold. who died there. REF: Mr. Schrum.

NOLAND, JAMES Vermillion
b. 1760, Liverpool, Eng.; d. 1835; m. 1785, Miss Emmerson; d.1830; chn. (at least): Susan, b. 1807; d. 1844; m. 1825, Joshua Dean, b. 1788; d. 1878. Service: pvt. in Col. Daniel Morgan's Regt. of Va. Riflemen, 1777-1779. REF: DAR Lineage Bk., v.158, p.130.

NORTH, JOHN Marion
b. 1754, S.C. Pens. appl. 3-30-1837, ae. ca. 83, Marion Co., Ind. After War liv. Ga.; 30 yr. in Ohio; 9 yr. in Ind. Service: enl. in S.C. ca. 1773-1774-1775 & serv. 1 mo. in the spring as a Ranger on the Frontier; Capt. Pollard; then mov. to Ga. & enl. again at Louisville (query: Ky.?) ca. 1774-1775-1776 or 1777 again as a vol. Ranger in Mil.; 2 yr. service under Capt. Alexander Irwin, Col. Triggs; had no clothes for the Comp. & got some ca. 1776-77-78-79 just after British had left Savannah. REF: Pens. R.7707 S.C.; Rej. Pens. List (1852) p.409--. Indian Wars before the Rev.

NUTT, LEVI Union
d. there; m. Sarah -----; chn. (at least): Aaron, b. Centerville, O.; m. there, Jane Forbes. Levi Nutt was one of 1st settlers in Union Co., Ind. He owned & cleared 160 ac. of land, where he d., having come here from Centerville, O.; was of an established Colonial fam. When son Aaron came, Levi gave him 80 ac. which he had entered; Aaron later bought out father & owned 240 ac. Service: "had been a soldier in the Revolution". REF: Beers--"Comm. Biog. Rec. of Indianapolis & Vicin." (1908) p. 370; Mrs. Irene Strieby, Indianapolis, Ind.

ODLER (OUTLER), FRANCIS Indiana
(Uncertain). His name is one of eight Revolutionary soldiers listed in a memorial to Congress, approved by the Legislature on 12-24-1830. There are pens. files for six of the eight. Odler may have died soon after---thus making it unnecessary to pursue the matter. REF: "Laws of Indiana, 1830-1831", p.176; Miss Dorothy Riker, Indianapolis, Ind.

OLINGER, JACOB   Carroll
b. 10-3-1763. Pens. appl. (undated) enclosed in letter dated
6-11-1832, Delphi, Ind. Settled early in Carroll Co., Ind., from
Tenn. Service: drf. 1781 while res. Augusta Co., Va.; Capt. John
Cunningham, Col. Samson Mathis; Portsmith, Va.; tr. to Capt.
Camel Camron; later under Capt. Samuel McCutchen & Col. William
Boyers. REF: Pens. R.7787 Va.; Rej. Pens. List (1852) p.409--
only 3 mo. & 20 da. service; "Hist. of Carroll Co., Ind." (1882)
page 169.

OVERLEESE, CONRAD   Rush
b. ca 1754, prob. Va.; d. 7-20-1834, ae. 80; bur. Overleese Cem.
near Milroy, Ind.; stone; m. 11-7-1788, Franklin Co., Va., Peggy
Hairston; chn.(all m. in Dayton, O.): Jacob;   Nancy m. Mr.
Small ;   Abraham b. 1796, Franklin Co., Va.; d. 1872, Dayton,
O.; m.(1) Mary -----; m.(2) 4-11-1854, Ruth Longwell;   Henry b.
1797, Va.; m. 7-22-1813. Mary Small;   Daniel b. 1798, Va.; d.
1868, Milroy, Ind.; m. 1-4-1819, Anna Margaret Hiser;   Mary b.
1801, Va.; d. 1879, east of Lucerne, Cass Co., Ind.; m. 4-4-1820,
George Foglesong, Jr.;   Elizabeth b. 1803, Va.; d. 1869, Milroy,
Ind.; m. 2-3-1822, David Witters;   Catharine b. 1803, Va.; d.
1874, Washington Twp., Cass Co., Ind.; m. Michael Bruner;   John
b. 1806, Va.; d. 1870, Milford (Milroy?), Ind.; m. 9-23-1830,
Susannah Sturgeon;   Susan b. 1809 (sic), Ky.; d. 1846, Cass Co.,
Ind. (Fry Cem.); m. 11-25-1830, William Sturgeon;   George b.
1809 (sic), Ohio; m. 4-1-1841, Hetty Zumbrum;   James b. 1810,
Ohio; m. 6-16-1834, Sharlotte Leonard. Abraham Overleese (son of
Conrad) has will dated 11-17-1868, rec. Dayton, O.; names bros. &
sists. & if deceased, their descendants (Estate Papers 10,039,
Probate Court, Montgomery Co., O.). John Foglesong, gr-son of
Conrad Overleese, states his gr-father on his mother's side fought
throughout the entire period of the Rev. War. REF: Kingman--
"Atlas Map of Fulton Co., Ind." (1883) p.56; Mrs. Hazel Overleese,
Rushville, Ind.

OWEN, HARRAWAY   Decatur
b. ca. 1763, Essex Co., Va.; d. 8-15-1834 (tombstone); m. spring
1802-1803, Scott Co., Ky., Elizabeth Gibson, b. ca. 1769. Pens.
appl. 2-25-1833, ae. ca. 70, Columbia Twp., Jennings Co., Ind.
After War, liv. Essex Co., Va.; 1788 to Fayette Co., Ky., for 9
yr.; Scott Co., Ind. (Ky.?); Decatur Co., Ind.; Jennings Co.,
Ind. Affid. of bro. Charles Owens, Scott Co., Ky.; that his
father's fam & sold.'s fam. mov. together in 1788 to Fayette
Co., Ky. Wid.'s pens. appl. 5-26-1853, ae. 83, Decatur Co., Ind.
Affid 1-3-1853, Decatur Co., Ind., of John Owens (rel. not
given) that he present at sold.'s mar. Wid. still alive Decatur
Co., Ind., ae. 84, 12-13-1853; 4-23-1855, ae. 86; also 9-11-1856.
Service: drf. 4-4-1781, Essex Co., Va.; Capt. Philip Lee, Col.
James Dabney. (Although pens. file gives res. as Jennings Co.,
Ind., and sold. died soon after, affid. in file says. he died in
Decatur Co., Ind. & has a tombstone). REF: Pens. W.5463 Va.;
BLW 26404; 1835 Pens. List, v.3, p.56, Jennings Co., Ind.

OWENS, EDMUND   Posey
b. 2-14-1755, Dorset Co., E. Shore, Md. Pens. appl. 8-11-1836,
ae. 81 last Feb. 14, Robb Twp., Posey Co., Ind.---Mov. with parents to Craven Co., near Newberry, N.C., till Rev. War. Service:
enl. Oct. 1778; Capt. Archibald Weeks, Col. William Caswell;
rendezvoused in Kingston, Lenoir Co., N.C. REF: Pens. R.7843
N.C.; Susp. Pens. List (1852) p.413--N.C. Militia service
overrated.

OWENS, WILLIAM   Indiana
(Uncertain). His name is one of eight Revolutionary soldiers
listed in a memorial to Congress, approved by the Legislature on
12-24-1830. There are pension files for six of the eight. Owens
may have died soon after---thus making it unnecessary to pursue
the matter. REF: "Laws of Indiana, 1830-1831" p.176; Miss
Dorothy Riker, Indianapolis, Ind.

PARNELL, STEPHEN   Decatur
b. ca. 1762. Pens. appl. 11-13-1832, ae. ca. 70, Decatur Co.,
Ind. Service: while res. of Anne Arundel Co., Md., enl. 4-3-1778, Ellicott's Mills, 4th Md. Regt.; Capt. Norwood. Name on
roll is Purnell; deserted on furlough, 5-5-1780. REF: Pens.
R.7976 Md.; Rej. Pens. List (1852) p.409--was a deserter.

PATTERSON, JOHN   Jackson
b. 1755; d. 9-2-1847, ae. 92; bur. Mitchell Cem., Owen Twp.;
mar.; chn. (surv. in 1849): John; Jane m. George Levinston;
Hugh. No pens. appl. Extant are the following affids., all
from Jackson Co., Ind. On 8-13-1849 of Travis Carter, ae. 30,
admr. in Prob. Ct.; that sold. was a Capt. in 2nd Regt., Pa.;
Col. Stewart; wife decd.; only surv. chn. (as listed above).
On 9-19-1849 of John G. Young, ae. 56; that sold. was a Capt. in
Rev. in Pa.; that sold.'s house burned ca. 14 yr. ago. On 12-27-1853 of James Ireland, Sr.; that sold. liv. Pa.; then a short
time in Ohio; then in Jackson Co., Ind. On 3-8-1854 of Samuel
Cutshaw of Washington Co., Ind.; that he (deponent) formerly liv.
Lancaster Co., Pa.; knew some of sold.'s sisters there & they
spoke of bro. John in Jackson Co., Ind.; that he later mov. to
Jackson Co. & met sold. Service: (as given by affids. above):
Capt. in 2nd Regt., Pa. (Lancaster Co.?); Col. Ctewart. REF:
Pens. R.8004 Pa.; Rej. Pens. List (1852) p.409--(deceased)--
claim for elleged service in this case already allowed.

PAVEY, SAMUEL   Madison
b. July 1761, Accomack Co., Va. Pens. appl. 8-12-1833, ae. 72
last July. After War, liv. a no. of yrs. in Dela., Ky., Ohio;
in 1818-1819 to Wayne Co., Ind.; liv. Wayne Co. & Fayette Co.,
Ind., till 12-14 mos. ago to Madison Co., Ind. Affids. supporting service records made by Bethuel F. Morris of Marion Co.,
Ind., & Olner (sp?) H. Smith of Fayette Co., Ind. O.H. Smith,
Senate, in letter of 12-5-1837, says that there were two men
named Samuel Pavy, the other a fifer who may have deserted; but
that this Samuel did not desert. Service: enl. 8-10-1781 (?),
Guilford Co., N.C., the August before the Battle of Eutaw Springs;

was in the Militia under Capt. Smith Moore; in Capt. Lytle's
10th Regt.; 1782.. REF: Pens. R.8017 N.C.; Rej. Pens. List (1852)
p.409--desertion.

    PAYNE, AUGUSTINE   Parke
b. 12-11-1761, Fauquier Co., Va.; d. 3-16-1844, Raccoon Twp.; m.
Jan. 1787, Culpeper Co., Va., Catharine -----, b. 7-12-1769;
chn (12? Bible gives only 11): John b.2-14-1790; Lewis b. 5-7-
1792; Sally T.(?) b. 12-4-1794; Delilah b.4-16-1796; James
b. 7-9-1799; Benjamin b. 10-9-1801; Harrison b. 10-23-1803;
William b 1-20-1806; Willis b. 1-31-1808; Lucinda b. 8-3-
1809; Joseph b. 9-18-1814. Pens. appl. 8-31-1832, ae. 70, Fauquier Co., Va.; in 1835 Pens. List, Fauquier Co., Va.; pvt. in
Va. Mil.; 6-10-1836, Parke Co., Ind., asks for pens. tr. to Ind.
as chn. mostly live in Ind. & wants to live with or near them;
attested by James Payne (rel. not given; son?); pens. tr. 7-7-
1836. Wid.'s pens. appl. 12-19-1844, ae. 74, Raccoon Twp., Parke
Co., Ind. Affid. of James Payne, Sr., ae. 55, distant rel. of
Augustine; had liv. within 3 mi. of him in Fauquier Co., Va.,
till he mov. to Parke Co., Ind., 1835; sold. had 12 chn., the
eldest near his own age, 55. After sold.'s death, his fam. rec.
went to son Joseph. Affid. 12-19-1844, Raccoon Twp., Parke Co.,
Ind., of dau. Delilah, ae. 48; affid. 12-19-1844, Parke Co.,
Ind., of son Joseph, ae. 30. Letter 9-18-1877 from son James
that he liv. now at Tipton, Manitou Co., Mo., and 9-27-1877, that
only 1 memb. of the fam. besides him is still alive. Service:
enl. Nov. 1780; Capt. John O'Bannon. REF: Pens. W.10850 Va.;
1835 Pens. List, v.2, p.133.

    PEARCE, THOMAS   Monroe
In 1835 Pens. List, ae. 84; pvt. in Va. Cont. Line. No pens.
file found at Natl. Archives. REF: Mr. Schrum; 1835 Pens. List,
v. 3, p. 60.

    PETERSON, LEMUEL   Delaware
Incorrectly given as Patterson. b. 2-22-1764. Pens. appl.
5-2-1835, ae. 71, Delaware Co., Ind. Papers withdrawn; letter
12-30-1836, Hon. W. Henderson.* REF: Pens. R.21900 N.J.; Susp.
Pens. List (1852) p.413--under age---privateer service, N.J.
Mil. Service overrated. *Service:left father's house in Cumberland Co.,N.J., to serve on a privateer vessel.

    PETTIT, JOHN   Clark
b. 1760; d 1853; bur. Turner Cem. on Flint Ridge Rd., 1½ mi. S
of Bethel Church; m. Catharine -----, b. 1760; d. 1853; bur. in
same cem.; chn. Was the first regular ferryman at mouth of Bull
Creek; it descended to his gr-son, John Pettit. The sold., John
Pettit & wife Catharine, with John & Sophia Fislar ("Roster"
p.142), founded oldest church in Ind. on 11-22-1798, Fourteen
Mile Church on Owens Creek (now Fourteen Mile Creek), later
called Charlestown Baptist Church, now called Silver Creek Bapt.
Church. No proof as yet of Rev. service. REF: Clark Co., Ind.,
Cem. Rec., I.S.L.; Baird--"Hist. of Clark Co., Ind." (1909) pp.
237-238, 63; "Hist. of Ohio Falls Cities & Their Cos." (1882)
v.2, pp. 378, 398.

PICKET, HEATHCOTE   Switzerland
Rev. sold. who died there. REF: Mr. Schrum.

PIERSON, MOSES   Vigo
b. 6-9-1765, Somerset Co., N.J.; d. Feb. 1834; mar. in Ky.;
chn. (heirs). Pens. appl. 2-10-1834, ae. 69, Vigo Co., Ind.
After War, liv. in Ky. (where serv. again in Indian Wars) till
1830 to Vigo Co., Ind. Affid. 7-5-1836, Pittsfield, Pike Co.,
Ill., of Moses & Isaac Riggs; that they knew Pierson, late of
Vigo Co., Ind., whose heirs now apply for pens.; that Pierson
was raised by their father in Somerset Co., N.J.; that they knew
Pierson was a waggoner in Rev. & that he was ca. 13 yr. old when
he first entered service in 1777. Letter 1-27-1838 that Pierson
d. Feb 1834 ca. 10-15 days after date of the orig. process in
court. Service: enl. Somerset Co., N.J., prob. summer 1778;
Capt. Henry Southard. REF: Pens. R.8247 N.J.; Rej. Pens. List
(1852) p.409--(deceased since)--not 6 mo. service.

PITCHER, WILLIAM   Johnson
d. 1831-1835 (will wr. 1831; pr. Nov. 1835); mar.; chn. (at
least): Susannah b. 9-1-1799; m. Mr. Swingle; Morgan; Franklin; William; Beny; Margaret m. Mr. McAbee; Ellender m.
Mr. Redwine. Liv. in Nineveh Twp., Johnson Co., Ind., in 1830.
Bible, said to be owned now by a desc. in Connersville, Ind., is
said to have notation: "Grandfather served in the Revolution."
Service: (from Adj. Gen.'s Office):"Copies of Virginia records
for the Court of Orange Co., Va., show under April 1782 that one
William Pitcher made claim for beef supplied for the public use
and his name appears on a list as a soldier of the Virginia Infantry, Revolutionary War." (Note: he is prob. the William Pitcher who in 1792 sold 50 ac. on North Fork Holston on Rattler's
Creek--"Annals of Southwest Virginia"). REF: Adj. Gen. Office;
Gwathmey--p.627; Mrs. Ira Tranter, Franklin, Ind.

PITTMAN, -----   Wayne
bur. in King Cem. on Charles Wilson farm, Wayne Twp., ca. 1 mi.
NW of Richmond, Ind., along the Chicago Division, Pa. Ry. A
descendant, Benjamin Pittman died a short time ago (summer 1953).
REF: Mrs. Forrest E. Kempton, Centerville, Ind.

POLLOCK, JOHN   Rush
Uncertain as to whether he d. in Ind. and as to Rev. War altho
sources would indicate the latter at least. No pens. file found
at Natl Archives except record that BLW 10040 & 10204 were issued 7-16-1795 to Margaret Pollock, admx. of John Pollock, pvt.
in Pa. Line. This would not seem to apply to the Rush Co. man
about whom the 1835 Pens List says ae. 69 (prob. in 1832); pvt.
in Va. Mil. (However, the disputed Va.-Pa. region might be remembered). REF: Mr. Schrum; 1835 Pens. List vol. 3, p. 66;
Natl Archives pens. files.

PORTER, NICHOLAS BRENT   Washington
b. 5-10-1763, Stafford Co., Va. (prob. son of Nicholas Porter,
Sr.; Sr. & Jr. both in 1782-1787 tax lists of Culpeper Co., Va.);
birth prob. rec. in Aquin (sp?) Church, Horton Parish; d. 1-4-
1835; m. Nancy ----- (alive 10-13-1835); Pens. appl. 4-16-1834,
ae. 70 on 5-10-1833, Washington Co., Ind. After War, liv. Horton
Par., Stafford Co., Va., with his mother's cousin, Col. William
Brent, ca. 5 yr. until his death; then in same parish with Dr.
Valentine Payton till 1792. Then joined Gen. Wayne in 1792 &
serv. 3 yr. in Light Horse. To Ky. ca. 1795; there till 1815; to
Washington Co., Ind. Service: enl. 1-12-1779, Stafford Co., Va.;
Capt. William Farrow; serv. 11½ mo. as pvt. & 13½ mo. as Sgt.Maj.;
dis. Oct. 1781; in Va. Troops; in Batt. of Cowpens. REF: Pens.
S.32454 Va.; Washington Co., Ind., Prob. Rec. B, p.291; Mrs.
Stan S. Brusnahan, Rensselaer, Ind.

PRATHER, BASIL R.   Clark
b. 1741-1742, Rockville, Montgomery (formerly Frederick) Co.,
Md.; son of Basil Prather I, b. Eng., to Rockville, Md., 1732;
m. ante 1765, Chloe (or Clorinda) Robertson (or Robinson) b. 8-
14-1748, Md.; d. 7-12-1812, Clark Co., Ind. Basil Prather d.
10-7-1822, Clark Co., Ind.; sold. & wife bur. New Chapel Cem.
(2nd M.E. Church) near Utica, Ind.; both have stones. (Note:
this may be the Basil Prather incorrectly given as died in Jefferson Co., Ky.). Chn.: (Maj.) William b. 8-17-1766 near Fincastle, Va.; m. 1795, Va., Lettice McCarroll; Thomas b. 1770;
m. 3-10-1790, Rachel Gaither; Walter m. 6-13-1791, Rowan Co.,
N.C., Martha Jacobs, b. 1-30-1777 (dau. of Jeremiah & Rebecca
(Dowden) Jacob) & liv. Clark Co., Ind.; (Jeremiah Jacob a Rev.
sold.; see this Suppl.); (Judge) Samuel m. Clark Co., Ind.,
Eda Holman (dau. of Isaac & Catharine (Wilcox) Holman; he a Rev.
sold.; "Roster" p.194); Lloyd m. 6-21-1824, Louisville, Ky.,
Nancy Redmon; John m. 9-10-1790 Rowan Co., N.C., Ann Campbell;
Sion m. 8-27-1813, Clark Co., Ind., Eliza Simmons; Basil R.,
Jr. (name added by Baird below). Service: name on 1st Mil. List
of Montgomery (formerly Frederick) Co., Md.; signed Oath of
Allegiance 2-28-1778 in Washington (formerly Frederick) Co., Md.
To Iredell Co., N.C., where again fought in Mil. In ca. 1798
bought 3,000 ac. in Clark's Grant, Ind. Terr. (now Clark Co.,
Ind.) & mov. fam. there. REF: 1945-1946 Yearbook of Ky. DAR,
pp.203-204; Newman--"Anne Arundel Gentry" p.437; Miss Thelma
Murphy, Indianapolis, Ind.; Mrs. Gustave B. Appelman (Mary
Prather), Tacoma, Wash.; Baird--"Hist. of Clark Co., Ind.",
(1909), pp.54, 674-675 & other pp. for descendants.

PRIDMORE, THEODORE   Lawrence
b. 4-17-1755, near Princeton, N.J. Pens. appl. 9-21-1833, ae.
78, Lawrence Co., Ind. With father, mov. to Md. when 10-12 yr.
old for ca. 2 yr.; to Bedford Co., Pa.; after War, liv. Pa. 4
yr.; to Va. on Holston & Clinch ca. 44 yr.; to Lawrence Co.,Ind.
Affid. 10-3-1835, Hawkins Co., Tenn., of Jonathan Pridmore, ae.
76 (rel. not given); that he enlisted Theodore. Service: enl.
spr. 1776, Frankstown, Bedford Co., Pa.; Capt. Paxton. REF:
Pens. S.32457 Pa.

PROTHERO, THOMAS   Jefferson
d. 6-28-1817; m. 8-19-1785 (bond dated;8-25-1786 according to
wid.'s affid.), Botetourt Co., Va., Hannah Miles, b. 1762; chn.:
poss. son Evan Prothero (in 1830 Cens., Jefferson Co., Ind.).
Wid.'s pens. appl. 8-23-1845, ae. 83, Jefferson Co., Ind. Affid.
1-11-1845, Ripley Co., Ind., but a res. of Shelby Co., Ky., of
Isaac Miles (rel. not given); that he knew they were mar.; she
nee Miles; she will be 83 next Mar.; she liv. Jefferson Co., Ind.
Same affid. 8-30-1845, Ripley Co., Ind., of Evan Miles (rel. not
given). Service: N.C. service. REF: Pens. R.8501 N.C.; Susp.
Pens. List (1852) p.419--for proof of service; this gives wid. as
of Ripley Co., Ind.; 1830 Cens., Jefferson Co., Ind., v.7,p,274.

PRUETT, ARCHIBALD   Scott
b. 12-25-1752. Pens. appl. 8-19-1840, ae. 88 next Dec. 25,
Vienna Twp., Scott Co., Ind. After War, liv. Randolph Co., S.C.,
ca. 21 yr.; mov. to ca. 15 mi. from Lexington, Ky., for ca. 8 yr.;
Washington Co., Ky., ca. 5 yr.; Elk Creek, Washington Co., Ind.,
ca. 10-12 yr.; then to Vienna Twp., Scott Co., Ind. Service:
enl. ae. ca. 21 yr., Aug. (can't read year) as subst. for friend,
John Cobb, in N.C. Mil.; Capt. Doswell, Col. Logan, Hillsborough,
N.C.; again enl. ae. ca. 23, Guilford Co., N.C.; Capt. Isaac
Norrell (sp?). REF: Pens, R.8503 N.C.; Rej. Pens. List (1852),
p.409--not under competent military authority.

PRY, JESSE   Spencer
b. 8-27-1767, Anne Arundel Co., Md., 14 mi. from Washington,
D.C. Pens. appl. 4-12-1847, ae. ca. 80, Spencer Co., Ind. At
enl., liv. ca. 12 mi. from Hagerstown, Washington Co., Md.; there
till 1810; to Green River, Ky.; to Spencer Co., Ind., 1816.
Service: drf. Mar. after Cornwallis' defeat, 1782, Hagerstown,
Md., 29th Regt., Mil.; Col. Rollins. REF: Pens. R.8509 Md.; Rej.
Pens. List (1852) p.409--did not serve 6 mo.

PUTNAM, HOWARD   Knox
b. 2-11-1760; d. 1-25-1834; m.(1); m.(2) Mrs. Caroline (--) ----,
b. ca. 1784; chn.: Sally b. 1817; Rufus b. ca. Feb. 1822.
Pens. appl. 6-18-1818, in 57th yr., Knox Co., Ind.; 6-28-1822, ae.
62, Knox Co., Ind.; wife Carline ae. ca. 40; 3 step-daus.: Roxey
16, Lavina 14, Malinda 12 & 2 own chn.: Sally 5, Rufus ca. 4 mo.;
3-26-1824, ae. 64 last Feb. 11, Knox Co., Ind.; wife Caroline 40;
3 step-daus.: Rosea 16, Lavina 14, Malinda 12; Sally 6, Rufus 2;
4-5-1825, ae. 65, Knox Co., Ind.; his 2nd wife ae. 43; Sarah 7,
Rufus 3. Sold. bought 80 ac. of land: N½-NW¼-Sec. 3-Twp. 10 N-
Range 10 W, Vincennes Land Dist., in 1817, sold by Otis Jones of
Vigo Co., Ind., but sold. never completed payments. Petition on
5-4-1829 of cits. of Vincennes, Ind. (1st sig. John Badollet) asks
for pens. for sold., res. of Knox Co., Ind., over 20 yr. On 8-
14-1829 sold. liv. 11 mi. from Vincennes, Ind.; on 9-3-1832, ae.
over 70. Service: enl. 5-15-1777, Capt. Jonathan Drury, 3rd. Regt.
Artill. Col. John Crane Mass. Cont. Line, Worcester Co., Mass.
REF: Pens. S.17032 Cont. (Mass.); 1835 Pens. List, v.3, p.57;
memorial to Congress in "Laws of Ind., 1830-1831",p.176; 1831
Susp. Pens. List, p.71--1818 pensr. stricken from pens. list under
Act of 1820--not in indigent circumstances.

-83-

RAINES, RICHARD   Fountain
b. 1756.   Pens. appl. 11-10-1834, ae. 78, Fountain Co., Ind.;
again 4-25-1835, Fountain Co., Ind. Service: drf. Aug. 1777 or
1778, Rockingham Co., Va., Mil.; Capt. James Frashier, Col. Campbell.   REF: Pens. R.8562 Va.; Rej. Pens. List (1852) p.409--did
not serve 6 mo.

RAINEY, J----   Daviess
(Uncertain).   Is in 1840 Pens. List, ae. 83, of Daviess Co.,Ind.
I could not identify him from the J. Rainey pens. files at Natl.
Archives.   It seems likely that he mov. to Ind. & died before an
application for pens. transfer went through --- thus making it
impossible for me to determine which of the J's he might have
been. Consequently, I did not abstract any of the J. Rainey
files.   There were John (b. 5-20-1750; Pens. S.4035 S.C.; liv. in
Tenn.); James (ae. 66 in 10-29-1818; Pens. S.35599 N.C.; liv. in
Pulaski Co., Ky.; letter in file implies that this one is the J.
Rainey of Daviess Co., Ind.). I also find a scribbled note that
there was a Joseph Rainey of Daviess Co., Ind. The unknown J.
would not seem to be the Jeremiah Raney of Martin Co., Ind. (in
"Roster", p.304), but Martin & Daviess Cos. adjoin. There is
the possibility that he mov. from Daviess Co., Ind. after 1840
to Martin Co., Ind.; this cannot be proved here as the "Roster"
does not give the death date for the Martin Co. Jeremiah Raney.
REF: 1840 Pens. List, p.182; Natl. Archives pens. files.

RANDALL, BENAGER   Owen
b. 7-14-1752,,on headwaters of the Yadkin in N.C.; m. in his
17th yr. Pens. appl. 4-16-1834, ae. 81, Owen Co., Ind. After
mar., mov. to Montgomery Co., N.C.; had a public place 15 mi.
from the county town, Henderson; Tories destroyed his provisions;
liv. there till ca. 2 yr. ago when mov. to Owen Co., Ind. Affid.
4-16-1834, Owen Co., Ind., of William Haltom, ae. 66; that he
had liv. near sold. in Montgomery Co., N.C.; that his bro., Joseph Haltom, decd., serv. with sold.; (see Mary Haltom, wid. of
Joseph, in widows' list, this Suppl.).   Service: drf. fall 1780,
Montgomery Co., N.C., on waters of Little Pedee; Capt. Thomas
Cotton, Col. Loftain. REF: Pens. S.32469 N.C.

RECTOR, JESSE   Lawrence
b. 12-26-1759, Fauquier Co., Va. Pens. appl. 11-11-1833, ae. 73
last Dec. 26, Shawswick Twp., Lawrence Co., Ind. After War, liv.
4-5 yr. in Va.; to N.C. ca. 5 yr.; Va. again ca. 30 yr.; in Ind.
last 13 yr. Service: drf. sum. or fall 1780, Fauquier Co., Va.,
Mil. REF: Pens. R.8639 Va.; Rej. Pens. List (1852) p.409--only
3 mo. & 10 da. service.

REEL (RIEL), JOHN   Gibson
b. ca. 1763; d. 3-3-1828, ae. 64; m. 11-14-1790, Jefferson Co.,
Ky., Catharine Stuckey (or Stokey); dau. of Martin Stuckey; she
b. 10-12-1771 (1772-1773); chn.: Frederick b. 1791;   Henry b.
1793;   Samuel b. 1795;   David b. 1797;   Elizabeth b. 1800;
Moris (or Mons?) b. 1801;   E..anuel b. 1802;   Nancy b. 1808;
Lucinda b. 1810;   James b. 1813;   1 other child. Wid.'s pens.

apl. 11-8-1842, Gibson Co., Ind.; attested by Henry Reel (rel. not given). Affid. 11-3-1842, Pike Co., Ind., of Samuel Stucky (rel. not given); that he present at sold.'s mar.; that chn. were as given above. On 12-3-1843, wid. 70 yr. old last Oct. Service: while liv. N.C., enl. as subst.; Col. Lees. (Note: a John Reel was commn. Ensign in 1st Regt., Ind. Terr. Mil., 8-11-1815; on 11-2-1818, Lieut. in 1st Regt.). REF: Pens. W.9619 N.C.; "Exec. Journ. of Ind. Terr., 1800-1816", p.237; "Exec. Proc. of Ind., 1816-1836", p.83.

REMKIN, BENJAMIN   Jefferson
(Uncertain --- he may not have died in Ind.) Pens. file could not be found at Natl. Archives under typographical error of Remkin or Lamkin. Widow was Nancy Hickey. REF: Susp. Pens. List (widows (1852) p.419--for proof of identity with the soldier of the L 90 certificate of depreciation.
RENNO, GEORGE--see p. 119.
RIDINGOUR, (JOHN) ANDREW   Morgan
(Also Ridenhour). b. 1761, Berks Co., Pa. Full name was John Andrew but evid. used Andrew only. Pens. appl. 5-12-1834, ae. 73, Morgan Co., Ind. Parents mov. to Rowan Co., N.C., when he ca. 14 yr. old. After War, sold. liv. Rowan Co.; N.C.; Burks Co., N.C.; Ohio; ca. 6 yr. ago to Montgomery Co., Ind.; now in Morgan Co., Ind. Says name may be John Andrew Ridingour on Muster Roll as he was sometimes called by that name. Service; drf. spr. 1780, Rowan Co., N.C.; Capt. John Barringer, Col. Tyler (Fyler?). REF: Pens. S.32486 S.C.

RILEY, JAMES   Orange
d. 4-20-1828, ae. 67; bur. Trimble Cem., Northeast Twp. Said to have been a Rev. sold. REF: "Orange Co., Ind., Cem. Rec."--Lost River Chap., DAR, Paoli, Ind. (1947) p.250.

ROBBINS, JOHN   Ohio
Rev. sold. who died there. This would not seem to be the one in "Roster", p.315 (died 1834 in Wayne Co., Ind.) since Ohio Co. was not formed until 1844 from Dearborn Co., Ind. REF:Mr. Schrum.

ROBERTS, HEZEKIAH   Switzerland
b. ca 1761; d. 2-23-1826; m. 1783, Culpeper Co., Va. (or Hanover Co., Va.; or Loudon Co., Va.), Agnes Robinson, b. ca. 1771; d. 9-23-1845 (2 affids.; 1848 in 1 afid.); chn.: one decd.; William b. 1788; m. 1810, Hamilton Co., O., Patsey Shepherd; John; Rebecca m Abisha McKay; Neely; Moses; Betsy; James; Andrew; Hezekiah d. 5-20-1852, Switzerland Co., Ind.; leaving 1 ch., Moses Perry Roberts. Pens. appl. 6-8-1821, ae. 60, Switzerland Co., Ind.; wife Agnes 50; chn.: Rebecca 16, Hezekiah 13, Moses 12. Affid. 11-4-1819, Dearborn Co., Ind., of Francis Cheek (Rev. sold. in this Suppl.); that he saw sold. in service. Affid. 8-19-1819, Nicholas Co., Ky., of Nehemiah Roberts, bro. of sold.; that sold. was in service. Affid. 6-29-1852, Switzerland Co., Ind., of William Roberts, ae. 66, & John Roberts, ae. 64; that mother d. 1848, ae. ca. 74; m. in one of the 3 Va. Cos. given above; that father liv. Culpeper Co., Va., & mother in Han-

over Co., Va.; that William the oldest ch. except the one that d. in infancy; that uncle Nehemiah Roberts had a Rev. pens. Two affids. that wid. d. 1845. Sold. & fam. liv. in or around Fayette Co., Ky., 1790, & Nicholas Co., Ky., 1810. Affid. 7-18-1853, Nicholas Co., Ky., of Henly Roberts (rel. not given); that he knew sold. & fam. from 1790 in Woodford Co., Ky., & mov. to Bourbon Co., Ky. Service: enl. 3-1-1777, Va. Cont. Line; Capt. William Fields. REF: Pens. W.9631 Va.; 1831 Rej. Pens. List, p.49-- "served in a regiment not on continental establishment."

ROBERTSON, NATHAN　　　　　　　　　　Clark
d. 1825; m. Elizabeth Speaks, d. 1821; (both bur. Robertson Cem. which adjoined Old Bethel Church, built by Nathan & his sons on their farm in 1808; reconstructed in 1925 by order of Ind. Meth. Conf. & moved to Charlestown for preservation); chn. (6 sons & 3 daus.): Robert b. 8-18-1772; m. Susanna Jones & mov. to Morgan Co., Ill., 1831; Middleton b. 6-17-1774; m. Cassandra Tucker & mov. to Jefferson Co., Ind., 1811; Eli b. 1-5-1776; m. Elizabeth Shawhan & stayed in Clark Co., Ind.; Zephaniah b. 1779-1780; m. Elizabeth Tucker; Nancy b. 1781-1782; m. Andrew Hughes & mov. to Ill.; Hezekiah b. 1-21-1784; m. Sarah Tucker; Elizabeth b. 1786; m. Thomas Gasaway (son of Nicholas & Margaret Gasaway) & mov. to Jefferson Co., Ind., ca. 1811; James b. 7-20-1791; m. Nancy Tucker; Mary b. 1793; m. Samuel Harrod (she d. in Clark Co., Ind., 1 yr. after her mar.). Son Robert serv. under Mad Anthony Wayne in 1794 & was in Batt. of Fallen Timbers; was a Col. in Home Mil. in 1812. Son James was in Batt. of Tippecanoe. Nathan Robertson brought his fam. from Montgomery Co., Md., to Bourbon Co., Ky., in 1787, & to Clark Co., Ind. Terr., in 1799. The four Tucker girls were sists. & daus. of Alexander Tucker. The Tucker & Speaks fams. had come to Ky. in 1785, 2 yr. before Nathan Robertson & his bro. Robert came; these fams. were also from Montgomery Co., Md. Elizabeth (Speaks) Robertson's bro., Hezekiah Speaks m. Eleanor Tucker, sis. of Alexander Tucker & a dau. of Edward Tucker. Another fam. coming with Nathan Robertson to Clark's Grant in 1799 was that of Nicholas & Margaret Gasaway, also from Md. (Informant has more data on them). Service: member of the Md. Mil.; also signed Oath of Fidelity & Support in Montgomery Co., Md.; he was enrolled for service during the Rev. in the Lower Battn. of Montgomery Co., Md., in Class 7, 1st Comp.; Capt. William Bailey, 7-15-1780; his name appears in the list of the Potomac Hundred, Frederick Co. (the lower part of which became Montgomery Co., after 1776), Md., 8-22-1776; below his name are his wife Elizabeth, ae. 22, & 2 oldest sons, Robert 4, & Middleton 2. REF: Mrs. Lewis Osterman, Seymour, Ind.; Brumbaugh & Hodge--"Rev. Rec. of Md.", v.1, p.7; "Mil. Lists, Montgomery Co., Md." (in Md. Hist. Soc.).

RODDY, CHRISTOPHER　　　　　　　　　Wayne
"He had fought through the whole seven years of the Revolutionary war. - - - Mr. Roddy emigrated with his family to the Territory of Indiana, and settled in what is now Wayne county in the year 1810 or 1811. - - - While Roddy was a non-commissioned officer in the army of the Revolution, on one occasion he gave a mortal

affront to a second lieutenant who challenged him to fight a duel. By the 'code of honor' the challenged party had the right to choose the weapons, the place, and the mode of fighting. Roddy accepted the challenge, and chose a heavy cavalry saber for his antagonist and a shoemaker's pegging awl for himself. The place of fighting was to be a large brick oven. The fight was not to commence till both were fairly in the oven. The idea was so novel and ridiculous that his antagonist withdrew the challenge, abandoned the fight, and there the matter ended. - - - Had he embraced religion in his youth and lived a pious life he might have accomplished good, and might have died in peace, but his life was a stormy one, his old age melancholy, and the day of his death dark." (Note: Mrs. Strieby suggests probability of Va. service & possibility of migration through Jefferson Co., Tenn.). REF: Rev. William C Smith--"Indiana Miscellany" (1867), Chap. X, pp. 84-88; Mrs. Irene Strieby, Indianapolis, Ind.

ROGERS, AQUILLA   Clark
d. 1838-1839 (will wr. 7-31-1838; pr. 2-16-1839); m.(1) mother of all his chn.: James; Philip; Isaac; Lewis; Aquilla; Nancy m. Jacob Iseminger; sold. m.(2) Phebe -----; no chn. Affid. 12-1-1845 of nephew David Rogers. Sold. in 1790 Cens., George Twp., Fayette Co., Pa. Service: Ill. Regt. with Gen. Clark at Kaskaskia & Vincennes. (Note: an Aquilla Rogers was appt. J.P. for Clark Co., Ind. Terr., 7-22-1806. An Aquilla Rogers was appt. J.P. for Bartholomew Co., Ind., 7-17-1821 (had resigned by Sept. 1822). An Aquilla Rogers was commn. J.P. for Monroe Co., Ind., 6-30-1825; same 9-8-1830; was appt. Prob. Judge, 9-3-1833. An Aquilla W. Rogers was commn. J.P. for Clark Co., Ind., 12-23-1831 (resigned by Oct. 1834); commn. J.P. for LaPorte Co., Ind., 12-18-1835.). REF: Va. State Libr.; Mrs. R.W. Valin, Newberg, Ore.; "Exec. Journ. of Ind. Terr., 1800-1816", p.135; "Exec. Proc. of Ind., 1816-1836", pp. 180, 237 n, 525, 527, 528, 386, 388 n,499.

RUBISON, CALZA   Washington
b. 11-19-1764, Charlotte Co., Va.; d. 9-25-1834; m. Lucinda -----; chn. (at least): Richard; Nancy (oldest dau.) m. Mr. Razor; Polly m. Absalom Chastain. Will wr. 7-4-1834 & pr. 10-13-1834 names these and "all the rest of my children"; son Richard was exec.; name also spelled Ruberson; Calza signed by X. Son Richard Ruberson, will wr. 7-5-1865; pr. 1-19-1866; names wife Mary Jane; sons: Thomas J., Jonah L., Rice M.J.(decd.), John S.; daus.: Lucy Meredith & Sally Stout. Pens. appl. 11-15-1832, ae. 68, Washington Co., Ind. Liv. Rowan Co.; N.C.; Guilford Co., N.C.; in Va.; in a few yrs. to Ky. for ca. 20 yr.; Washington Co., Ind., for last ca. 14 yr. Father d. when sold. was very young. Affid. 11-15-1832, Washington Co., Ind., of Richard Rubison (rel. not given) & Robert Smith; Richard has known sold. over 30 yr. Service: enl early in spring 1781 at Ramsey's (query: Ramsour's?) Mill; Col Reed, Guilford Co., N.C. REF: Pens. S.16240 N.C.; Washington Co., Ind., Probate Book B, pp. 212, 213, 571, 572.

RUMINGER, GEORGE   Daviess
b. Feb. 1763, Rowan Co., N.C.; apparently still alive 8-19-1843
(letter in Frederick Stipe's pens. file; see later, this Suppl.).
Pens. appl. 11-12-1833, ae. 71, Bogard Twp., Daviess Co., Ind.
When very young, mov. to Lincoln Co., N.C., where res. dur. Rev.
& till 1812; mov. to Jefferson Co., Ky.; then to Hardyman (?)
Co., Tenn., for 7 yr.; to Daviess Co., Ind. (Note: see 1835 Pens.
List, v.3, p.3, Daviess Co., Ind., for probable bro., Daniel
Ruminer; Tenn. Mil.; tr. from West Tenn.; sett. in Bogard Twp.,
Daviess Co., Ind., 1818). P of A, 7-6-1854, Daviess Co., Ind.,
from John Rumingher (rel. Not givem, but prob. son). Service:
enl. Mar. 1780; Capt. Joseph Collins, Lt. David McMicking (sp?).
REF: Pens. R.9071 N.C.; Rej. Pens. List (1852) p.409--Bogard Twp.-
served only a little upwards of 5 mo.; "Hist. of Knox & Daviess
Cos., Ind." (1886) p.600.

RUSSELL, JOHN   Clark
Not the John Russell, b. 1765, of Clark Co., Ind., in "Roster",
p. 331; nor the one of Jackson Co., Ind., below).   b. 1743; d.
prob. soon after 1827. The following petition signed by Joseph
Bower, J.P., and 18 others: "To His Excellency James Brown Ray,
Governor in and for the State of Indiana -- The undersigned your
petitioners of the County of Clark Would beg Leave To Represent
to your Excellency that John Russell aged 83 years a Revolutionary Soldier was on the 18th day of September 1826 fined before
Joseph Bower a Justice of the Peace in and for the County of
Clark in the Sum of Seven Dollars for Profane Swearing we would
farther beg Leave to Represent to your Excellency that the Informant against the said Russell was as we verily believe actuated by
Malice inasmuch as the said Russell and him are and have for some
time been personal Enemies now if your Honor can consistently
Remit said fine we as in duty bound will ever pray (done) this
30th Nov. 1826." (19 signatures). Fine was remitted 12-16-1827.
"John Russell lived in Washington village (in Washington Twp.) in
1811. He was a Revolutionary soldier, and died many years ago.";
(from 1882 Hist. below). REF: "Pardons and Remissions of Fines"
(Ind. State Archives); "Exec. Proc. of Ind., 1816-1836", p. 332;
"Hist. of the Ohio Falls Cities & Their Counties" (1882), v. 2,
p. 421.

RUSSELL, JOHN   Jackson
Rev. sold. who died there. Intestate rec. on file at courthouse.
Prob. liv. in Grassy Fork Twp., where the Russell family were
prominent. REF: Ft. Vallonia Chap., DAR, Seymour, Ind.

RUSSELL, WILLIAM   Posey
b. 1755-1756, N.C.; d. May 1850, Black Twp., ae. 94; widower. No
proof that he was a Rev. sold., but certainly was of the right
age. REF: 1850 Mortality Schedules, Posey Co., Ind., v.2, p.138;
Miss Thelma Murphy, Indianapolis, Ind.

RUTH, JOHN   Crawford
b. ca. 1751. Liv. in Patoka in 1825. No pens. file found at
Natl. Archives under this spelling --- name may be Reeth, etc.
If any reader knows the right name, please notify the compiler.
REF: 1840 Pens. List, p. 181, ae. 89; Pleasant--"Hist. of Craw-
ford Co., Ind." (1926) pp. 74, 84, 99.

RUTHERFORD, JOHN   Johnson
b. 1749; d. 1821 or 1823; bur. in Smiley Cem. Prob. came from
Washington Co., Ky. REF: Mrs. Ira Tranter, Franklin, Ind.

SACREE, W-----   Hendricks
(Uncertain). Said to be Rev. sold. who died there (on Mr.
Schrum's list). Is in 1840 Pens. List, ae. 73, living with Abram
Spicklemore. (Unless age is wrong, he is rather young to have
been a Rev. sold. although it is possible. However, there is no
pens file at Natl Archives. There was an Isaac Sacrey who d.
1807, Franklin Co, Ky., and whose widow, Elizabeth (George)
Sacrey, later lived in Hendricks Co., Ind., and drew Pens.
W.10247 Va. REF: Mr. Schrum; 1840 Pens. List, p. 182.

SAMPLE (SEMPLE), THOMAS   Vigo
b. 6-22-1746; m. Margaret ----- (ae. 55 in 1818). Pens. appl.
6-19-1818, ae. 71 last June 22, Gibson Co., Ind. Pens. granted
7-7-1819 (1818 Law). Again appl. 10-19-1820, ae. 74, Gibson Co.,
Ind., resident of the District. Evid. mov. to Vigo Co., Ind.,
where is in 1835 Pens. List, ae. 87; pvt. in S.C. Line. Service:
enl. spr. 1777; Capt. John Buoy (or Baugh) in 2nd or 3rd S.C.
Regt., Col. Hughgee (sp?); again enl. at the White Horse in
Chester Co., Pa.; 1st Pa. Regt.; Col. James Chambers, Capt. James
Wilson. REF: Pens. S.36750 Pa., S.C.; 1835 Pens. List, v.3, p.34.

SARGEANT, WILLIAM   Washington
(Uncertain). Name obtained after this Suppl. was started. A
William Sargeant of Indiana is on the 1831 list of rejected Pensions, reason: "no proof of his having been an enlisted soldier
exhibited". There is a William Sargeant in the 1820 Cens. of
Washington Co., Ind., v.5, p.364. REF: "Rej. Appl. for Pens."
(1831) p.49 (see note at end after Daniel Zink.).

SCOTT, JUSTUS   Hamilton
b. 1766, Waterburg, New Haven Co., Conn. Pens. appl. 5-12-1834,
ae. ca. 68, Hamilton Co., Ind. Since War has liv. Conn. 17-18
yr.; Vt., 25 yr.; Ohio, 5-6 yr.; Hamilton Co., Ind., last 4-5 yr.
(Sett. in Hamilton Co., Ind., in 1829). Service: enl. Apr. 1781
or 1782, Waterbury, Conn., in Conn. Troops; Capt. Treadway. REF:
Pens. R.9305 Conn.; Rej. Pens. List (1852) p.409--did not serve
in a military capacity; "Hist. of Hamilton Co., Ind." (1880),118.

SCOVELL, OORR   Henry
Rev. sold who d there.; at death, liv. on what is now called
Graham Farm, near the "Old Stone Quarry Mill", in Spiceland Twp.
Was an early settler of Henry Co. Had a son, Elisha. Served in
a N.J. or Conn. Regt. REF: Mr. Schrum; Hazzard--"Hist. of Henry
Co., Ind." (1906) pp. 699, 1067.

SHANNON, JOHN   Jefferson
Rev. sold. who died there. (Might possibly have been the
George Shannon of Jefferson Co., "Roster", p. 327). REF: Schrum.

SHARP, -----   Monroe
Rev. sold. who died there. REF: Mr. Schrum.

SHELDON, GEORGE   Dearborn
b. Oct. 1757; mar.; chn. Pens. appl. 3-1-1833, ae. 75 last Oct.,
Sempronius, Cayuga Co., N.Y. Attested by Ichabod Sheldon (rel.
not given), a clergyman of Sempronius, N.Y. On 8-12-1837, sold.
asks for pens. tr. to Dearborn Co., Ind., as all his chn. came;
pens. tr. from Albany, N.Y., Agy., 3-1-1838. On 2-19-1838, Dearborn Co., Ind., Ichabod Sheldon identifies the sold. Service:
enl. 1777, Stephenstown, Rensselaer Co., N.Y.; Capt. James Dennison; later enl. in a Comp. in which Isaac Sheldon (rel. not
given) was Ensign. REF: Pens. S.17084 N.Y.

SHELTON, WILSON   Parke
b. 1747, Charles Co., Md.; mar.; chn.: at least dau. Margaret, m.
Mr. Harden (or Harding). Pens. appl. 12-20-1833, ae. 86, Henry
Co., Ky. To Shelby Co., Ky., 1810. In 1835 Pens. List, Henry
Co., Ky.; pvt. in Va. Mil. On 3-26-1838, Parke Co., Ind., asks
for pens. tr. to Ind. as came spr. 1837 to Parke Co. to live with
dau., Mrs. Margaret Harden (another place, Harding) with whom he
had liv. ca. 27 yr.; pens tr. 7-31-1838. Affid. 1838, Parke
Co., Ind., of Mason Harden (query: husb. of Margaret?). Service:
enl. Aug. 1780, Stafford Co., Va.; Capt. Charles Rolls, Col. Samuel Payton. REF: Pens. S.31955 Va.; 1835 Pens. List, v.3, p.105.

SHIELDS, -----   Greene
Rev. sold. who died there. REF: Mr. Schrum.

SHOEMAKER, JOHN   Dearborn
b. 1-1-1745, Hunterdon Co., N.J. (in what looks like Amil Twp.
or Arril Twp.). Pens. appl. 4-2-1834, ae. 89, Randolph Twp.,
Dearborn Co., Ind.; also 2-6-1834. After War, liv. 10 yr. near
Cumberland, Md.; 5 yr. in Fayette Co., Pa.; 11 yr. in Ohio near
mouth of the Big Scioto; last 10 yr. in Randolph Twp., Dearborn
Co., Ind. Letter in file*says that he has not called for his
pens. for over a year. Service: drf. Oct. 1776, Hunterdon Co.,
N.J., in N.J. Mil.; Gen. Herd, Cols. Beaver & Taylor. REF:
Pens. S.32515 N.J.   *3-15-1838

SHUTTLE, JOHN   Decatur
b. 9-10-1754, Hunterdon Co., N.J. Pens. appl. 11-9-1835, ae. 81,
Adams Twp., Decatur Co., Ind. Mov. with father in 1760 to Bedford Co., Va.; there till 1806 to Washington Co., Va.; there till
Aug. 1834 to Dearborn Co., Ind., where arrived last of Sept.;
sister in Campbell Co., Va., has father's Bible. Service: enl.
Mar. 1775, New London, Bedford Co., Va.; Capt. Jacob Moon, Lt.
Amos Galloway. REF: Pens. R.9556 Va.; Susp. Pens. List (1852)
p. 413--for proof of service.

SIMMONS, SAMUEL   Shelby
Rev. sold. who died there. REF: Mr. Schrum.

SMITH, GEORGE   Indiana
Service: enl. Nov. 1777, Pa. Cont. Line; Col. Jacob Hillsumer
(sp?), Maj. George Grace, Capt. Philip Hinkley. (No other papers
in file; sent 12-11-1846 to Hon. J.W. Davis). REF: Pens.
R.9737 Pa.; Susp. Pens. List (1852) p.413--for proof of service.

SMITH, JACOB   Indiana
(Uncertain). Name obtained after this Suppl. was started. A
Jacob Smith of Indiana is on the 1831 list of rejected pensions,
reason: "deserted the service". There are Jacob Smiths in the
1820 Censuses of the following Indiana counties: Fayette, Floyd,
Franklin, Orange, Dearborn; 1830 Censuses for: Decatur, Fayette,
Floyd, Franklin, Greene, Lawrence, Pike, Switzerland, Warren,
Washington, Wayne. REF: "Rej. Appl. for Pens." (1831) p.49 (see
note at end after Daniel Zink).

SMITH, JACOB   Washington
b. 1749 or 1750, Bucks Co., Pa.; d. 2-3-1835. Pens. appl. 11-16-
1832, ae. 83, Washington Co., Ind. After War, liv. Botetourt
Co., Va., till ca. 1819; to Ill. ca. 3 yr.; then to Washington
Co., Ind. Service: enl. 1777, Berkeley Co., Va.; Capt. Porterfield, Va. Mil.; Col. Pendleton; again late 1780 or early 1781,
Botetourt Co., Va. REF: Pens. S.16253 Va.

SMITH, JOHN   Harrison
b. ca. 1761; liv. 1-21-1843, ae. 82, Harrison Co., Ind., when he
made affid. that he was in War at same time as sold., George
Foote, who served from Caswell Co., N.C.; see forward. (Note:
this man is not on I.A.R. as a pensioner paid in Indiana; so I
did not read the many John Smith pension files at Natl. Archives).
REF: Pens. W.10032 N.C. (of George Foote).

SMITH, NATHAN   Washington
b. ca 1754, Frederick Co., Va.; mar. in Frederick Co., Va.;
chn. (at least 3 incl.): Allen. Pens. appl. 3-31-1836, ae. ca.
82, Franklin Twp., Washington Co., Ind. Mother d. Frederick Co.,
Va., when he ca. 4 yr. old; father apprenticed him when ca. 15
yr. old to Benjamin Agin in Frederick Co., Va.; father d. Frederick Co., Va., when Nathan ca. 18 yr. old; apprenticeship over
at age 21, so he enlisted; liv. Frederick Co., Va., till 4-5 yr.
after disch. from service; with wife & 3 chn. to Wilkes Co.,
N.C., for ca. 6 yr.; liv. ca. 18 mi. below Wilkes Co. Ct. Hse.;
to Burke Co., N.C., for ca. 20 yr.; to Knox Co., Tenn., ca. 10
mi. from Knoxville ca. 4 yr.; to Adair Co., Ky., ca. 4-5 yr.; in
Franklin Twp., Washington Co., Ind., for last 8-9 or more yr.
P of A, 2-15-1854, Washington Co., Ind., from Allen Smith, son &
heir. Service: enl. in or ca. 1775 immed. after he 21 yr. old,
Frederick Co., Va., Mil.; Capt. Arbuckle. REF: Pens. R.9816 Va.;
Susp. Pens. List (1852) p.413--for further proof & specifications.

SMITH, ROBERT B.   Jackson
d. 6-18-1845. Intestate rec. on file at Ct. Hse. REF: Fort Vallonia Chap., DAR, Seymour, Ind.; Prob. Will Bk. C, p. 36; administratrix, Jessie Matthews.

SMITH, STAFFORD   Greene
b. fall 1752, Co. Antrim, Ire. Pens. appl. 4-3-1833, ae. 80 last fall (discrepancy). To Amer. ae. ca. 18; landed Baltimore late Aug. 1770; mov. to Cumberland Co., Pa.; there till fall 1776; went on trip south to see the country; enl. while on trip; after disch., retd. to Cumberland Co., Pa., 1 yr.; to Washington Co., Ky.; other places in Ky. for ca. 30 yr.; to Harrison Co., Ind., ca. 12 yr.; to Washington Co., Ind., 3 yr.; to Greene Co., Ind. Service: enl. Sept. 1776, New Town, Berkeley Co., Va.; Capt. Joseph Mitchell, Col. Woods, 12th Regt., Va. Line. REF: Pens. R.9859 Pa., Va.; Susp. Pens. List (1852) p.414--not on the rolls-- no proof of service.

SMOCK, JACOB   Jefferson
b. 5-20-1744, Raritan, N.J.; son of John & Leah (Fontine or Fonteyn) Smook; d. 1820-1829, at home of son Samuel; bur. Hanover, Ind.; m Catharine Demaree (or Demarest), who also prob. d. 1820-1829; chn.: Leah b. 4-9-1774, bap. 5-15-1774, Conewago, Pa.; m. 5-5-1791, Mercer Co., Ky., Gerardus Ryker (son of Rev. sold., Gerardus Ryker, killed in Ky. by Indians, & Rachel Demarest); both bur. in Ryker's Ridge Cem., Jefferson Co., Ind. Matthew d. unm.; Samuel b. 10-7-1776, Berkeley Co., Va.; d. 7-5-1833; m. as 3rd husb., 11-18-1797, Shelby Co., Ky., Mrs. Rachel (Ryker) Houghland Robins, b. 6-19-1773 (or 1772); d. 1858;(dau. of Rev. sold. above, Gerardus & Rachel Demarest Ryker); she having m.(1), 1-5-1791, Jefferson Co., Ky., Henry Houghland & m.(2), 12-31-1793, Shelby Co., Ky., William Robins; John b. 10-7-1779; m. Catharine Carnine; Jacob m. Sallie Salyers; Abraham b. 7-8-1790; m.(1) Ann Smock; he m. (2) Catharine Goth; Peter b. 1-27-1781; m. Sallie Arbuckle; Mary ("Polly") m. Cornelius Seburn; Catharine b. 7-24-1793; m. John V. Seburn. Sold. & fam. came to Shelby Co., Ky., after 1780; later to Jefferson Co., Ind., where he & wife, both ae. 45 plus, are in 1820 Cens. with 1 son ae. 26-45 & 1 dau. ae. 10-16. Service: Sgt. in 1777-1779; Capt. Robert Higgins, Maj. Jonathan Clark, 4th Regt., Va. Troops; Sgt. in 3rd & 4th Regts., Cont. Line. REF: DAR Lineage vols. 51, 72, 73; Gwathmey- "Hist. Reg. of Va. in Rev." (1938); Brumbaugh--"Rev. War Rec. of Va.", v.1, p.496; Dunn--"Hist. of Greater Indianapolis" (1910), v.2; "Indianapolis & Vicinity" (1908) pp. 177-178; John Conover Smock--"Gen. Notes on the Smock Fam." (1922), Albany, N.Y.; "Fam. Rec. of Members of Manitou Chap., DAR" (ts in ISL); Demarest-- "Demarest Fam." (1938) p.109, & Suppl. (1944) p.4; 1820 Cens., Jefferson Co., Ind., v.3, p.294; A.M. Tuttle--"Notes on Jacob Smock & Gerardus Ryker" (ts in ISL); Miss Mary Hill, Madison, Ind.

SNELLING, WILLIAM — Decatur
b. 3-17-1760, Fauquier Co., Va. Pens. appl. 6-22-1836, ae. 76 last Mar. 17, Decatur Co., Ind. Liv. Fauquier Co., Va., till 1790; Fayette Co., Ky., till 1822; to Decatur Co., Ind. Original member of Salt Creek Church of Christ, 2 mi. E of Clarksburg, Ind.; church org. 11-16-1831. Service: drf. Apr. 1777, Fauquier Co., Va., Mil.; Capt. Davis. REF: Pens. R.9899 Va.; Rej. Pens. List (1852) p.409--did not serve 6 mo.; Harding--"Hist. of Decatur Co., Ind." (1915) p.261.

SNOW, JOHN — Monroe
b. ca. 1760, Kent Co., Del.; mar.; chn. Pens. appl. 4-18-1833, ae. 73, Stokes Co., N.C. Mov. to Surry Co. (now Stokes Co.) in Mar. 1777. Had a bro. who took the fam. Bible West. On 10-10-1834, Monroe Co., Ind., asks for pens. tr. a s now lives with his chn. who live here; pens. tr. from N.C., 7-13-1835. Service: enl. sum. 1779 at Old Richmond; Capt. Samuel Moseby. REF: Pens. S.17690 N.C.

SOFIELD, LEWIS — Fayette
d. 8-29-1836, Connersville, Ind.; intestate; m. 10-13-1785, Connecticut farm, N.J., Phebe Woodruff, b. 6-5-1767; d. 6-4-1872; no chn. (at least surv.). Wid.'s pens. appl., ae. 103 last June 5, 102 N. Franklin St., Richmond, Wayne Co., Ind. Wid.'s will names sole legatee, niece Susan R. Moore, Richmond, Ind. Service: enl. Elizabeth Town, N.J., Comp. B., Jersey Blues. REF:Pens. W.8297NJ.

SPEECE, LUDWIG (LOUIS) — Carroll
d. intestate. Served in Pa. Mil. From Dayton, O., to Carroll Co., Ind. REF: Miss Gertrude I. McCain, Delphi, Ind.

STEEL, JOHN — Harrison
b. Aug. 1762 or 1763, Washington, N.H. Pens. appl. 10-14-1834, ae. ca. 72, Harrison Co., Ind. Ran off from his father in 1779 or 1780 to his Uncle John Scott's in Sheffield Co., Conn., & enl. there as a subst.; Capt. Hinkle, Col. Hoyt. REF: Pens. R.10095 Conn.; Rej. Pens. List (1852) p.409--did not serve 6 mo.

STEWART, THOMAS — Monroe
b. 4-19-1755 or 1756, Rowan Co., N.C.; mar.; chn. (4 sons surv. 1854); incl. Lazarus. Pens. appl. 8-14-1832, ae. 76-77 last Apr. 19, Monroe Co., Ind. In fall 1781, mov. to E. Tenn. (then N.C.) where liv. ca. 28 yr.; to W. Tenn. ca. fall 1809 for ca. 20 yr.; fall 1829 to Monroe Co., Ind. Again; appl. 8-12-1833, ae. 77-78, Monroe Co., Ind.; serv. in War with William Clements of Ky. & David Clements of Monroe Co., Ind. ("Roster" p.98); knew them in N.C. & here. Affid. 4-15-1830 (?), Monroe Co., Ind., of David Clements; that he knew Stewart enl. under Capt. Knox in N.C. Troops, Col. Alexander Martin; that he saw sold. mustering & serving in Capt. George Davidson's Comp, in 1st Regt. of N.C. Troops, Col. Alexander Martin, Aug. 1775. Same affid. 2-20-1830, Monroe Co., Ind., from William Clements, ae. 76. P of A, 2-25-1854 (no place given) of Lazarus Stewart, one of 4 sons, the only liv. chn. REF:Pens. R.10172N.C.;Susp.Pens.List(1852)p.413-for further proof & specif.;1831 Rej.Pens.List,p.49-did not serve 9 mo. under 1 engagement.Serv:enl.Aug.1775 Rowan Co,NC Line,Capt.George Davidson,Col.Alex.Martin

STEWART, WILLIAM   Washington
b. 1755-1756; d. 3-4-1831; mar.(wife d. by 1819); chn.: at least
2. Pens. appl. 6-22-1819; ae. 64, Fayette Co., Ky., a res. of
Washington Co., Ind.; 2-28-1821, ae. 65, Washington Co., Ind.;
no fam. except.2 chn. with whom he lives. Affid. 6-22-1819, Fayette Co., Ky., of James Morrison who was an officer in the 8th
Pa. Regt.; knew sold. in War & many yrs. later where he liv. near
Pittsburgh, Pa., & later in Ohio; sold. now lives with his chn.
in Ind. Service: enl. spr. 1776, McKeesport on the Monongahela
in Pa.; Capt. James Montgomery, Col. McCoy, 8th Pa. Regt., Pa.
Line. REF: Pens. S.36803 Pa.; 1835 Pens. List, v.3, p.36.

STINSON (STEVENSON), WILLIAM   Hendricks
(Uncertain). His affid. is in file of his bro., John Stinson
(or Stevenson). John's data given here to help for William: John
b. 7-6-1755, Bucks Co., Pa.; father mov. to Md. ca. 9 yr. later;
John mov. to Va. 1783, leaving father in Md., John to Clark Co.,
Ky., 1793. Service (John): ensign in Capt. Barr's Comp., Linganore Battn., Frederick Co., Md., Mil.; commission dated 6-22-
1778, signed Thomas Johnson. John was res. of Frederick Co.,
Md., when he entered service; first tour in Capt. Peter Little's
Comp., Linganore Battn.; he vol. & serv. 2 mo. Pens. appl. (John)
10-3-1832, ae. 77, Clark Co., Ky. Affid. from bro. Isaac Stevenson, Clark Co., Ky.; that John serv. in War. Affid. of bro. William Stinson, Hendricks Co., Ind.; that bro. John Serv. 3 tours
& that he (William) was along with John on the one at Fredericktown, Md., guarding the British prisoners taken at the surrender
of Cornwallis; and that John acted as Lieut. in Capt. Gabble's
Comp. during said tour which was in the latter part of 1781,
altho he was only commn. as ensign. REF: Pens. S.30741 Md, (of
John Stinson); Bell--"Md. Sold. of the Rev. War, War of 1812, or
Indian Wars Who Drew Pens. While Residing in Ky." pp. 28-29.

STIPE, FREDERICK   Daviess
b. 4-11-1759, 18 mi. from Philadelphia, Pa.; mar.; chn. Sold.
was still alive 8-19-1843. Pens. appl. 3-25-1837, ae. 77 last
Apr. 11, Daviess Co., Ind. Mov. when 7 yr. old with parents to
Frederick Co., Va., where liv. till. 1790; to Jessamine Co., Ky.,
till ca. 12 yr. ago; to Knox Co., Ind., till ca. 1 yr. ago, to
Daviess Co., Ind. Had his disch. till 1831 or 1832 when it was
accid. torn up by his idiot dau. Serv. in War with William Pollard of Anderson Co., Ky. Affid. from Pollard, 11-23-1836, Anderson Co., Ky. Service: drf. Sept. 1780, res. of Winchester, Frederick Co., Va., in Va. State Troops; Capt. John Smith, Lt. Colmes
(sp?), another minor officer named Bell. REF: Pens. R.10193 Va.;
Rej. Pens. List (1852) p.409--only 3 mo. service.

STONE, WILLIAM   Vermillion
(Uncertain if he d. in Ind.). d. 12-27-1824; m. 10-12-1775-1776,
Person (sp?) Co., N.C., Sarah -----, b. ca. 1759; chn. (16 incl.):
David; Job (3rd ch., killed by a horse ae. ca. 24-25, Halifax
Co., Va.). Wid.'s pens. appl. 8-17-1843, ae. 84, Vermillion Co.,
Ind. Husb. was drf. when she had 1 ch.; while he was on 3rd
tour, she had her 3rd ch., Job; fam. Bible may be at her son.

David's in Wilkes Co., N.C.; immed. after her mar. in Person (?) Co., N.C., mov. to Halifax Co., Va., the adjoining Co.; fellow solds. of her husb. were: Abram Gregory, Job Gray, Thomas Branan (sp?), & William Gill. Service: drf. ca. 1777 or 1778, Halifax Co., Va., Mil.; was a drummer on 2nd tour; 3rd tour 1781, May after Batt. of Guilford. REF: Pens. R.10220 Va.; Susp. Pens. List (1852) p.416--for period, length & grade of service, & names of company & field officers, & proof of marriage.

STONEBERGER, JOHN   Bartholomew
b. 1760; d. 1821; bur. Union Cem., Taylorsville, Ind. REF: DAR Rept. 51, p. 107.

STORM, JACOB   Scott
b. 6-3-1762, York Co., Pa. Pens. appl. 11-7-1832, ae. 70 last June, Scott Co., Ind. Kinard & Catharine Ferguson will testify as to his service. Affid. 11-7-1832, Scott Co., Ind. of Catharine Ferguson, ae. 88; that she knew he enl. & that she helped her father make clothing for Jacob Storm when he went into the service. (Query: might she be a sister?). P of A, 9-29-1834, Scott Co., Ind., of Jacob Storm, who appts. George Samgster of Marion Co., Ind., & Thomas Sangster of Fauquier Co., Va., to carry on with his claim. Letter 11-21-1854 mentions "heirs". Service: enl. 2-7-1780; Lt. William Goodson, recruiter, Col. Skillard (sp?), Capt. Mills, Botetourt Co., Va. REF: Pens. R.10229 Va.; Rej. Pens. List (1852) p.409--not 6 mo. service.

STOUT, PETER   Clark
b. 9-3-1757, Chester Co., Pa.; mar. Pens. appl. 4-27-1833, ae. 76 next Sept. 3, Clark Co., Ind.; 5-25-1835, ae. 78, Clark Co., Ind.; wife old. From N.C. he mov. to Ga.; to Ind. ca. 23 yr. ago; disch. burned 1828 in his house in Washington Co., Ind. Service: enl. June in yr. of Batt. of Guilford; Guilford Co., N.C.; liv. in Orange Co., N.C.; Capt. Thompson, Col. John Lane. REF: Pens. S.32541 N.C.

STROTHER, DANIEL   Knox
b. 1765, S.C. Pens. appl. 3-10-1834, ae. ca. 68, Knox Co., Ind.; reared in Anson Co., N.C., near Yadkin River. Service: enl. 1-8-1781, Cont. Army, Charlotte Co., Va., as a waggoner. Service attested by pensr., Peter McAnnelly (negro); "Roster" p.264) who knew him in War; 11-6-1844, Knox Co., Ind., by pensr., Andrew Ferguson (negro; "Roster" p.139) who recently saw the old acquaintance he knew dur. the Rev. Pens. file of John LeMountain (see this Suppl.) has Daniel's affid. that he knew LeMountain was a Rev. sold. REF: Pens. R.10275 Va.; Rej. Pens. List (1852) p 409--did not serve 6 mo. in a military capacity.

SUMMERS, JAMES   Putnam
Rev. sold. who died there. REF: Mr. Schrum.

SWINDELL, PERRY   Madison
Rev. sold. who died there. (See Willis Swindell of Madison Co., Ind., in my 1949 compilation, p.33). REF: Mr. Schrum.

TATE, SAMUEL   Clark
(Uncertain). Name obtained after this Suppl. was started. A
Samuel Tate of Indiana is on the 1831 list of rejected pensions,
reason: "On account of amount of his property". (By the 1820
law, indigents under the 1818 law, or new applicants, had their
pensions suspended, or rejected, if they had too much real or
personal property). There are two Samuel Tates in the 1820 Cens.
of Clark Co., Ind., v. 1, pp. 6, 8. (Note: this may be the Samuel Tate below altho the second one is said to have received a
pension and to have died in Spencer Co., Ind., while on a visit.
There is no Samuel Tate on the Ind. Agy. Rolls; so the second one
may have been pensioned in Ky.). REF: "Rej. Appl. for Pens."
(1831) p.49 (see note at end after Daniel Zink).

TATE, SAMUEL   Spencer
b. Pa.; d. ae. 91, while on a visit (prob. from Ky.) to his dau.,
in Spencer Co., Ind.; m. Nancy Johnson, b. Pa.; chn. (7, incl.):
David b. 8-24-1799, Jefferson Co., Ky.; m.(1) Jefferson Co., Ky.,
Elizabeth Blaine, d. 5-5-1831; he m.(2) 10-13-1831, Perry Co.,
Ind., Lucy Seaton, d. 9-10-1846; he m.(3) 7-22-1847, Perry Co.,
Ind., Catharine Cart, d. 2-23-1862; m.(4) 1-15-1863, Perry Co.,
Ind., Mary A. Stinnett; chn.: 6 by 1st w.; 8 by 2nd w.; 3 by 3rd
w.; 6 by 4th w. (full acct. in Co. Hist. below; has 23 chn., eld-
est 65, youngest 8; 76 gr-chn.; 46 gt-gr-chn. David Tate, oldest
res. of Tobin Twp., Perry Co., Ind.; came to Polk's Bottom after
his 2nd mar. The sold., Samuel Tate, recd. Pens. for Rev. serv.
(This name recd. too late by me to check for pens. file). Note:
see above, Samuel Tate of Clark Co., Ind. REF: "Hist. of Warrick,
Spencer, & Perry Cos., Ind." (1885) pp. 795-796.

TAYLOR, BAILIE   Gibson (?)
(Uncertain). While reading another man's pens. file, I found a
reference to Bailie Taylor. The reference (now lost) indicated
service in a Southern state for Taylor. I find that a Bailey
Taylor m. 7-18-1815, Gibson Co., Ind., Winney Bass. They appear
in the 1830 Cens. for Gibson Co. Ind., as: 1 male ae. 60-69,
1 female ae. 60-69. Thus, having been born about 1761 or a little later, Taylor would have been of an age to serve in the Rev.
The pens. file in which I found the reference to him concerned a
Vanderburgh Co., Ind., man; so the location is correct. REF:
Natl. Archives pens. files; 1830 Cens., Gibson Co., Ind., v.5,
p.320; Tartt--"Hist. of Gibson Co., Ind." (1884) p. 64. Note: ref.
finally found; see Jeremiah Wyatt, p. 154.

TAYLOR (TYLER), JACOB   Dearborn
b. 11-12-1758-1759, 5 mi. from Winchester, Frederick Co., Va.;
d. 8-23-1849, Kelso Twp.; m. (wife surv.). Pens. appl. 5-21-
1833, ae. 74, Sullivan Co., Tenn.; 6-18-1849, ae. 90-91, Kelso
Twp., Dearborn Co., Ind.; was under 18 when enl.; at div. of his
father's estate, his youngest sis. got the father's fam. Bible;
she last heard of liv. in Va.; after War, he later liv. Sullivan
Co., Tenn., for 31 yr.; was usually called Tyler in place of Taylor. Letter 10-18-1849, New Alsace, Dearborn Co., Ind., of Daniel Taylor (rel. not given); that sold. d. 8-23, ae. 91 (altho
Mort. Sched. below say 8-22, ae. 90), Service: enl. 1777, Fred-

erick Co., Va., 7th Regt., Col. Mecklenburg.   REF: Pens. R.10416½
Va.; 1850 Mortality Schedules (ISL), v.1, p.235; "Madison Daily
Courier", 9-3-1849, abstr. by Miss Mary Hill, Madison, Ind.

TEVEBAUGH, JACOB   Knox
b. 1764, Hampshire Co., Va. (or in Holland); d. Apr. 1790, killed
by Indians; mar.; chn.: only 1 known is Jacob who m. Mary -----
and had Solomon, Abraham, George, Barbara, Jacob, Nimrod, Mary
(m. David Reaugh), Drusilla (m.1st, Alexander McCray & m.2nd,
William Sullivan). To Vincennes, Ind., 1785; in Knox Co. Mil.
Service: in Rev. under Capt. Zadock Wright, Washington Co., Pa.,
1782. REF: Eckenrode (1912) p.432; Gwathmey--"Va. in Rev.",
p.775; "Pa. Arch.", 6th Ser., v.2, pp.80, 256; Pens. S.16072 of
Philip Catt ("Roster" p.91); Mrs. Eva B. Davenport, Vincennes.

THOMAS, JOHN   Vigo
b. 4-10-1763, Frederick Co., Va.; d. ca. 1836; mar. twice (one
time was in 1786 in Hardin Co., Ky.) to 2 daus. of Robert Hodgen
(founder of Hodgenville, Ky.). Pens. appl. 2-9-1836, ae. 73,
Vigo Co., Ind. When 8 yr. old, mov. with father to Fayette Co.,
Pa.; dur War, was stationed at Louisville (Ky.) & never retd. to
Pa.; after 1782 service, liv. in what is now Hardin Co., Ky.; in
1831 to Floyd Co., Ind.; 1833 to Washington Co., Ind.; 1834 to
Vigo Co., Ind. Was also in Indian Wars; in 1791 raised a Comp.
& commanded it at St. Clair's defeat; in 1793 commanded a Comp.
under Gen. Wayne.. Owned land on Green River, 1786; one ref. says
liv. LaRue Co., Ky., 50 yrs. Quoted: "Thomas was the most veteran soldier of them all -- a Captain in the American Revolution
and in St. Clair's ill-starred expedition against the Indians
under Brandt and Little Turtle in 1791, he arose to Colonel and
on to Major General in the War of 1812. General Thomas lived as
a quiet farmer until his death in Vigo County, Indiana twenty
years after" (his retirement). Service: enl. 1781, Fayette Co.,
Pa.; Gen. Clark, Capt. Robert Ferrel, Col. Zachariah Morgan, Maj.
Lowder; stationed at Louisville. REF: Pens. R.10503½ Pa. & Va.;
Rej. Pens. List (1852) p.409--did not serve 6 mo.; "Reg. of the
Ky. Hist. Soc." v.29, Oct. 1951, p.362; Mather--"Six Generations
of LaRues & Allied Fams." (1921) pp.128, 133; Miss Thelma Murphy,
Indianapolis, Ind.

THOMAS, RICHARD   Union (?)
b. ca. 1745; d. Jan. 1839, Union Co., Ind. (or Fayette Co., Ind.);
bur. near Connersville, Fayette Co., Ind.; m. Jane (or Rhoda or
Rhoda Jane) Porter, d. 7-14-1840, Fayette Co., Ind.; chn.: Hannah b. 1781, Md.; d. 1-8-1857, ae. 76, Union Co., Ind.; bur. Sims
Cem ca. ½ mi. N of Fairfield, Ind.; m. Jacob Bloyd, d. 4-15-
1845;* Thomas b. 1790, Md.; d. 1873; m. Franklin Co., Ind., Jane
Harlin; both bur. Sims Cem.;(he in War of 1812, Ind.); Susannah
m.(1) 10-26-1815, Franklin Co., Ind., John Adair; m.(2-3 or re-
verse) Mr. Barrackman & John Ferris; John d. ante 1840 & left
several heirs liv. then in Harrison & Floyd Cos., Ind.; Mary,
unm.; d 1-15-1843, Rush Co., Ind.; Richard b. 1783; m. 8-8-
1821, Fayette Co., Ind., Mary Ann Risk; Rebecca m. Mr. Hollingsworth & liv. 1840 Vermillion Co., Ind.; Elizabeth d. ante 1840;
  *ae. 68-7-5

m. James Abernathy & liv. Rush Co., Ind.; Hannah (Note: I just
caught discrepancy with first child above) m. 11-21-1828, Union
Co, Ind., David Lynch. (Note: there were 2 daus. named Hannah;
both are named in mother Jane Thomas' estate papers in Connersville, Ind.) Richard Thomas entered the NE¼ of Sec. 6, Twp. 13,
Range 13 East, Fayette Co., Ind., on 9-15-1813; land to heirs in
1840; he is in 1820-30 Cens., Fayette Co., Ind. Service: pvt.
in Md. Troops, 5th Md. Regt.; enl. 6-4-1778; disch. 3-20-1779;
Capt. Josiah Johnson, Col. William Richardson. REF: "Md. Arch.",
v.18, p.251; Adj.-Gen. Office, Washington, D.C.; "Harlan Geneal.";
Mrs. Hazel Overleese, Rushville, Ind.

THOMPSON, JAMES   Johnson
b. 11-17-1761, in Md., not far from the Mine banks on the oppo-
site of the Susquehanna River in Cecil Co., near Charley Brook-
ens Mill; still alive 9-27-1845 (see note below); mar. Pens.
appl. 11-11-1834, ae. ca. 73, Jackson Co., Ind. When ca. 4-5 yr.
old, mov. with father (John Thompson, Sr.) to Carlisle, Pa., for
ca. 3 yr.; to Braddocks fields (then in Westmoreland Co., now
prob. Alleghany Co.) near mouth of Turtle Creek on Monongahela
River in Pa.; liv. there till ca. 19 yr old & married & later
mov. to Lexington, Ky.; there ca. 7 yr.; to near mouth of Great
Miami River in Dearborn Co., Ind., for 3-4 yr.; to near Harrison
on E side of Whitewater in Hamilton Co., O., for ca. 14-15 yr.;
till ca. 14-15 yr, ago to Stringtown, Jackson Co., Ind.; for ca.
1 yr.; then to Hamilton Twp., Jackson Co., Ind., where now lives.
Affid. 11-11-1834, Hamilton Twp., Jackson Co., Ind., of James
Guffy ("Roster" p.167); that he knew Thompson dur. Rev. when he
serv. with him in Capt. Rolliter's Comp. in which he (Guffy) was
Ensign, & afterward in Capt. Myers' Comp. in Pa. Mil. of what is
now Alleghany Co., Pa.; that he knew Thompson's father. Similar
affid., but more in detail, of William Thompson (might be a bro.
or cous. of Hamilton Twp., Jackson Co., Ind. Sold. again appl.
11-12-1838. ae. 77, Hensley Twp., Johnson Co., Ind.; pretty much
sama data as in orig. appl. Letter from him 9-27-1845 again saying he is now of Johnson Co., Ind.: Service: was ca. 12-14 yr.
old when War began; when ca. 15-16 yr. old, enl. in Pa. Mil.;
Capt Rolliter, Lt. Burrows Ens. James Guffy; Col. Gibson, Westmoreland Co. (now Alleghany Co.) Pa. (Note: the Rej. Pens. List
gives a James Thompson of Jackson Co. & one of Johnson Co., too.
The Ft. Vallonia Chap., DAR, Seymour, Ind., feels that the Jackson Co. one is the man whose will was pr. 6-28-1835, Bk.1, p.17,
and who is bur. in Driftwood Cem., Jackson Co., Ind. I feel that
this must be another man of the same name & that the Jackson Co.
sold. mov. to Johnson Co. as this pens. file would indicate).
REF: Pens. R.10534 Pa.; Rej. Pens. List (1852) p.409 (Jackson Co.)
not under competent military authority or organization; p.409
(Johnson Co.)-not 6 mo. actual service; Mrs. Claude E. Gilliatt,
Seymour, Ind.

THOMPSON, JOHN   Harrison
(Not to be confused with the one below or with the one in the
"Roster" p.354). b. ca. 1757; d. 11-15-1827 (or 10-15); mar.;
(wife ae. 45 in 1822); chn. (at least): John, 18; Jane, 15;

both liv. with sold. 1822. Pens. appl. 9-23-1822, Nelson Co., Ky., ae. 65. Affid. of John Cullett that he was in same Comp. with Thompson, 11th Va. Regt. Affid. 3-3-1824, Harrison Co., Ind. of William Madden ("Roster" p.243) that he knew sold. dur. War. Letter 3-4-1824, Corydon, Harrison Co., Ind., from Thomas Posey to Jonathan Jennings that sold. now lives here, having mov. from Ky. where he first appl. Note in pens. file says d. 11-15-1827; 1835 Pens. List says 10-15-1827. Service; enl. 1776 in Va.; Capt. Charles Porterfield, Col. Daniel Morgan, Va. State Line. REF: Pens S 36828 Va.; I.A.R. #19,268 (5-31-1824); 1835 Pens. List, v. 3, p. 19.

THOMPSON, JOHN Indiana
(Not to be confused with the one above nor with the one in the "Roster" p.354). b. ca. 1759; d. Sept. 1830; mar.; chn.: at least 1 boy & 1 girl. Pens. appl. 6-9-1819, ae. 60, Mercer Co., Ky.; 1-1-1821, ae. 69, Mercer Co., Ky.; pens. tr. from Mercer Co., Ky., to Ind. (no date); wrapper has Ky. crossed off & Ind. written in in red but no county given. Service: enl. 1776, Va. State Troops; later in Aug. 1776, in 12th Va. Regt., Continental Establishment; Col. James Wood, Capt. Michael Bowyer. REF: Pens. S.36826 Va.; I.A.R. #16,406 (1-27-1820); 1835 Pens. List,v.3,p.37.

THOMPSON, SETH Dearborn
Rev. sold. who died there. REF: Mr. Schrum.

THOMPSON, THOMAS Delaware
b. 6-24-1757 (note discrepancies), Chester Co., Pa. Pens. appl. 6-19-1834, ae. 77, Hamilton Co., O., where has liv. over 20 yr. Again appl. 2-9-1839, ae. 84 last June 24. Since service, has liv. Lycoming Co., Pa.; 30 yr. in Hamilton Co., O.; now Delaware Co., Ind. P of A, 1-20-1854, De;aware Co., Ind., of Jesse W. Thompson (rel. not given, but prob. son), heir to Thomas Thompson deceased. Service: enl. as a subst. for his bro., Robert Thompson, who enl. 1776; as a subst., serv, under Col. Shives, Capt. Cummins, Lt. Conn; 2nd N.J. Regt.; enl. Dec. 1776 at Princeton, but a res. of Pitchgrove Twp.; Salem Co., N.J. REF: Pens. R.10557 N.J.; Rej. Pens. List (1852) p.409--not 6 mo. service.

THORN, ASA Indiana
(Uncertain). His widow, Zenion Thorn, is on Ind. Agy., Revolutionary Pens. Rolls, certif. #152 (law of 1836), husb. a Lieut. However, Natl. Archives could not find pens. file. (Note: an Asa Thorn was commn. Lieut. on 11-2-1818 in the 1st Regt., Knox Co., Ind., Mil.). REF: I.A.R.; "Exec. Proc. of Ind., 1816-1836" p.83.

THRASHER, JOSIAH Rush
b. Jan. 1763, Frederick Co., Md. Pens. appl. 10-12-1842, ae. 80, Rush Co., Ind.; had appl. for pens. in 1834 or 1835 & nothing ever heard. (Note: this appl. was not in pens. file). Since War, has liv. Pa., Ky., Ind., now Rush Co., Ind. Affid. 7-19-1842, Pendleton Co., Ky., of James Preble; has known Thrasher, formerly of Pendleton Co., Ky., since small boy; saw Thrasher in

service at Jackson's Fort when he (Preble) was in service at same
time under Capt. Jesse Pigman at Ancrom's Fort ca. 3 mi. away;
often went over to Jackson's Fort & saw Thrasher there in service
under Capt. James Archer. Affid. 10-17-1842, Pendleton Co., Ky.,
of Mary Boner, ae. 74; that Thrasher is her bro. & is ae. ca. 79;
that fam. liv. Jackson's Fort ca, 2 yr.; that she remembers her
bro. & many others as guards against Indians. Service: enl. at
Fort Jackson, Washington Co., Pa.; Capt. James Archer; in his 17-
18- or 19th yr. REF: Pens. R.10578 Pa.; Rej. Pens. List (1852)
p. 409--not under competent military authority or organization.

 THURIE, EDWARD   Randolph
Rev. sold. who died there. REF: Mr. Schrum.

 TIPPS, CONRAD   Washington
Rev. sold. who died there; bur. in Little York Cem. Liv. in
Gibson Twp. Was also in War of 1812. REF: Mr. Schrum; Morris--
"Arch. & Hist. Survey of Washington Co., Ind." (1925) pp.91, 95;
Stevens--"Hist. of Washington Co., Ind." (1916) p.633.
 TRAINER, ISAAC--see p. 119.
 TRANTER, JOHN   Daviess
d. post 1821 (signed deed); m. Magdalene -----; d. post 1821
(deed); chn. (at least): John, Jr., b. ca. 1789; m. 6-6-1809,
Jessamine Co., Ky., Martha Bruner, dau. of Henry Bruner. Fam.
liv. Chester Co., Pa.; sold. was one of pioneer settlers of Liv-
erpool (now Washington), Daviess Co., Ind.; may have had a son
George & also either dau. or sis., Elizabeth, who m. David Hoov-
er (Moravian missionary to Jessamine Co., Ky.). Service: pvt. in
Chester Co., Pa., Mil.; Capt. John Harris' Comp., 1780-81-82.
REF: "Pa. Arch.", 5th Ser., v.5, pp.605, 639; "Johnson Co.,Ind.,
Rec.", v.2, pt.4, p.254 (the following pp. have desc. of John,
Jr.), Alexander Hamilton Chap., DAR, Franklin, Ind.; Mrs. Ira E.
Tranter, Franklin, Ind.

 TUFTS, WILLIAM   Lagrange
Rev. sold. who died there. In 1840 Pens. List, ae. 92, of Elkhart Co., Ind. REF: Mr. Schrum; 1840 Pens. List, p. 182.

 VANARSDALL, CHRISTOPHER   Gibson
b. 1739; mar.; chn. Pens. appl. 10-17-1834, ae. 95, Mercer Co.,
Ky. Affid. 10-17-1834, Mercer Co., Ky., of Lt. Cornelius Vanarsdall, ae. 87; that he & sold. were raised boys together in
Somerset Co., N.J., & serv. together in War. Same of Cornelius
O. Vanarsdall, ae. 74, Rev. sold. Same of Peter Huff, Rev. sold.;
that he liv. in adjoining Co. in N.J. before War & knew sold.
then & later serv. in War with him. Service: drf. fall 1775;
Capt. Conrad Teneych, Col. Vroom, Somerset Co., N.J.; well remembers being stationed at Millstone when his oldest son fell in the
Batt. of Brandywine. Ca. 2 yr. ago sold. spoke to a Judge Hall
of Ind., where he was then liv., to make pens. appl. for him; but
it was not done; since wife long dead, sold. went to live with son
in Mercer Co.,Ky.,where were others who had serv. with him. On
3-12-1836, Gibson Co.,Ind.,asks for tr. to Ind. to live with chn.
who have mov. here.; tr. 10-1-1836. REF: Pens. S.32567 N.J.

VANCE, SAMUEL   Fayette
This man has often been confused with Samuel Colville Vance, and
descendants have joined the DAR under the latter man, incorrectly.
Samuel C. Vance was b. in 1770 in Pa.; serv. in the Indian Wars
under Wayne; laid out Lawrenceburg, Dearborn Co., Ind., in 1802;
d. Feb. (or Mar.) 18, 1830, ae. 60; was the son of David Vance.
Samuel C. Vance m. Sarah Lawrence, gr-dau. of Gen. St. Clair.
REF: "Indianapolis Star", 6-25-1944, p.4; Vance papers in Ind.
Hist. Soc. Libr.   The Samuel Vance of Fayette Co., Ind.,
was b. 6-18-1762, Bucks Co., Pa.; d. 3-1-1843, Connersville, Ind.;
bur. on home farm near Connersville; son of Samuel & Agnes (Penquite) Vance of Baltimore Co. & Harford Co., Md.; m. 10-14-1798,
Bel Air, St. James Parish, Baltimore Co., Md., Mary Ann Waters,
b. 3-29-1779, Harford Co., Md.; d. 11-7-1857 (or 1856); bur. by
husb.; chn. (at least): twins, Elijah b. 1801; & Elisha b. 1801,
Harford Co., Md.; d. 7-5-1864, Connersville, Ind.; m. Oct. 1820,
Butler Co., O., Mary Harper, b. 3-15-1801, Ohio; d. 4-22-1882,
Connersville, Ind.; dau. of Samuel & Catharine (DeMoss) Harper of
Fauquier Co. & Berkeley Co., Va., respectively; they had 10 chn.
Pens. appl. first made in 1818 under indigent law; again 6-25-
1834, ae. 72 on June 18, Chester Twp., Clinton Co., O. In 1809
mov. from Md. to Greene Co., Pa.; 1818 to Ohio; for last 3 yr. in
Chester Twp., Clinton Co., O.; did not move to Ind., until son
sett. there in Fayette Co., Ind., in 1825. Affid. 6-26-1834,
Clinton Co., O., of E. Vance (rel. not given, but undoubtedly one
of his twin sons); that he has frequently seen rec. of sold.'s
age, etc. Letter 3-18-1839 from Eli Vance, Connersville, Ind.,
saying sold. now liv. Connersville & mail to him should be addr.
Samuel Vance, Senr., as there are two others of the same name
here. (Note: sold. also had a nephew named Samuel Vance; see
1840 Cens., Waterloo Twp., Fayette Co., Ind., v.3, p.116, 4 entries). Service: res. Harford Co., Md., in Rev.; father made
Supt. of Warehouses at Otter Point, Harford Co., Md., fall 1778,
under Col. Richard Dallum (Dellum? Dullum?), Md. Mil. Samuel,
ae. 16-17, helped salt beef & pork for Army, 1778-1779 & help
guard warehouses; fall 1779 was ordered to Bush (Buck?) Town,
Harford Co., Md., to clean the public arms; here for 5 mo. & was
assisted only by a younger bro. Later he says he enl. Sept. 1778
& was pvt. 12 mo. in Capt. William Bradford, Col. Dallum; fall
1779, 5 mo. under Col. Dallum; fall 1780, 1 mo. under Capt.
McComas. (Informant below has earlier & later data on Vance &
Penquite fams.). REF: Pens. R.10836 Md.; Rej. Pens. List (1852)
p.409--not military service; Mrs. Alice Vance Robinson, Seattle,W.

VAN GORDEN, WILLIAM   Lake
b. 10-17-1758, New Windsor, Orange Co., N.Y. Pens. appl. 3-8-
1833, ae. 75, Tioga Co., N.Y., but a res. of Athens, Bradford
Co., Pa. Dur. War, liv. Walpeck, Sussex Co., N.J. & after till
1799, to Tioga Co., N.Y. & "in its neighborhood just over the
Penna. line" has liv. ever since. Affid. 4-10-1833, Tioga Co.,
N.Y., of John Swartwood, ae. 79, Cayuta, N.Y.; that he knew sold.
in War; same of Samuel Westbrook, who was the Major. Service:
enl. May 1779, Walpeck, Sussex Co., N.J.; Capt. Emanuel Hoover.
I.A.R. says Sergeant; 1835 Pens. List says pvt. in N.Y. Mil. On

5-27-1837, Lake Co., Ind., asks for pens. tr. to be with his relations in Lake Co., where he has been since Nov. 1836; pens. tr. from Albany, N.Y., Agy., 6-28-1837. REF: Pens. S.17743 N.J.; 1835 Pens. List, v.2, p.434; Tioga Co., N.Y.

VAN VLAIR, ADAM   Fayette
b. 1762-1763, Sussex Co., N.J.; m. Mar. or Apr. 1798, Mary -----, b. ca. 1786; he d. Mar. 1840. Pens. appl. 2-10-1836, ae. 73-74, Connersville Twp., Fayette Co., Ind. His oldest bro. has the fam. Bible but d. several yrs/ ago in Va.; bro.'s wid. now liv. in N. Ind. & prob. has Bible. Last fall sold. visited a sis. in Ohio. Some yrs. after War, he mov. to Va. near mouth of Little Kanawha; there 18-20 yr.; then Butler Co., O., ca. 5 yr.; Union Co., Ind., 4-5 yr.; since then here in Fayette Co., Ind., 12-13 yr except 1 yr. in Henry Co., Ind. Affid. & P of A, 5-24-1855, Fayette Co., Ind., of Mary Tell (Lell?), wife & heir; that she m. in Mar. or Apr. 1798; he d. Mar. 1840; she ae. 69. Service: drf 1778, Col Bloomfield, Maj. Ogden Capt. Beesley, Sussex Co., N.J. REF: Pens. R.10896 N.J.; Rej. Pens. List (1852) p.409- was employed principally as a cook.

VAUGHN, JOHN   Washington
Rev. sold. who died there.; bur. in Mounts Cem., south of Little York, in Gibson Twp. Was a Captain. REF: Mr. Schrum; Stevens-- "Hist. of Washington Co., Ind." (1916) p.634.

VINNEDGE, ADAM   Wayne
bur. in King Cem. on Charles Wilson farm, Wayne Twp., ca. 1 mi. NW of Richmond, Ind., along the Chicago Division, Pa. Ry.; m. (prob. S.C.), Margaret Simonton of S.C. (Charleston?); chn.: Elizabeth b. 8-27-1776; d. 9-18-1833; m. Samuel Russell, d. 4-15-1835; John b. 4-4-1774, Pa.; d. 4-16-1868; m. Rosannah Moore (& had son John); David b. 1-13-1793 (liv. Hamilton Co., O., & many desc. there); Margaret m. Mr. Spivey; Mary m. Jacob Miller (Rev. sold.; see forward this Suppl.). In cem. are stones of William Vinnedge, d. 3-21-1839, ae. 39 yr., 10 mo., 17 da.; Margaret Vinnedge, d. 9-8-1839, ae. 37 yr., --(?) mo., 19 da. Next to William is a grave with a flat, rough-hewn marker (may be Adam's). Sold.'s son, John, to Ohio 1794 in Gen. Wayne's army; also in War of 1812; his wife came to Cincinnati, O., 1789. Service: patriot who rendered material aid. Records show that Adam Vinnedge was paid by Quartermaster-General's Dept. on 5-25-1782 & 9-2-1782 for hay, oats, & pasture and for carting military stores to Philadelphia. Also, his name on a receipt dated 8-17-1782 for 10 shillings for pasturing 3 horses. Info from Adj.-Gen. of N.J.; Trenton State Librarian; Harrisburg, Pa.; Commissioner of Pensions, Washington, D.C. REF: Mrs. Forrest E. Kempton, Centerville, Ind., whose husband's aunt, Mrs. Clara Kempton, ae. 88, has the above receipt.

WALKER, DANIEL   Indiana
(Uncertain) Name obtained after this Suppl. was started. A Daniel Walker of Indiana is on the 1831 list of rejected pensions, reason:"served in a regiment not on continental establishment". A

Daniel Walker is in the 1820 Cens, of Dearborn Co., Ind., v.1, p.
98. In the 1830 Cens., there is one in Clay Co., Ind., v.1, p.
544, and one in Johnson Co., Ind., v.7, p.56. REF: "Rej. Appl,
for Pens." (1831) p.49 (see note at end after Daniel Zink).

  WALLACE, OLIVER   Vermillion
b. 2-14-1763, Shenandoah Co. (now Rockingham Co.), Va.; d. 11-30-
(or 11-13)-1842; m. 9-14-1780, Rockingham Co., Va., Mary -----,
b. ca. 1766; chn. (others besides): John b. ca. 1786, Tenn.;
Thomas R., b. Dec. 1790, Ky.; William; Sarah. Pens. appl.
10-5-1832, ae. 69, Warren Co., Ohio; again 8-8-1836, ae. 74, in
Warren Co., Ind. Dur. War., liv. on Smith's Creek, Rockingham
Co., Va.; later in Tenn.; in Ky.; Warren Co., O.; now Warren Co.,
Ind. Wid.'s pens. appl. 2-23-1844. ae. 78, Edgar Co., Ill.
Affid. 8-14-1846, Edgar Co., Ill., of William Runion, ae. 69;
that he knew sold. & wife for 40 yr. & in Warren Co., O.; that
sold. came there 2-3 yr. later than deponent did in 1802-1804;
that sold. had grown chn. 40 yr. ago & that wid. now has grown
gr-chn. Affid. 6-9-1846, Edgar Co., Ill., of John McCartney, ae.
46; that he knew sold.'s fam. in Warren Co., O.; 23 yr. ago; that
5 chn. are still liv.; that sold.'s son John must be at least 60
yr. old. Affid. 6-27-1846, Edgar Co., Ill., of William Bush, ae.
62; that he knew John Wallace & Thomas R. Wallace for 28 yr. &
that he knew sold. & fam. that long; that sold. had large fam.
Affid. 6-27-1846, Edgar Co., Ill., of Thomas R. Wallace, ae. 53;
that John Wallace, ae. 59, is oldest ch. of sold. Affid. 8-18-
1845, Warren Co., O., of John Wallace, son, ae. past 60, b. Tenn.;
was ca. 8 yr. old when fam. mov. from Tenn. to Ky., where liv.
for ca. 16 yr., & then to Warren Co., O., until ca. 10 yr. ago
when he mov. to Ill.; that Thomas Wallace, ae. ca. 55 next Dec.,
b. Ky., is a son of sold.; that they had other chn. older than
Thomas, namely: William, Sarah, John, & 1 dead. As an orphan,
sold. was bound out to Thomas Lookey of Rockingham Co., Va. Service: enl Winchester, Va., as subst. for Elijah Russell, a bro-
in-law of James Lookey (son of Thomas Lookey); 8th Va. Regt.,
Col. Campbell REF: Pens. W.22543 Va.

  WALLACE, SAMUEL   Bartholomew
b. 2-19-1761, Albemarle Co., Va.; d. 12-4-1843; m. 3-2-1831, Bartholomew Co., Ind., Lilly Ann -----, b. ca. 1789. Pens. appl.
9-13-1842, ae. 81 on Feb. 18, Flat Rock Twp., Bartholomew Co.,
Ind. Service: enl. fall 1779, Albemarle Co., Va.; Capt. Andrew
Wallace (no rel. given), Col. Morgan. After War, liv. in Ga. 8
yr.; Ky. 12 yr.; now Ind. Wallace is mentioned in a letter in
pens. file of William Campbell, Pens. R.1632. Wid.'s pens. appl.
2-10-1851, ae. 62, Wabash Co., Ind.; she prev. appl. from Bartholomew Co., Ind., after husb. died. REF: Pens. R.11071 Va.;
Susp. Pens. List (1852) p.414--no proof of service.

  WAPSHOTT, GRAVES   Perry
b. 7-16-1750, Old Style, London, Eng. Emigr. to Amer. & landed
6-28-1773, Dumfries, Va.; liv., Prince William, Loudon, Fauquier,
& Hampshire Cos., Va., 1773-1780, when left for Louisville, Ky.,
where landed 6-4-1780 & where was liv. when enl. After War, liv.

Jefferson, Nelson, & Washington Cos., Ky.; last 15 yr. in Perry Co., Ind., where appl. for pens. 11-14-1832, ae. 82. Service: he had hired late in 1779 a Mr. Fagan of Hampshire Co., Va., to serve as a subst. for him for $2,500 for whole term of War in 3rd Va. Regt.; Capt. Robert Higgins; later he himself was drf. June-July 1780, George Rogers Clark, Capt. John Askins, Lt. John Hanley; was an Orderly-Sergeant. REF: Pens. R.11111 Va. (also 1786 & 1790 service); Rej. Pens. List (1852) p.410--did not serve 6 mo.; Mr. Wallace Weatherholt, Tell City & Indianapolis, Ind.

WARD, WILLIAM M. Indiana
Uncertain if he died in Ind. His wid., Rebecca Ward, is on Ind. Agy. Rolls, certif. #400, 9-4-1849. Natl. Archives could not find pens. file. Name may be wrong--Wood, Wand, etc. If any reader knows the correct name, please notify the compiler. REF: Ind. Agy. Rolls.

WASHBURN, GEORGE Montgomery
b. prob. Penna.; d. 3-9-1850; bur. Round Hill Cem., Coal Creek Twp.; m.(1) Azuba Robins; chn.: Jeremiah m. Nancy McDaniels; Isaac b. Ky. (or Pa.); d. 1828 (or 1825), Brown Co., O.; m. 10-9-1804, Rachel Laycock, b. 5-9-1786, Va. (& had 11 chn.); he was in War of 1812; wid. m.(2) 12-16-1828, Vincent Calvin; mov. to Pulaski Co., Ind., & d. at nearly 100; Cornelius m. Susan Dunn, dau. of James Dunn; Sarah m. James Holmes; Rebecca m. John Stansbury; Rachel m. Samuel G. Sperry; Azuba m. James Hass; Phoebe m. William Grant; Nancy m. Andrew Lowderback. The sold. m.(2) Eleanor (Tong or Tongue) Rankins, wid. of Daniel Rankins (who had d. 4-30-1833, Brown Co., O., & had Rev. pens. After War, sold. liv. Madison Co., Ky.; to Brown Co., O., to east side of Straight Creek, on what was called Cherry Bottom, Franklin Twp.; then to Wardlow's Run; later to Ind. Wid., Eleanor, liv. Montgomery Co., Ind., & Tippecanoe Co., Ind. Service: from beginning to end of War; was later with Boone in Ky. REF: "Hist. of Brown Co., O." (1883) pp.531-534, 605; "First Cens. of Ky."; pens. file of Daniel Rankins; Miss Mary Whitehouse, Cathedral City, Calif.

WATSON, WILLIAM Clark
b. ca. 1747; d. ca. Nov. 1819, Charlestown, Ind., ae. 72. Was a sold. of the Rev. Mov. with fam. from Ky. to Charleston, Ind. Death notice in Lexington, Ky., "Gazette" on 12-5-1819. REF: "Ky. Hist. Reg." Apr. 1947, p.198; Miss Thelma Murphy, Indianapls.

WATSON, WILLIAM Posey
b. 9-5-1742, Louisa Co., Va.; d. 9-2-1846; mar.; chn. (at least): John; William H.; Francis M. Pens. appl. 9-12-1832, ae. 90, Madison Co., Ky.; has liv. Ky. ca. 28 yr. Affid. 1-1-1841, Madison Co., Ky., of Daniel Breck; that sold. mov. to Ind. in winter 1833 with his son. Affid. 5-27-1841, Posey Co., Ind., of sold.; that he mov. to Posey Co., Ind., in winter 1833 or late 1832; wife dead; liv. with son John, who mov. to Posey Co. In 1835 Pens List, Madison Co., Ky., as Lieut. in Va. Line. Pens. tr. to Ind 7-7-1841. Service: enl. fall 1780; Capt. Thomas Smith,

Col. Robert Smith, while liv. Pittsylvania Co., Va. (Note: may be the bro. William of Ind. mentioned in pens. file S.15695 of John Watson of Anderson Co., Ky. REF: Miss Thelma Murphy, Indianapolis, Ind.). REF: Pens. S.17752 Va.; 1835 Pens. List. vol. 3, p. 117.

WATTS, CHARLES   Parke
b. 4-14-1761, Albemarle Co., Va. Pens. appl. 2-22-1836, ae. 75, Washington Twp., Parke Co., Ind. Fam. rec. prob. still in Albemarle Co., Va., 8 mi. below Charlotteville. A few yrs. after service, mov. to Rockbridge Co., Va., where liv. till came to Ind. Service: drf. Oct. 1778, Albemarle Co., Va.; Capt. Robert Sharp, Ens. Harry Qualls; when he was ae. ca. 16. REF: Pens. R.11215 Va.; Rej. Pens. List (1852) p.409--did not serve 6 mo.

WATTS, WILLIAM   Washington
b. ca. 1758; d. 7-20-1834. Pens. appl. 9-26-1832, ae. 74, Washington Co., Ind. Service: enl. 1775, 8th Regt., Va. Line; Capt. Abraham Hite; recruited at New London, Campbell Co., Va. REF: Pens. S.16286 Va.

WAYMAN, EDMOND   Washington
Affid. 4-4-1856, Jackson Co., Ind., of Charles L. Wayman, ae. 50, in pens. file of Thomas Alexander of Washington Co., Ind. (see forward, this Suppl.) states that he (Charles) knew Alexander 30 yr. ago in Washington Co., Ind. & later in Jackson Co., Ind.; and that he often heard Alexander & his father, Edmond Wayman, now decd., talk about their respective service in the War. (See Thomas Alexander's record, this book, for possible clue as to Edmond Wayman's service). REF: Pens. R.90 Pa. (of Thomas Alexander); 1820 Cens., Washington Co., Ind., v. 5, p. 364.

WEAVER, MICHAEL   Washington
b. 8-15-1756, Northampton Co., Pa. Pens. appl. 11-12-1832, ae. 76, Washington Co., Ind. Service: enl. Sept. 1776, Berks Co., Pa.; Capt. Powell Grosscup, Col. Paulsen Kerr. After War, cont. liv. in Berks Co., Pa., 4 yr.; to N.C. ca. 10-12 yr.; to Pulaski Co., Ky., 6 yr.; to Washington Co., Ky., ca. 3 yr.; to Orange Co., Ind.; for last 14 yr. in Washington Co., Ind. REF: Pens. S.16290 Pa.; Mr. Schrum.

WEBB, BARRUCH   Wayne
(Uncertain. There is no request in his pens. file for a trans. to Ind from Ohio; he may have mov. to Ind. & died before a trans. could be effected --- or he may have mov. to Ind. & have had pens payments continue from Ohio because of convenience or some other reason. Although he appears in "Ohio Rev. Sold.", I see no proof that he died there). b. 1760; mar. Mary -----, b. Feb. 1776; chn. (6 liv. with him in 1820): Harriet 12; Noah 9; Asaph 7; Maria 6; Thomas 4; Manassah 5 (deaf & dumb). Pens. appl. 5-25-1818, Clark Co., O.; again 9-1-1819, ae. 58; again 8-14-1820, ae. 60. Appears in the 1835 Pens. List for Wayne Co., Ind., ae. 74; pvt. in Md. Line. Service: enl. June-July 1780, Bladensburg, Md.; Col. Joshua Bell; Md. Mil., Cont. Estab.,

1st Comp., State Regt. of Md.; Capt. Goulder. REF: Pens. S.40654
Md.; 1835 Pens. List, v.3, p.37; "Ohio Rev. Sold.". v.2, p.357.

WEBB, JEREMIAH   Indiana
(Uncertain). Name obtained after this Suppl. was started. A
Jeremiah Webb of Indiana is on the 1831 list of rejected pensions,
reason: "served in a regiment not on continental establishment".
There is no Jeremiah Webb in either the 1820 or 1830 Cens. of
Ind. He may have lived in the household of someone else, may have
lived here in an interim period between censuses and have died, or
may have moved away. REF: "Rej. Appl. for Pens." (1831) p.49 (see
note at end after Daniel Zink).

WEBB, JONATHAN   Franklin
b. 9-3-1753; d. fall 1815; m. 1787, Goshen, Orange Co., N.Y., Mrs.
Amy (-----) Basset, b. 3-13-1761; chn. (from Bible): Mary b. 4-4-
1789; Barzillai b. 4-2-1791;   Rebekah b. 8-22-1793; m.(Daniel?)
Budd; Jonathan Bassett b. 10-4-1795;   Matilda b. 5-30-1798;
Elizabeth b. 11-15-1800;   Nathaniel b. 3-24-1803. Wid.'s pens.
appl. 7-22-1843, ae. 82, Franklin Co., Ind. Fam. mov. from
Orange Co., N.Y., to Franklin Co., Ind., where husb. d. in same
year; she lives Brookville, Ind.; Bible written by husb. ca. 1790;
she had prev. mar. Jonathan Basset, by whom she had 2 chn.: John
Basset b. 1-11-1779 & Hannah Basset b. 10-2-1781. Jonathan Webb
put his step-chn. in his Bible; other chn. are hers & Webb's.
Affid 7-22-1843, Franklin Co., Ind., of Rebecca Budd, ae. 49,
dau of Jonathan Webb, re Bible. Affid. 7-22-1843, Franklin Co.,
Ind., of Daniel Budd, re sold.'s death. P of A, 9-28-1843, Frank-
lin Co., Ind., of wid., Amy Webb; that husb. prob. serv. under
Capt. Weasner (sp?), Col. Hatfield; other officers were Job
(John?) Wood & a man named Hatfield. P of A, Jan. 1854, Decatur
Co., Ind., of Abel Webb & Joseph Webb (rel. not given). Service:
orderly sgt. in N.Y. Mil., prob. while res. of Orange Co., N.Y.
REF: Pens. R.11244 N.Y.; Susp. Pens. List (1852) p.420--for proof
of identity with the Jonathan Webb of the Conn. & N.Y. Troops;
Reifel--"Hist. of Franklin Co., Ind." (1915) pp. 94, 101, 178.

WEBB, THEODORE   Decatur
Rev. sold. who died there. REF: Mr. Schrum.

WEDDING, R. H.   Parke
Rev. sold. who died there. (Note: a Randolph H. Wedding was
commn. J.P. for Parke Co., Ind., 3-5-1834; sold. or son?). REF:
Mr. Schrum; "Exec. Proc. of Ind., 1816-1836", p.554.

WEIST, HENRY   Switzerland
b. 1-1-1754, Hopewell Twp. (formerly Shrewsbury Twp. till 1767),
York Co., Pa.; d. 11-18-1845, in 91st yr. (obit says died in
Ohio; this might be an error for Ohio Co., Ind.; anyhow, was bur.
near Patriot, Ind., with tombstone, now nearly illegible; elderly
relatives remember as children that stone stated he was a Rev.
sold. & gave the Regt.; obit also says Rev. sold.); m. in 20th yr.
(prob. York Co., Pa., or Baltimore Co., Md.), Elizabeth Reister,
b. 7-3-1755; d. 7-3-1838, Switzerland Co., Ind.; dau. of John

Reister; chn.: Margaret b. 1-7-1795, Md. (prob. Baltimore Co.);
d. 11-3-1873, Switzerland Co., Ind.; m. 10-1-1827, Switzerland
Co., Ind. (as 1st wife), Peter Davis, b. 1805-1806, N.Y.; d. 1886
(will pr. Aug. 4), Posey Twp., Switzerland Co., Ind.; son of James
& Catharine Davis. Henry Weist (Wiest-Weast-Weest) lived in the
disputed Penna.--Md. region settled by the Mason-Dixon Line in
1768. Titles to lands in this region were granted by Maryland.
He appears in the 1779-80-81-82-83 Tax Lists of Hopewell Twp.,
York Co., Pa. By 1790 he had moved to Baltimore Co., Md., where
he later was executor of the estate of his father-in-law, John
Reister. One of John Reister's heirs was Margaret Trine (dau.?)
& Henry Weist, as executor, conveyed land to Peter Trine of York
Co., Pa. It is not known when Henry Weist came West, His obit
states that he helped to build the Block House at Cincinnati. He
is said to have come to Switzerland Co., Ind., in 1813, from
Reistertown, Baltimore Co., Md. Service: name is on list of John
Travis' Comp. of York Co., Pa., Mil., 5-27-1778. REF: "Pa. Arch."
6th Ser., v.2, p.620; 3rd Ser., v.21, pp. 46-312-471-541-780;
1790 Cens., Baltimore Co., Md., p.32; 1820 Cens., Switzerland Co.,
Ind., v.5, p.282 A, Posey Twp.; 1830 Cens., Switzerland Co.. Ind.,
v.14, p.144; Waters--"Ind. Land Entries", v.1, pp.2, 4; Knox---
"Switzerland Co., Ind., Marriages", p.7; Switzerland Co., Ind.,
Will Bk. 3, pp. 1, 301, 317; Will Bk. 4, p.237; "Western Christ-
ian Advocate", v.12, p.188; 3-6-1846 (obit); Miss Dorothy Mae
Davis, Dallas, Tex.

  WELLS, PETER   Vermillion
b. 10-23-1759, Bucks Co., Pa.; mar. Pens. appl. 7-3-1834, ae.
75 next Oct. 23, Warren Co., Ind. Since War, has liv. Md.; Ross
Co., O.; last 3 yr. in Ind., now Warren Co., Ind.; sometimes
lives in the upper end of Vermillion Co., Ind., ca. 17 mi. from
Co. seat; couldn't hire horse & wagon to take him there so came
to Warren Co.; one leg off after War as result of leg broken in
War. Again appl. 7-22-1835; same data except William Wilmeth,
Probate Judge of Warren Co., Ind., says sold. lives N end of Vermillion Co., Ind., near the line dividing Vermillion Co. & Warren
Co., ca. 16 mi. from Co. seat of Vermillion Co. & ca. 18-19 mi.
from Co. seat of Warren Co.; only 1 leg; no means to hire waggon
(so evid. the Judge went to Wells' house). Again appl. 7-22-
1835, ae. 76. Affid. 7-22-1835, Warren Co., Ind., of Robert Beaver; has known sold. ca. 35 yr., first in Hampshire Co., Va.,
where he was nearest neighbor; sold.'s father-in-law was a Rev.
sold.; other soldiers were Peter McMahan, now of Cumberland, Alleghany Co., Md., and John Boyd. Service: drf. Mar. 1781, Tanney
Town, Frederick Co., Md.; Capt. Thomas Purkison, Lt. Havins, Ens.
Benjamin Jefferson, Col. Norman Bruce. REF: Pens. R.11317 Md.;
Rej. Pens. List (1852) p.410--did not serve 6 mo.

  WELLS, THOMAS   Marion
Rev sold who died there. In 1840 Pens. List, Franklin Twp., ae.
74. REF: Mr Schrum; 1840 Pens. List, p. 183.

WELTON, JONATHAN   Knox
d. 3-9-1823; m. 4-5-1785, Hampshire Co., Va., Margaret Miles; chn.: at least a dau. Wid.'s pens. appl. 11-16-1839, ae. nearly 74, Knox Co., Ind. Affid. 9-19-1842, Clay Co., Ind., of David Thomas; that he knew sold. in Hardy Co., Va., in 1779 & knew when sold. enlisted. Wid. mov. to Clark Co., Ill., 1842, to live with a dau. Service: res. near Moorefield, Hampshire Co., Va.; enl. in Va. Mil. REF: Pens. R.11320 Va.; Susp. Pens. List (1852) p.420--not 6 mo. service established in this case; 1820 Cens., Knox Co., Ind., v. 3, p. 119.

WEST, NICHOLAS   Perry
b. 1752, near Easton, Pa. Enl. 1775, S branch of Potomac, Hampshire Co., Va.; Capt. Maderinamer, Col. John Bell. Liv. 20 yr. in Nelson Co, Ky. Pens. appl. 11-14-1832, ae. 80. REF: Mr. Wallace Weatherholt, Tell City & Indianapolis, Ind.

WESTFALL, ABRAHAM   Knox
b. Hampshire Co., Va.; d. Dec. 1832 or Jan. 1833; son of John & Sarah Westfall; bro. of Isaac, Jacob ("Roster" p.378), Abel (see my 1949 compilation), Cornelius ("Roster" p.377), John (see this Suppl.); m. 10-11-1789, Vincennes, Ind. Terr., Massey Harbin, ae. 69 in her pens. appl. of 11-12-1839, Knox Co., Ind.; dau. of Joshua (see this Suppl.) &.Elizabeth Harbin; chn. (7; 4 dead by 1840) including: Abraham H. (youngest son) m. Elizabeth Harbin; James m.(1) Rebecca Ferguson & m.(2) Mary Bedell & m.(3) Prudence Flowers; Thomas m. Polly Springer; Sally m. William Scott; Isaac; Joshua. Affid. of Michael Thorn, ae. 76 ("Roster" page 355) that dur. War he knew Abel, Cornelius, & Abraham Westfall, brothers; that Abel was a Capt., Cornelius his Lieut., Abraham a pvt.; that he heard the late Abel say that Abraham was eligible for a pens. but Abraham refused; that he was present at mar. of Abraham to Massey Harbin in her father's home. Affid. Knox Co., Ind., of Sarah Harness, ae. 81, b. Hampshire Co., Va.; that she knew the Westfalls where they had liv. near her on S branch of Potomac; that Abel, elder bro. of Abraham, enl. a Comp. in neighborhood near what is now called Moorfield on 2-28-1776 & that Abraham joined. (See service of his brothers). Service: sgt. in Rev. (Note: Abraham Westfall was appt. Judge of the Probate Ct., Knox Co., Ind., 1-14-1801). REF: Pens. W.9883 Va.; Am. Leg.; Eckenrode, p.465; father's will in Judy--"Hist. of Grant & Hardy Cos., W. Va." (1951) p.303; "Exec. Journ. of Ind. Terr., 1800-1816", p.95; Mrs. Eva Davenport, Vincennes, Ind.

WESTFALL, JOHN   Knox
(Not to be confused with the one of Harrison Co., Ind.). b. Hampshire Co., Va.; d. 1808, will wr. Sept. 1808 & pr. Oct.1; bur Indiana Church Cem., Gr. 43, Blk. 20; son of John & Sarah Westfall; bro. of Isaac, Jacob ("Roster" p.378) Abel (see my 1949 Compilation), Cornelius ("Roster" p.377), Abraham (see above); mar. (wife d. ante will wr.); chn.: Abram (oldest son); John (youngest son); Sarah; Katharine. Service: Hampshire Co., Va., Mil. Later in Knox Co,Ind.,Mil.,1790. REF:"Va.Sold.of the Rev."; father's will (see Abraham(s rec. above); Mrs. Davenport.

WESTON, EDMUND   Lagrange
b. ca. 1758; d. poss. 1837; mar. (wife liv. 1818). Pens. appl.
4-20-1818, ae. nearly 60, Mercer Co., Pa., having lately moved
there; also 10-2-1820, ae. 61 yr., 9 mo., Mercer Co., Pa. In
1835 Pens. List, Mercer Co., Pa.; pvt. in Mass. Cont. Line. On
3-31-1836, Lagrange Co., Ind., asks for tr. from Pa. to Ind.,
having mov. "to better his condition and that of his family"; tr.
from Pa. 628-1836. May have d. 1837 as letter 6-16-1837 from
Indianapolis Agy. says over 60 days have elapsed since transfer.
Service: enl. 1st Regt., Mass. Line; Col. James Vosse, Capt.
George Smith . REF: Pens. S.36843 Mass.; 1835 Pens. List,v.2,p.104

WHEAT, JAMES   Montgomery
d. 8-10-1852; bur. Union Hill Cem., Walnut Twp., Gr. 1, Lot 4.
REF: Am. Leg.; "List of Soldier Dead of Montgomery Co." (1941),
p. 19. Note: I question this. The James Wheat in the 1850 Cens.
is too young to have fought in the Rev. From the cens.: family
#377, p. 499½, Walnut Twp.--George Wheat, 27, b. Ohio; Mary E.,
22, Md.; Hannah, 4, Ind.; Grant 2, Ind.; Sarah F., 2/12, Ind.;
James Wheat, 72, b. Conn., shoemaker.

WHEELER, ISAAC   Shelby
(Uncertain). b. 1762. Pens. appl. 6-11-1817, ae. 55, Bradford
Co., Pa.; again appl. 9-13-1820, ae. 57. On 4-8-1825 asks for
tr. from Pa. Agy. at Philadelphia to Ohio Agy. at Chillicothe as
has since mov. to Ohio. (Note: I think he later mov. to Shelby
Co., Ind., where he appears in the 1840 Pens. List, ae. 78, in
Liberty Twp. He may not have asked for a tr. from Ohio since it
may have been convenient enough to be paid in Ohio, or he may
have died before he could ask for a tr. He is listed as a Rev.
sold. who lived in Ohio but not as one who died there). Service:
enl. Nov. 1778, Johnston in what is now Montgomery Co., N.Y.;
Capt. Van Ransalear, 1st Regt., Col. Goose Vanscork, N.Y. Line.
REF: Pens. S.40681 N.Y.; 1840 Pens. List., Shelby Co., Ind.,
p.185; "Ohio Rev. Sold.", v. 2, p. 361, Scioto Co., Ohio.

WHITACAR, JOHN   Ripley
(Note: not to be confused with John Whittaker or Whitacre in
"Roster", p.381, given as of Ripley Co., Ind., and who, I think,
should be of Switzerland Co., Ind. He is given in the 1835 Pens.
List, v.3, p.33, as of Switzerland Co., Ind.; was placed on pens.
roll 7-22-1819, I.A.R. certif. #12,571, Pens. S.36845 Va.). The
correct Ripley Co., Ind., man is John Whitacar or Whitacer, b.
1754-1757; d. 1833; mar. (wife ae. 60 in 1822); chn.: at least
1 son (18 in 1822) 1 dau. (12 in 1822). Pens. appl. 7-21-1818,
ae. 64, Ripley Co., Ind.; again 2-6-1822, ae. 65, Ripley Co.,Ind.
Service (1st appl.): enl. 1778, 8th Regt., Va. Line; Capt. Thomas
Boyears; (2nd appl.): enl. ca. 1777, Inf. Regt.; Col. Guess
(Gist?), Capt. Thomas Boyer. Placed on pens. roll 12-7-1818;
I.A.R. certif. #4,786. REF: Pens. S.36844 Va.; 1835 Pens. List,
Ripley Co., Ind., v. 3, p. 29.

WHITE, THOMAS   Franklin
b. 1756, Middlesex Co., N.J.; d. 8-16-1838; m. Mary ----- (liv. 1841; see below). Pens. appl. 8-2-1832, ae. 76, Butler Co., O. After War, liv. in Md. till 9 yr. ago to Butler Co., O. In 1835 Pens. List, Butler Co., O.; pvt. in N.J. Mil. On 3-8-1836, Franklin Co., Ind., asks for tr. to Ind. because has bought 2¼ ac. of land near Brookville; pens. tr. 4-2-1836. (Thomas White land entries: SW¼-SW¼-Sec. 35, Twp. 11 N, Range 11 E of 2nd P.M., Jan. 12, 1836 & NW¼-SW¼ of same, June 6, 1836. Note; these should be 40 ac. each). Letter 1-6-1841, Ft. Wayne, Ind., saying wid. Mary is applying for a pens. Service: enl. 7-6-1776, Middlesex Co., N.J., in Flying Camp; Capt. Vincent Wetherly, Col. David Finnan (Firman?). REF: Pens. S.16291 N.J.; 1835 Pens. List, v.3, p.108; "Ohio Rev. Sold." v.2, p.363; Waters--"Indiana Land Entries, v.1, Cincinnati District" (1949), p. 157.

WHITE, WILLIAM   Tippecanoe
Rev. sold. who died there. (This would not seem to be the one of Switzerland Co., Ind., nor the one of the "Roster", p. 381, of Dearborn Co., Ind., who, incidentally, had his pens. tr. to Cincinnati Agy as he had been living there for some years past & who was dead by 3-19-1856). REF: Mr. Schrum.

WILCOX, ISAAC   Perry
b. 3-27-1761, Dutchess Co., N.Y.; d. 9-3-1839. Pens. appl. 11-12-1834, ae. 73, Perry Co., Ind. Letter 11-19-1845, Parry Co., Ind., in which Co. Clerk says that Reuben Bates is exec. of last will & testa. of Isaac Wilson, U.S. pensr., decd.; that he died leaving no wid., chn., or legal heirs. Service: enl. spr. 1777, Dutchess Co., N.Y.; Capt. Wood, Col. Pawling. REF: Pens. S.32598 N.Y.

WILKERSON, WILLIAM   Greene
Rev. sold. who died there. (This is NOT the one of Brown Co., Ind., in "Roster" p.382; but is prob. the one of Monroe Co., Ind., ae. 105, in 1840 Pens. List. Monroe Co. & Greene Co. adjoin. REF: Mr. Schrum; 1840 Pens. List, p. 184.

WILLHEIM, MICHAEL   Fayette
b. 1756, Germany. Pens. appl. 11-1-1837, ae. 81, Fayette Co., Ind. Liv. in Pa. 40 or more yrs.; Rockbridge Co., Va.; now Fayette Co., Ind.; his sister has the family record. Service: as a res. of Bucks Co., Pa., vol. to drive with a wagon-master to Boston; there he vol. on vessel "Nancy"; Capt. Ross. REF: Pens. R.11540; Rej. Pens. List (1852) p.410--privateer service.

WILLIAMS, BARNEY   Spencer
Rev. sold. who died there. REF: Mr. Schrum.

WILLYARD, HENRY   Ripley
b. ca. 1750; d. 1-20-1830; m. 11-2-1790, Ligonier Valley, Westmoreland Co., Pa. (later, wid. says Bedford Co., Pa.), Agnes Bridges, b. (see varying ages); alive 3-29-1855, ae. 88, Ripley Co., Ind. Pens. appl., Cincinnati, Hamilton Co., O., in 70th yr. (1820?); 12-23-1823, ae. 73, Hamilton Co., O.; wife 65; chn. grown up. Affid. 1-3-1820, Switzerland Co., Ind., of John Gullion ("Roster" p.167); that he serv. with Willyard; same of Alexander Lemmon of Hamilton Co., O. Affid. 8-21-1820, Hamilton Co., O., of John Willyard, bro. of Henry, who was under age at enlistment & whose father went to camp to try to get Henry released. Wid.'s appl. 7-7-1838 & 1842, ae. 74 on May 7, 1842, Ripley Co., Ind.; other ages: 11-14-1839, ae. 72; 5-8-1843, ae. 75; 9-15-1849, ae. 82; 3-29-1855, ae. 88; all Ripley Co., Ind. Affid. 11-14-1839, Ripley Co., Ind., of Esther Early; that she knew sold. & wife for 40-41 yr. Affid. 6-24-1842, Ripley Co., Ind., of John Willyard, ae. 72, bro. of Henry. Service: enl. spr. 1777, 8th Regt., Pa. Line; Capt Wendal Owry (Owey?), Col. Bayard. REF: Pens. W.9892 Pa.; BLW 26151-160-1855.

WILSON, ROBERT   Hancock
b. 1749, Augusta Co., Va., 6 mi. from Stanton. Pens. appl. 8-29-1833, ae. 84, Hancock Co., Ind. After War, liv. Ky. several yrs.; in Ind. in Dearborn, Switzerland, Wayne, Henry Cos. & finally Hancock Co., Ind. Affid. 12-18-1839, Hancock Co., Ind., of William Wilson & Samuel Wilson (rel. not given). In 1835 Pens. List, Hancock Co., Ind.; pvt. in Va. Mil.; in 1840 Pens. List, ae. 95, Center Twp., Hancock Co., Ind. ("Roster" p.405, says he tr. to Ill.; but I could not find such a notation in pens. file, nor does I.A.R. carry this notation. Co. Hist. below has several Robert Wilsons; the following data may be for this man: Robert & Sarah (Friend) Wilson of N.C.; to Ind.; among 1st sett. of Green Twp., Hancock Co., Ind.; 40 ac. here & both d. here; among chn.--Samuel, b. N.C.; m. Elizabeth Bolden, b. N.C. (dau. of Hugh & Sarah Bolden, from N.C. to White Water River, Hancock Co., Ind.; Samuel d. ca. 25 yr. ante wife; they had: Frances, John (d. young), Robert F. (b. 1844), James, Noah, William J., & Isabel. A Robert Wilson was commn. J.P. for Hancock Co., Ind., 2-5-1835). Service: enl. Augusta Co., Va.; Capt. Long; as a subst. for man named Calwell 2 yr. before Batt. of Blue Licks, Ky., at which batt. his bro., John Wilson, was killed. Next yr. went to live with bro. John to the Catawba in Carolina; later with bro. John & 40-50 fams. to Wilson's Station on Salt River in Ky. in the winter before the Batt. of Blue Licks. He helped guard the fort while his bro. & 4 others went on a scout & were killed. REF: Pens. S.32603 N.C., Va.;.1835 Pens. List, v.3,p.51; 1840 Pens. List, p.183; Richman--"Hist. of Hancock Co., Ind." (1916) p. 1095; "Exec. Proc. of Ind., 1816-1836", p. 682.

WINCHELL, JOHN   Perry
b. 1760, "Great Nine Partners", Dutchess Co., N.Y.; son of Stephen & Mary (Rouse) Winchell; d. 9-14-1811, ae. 51, Tobinsport, Ind.; m. Rachel Avery, b. 1762; d. 8-19-1815, ae. 53, Tobinsport, Ind.; dau. of Alpheus Avery; chn. (all b. Ulster Co., N.Y.):

Catharine b. 1-24-1784; Smith b. ca. 1786; Phebe; Uriah
Avery b. ca. 1790; Charity; Margaret; John (or Jerome) b.
1793; Roxana b. 11-24-1799; Mary; Cassandra. Migr. from
Dutchess Co., N.Y., to Ulster Co., N.Y.; to Delaware Co., N.Y.;
ca. 1808-09 via Pittsburgh westward; Cincinnati, Louisville; to
Perry Co., Ind., ca. fall 1809. "John served in the Revolutionary army." See fam. geneal. for more data on chn. REF: Winchell-
"Winchell Gen." (1917) pp. 101-102, et al.; Mr. Wallace Weatherholt, Tell City & Indianapolis, Ind.

    WOOD, W-----   Clark
Rev. sold. who died there. (Note: it is possible that this man
may be the following one of Harrison Co., Ind.). REF: Mr. Schrum.

    WOOD, WILLIAM   Harrison
b. 7-1-1761, Augusta Co., Va. Pens. appl. 11-10-1834, ae. 73,
res. of Franklin Twp., Harrison Co., Ind. After War, liv. Augusta Co., Va., till 1816 to Harrison Co., Ind. Service: enl.
Apr. 1776, Augusta Co., Va.; Capt. John White, Va. State Troops.
REF: Pens. S.32615 Va.

    WOOLCOTT, JOSEPH   Switzerland
b. 7-27-1764, Newington, Conn. (pens. appl.) or b. 7-27-1760,
Steuben Co., N.Y. (see below); son of Augustus (or Justus) Woolcott. Pens. appl. 5-17-1833, ae. 68, Switzerland Co., Ind.; &
5-16-1836, ae. ca. 74, Switzerland Co., Ind. After War, continued to live in Rensselaer Co., N.Y., for many yrs. Affid. 1-30-
1834 of Charles Woolcott, 66, & of Norman Woolcott, 68; that they
are bros. of Joseph; that they now (I think) live in Rensselaer
Co., N.Y.; that Joseph was b. 7-27-1760, not 1764, in Steuben
Co., N.Y.; that sold. made his home at their father's house in
Rensselaer Co., N.Y.; that sold. is 6 yr. older than Norman & 8
yr. older than Charles; that sold. served as a subst. for their
father, Justus Woolcott. Service: enl. 1776; Capt. Turner; later
serv. as subst. for father, Augustus Woolcott, who had been
called out for 9 mo.; Joseph subst. 6 mo. & father serv. the balance   At enl., liv. Stephentown, Albany Co., N.Y.; there for ca.
29 yr.; to Ky.; then to Ind. REF: Pens. S.32610 N.Y. (See p.119).

    WORK, JOHN, Sr.   Clark
b. 1760; d. 2-14-1832, ae. 71; bur. Faris Cem., Tunnel Mill Rd.;
m. Sarah -----, b. 1769; d. 3-24-1854, ae. 85 yr., 3 mo.; bur.
same cem.; chn.: at least John, Jr., b. Pa. (was appt. Lieut. in
Clark Co., Ind. Terr. Mil., 1-10-1806). Fam. sett. 1804 in
Charlestown Twp., Clark Co., Ind. John Work, Sr., constructed
the famous tunnel millrace in Clark Co., Ind.; operated early
mill in Charlestown Twp.; deeded ground for Presby. Ch. in Charlestown, Ind.; was from Penna.; son John continued father's mill
till 1854. Service: no proof given. REF: Clark Co. Cem. Rec.,
ISL; "Exec. Journ. of Ind. Terr., 1800-1816" p.132; Baird--"Hist.
of Clark Co., Ind." (1909) pp. 604-71-78-260; "Hist. of the Ohio
Falls Cities & Their Counties" (1882) v. 2, pp. 343-344.

WRIGHT, JOHN   Tippecanoe
(Uncertain). He appears in the 1840 Pens. List, ae. 80, Sheffield Twp., Tippecanoe Co., Ind. I could not identify any pens. file from available data. REF: 1840 Pens. List, p. 185. May have lived with John Stean.

    WYCOFF, ISAAC   Ripley
Rev. sold. who died there. In 1835 Pens. List, ae. 76; pvt. in N.J. State Troops. REF: Mr. Schrum; 1835 Pens. List, v. 3, p.65; Stryker--"Official Reg. of N.J. in Rev. War", p. 830.

    WYMAN, HENRY, Sr.   Washington
b. 1760, Germany (maybe Hesse); d. 1840; bur. Wyman Cem. on the O. P. Graves farm, Sec. 3; m. Catharine Carnes (or Karnes), b. 1762; d. 1831; bur. same cem.; chn.: Margaret m. Mr. Smith; Susan m. William Brooks; Frederick m. Miss Baker; Henry m. 5-3-1817, Washington Co., Ind., Catharine Boss; Molly m. 4-13-1821, Washington Co., Ind., Philip Boss (& had dau. Peggy); Catharine m. Henry Sherley; Elizabeth m. Stephen Elrod; Henry, Jr., b. 2-22-1793; d. 4-22-1873; m. Anna Catharine -----, b. 5-25-1795; d. 9-29-1852; Leonard b. 4-17-1794, N.C.; d. 5-20-1864; m. 4-1-1824, Washington Co., Ind., Jane Baker, 1st w.; he m.(2) 2-25-1831, Washington Co., Ind., Eliza Leach, b. 9-13-1808, Ky.; d. 7-28-1888; Solomon b. 1806; d. 2-27-1874; m. Catharine -----, b. 9-13-1813; d. 11-23-1897. Sold.'s will wr. 4-17-1837, pr. 11-16-1838, names the above chn. & also decd. son Frederick's chn.: Lewis, Henry, Noah, Anna, Jane, & Samuel. Service: sold. was a Hessian captured at Batt. of Trenton; made shoes for Washington's army to the end of the War. Then mov. to N.C.; to Washington Co., Ind., 1804, & bought land in Jackson, Pierce, & Polk Twps.; first settler in Jackson Twp. REF: Morris- "Arch. & Hist. Survey of Washington Co., Ind." (1925) pp. 167-175-179; Stevens--"Hist. of Washington Co., Ind." (1916) pp. 907-908-735; Washington Co., Ind., Prob. Bk. C, pp. 71-73; Mar. Bk. A, pp. 19-29-112; Mar. Bk. B, p. 43.

    WYSONG, VALENTINE   Randolph
Rev. sold. who died there. REF: Mr. Schrum.

    YORK, JOSHUA   Franklin
b. 1-22-1856; mar.; chn.: at least son Valentine. Pens. appl., ae. 62, Mason Co., Ky.; again 8-25-1820, Mason Co., Ky., ae. 64 on 1-22-1820; liv. with him is 1 son, Valentine, ae. ca. 21; also gr-son, Aquilla York, is at present liv. with him. Was still in Mason Co., Ky., Feb, 1829. Was placed on pens. roll 9-23-1819; dropped under Act of 5-1-1820; restored commencing 2-4-1829. In 1835 Pens. List, Mason Co., Ky.; pvt. in Pa. Line. On 1-20-1836, Franklin Co., Ind., asks for tr. to Ind. because (1) his sons live here; (2) he wants to live in a free state; pens. tr. 3-8-1836. Service: enl. Aug.-Sept. 1777, 8th Pa. Regt.; Capt. John Picket, Col. McCoy. This service is attested by John Waugh, who also served. REF: Pens. S.36864 Pa.; 1835 Pens. List, v.3, p.48.; Waters--"Indiana Land Entries, Vol. 1, Cincinnati District" (1949) pp. 119 (2), 120.

YOUNG, THOMAS   Indiana
(Uncertain)   Name obtained after this Supplement was started.
A Thomas Young of Indiana is on the 1831 list of rejected pens-
ions, reason: "wagon-master, case not proved by law". There are
Thomas Youngs in the 1820 Census of these Indiana counties: Pike,
Harrison, Washington; 1830 Census: Fountain, Harrison, Pike, Put-
nam, Washington. REF: "Rej. Appl. for Pens." (1831) p.49 (see
note at end after Daniel Zink).

YOUNGER, KANARD   Ripley
b. 1760, Frederick Co., Md.; d. 8-2-1851; mar. Pens. appl. 9-21-
1833, ae. 73, Henry Co., Ky. After Md. service, ca. Feb. 1783
mov. to Ft. Pitt & serv. there; later mov. to Falls of Ohio at
Louisville, Ky. In 1835 Pens. List, Henry Co., Ky.; pvt. in Va.
Mil.; in 1840 Pens. List, Trimble Co., Ky. On 5-30-1850, Ripley
Co., Ind., asks for tr. to live with step-son-in-law who has recently mov. to Ripley Co., Ind.; pens. tr. 6-22-1851. Service:
enl. Feb. 1778, Frederick Co., Md. REF: Pens. S.32620 Md.; 1835
Pens. List, v.3, p.105; 1840 Pens. List, p.167.

ZINK, DANIEL   Washington
Rev. sold. who came from Ky. early to Washington Co., Ind., and
died there: prob. bur. at Salem. Sett. on farm where son Peter
later liv. for many yrs., 2½ mi. SW of Salem. Son Peter, b. Va.;
m. Sarah Wright, b. 9-14-1799, N.C.; dau. of Philburd & Molly
(Sears) Wright. Sold. also had son John, wounded in the Pigeon
Roost Massacre (Scott Co., Ind.; Col. Dewalt's Comp. of Rangers);
John d. 9-6-1812, Fort Vallonia (Jackson Co., Ind.) & was retd.
for burial to first graveyard in Washington Co., Ind., in Brock
settlement, just north of Salem. Daniel Zink also had other sons.
REF: Mr. Schrum; Stevens--"Hist. of Washington Co., Ind." (1916)
pp. 544-545-633-669-688-804.

- -

                              NOTE

Last summer (1953) I came across the "Rejected Applications for
Pensions", published in 1831 as one of the Senate Documents.
This had previously escaped my notice in my search for various
lists of soldiers. It includes men who were rejected because
their type of service did not qualify them under the existing law
at the time (but some of whom later did receive pensions) and men
whose pensions were discontinued because they had too much property (after the law pertaining to indigents in 1818). I was able
to insert some of these names in their correct alphabetical order;
others are listed in the section following. I plan to read and
abstract the pension files of these 1831 list men on my next trip
to the National Archives this summer. Interested persons may
wish to write me concerning them.

NAMES RECEIVED TOO LATE FOR ALPHABETICAL ORDER

BOREN, NICHOLAS   Gibson
b. 1756, Ireland; d. 1836, Union Twp.; bur. in New Mt. Moriah
Cem., 4 mi. NE of Cynthiana, Ind. & 2 mi. N of New Liberty Church;
stone; m. post War, Mary Catharine Hampson, b 1759, Ireland; d.
1837; bur. same cem.; chn.: Polly m. Andrew Blythe; Margaret m.
Chane Boren; Absalom m. Katie -----; Hester Ann m. Frank Jordan; Ezekiel b. 1792; d. 1873; m. Rosa Evans, b. 1797; d. 1863
both bur. in above cem.;   John b. 8-25-1796; d. 7-80-1870; m.
Polly McCrary, b. 3-17-1797; d. 7-3-1876, both bur. in New Liberty Cem.; James b. 1781; d. 1864 (Capt. in 1812 War); m. Jane
Blair, b. 1791; d. 1866;   Ruth m. James West; Temperance m.
Nathan Knowles. Nicholas Boren came as a child to U.S. with parents; sett. in Chester Co., Pa., near the Md. line. Mary Hampson
came as a child to U.S. with parents & sett in Cecil Co., Md.,
near the Pa. line. After mar., Nicholas & wife to Ky.; then Tenn.
where chn were reared. Desc. of Scotch-Irish Presby., in Tenn.
the Borens helped to org, the First Christian Ch. In old age,
came to Gibson Co., Ind., where Nicholas entered the SW¼ of Sec.
21, Twp. 3 S, Range 11 W, on 12-9-1816. Service: under George
Washington; wounded at Batt. of Brandywine. REF: Massey--"Desc.
of Nicholas Boren & Mary Hampson Boren" (1939); Waters--"Ind.
Land Entries", v.2, p.84 (1949); Mr. A.C. Boren, Cynthiana, Ind.

BOSTON, ELIJAH   Madison
b. Md.; d. when over 70 yr. of age; mar.; chn. (had a small Fam.)
including: Hiram; Elizabeth R. m. Hezekiah M. Gce, b. Fayette
Co., Pa. (son of William Gos, to Hamilton Co., Ind., 1816).
Elijah Boston came early to Pendleton, Ind.; had been a merchant
in the East. Service: "served as an officer in the Revolution".
REF: Beers--"Comm. Biog. Rec. of Indianapolis & Vicinity" (1908)
pp. 643-644; Mrs. Irene Strieby, Indianapolis, Ind.

BRIDGES, JOHN   Jennings (?)
(Uncertain). Name obtained after this Suppl. was started. A
John Bridges of Indiana is on the 1831 list of rejected pensions
reason: "served in a regiment not on continental establishment".
He is prob. Pens. R.1194 Pa., on "Natl. Gen. Soc. Quart." pens.
index. There is a John Bridges in the 1820 Cens. of Jennings
Co., Ind., v. 3, p.17, who is also in the 1830 Cens, v.7, p.283
as Sr. There is also a John Bridges in 1820 Cens., Franklin Co.,
Ind., v.2, p.201, and another in 1820 Cens., Delaware Co., v.2,
p.30. (Note: The Delaware Co., Ind., of 1820 was an unorganized
county which covered all present counties in the middle third &
northeastern parts of the state, excluding the northern tiers of
counties which had not yet been purchased by Indian treaty). REF:
"Rej. Appl. for Pens." (1831) p.48.

BROOKS, WILLIAM   Franklin
"It is believed that William was a soldier in the Revolutionary
war". Chn.: John; Elias; William; Walter; Lottie; Malinda.
"John Brooks was a son of William, who came from English ancestors, and moved to Indiana in very early times, settling in Frank-

NAMES RECEIVED TOO LATE FOR ALPHABETICAL ORDER

lin county, where he died....John Brooks was probably born in America, and it is known that he married, in North Carolina, Sarah Elizabeth Heath, daughter of Samuel and Lucy (Austin) Heath. Samuel Heath was a farmer of Franklin county, who moved to Jefferson county, Ind., where he cleared a farm of 160 acres, on which he passed the rest of his life. His children were: William; Samuel; Edward; Sarah Elizabeth; and Lucy". Abstracted: John Brooks, mov. from N.C. ca. 1814 to Franklin Co., Ind.; fall 1832 to Hancock Co., Ind.; d. ae. 65. (Long acct. of the fam. in these Cos., plus Hamilton & Madison Cos., Ind). REF: Beers-- "Comm. Biog. Rec. of Indianapolis & Vicinity" (1908) pp. 1045-1046; Mrs. Irene Strieby, Indianapolis, Ind.

BROTHERTON, JOHN   Washington
(Uncertain). Name obtained after this Supplement was started. A John Brotherton of Indiana is on the 1831 list of rejected pensions, reason: "served in a regiment not on continental establishment" There is a John Brotherton in the 1820 Cens. of Washington Co., Ind., v.5, p.358. Several Brothertons are in the 1830 Cens. of Vigo Co., Ind. REF: "Rej. Appl. fpr Pens." (1831) p.48.

CHAMBERS, JOHN THOMAS   Monroe (?)
(Uncertain; see note below   However, this is not the John Chambers of "Roster" p.92).   b. ca. 1760, Va.; m. 1786, Greenbrier Co., (W.) Va., Margaret Feamster, b. 10-23-1767, Augusta Co., Va. (dau. of William Feamster & Margaret Black); chn.: William S. b. 1787, Madison Co., Ky.; d. 1-16-1855, Monroe Co., Ind.; m. 12-30-1806, Madison Co., Ky., Mary Meadows (sis. of Sarah below); Rachel m. 3-17-1806, Estill Co., Ky. (bond in Madison Co., Ky., 3-15-1806), William Meadows;   Nancy m. 7-6-1807, Madison Co., Ky., Ebenezer Jackson;   John m. 3-7-1808, Madison Co., Ky., Sally Johnson;   David b. 10-22-1792, Madison Co., Ky.; d. 9-6-1861, Monroe Co., Ind.; m. 8-29-1814, Estill Co., Ky., Sarah Meadows (sis. of Mary above), b. 8-20-1796, Va.; d. 8-5-1877, Monroe Co., Ind.;   Anthony b. 1797, Madison Co., Ky.; d. 4-25-1848, Monroe Co., Ind.; m. 4-29-1823, Jefferson Co., Ind., Mary Roseberry, b. 1805; d. 2-24-1859.   Service: served in a Va. Regt.; was shot thru the hip at Batt. of Monmouth, 6-28-1778, and was a cripple ever after. REF: Emery--"Chambers & Feamster Gen." (1953) pp.1-17-23-26-32-33-34-38. (Note: Miss Thelma Murphy says that a woman in Paris, Ky., told her that John Chambers died in Indiana. Mrs. Emery seems to feel that this is the case, too. However, later Miss Murphy talked with someone who says that John Chambers returned to Greenbrier Co., (W.) Va., where he died.)

CRANE, EDMUND   Ripley
(Uncertain). Name obtained after this Suppl was started. An Edmund Crane of Indiana is on the 1831 list of rejected pens., reason: "deserted the service". He is prob. Pens R.2443 N.J. on Natl. Gen. Soc. Quart. pens. index. There is an Edmund Crane in 1820 Cens of Ripley Co., Ind., v.6, p.72. REF: "Rej. Appl. for Pens." (1831) p. 48.

CROSS, JOHN -- see p. 119.

DOUGHERTY, JOHN   Indiana
(Uncertain). Name obtained after this Suppl. was started. A
John Dougherty of Indiana is on the 1831 list of rejected pens.,
reason:"deserted the service". The name appears in the 1820 Cens.
in these Indiana counties: Orange (3 men, one as Sr.), Spencer,
Sullivan (2 men), Vanderburgh; in the 1830 Cens.: Henry, Harrison, Lawrence, Monroe, Orange (2 men, one as Jr.), Perry, Putnam,
Ripley, Spencer. REF: "Rej. Appl. for Pens." (1831), p. 48.

FANCHER, WILLIAM   Switzerland
(Uncertain). This name was received too late for me to check.
His appl. for a pens. was accompanied by affidavits signed by
John Pavy & Isaac Nash. William Fancher signed the pens. appl.
of Jemima Nighswonger, wid. of Solomon Nighswonger (see later in
this Suppl.). The soldier may not have died in Switzerland Co.
REF: Switzerland Co., Ind., Probate Bk. A, p.330 (name has Sr.);
Probate Ord. Bk. A (1831-1837), p.101; Mary Hill, Madison, Ind.

GREEN, RICHARD   Clark
(Uncertain). Name obtained after this Suppl. was started. A
Richard Green of Indiana is on the 1831 list of rejected pens.,
reason: "Served in a regiment not on continental establishment".
There is a Richard Green (only one in the whole state) of Clark
Co., Ind., in the 1820 Cens., v.1, p.44. REF: "Rej. Appl. for
Pens." (1831), p. 48.

GUDGELL (GUTCHELL), JOHN   Jefferson
(Uncertain). Name obtained after this Suppl. was started. A
John Gutchell of Indiana is on the 1831 list of rejected pens.,
reason: "served in a regiment not on continental establishment".
He is prob. the John Gudgell of Jefferson Co., Ind. in 1820
Cens., v.3, p.284 & 1830 Cens., v.7, p.196. There are several
Gudgell families in the 1850 Cens. of Jefferson Co. REF: "Rej.
Appl. for Pens." (1831) p. 48,

GUMP, FREDERICK   Wayne
(Uncertain). Name obtained after this Suppl. was started. A
Frederick Gump of Indiana is on the 1831 list of rejected pens.,
reason: "served in a regiment not on continental establishment".
The name is so unusual that he is prob. the Frederick Gump of
Wayne Co , Ind., in the 1820 Cens., v.6, p.216 (the only man of
that name in the whole state). REF: "Rej. Appl. for Pens."
(1831), p. 48.

HAYS, JOSHUA   Washington
(Uncertain). Name obtained after this Suppl. was started. A
Joshua Hays of Indiana is on the 1831 list of rejected pens.,
reason: " served in a regiment not on continental establishment".
There is a Joshua Hays. Sr. (only one in the whole state) of
Washington Co., Ind., in the 1820 Cens., v.5, p.354, & on the
same page a Joshua Hays, Jr.; a Joshua Hays in 1830 Cens., v.11,
p.196, of Parke Co., Ind. REF: "Rej. Appl. for Pens." (1831),
page 48.

HENDERSON, DAVID   Jackson
(Uncertain). Name obtained after this Suppl. was started. A
David Henderson of Indiana is on the 1831 list of rejected pens.,
reason: "served in a regiment not on continental establishment".
There is a David Henderson (only one in the whole state) of Jackson Co., Ind., in 1820 Cens., v.3, p.81. REF: "Rej. Appl. for
Pens." (1831), p. 48.

HEROD, WILLIAM   Bartholomew
b. Va.; mar.; chn. (at least): William, b. Bourbon Co., Ky.; d.
1871, Columbus, Ind., ae. 71; m. Cassandra Wingate, b. Hamilton,
Butler Co., O.; d. 1864, ae. 54 (dau. of Brig.-Gen. John Wingate
& 1st wife). "William Herod...was born in Virginia, of an agricultural family that owned large estates. He served as a soldier
in the Revolutionary war. In the very early days he came as a
pioneer to Bartholomew Co., Ind., where the balance of his life
was spent." (After liv. in Bourbon Co., Ky., fam. liv. for a
while in Boone Co., Ky.)   REF: Beers--"Comm. Biog. Rec. of Indianapolis & Vicin." (1908) p. 1229; "Hist. of Bartholomew Co.,
Ind." (1888) pp. 428-429; Mrs. Irene Strieby, Indianapolis, Ind.

JOHNSTON, JOHN   Knox
b. ca. 1750; d. 1-21-1816, in 66th yr. Member of the Shaker Ch.
at Union Village, Busseron Twp., ca. 16 mi. N of Vincennes.
"Another valiant revolutionist and a good cleaver old man." REF:
from diary of Benjamin Seth Youngs, a member of the first Shaker
propaganda to the West; diary given in full in MacLean--"Shakers
of Ohio" (1907) p.313; Miss Caroline Dunn, Indianapolis, Ind.

KNOX, JOHN   Knox
b. ca. 1755; d. 11-10-1815, ae. 60. Member of the Shaker Ch. at
Union Village, Busseron Twp., ca. 16 mi. N of Vincennes. "He had
been in revolutionary service a number of years, and found in the
Gospel that Liberty for which he had contended so long ago." REF:
from diary of Benjamin Seth Youngs, a member of the first Shaker
propaganda to the West; diary given in full in MacLean--"Shakers
of Ohio" (1907) pp.312-313; Miss Caroline Dunn, Indianapolis,
Ind. NOTE: Mr. Schrum might have confused forename with one of
the other Knox men of Knox Co.; see Sec. I of this Suppl.).

NIGHSWONGER, SOLOMON   Switzerland
(Uncertain). Name obtained too late to get data. Died prob. in
1820's; m. Jemima -----; chn.: possibly sons John & Solomon.
Wid.'s pens. appl. is supported by affids. signed by William
Fancher (see this Suppl.) & Joseph Boesea (sp?). Solomon Nighswonger entered the SE¼ of Sec. 32 in Twp. 2 N, Range 2 W of the
1st P.M. on 7-20-1815; he later relinquished it & it was reentered by Isaac Matts, the W½ on 8-20-1828, the E½ on 9-10-1828.
Solomon Nighswonger entered the NW¼ of Sec. 36 in Twp. 3 N, Range
3 W of 1st P.M. on 1-26-1814. It is poss. that these entries
may have been made by a son, Solomon, Jr., & that the soldier may
have died elsewhere (even before the fam. mov. to Ind.); the 1820
Cens. of Switzerland Co., Ind., has a John Nighswonger & the 1830
a Solomon. REF: Switzerland Co., Ind., Probate Book A, p. 413;

Probate Order Book A (1831-1837) p.172 (widow's pens. appl.); Waters--"Ind. Land Entries", v.1 (1949) pp.43, 72; Miss Mary Hill, Madison, Indiana.

RENNO, GEORGE   Switzerland
(Uncertain) Name received too late to get data. He may not have died in Ind. altho he appl. for pens. here. A Presley Reno entered the E½ of the NW¼ of Sec. 2 of Twp. 3 N, Range 3 W of the 1st P.M. on 2-26-1818, & a Presley Q. Reno the NW¼ of the SW¼ of Sec. 28 in Twp. 4 N, Range 3 W of 1st P.M. on 2-10-1837. REF: Switzerland Co., Ind., Probate Bk. A, p.429; Waters--"Ind. Land Entries" v. 1 (1949) pp. 69, 148.

TRAINER, ISAAC   Switzerland
(Uncertain). Name received too late to get full data. He died in 1819 (but poss. not here); m. Elizabeth -----; chn. (at least): Maria; Cynthia; John; James H. (deposition in ref. below); Jane; Hiram; Amaline. Service: pvt. in 2nd Regt. of Riflemen in U.S. army. REF: Switzerland Co., Ind., Probate Ord. Bk. A (1831-1837) p.444; Miss Mary Hill, Madison, Ind.

CROSS, JOHN   Boone
d.4-22-1847,ae.85-1-20. Liv. near Mt.Zion Mtg.Hse.;Royalton Circuit."He was a Rev. War sold. for 3 yrs."(Mt.Zion Ch.,Jackson Twp. REF:Meth "Western Christian Advocate"v.14-p.48;obituary-7-2-1847.

ADDITIONAL NOTES TO SOLDIERS IN SECTION I

BECKES, PARMENAS-p.11. Elizabeth Harvey m.(1) Hon. Will Clarke; m.(2) Parmenas Beckes; m.(3) 1-7-1817, as 2nd wife, at Vincennes, Ind., General W. Johnston (General was his forename; see Section VIII, this Suppl.).

ELKINS, SHADRACK-p.30. Pens. file R.3285 N.C. had no papers mentioning Indiana. All papers were Tenn : Marion, Sumner, & Bedford Cos. Correct surname may be Alkins or some variation.

HALL, BENJAMIN-p.44. Confusion between a Rev. sold., Benajah Hall, d. 11-4-1840, Cayuga Co., N.Y., who liv. after Rev. at Hartford, Conn., & Dutchess Co., N.Y.; had pens.; had son Benajah who is incorrectly given as Benjamin Hall, 61, Conn.; wife Margaret, 54, N.Y.; chn.: Simon, 26, N.Y.; George W., 19, N.Y.; Margaret C., 16, N.Y.; Lewis, 12, Ohio, in 1850 Cens., Ripley Co., Ind., Washington Twp., p.312½, fam. 70. The Rhode Island man in "Roster", p.170, should be Benjamin and not Benajah.

HENSON, JOHN-p.49. See Section VI of soldiers who moved from Ind. to other states. John, William, & Jesse Henson were brothers.

LEDGERWOOD, JAMES-p.63. More info in "Reg. of Ky. Hist. Soc.", Jan. 1954, v.52, no.178, p.68.

WOOLCOTT, JOSEPH-p.112. Switzerland Co., Ind., Probate Order Book A (1831-1837), page 129.

STATE
Bower, Benjamin
Bushman, Jacob
Butten, Daniel
Couch, John
Dougherty, John
Fott, John
Goodwin, William
Henry, John
Hicks, Dempsey
Hinkley, Seth
Lanker, Jacob
Maxwell, Thomas
Odler, Francis
Owens, William
Smith, George
Smith, Jacob
Thompson, John
Thorn, Asa
Walker, Daniel
Ward, William M.
Webb, Jeremiah
Young, Thomas
BARTHOLOMEW
Adams, Gavin
Herod, William
Jones, Nicholas
Jones, Thomas
Lytle, Francis
Stoneberger, John
Wallace, Samuel
BOONE
*Lawrence, Isaac
BROWN
Hampton, John
CARROLL
Davis, Daniel
Galloway, Peter
Lusher, John
Olinger, Jacob
Speece, Ludwig
CASS
Hubbell, Hezekiah
CLARK
Biles, Charles
Bullock, William
Burke, John
Bush, George
Douthitt, Thomas
Green, Richard
Griffin, William
Hartley, Daniel
Jacob, Jeremiah
Lewis, George
*Cross, John

Pettit, John
Prather, Basil R.
Robertson, Nathan
Rogers, Aquilla
Russell, John
Stout, Peter
Tate, Samuel
Watson, William
Wood, W----
Work, John
CLAY
Bell, Benjamin
Case, Joseph
Case, Obadiah
Cunningham, Richard
LePerra, Latasco
Luther, Jacob
CRAWFORD
Keysacker, George
Ruth, John
DAVIESS
Rainey, J----
Ruminger, George
Stipe, Frederick
Tranter, John
DEARBORN
Angevine, John
Ansley, John
Arnold, Richard
Barlow, John
Cheek, Francis
Ewing, George
Kincaid, -----
Lambert, James
Lamphear, Abel
McKnight, David
Sheldon, George
Shoemaker, John
Taylor, Jacob
Thompson, Seth
DECATUR
Bennet, Archibald
Burton, Absalom
Cassell, Ralph
Devore, Elijah
Hobbs, James
Layton, William
McIntosh, Francis
Newton, John
Owen, Harraway
Parnell, Stephen
Snelling, William
Shuttle, John
Webb, Theodore

-120-

DELAWARE
Andrews, James
Barnes, John
Dale, Campbell
McCallister, Alex.
Peterson, Lemuel
Thompson, Thomas
ELKHART
Johnson, Jacob
FAYETTE
Farmer, Nathaniel
Hames (Hamer), James
Harner, James
Kilander, Philip
Sofield, Lewis
Vance, Samuel
VanVlair, Adam
Willhelm, Michael
FLOYD
Hickman, Jacob
Keller, Daniel
FOUNTAIN
Covenhover, Thomas
Dixon, Peter
Ewen, Timothy
Raines, Richard
FRANKLIN
Allen, John
Brooks, William
Burch, Daniel
Davison, Samuel
Haymond, Calder
Johnson, James
Layton, Thomas
Lewis, William
Low, John
McCarty, Benjamin
Newkirk, Henry C
Webb, Jonathan
White, Thomas
York, Joshua
GIBSON
Boren, Nicholas
Fitzjarrell, James
Kitchen, Thomas
Taylor, Bailey
Reel, John
Vanarsdall, Christ.
GRANT
Grimes, Ben
GREENE
Burnett, John
Ellis, George
Ellis, Robert
*Leftyear, Uriah

Shields, -----
Smith, Stafford
Wilkerson, William
HAMILTON
Allen, John
Cary, Saul
Scott, Justus
HANCOCK
Cooper, Vincent
Franklin, Joseph
Wilson, Robert
HARRISON
Applegate, Robert
Bliss, Charles
Bliss, James
Cook, Elihu
Denbow, -----
Evans, Robert
Foote, George
Funk, Daniel
Henson, William
Johnson, James
Smith, John
Steel, John
Thompson, John
Wood, William
HENDRICKS
Brown, John
Hunt, Israel
McCoy, John
Newnam, Joshua
Sacree, W----
Stinson, William
HENRY
Gee, Parker
Scovell, Orr
HOWARD
Heaton, Daniel
JACKSON
Alexander, Thomas
Alsup, John
Applegate, Samuel
Davis, Levi
Henderson, David
Langdon, Philip
Lee, Samuel
Medlock, Richard
Newkirk, Benjamin
Patterson, John
Russell, John
Smith, Robert B.
JAY
Butler, Joel
Chapman, William
Clark, William

JEFFERSON
Arbuckle, David J.
Banta, Cornelius
Booth, John
Broadhead, William H.
Gudgell, John
Lee, John
Littlejohn, John
Morrow, John
Prothero, Thomas
Remkin, Benjamin
Shannon, John
Smock, Jacob
JENNINGS
Ballard, John M.
Bridges, John
Haney, Charles
Howell, William E.
Loyd, Robin
Midcap, John
JOHNSON
Armstrong, Ambrose
Harney, Hiram
McCool, William
Pitcher, William
Rutherford, John
Thompson, James
KNOX
Beckes, Benjamin
Curry, John
Harbin, Joshua
Hodgens, Robert
Johnston, John
Knox, George
Knox, John
Knox, James
LeMountain, J.Henry
McCormick, Robert
Putnam, Howard
Strother, Daniel
Tevebaugh, Jacob
Welton, Jonathan
Westfall, Abraham
Westfall, John
LAGRANGE
Clark, John
Elmer, Elijah
Maybee, Philip
Tufts, William
Weston, Edmund
LAKE
VanGorden, William

LAWRENCE
Baker, Nicholas
Blevins, Daniel
Evans, Edward
Pridmore, Theodore
Rector, Jesse
MADISON
Boston, Elijah
Jackson, Andrew
Noble, Jonathan
Pavey, Samuel
Swindell, Perry
MARION
Allison, John
Bogan, Samuel
Clements, Bernard
Coonrod, -----
George, James
Griffin, Thomas
Hanna, John
Hanna, Thomas
Klingensmith, Jacob
Lingenfelter, Michl.
Lucas, Thomas
Miller, Benjamin
North, John
Wells, Thomas
MARTIN
Blake, John
Demoss, Reuben
Henson, Jesse
MIAMI
Flint, John
MONROE
Blaine, John
Bryant, John
Buskirk, Aaron
Chambers, John T.
Davis, David
Dock, John
Graham, Thomas
Holman, William Nye
Houston, Peter
Johnson, Joseph
Massy, Charles
Pearce, Thomas
Sharp, -----
Snow, John
Stewart, Thomas
MONTGOMERY
Alexander, Joseph
Armantrout, Fredk
Betts, Joseph
Bivins, William
Fields, Samuel

Hitch, Gillis
Largent, Nelson
McNulty, Samuel
Washburn, George
Wheat, James
MORGAN
Jones, William
Landers, Jonathan
Ridingour, J. Andrew
OHIO
Robbins, John
ORANGE
Brown, James
Cowherd, -----
Fleck Christopher
Glover, Uriah
Hally, Joel
Henry, Joseph
Holt, Elisha
Killion, John
Riley, James
OWEN
Brenton, Adam
Dunnigan, Thomas
Franklin, Mordecai
James, Joseph Rog.
Keisinger, Andrew
Maness, Ambrose
Randall, Benager
PARKE
Alisla, Coonrod
Blue, David
Hiatt, Asa
Payne, Augustine
Shelton, Wilson
Watts, Charles
Wedding, R. H.
PERRY
Adams, John
Cotton, J. A.
Hiley, George
Kepler, Jacob
Wapshott, Graves
West, Nicholas
Wilcox, Isaac
Winchell, John
PIKE
Frederick, Sebastian
POSEY
Elkins, Shadrack
McCollum, Daniel
Moore, Asa
Owens, Edmund
Russell, William
Watson, William

PUTNAM
Gorrell, John
Harrison, George
Hutchinson, Thomas
Lucas, William
Mills, Hardy
Summers, James
RANDOLPH
Borders, William B.
Dwiggins, Robert
Johnson, Zachariah
Morris, Thomas
Thurie, Edward
Wysong, Valentine
RIPLEY
Crane, Edmund
Fox, Adam
Hall, Benjamin
House, Levi
Whitacar, John
Willyard, Henry
Wycoff, Isaac
Younger, Kanard
RUSH
Bebout, Daniel
Boyer, John
Collins, John
Grant, Daniel
Huddleston, William
Hunt, James
Overleese, Conrad
Pollock, John
Thrasher, Josiah
SCOTT
Blads, Eli
Bridgewater, Saml.
Haas, Michael
Mulberry, John
Pruett, Archibald
Storm, Jacob
SHELBY
Connor, Abner
Emett, William
Ensminger, Joshua
Gorsage, John
Neal, Benjamin
Simmons, Samuel
Wheeler, Isaac
SPENCER
Findley, Samuel
Miller, Barney
Miller, Nicholas
Pry, Jesse
Tate, Samuel
Williams, Barney

SULLIVAN
Carrithers, William
Haddon, John
Ledgerwood, James
SWITZERLAND
Brown, Samuel
Cotton, Ralph
Ellis, Robert
Fancher, William
Ford, John
Gray, Moses
Hammond, Lewis
Lanham, Henry
Morgan, Daniel
Neal, Charles
Nighswonger, Solomon
Picket, Heathcote
Renno, George
Roberts, Hezekiah
Trainer, Isaac
Weist, Henry
Woolcott, Joseph
TIPPECANOE
Alexander John
Blue, Cornelius
Buck, John
Cox, Nathaniel
Jeffries, John
White, William
Wright, John
UNION
Fall, Christian
Flint, John
Lemon, Moses
Nutt, Levi
Thomas, Richard
VANDERBURGH
Griffis, John G.
Harrison, Zephaniah
Henson, John
VERMILLION
Chenoweth, John
Dickinson, John
Noland, James
Stone, William
Wallace, Oliver
Wells, Peter
VIGO
Brady, Joseph
Cruse, Alison
Durham, William
Eagelton, Alexander
Macom, Joseph
Pierson, Moses
Sample, Thomas
Thomas, John

WARREN
Mann, John
WARRICK
Gray, Benjamin
Knight, William
WASHINGTON
Blunt, Samuel
Bowman, William
Brock, George
Brotherton, John
Buckman, James
Bush, Daniel
Carter, Henry
Deremiah, John
Donahue, John
Dukes, Richard
Gallamore, John
Garriott, Ambrose
Garrison, James
Goold, John
Hall, George

Hays, Joshua
Hensley, Richardson
Hogg (Hoggatt) ----
Holler, John
Johnson, Joseph
Johnson, Josiah
King, William
Long, George (Saml.,?)
Long, Joseph
Lusk, William
McGill, James
McWhorter, Robert
Monical, Moses
Mull, -----
Porter, Nicholas B.
Rubison, Calza
Sargeant, William
Smith, Jacob
Smith, Nathan
Stewart, William

Tipps, Conrad
Vaughn, John
Watts, William
Wayman, Edmond
Weaver, Michael
Wyman, Henry, Sr.
Zink, Daniel
WAYNE
Chance, Samuel
Doddridge, Philip
Fort, Benjamin
Gallion, Thomas
Gump, Frederick
Healey, Hugh
Lamb, Joseph B.
Miller, Jacob
Pittman, -----
Roddy, Christopher
Vinnedge, Adam
Webb, Barruch

The following 190 soldiers are mentioned in affidavits or depositions in the pension files of soldiers in Sections I and II. These 190 soldiers served from and lived in many different places. Most of them have no connection with Indiana (although 38 of them, marked with an asterisk, are in the "Roster"). They are being listed here to show how valuable the many papers in the pension files are and in the hope that even just one name will help a reader to prove service which he has heretofore been unable to find in published records.

Acres, Austin-46
Acres, Valentine-46
Adams, Bartholomew-51
Adams, Simon-69
Alexander, Thomas-71-105
Alexander, William-9
Allen, John*-36
Applegate, ---- 9
Arnold, Ziba-42
Barnes, David-64
Beall, Ninian*-37
Bell, Nathaniel*-12
Biles, Charles-65
Blake, John-28
Blevins, James*-31
Blue, Jacob-14
Boyd, John-107
Branan, Thomas-95
Burch, John-19
Calwell, ---- 111
Calwell, see Colwell
Campbell, Enos-64
Campbell, William-103
Carrenton, George-61
Cassell, Abraham-66
Catt, Philip*-38-97
Charley, George*-36
Cheek, Francis-85
Claycomb, Frederick*-59
Clements, David*-93
Clements, William-93
Cliffen, Joshua-51
Cobb, John-83
Colwell, John*-26-30-71
Cruse, Alison-30-71
Cullett, John-99
Davis, Forrest-41
Davis, John-27
Davis, Lodowick*-41
Davison, James-28

Demoss, Reuben-13
Dixon, George*-29
Dow, Henry-64
Duncan, Charles-50
Duncan, Robert-50
Durham, William-71
Eagelton, Alexander-30-71
Ewen, Catharine(Campbell)-32
Fagan, ---- 104
Fancher, William-118
Farr, Nicholas-74
Farriss, Thomas-32
Ferguson, Andrew*-95
Fislar, John*-80
Flint, ---- 36
Foote, George-91
Foote, Newton-36
Ford, Warner-64
Frazee, Jonas-10
Gaddis, Thomas-40
Gallamore, ---- 38
Garner, Thomas-49
Garrett, Robert-70
Gilbert, Michael-28
Gill, William-95
Gray, Job-95
Gregg, Johnson-21
Gregory, Abram-95
Grimes, James*-67
Guffy, James*-98
Gullion, John*-111
Hall, John-44
Hall, William*-52
Haltom, Joseph-84
Hamblen, Job*-57
Hammond, Thomas-74
Harbin, Joshua-108
Haymond, Edward-47
Haymond, Owen-47
Haymond, Thomas-47

Henry, John-48
Henry, Moses*-48
Henson, Jesse-49-50
Hines, John-50
Holiday, ----60
Holloway, Levi*-21
Holman, Isaac*-54-82
Huff, Peter-100
Hungerford, Lemuel-61
Jacobs, Jeremiah-82
Jacobs, John-76
Johnson, David*-27-56
Jones, Griffin-57
Jones, James-19
Joy, James-64
King, Arra-60
Kisler, Philip-52
Lamb, James*-61
Lawrence, William-61
Lawson, James-16
Lee, Joseph*-64
Lemmon, Alexander-111
LeMountain, John-95
Levi, Isaac*-74
Lindsey, John-14
Littleton, Charles-17
Littleton, Mark-17
Littleton, Savage-17
Lorance, William-61
Lore, Andrew-46
Lore, Henry-46
Low, Nelus-67
McAnnelly, Peter*-95
McGahey, William*-41
McMahan, Peter-107
McWhorter, Robert-6
McWhorter, William-71
Macon, Joseph-30
Madden, William*-99
Malone, Francis*-5
Massey, Thomas-72
Matney, Thomas-51
Mays, James-60
Meads, William-42-43
Meredith, Samuel*-29
Miller, Barney-59
Miller, Jacob-102
Morrison, James-94
Mounts, Thomas-64
Neal, Campbell-21
Newton, Basil-72
Nighswonger, Solomon-117
Paul, George-73
Pollard, William-94
Pope, Elijah-57
Prather, Basil-54

Preble, James-99-100
Price, Stephen-64
Pridmore, Jonathan-82
Purdy, John-16
Rainey, James-84
Rainey, John-84
Rains, Anthony-50
Raney, Jeremiah*-84
Rankins, Daniel-104
Reede, Henry-37
Roberts, Hezekiah-22
Roberts, Nehemiah-85-86
Russell, Elijah-103
Ryker, Gerardus-92
Sacrey, Isaac-89
Saunder, Jacob-52
Smith, John-36
Smith, Thomas-61
Starrs, Richard-51
Stephens, John-50
Stephens, Robert-50
Stiffey, Isaac-46
Stiffey, Peter-46
Stinson, John-94
Stinson, William-94
Stipe, Frederick-88
Swan, John-55
Swartwood, John-101
Swindell, Willis-95
Taff, James*-47
Thompson, Robert-99
Thompson, William-98
Thorn, Michael*-38-46-108
Triplett, Daniel-36
Vanarsdall, Cornelius-100
Vanarsdall, Cornelius O.-100
Vinnedge, Adam-73
Warrenton, Alexander-21
Watson, John-105
Waugh, John-113
Wayman, Edmond-6
Welch, James-64
Westbrook, Samuel-101
Westfall, Abel-108
Westfall, Abraham-46-108
Westfall, Cornelius*-108
Westfall, Jacob*-108
Westfall, John-108
Wilson, John-111
Wood, Ebenezer-29
Woodworth,* Dyer-76
Woolcott, Augustus-112
Wright, Evans-50
Wright,* William-49-64
Yarberry, ----13
York, Jerry (or Shubel)-50

The following 55 soldiers at one time lived in Indiana but moved
to other states where they presumably may have died. With one
exception they all have pension files. Since the soldiers did
not die in Indiana, I did not abstract the pension files but jotted down only the briefest of notes. I made no p rticular effort
to ascertain the Indiana county of residence but have given it if
I found it easily. No references are given since full data can
be obtained from the pension files. These 55 men are not listed
in the "Roster", pages 404-405.

ANGEL, LAWRENCE — Johnson
To Ark., May 1834. In 1835 Pens. List of Independence Co., Ark.

BARR, HUGH — Daviess
To Ill.; d. 4-24-1842, Edgar Co., Ill., at home of son, Michael.
Was son of Michael Barr of Montgomery Twp., near Washington,
Ind. Pens. 32110 N.C. & Va.

BEAN, DANIEL — Marion
From Ohio to Ind., 5-15-1837; from Ind. to Iowa, 9-15-1840; d.
11-1-1840, Burlington, Iowa. Pens. W.8124 Pa. More data in
"Ohio Rev. Sold.", v. 2, p. 53.

BRACKENBAUGH, LEONARD — Union
To Ohio, 10-4-1839. In 1835 Pens. List, ae. 70, Union Co., Ind.

BRONSON, PHINEAS
From Pittsburgh, Pa., Agy., to Ind., 8-13-1838; to Ill., 4-17-1839. In 1840 Pens. List of Peoria Co., Ill.

BRYANT, WILLIAM G. — Greene, Ripley, Marion
To Jonesborough, East Tenn., Agy., 1-21-1840, having mov. to
Smith Co., Tenn., in 1837.

BURNETT, JOSHUA — Greene
To Ill., 1-11-1840.

BURNHAM, JOHN — Floyd
To Ohio, 1821; Hamilton Co., O.

BURRELL, FRANCIS — Jackson
d. Decatur Co., Iowa. Rejected pens.; service accepted by DAR.

CAULKINS, JOEL — Washington
From Albany, N.Y., Agy., to Ind., 1-17-1837; back to N.Y., 3-18-1843. In 1835 Pens. List of Jefferson Co., N.Y.; in 1840 Pens.
List, ae. 81, Brown Twp., Washington Co., Ind. Pens. 23567 Conn.

COOPER, ELIJAH — Marion
To Ill. Pens. W.9802 N.H.

COY, CHRISTOPHER   Harrison
d. 10-12-1839, Lawrence Co., Ill. Pens. R.9798 Md. Widow lived
Greene Twp., Parke Co., Ind., 1 mo. after his death. (See that
Section in this Suppl.)

CRESSEY, BENJAMIN   Washington
From Mass. to Ind., 4-5-1831; back to Mass., 1-5-1832; d. 7-10-
1834, Middlesex Co., Mass. Pens. S.34260 N.H.

CUNNINGHAM, RICHARD
From Ohio, 1-18-1838, to Ind.; back to Ohio, 9-6-1847.

CUNNINGHAM, THOMAS
Pens. S.42664 Va. (Notes re residence & transfer lost).

DAVIDSON, Isaac   Johnson
To Ohio, 2-25-1841, Clark Co., O.; d. 10-17-1842, South Charleston, O. Pens. S.2509 Va. More data in "Ohio Rev. Sold.",v.1,107.

DICKINSON; WAITSTILL   Lagrange
From Albany, N.Y., Agy., to Ind., 5-30-1836; from Ind. to Pa.,
9-25-1839. In 1835 Pens. List of Ontario Co., N.Y.

DOLLAR, WILLIAM
To Ill., 11-15-1828; Fulton Co., Ill.

DUNCAN, JESSE   Parke
To Va., Feb. 1836.

DUNKAN, EDWARD   Decatur
To Ohio, 5-14-1841.

FELLOWS, WILLIS   Greene
To Ill., 1-10-1829.

FRITTS, JOHN
From Jonesborough, East Tenn., Agy., to Ind., 12-30-1837; from
Ind. to Va., 6-3-1843. In 1835 Pens. List, Hawkins Co., Tenn.

GRAVES, JEDIDIAH
From Albany, N.Y., Agy , to Ind., 3-23-1838; back to Albany, N.Y.
Agy., 9-27-1839.

GRIER, JOHN
From Jonesborough, East Tenn., Agy., to Ind., 12-8-1835; back to
E. Tenn., 6-8-1840. In 1840 Pens. List, Sullivan Co., Tenn.

HALL, JOHN   Johnson
d. Ohio. Pens. R.4470½ Pa. From Pa. to Hardin Co., Ky. From
Ky. ca. 1826-1830 to Johnson Co., Ind.; may have liv. for a
while in Owen Co., Ind.

HARDESTY, HEZEKIAH
From Ill., 4-25-1836; back to Ill., 7-16-1839. In 1835 Pens. List
of Lawrence Co., Ill. & 1840 of Fulton Co., Ill.

HAWLEY, SAMUEL   Floyd
To Miss., 5-7-1828.

HENSON, JOHN   Vanderburgh
d. 7-25-1835, Wayne Co., Ill. Pens. appl. 1829, Vanderburgh Co., Ind. Pens. W.2130 N.C. Wid., Jane (Goodbread) Henson, m. 1787, Rutherford Co., N.C. Son Reuben. Sold. had bros.: William and Jesse (see Section I, this Suppl.); nephew William Henson Also named is Bartlett Henson (rel. not given).

HIGGINS, DANIEL
From Ohio, 4-5-1837; to Wheeling, W. Va., 3-16-1840 (poss. convenient for Ohio residence). In 1835 Pens. List, Butler Co., O. More data in "Ohio Rev. Sold.", v.2, p.175. (Not the man in the "Roster", p. 186).

KELLEY, MOSES   Clark
To Ohio, 4-20-1835.

LIVINGSTON, DAVID
To Ohio, 6-21-1821. In 1835 Pens. List, Hamilton Co., O.; died 1-27-1831. More data in "Ohio Rev. Sold.", v 1, p. 229.

LONG, WILLIAM   Parke
To Shelby Co., Ky., 1853, ae. 95, to live with son Jeremiah. In 1840 Pens. List, Parke Co., Ind., ae. 80.

McCLURE, SAMUEL   Franklin & Vigo
To Clark Co., Ill. Pens. S.33079 Va. Never pensioned in Ind., but liv. Franklin Co., Ind., for a time & while liv. Vigo Co., Ind., made affid. for pens. appl. of John Colwell ("Roster" p.82) that he served with Colwell.

McCORMICK, JOHN   Fayette
To Mo., 8-28-1845.

MITCHELLER, JACOB   Ripley
To Ohio, 9-2-1835.

MONTGOMERY, ALEXANDER   Jefferson, Scott, &
To Mercer Co., Ill., where d. 1-9-1837.   Montgomery
In 1835 Pens. List, Montgomery Co., Ind. Poss. clue to poss. son, Alex Montgomery, b. 1790; 1st Lt., Co. E, 80th Ind. Inf., Civil War; bur. Linden Cem., Madison Twp., Montgomery Co., Ind. Soldier's wid. liv. Johnson Co., Iowa.

MORGAN, WILLIAM   Johnson
From Shelby Co., Ky., post 1828; back to Shelby Co., Ky., 4-7-1837. Pens. S.18985 Va.

MOSS, ZEALLY
From Ky. to Ind. to Peoria Co., Ill. Pens. to 2nd wife, Jeanette Glasscock. See DAR Mag., v.48, p.54.

MURRAY, RICHARD
Pens. S.38253 paid from Corydon, Ind., Agy.; by 10-28-1822 had
mov. to Va.; on 9-5-1837 liv. Belmont Co., Ohio.

OGDEN, STEPHEN D.   Floyd
d. Edgar Co., Ill. See "Ill. Rev. Sold.", p.34. As I remember,
this man is the only one in this Section who may have had no
pension file although my 1949 compilation, p.25 (from which he
should be deleted) says he appl. for a pens.

RANSTEAD, JAMES
To Ohio, 10-27-1830; incorrectly given as Rauskad.

REEVES, SAMUEL
To Lincoln Co., Tenn.; d. 10-12-1834. Debatable if sold. lived
in Ind.; died in Ind.; or trans. to Tenn. & died in Tenn. Wid.,
Susanna (Brack or Brock) Reeves liv. Tenn. in 1838 & 1842.

ROSE, RICHARD
To Ill. In 1835 Pens. List, Adams Co., Ill.; then liv. Schuyler
Co., Ill.; d. 2-14-1842, Hancock Co., Ill. More data in "Ill.
Rev. Sold.", p. 54.

ROSE, WILLIAM   Floyd
To Mo., 5-7-1827.

SCOTT, SAMUEL   Boone
d. 8-8-1833, Lee Co., Va.; pens. R.9312 Va. There are three, if
not four, Samuel Scotts connected with Ind. I think papers in
the pens. files may have been misfiled (I have proved this in several other instances), thus resulting in telescoping some of the
men. The Ind Agy. Rolls show no pens. ever paid to any Samuel
Scott nor for the wid. of any Samuel Scott. The 1852 Rejected
Pens. List gives a rejected pens. for only one Samuel Scott, but
I have personally seen the two rejected pens. files for two different Samuel Scotts. The best interpretation I could make in my
limited time is this.   No.1-Samuel Scott liv. Boone Co., Ind.;
mov. to Lee Co., Va., where he d. 8-8-1833; pens. R.9312 Va. REF:
1852 Rej. Pens. List, p.413.   No.2-Samuel Scott liv. West
Tenn.; mov. to Posey Co., Ind., where he d. 1849; is in my 1949
compilation, p.30, & should be deleted since service was in War
of 1812.   No.3-Samuel Scott, "Roster", p.405, says liv. Parke
Co., Ind., & had pension; then mov. to Ky., where he d. 1820. My
notes show that this man was not pensioned; pens. R.9307 Va. was
rejected; he d. Jessamine Co., Ky.; wid. Martha liv. Montgomery
Co., Ind., 1854; probability of his ever living in Parke Co.,
Ind., seems remote if he d. 1820 in Ky. The trouble with this
is: the "Roster" has him as pensioned & I found no Samuel Scott
(nor widow) as a pensioner on Ind. Agy. Rolls; I have him with a
rejected pens. & there is only one Samuel Scott on the 1852 list
& he is R.9312 Va., of Boone Co., Ind., No.1 above. This still
leaves unidentified the man (No.4?) in the 1835 Pens. List, v.3,
p.8, who trans. from Penn.; pens. began 9-4-1791 under Law of
6-7-1785; he is listed as of Parke Co. Ind., so he would seem to

be No.3 above, a pensioner, except that the Ind. Agy. Rolls have
no pensioned Samuel Scott & that I have found him with a rejected
pension.

SIMPKINS, JOHN G. Vigo
From Ill., 3-23-1838; back to Ill., 11-25-1849 (sic). In 1835
Pens. List, Franklin Co., Ill.; d. 7-22-1843 (sic), Williamson
Co., Ill. More data in "Ill. Rev. Sold.", p. 175.

SMITH, PHILIP D.
To Ohio, 5-3-1828. In 1835 Pens. List, Hamilton Co., O. More
data in "Ohio Rev. Sold.", v.1, p. 342.

SPRAGUE, JAMES
From Ohio, 3-16-1836; back to Ohio, 7-10-1840. In 1835 & 1840
Pens. Lists, Muskingum Co., O. More data in "Ohio Rev. Sold.",
v. 1, p. 347.

THOMAS, JAMES
To Ky., 11-24-1825.

TRACY, SOLOMON Bartholomew
To Ky., 12-1-1838.

TUCKER, JOHN Ripley or Parke
To Ky., 10-26-1839. (Two men in "Roster", p. 360; this would
seem to be the Parke Co. man. Ind. Agy. Rolls number would
prove which man).

TULLIS, MICHAEL
To Ohio, 6-28-1850.

WALKER, BENJAMIN Dearborn
To Ill., 11-7-1840; back to Ind., 2-4-1842; back to Ill., 9-4-
1845.(where died). His wid., Mary, trans. from Ind. to Ohio,
2-10-1860; from Ill. to Ind., 6-21-1865., More data in "Ill. Rev.
Sold.", p. 99, and in "Western Christian Advocate--Abstracts of
Obituaries & Marriages" by Waters & Millikan (copies in DAR
Library and I.S.L.).

WARREN, JAMES Johnson
To Green Co., Ky., 5-13-1840, where had formerly lived.

WYMAN, REUBEN
To Maine, 9-25-1821. In 1840 Pens. List, Somerset Co., Maine.

The following 121 soldiers did not die in Indiana. Their widows later moved to Indiana. Of the 121 widows, there are pension files for 120. Since these are not Revolutionary soldiers who died in Indiana, I jotted down only the sketchiest of data which may, however, help some reader. When known, Indiana residence is given for widow.

  ADAMS, AARON & SARAH (HARD)   Johnson
He d. 12-13-1833. Pens. file does not say where; DAR Lineage Bk., v. 155, p. 283 & v. 166, p. 70, say in Tenn., but I think this unlikely. He may have d. in Ohio. His dau., Charlotte (Mrs. Ebenezer Merry) liv. Norwalk, Huron Co., O., 8-27-1841. Sold.'s son Aaron mov. to Ohio, then to Ind., ca. 1839. Sarah in Johnson Co., Ind., 8-6-1840; by 3-25-1851, she in Milan, Erie Co., O. Son, Aaron, Jr., on 11-4-1841 was in either Franklin Co., Ind., or Franklin, Johnson Co., Ind. Pens. W.9393 Vt.

  ARGENBRIGHT, GEORGE & CHRISTINA (EATON)   Cass
He d. 2-22-1840, Rockingham Co., Va. Pens. W.25357 Va.

  BERRY, WILLIAM & HANNAH   Scott
He d. Ohio. Pens. W.9724 Cont. (Md.) Navy.

  BIVINS, ABNER & HANNAH (WATTERHOUSE)   St. Joseph
He d. 11-5-1833, Savannah, Wayne Co., N.Y. Pens. W.2432 Mass,R.I.

  BLACKBORN, JOHN & ELIZABETH   Morgan
He d. 1-15-1835, Shelby Co., Ky. Pens. W.1367 Cont., Pa.

  BLACKMER, EPHRAIM & MARY (JONES)   Rush
A Mary Collins is in 1840 Pens., List, p. 185, Posey Twp., Rush Co., Ind., ae. 75. She may be the wid. of Ephraim Blackmer who d. 2-27-1796, Westmoreland; she m.(2) 1-9-1798 Samuel Collins who d. July 1837; in 1842 she liv. Oneida Co., N.Y.; Pens. W.16925 Vt. (I question this because there is no Mary Collins on the Ind. Agy. Rolls.

  BLADES, JOHN LEVY & SARAH   Switzerland
He d Jan.-Feb. 1784, Worcester Co., Md. Pens. W.9502 Md. She m.(2) William Lancaster (Pens. S.16912 Va.) who d. 11-4-1843 ("Roster", p. 226.

  BOTTORFF, HENRY & SOPHIA (FRICKER)   Clark
He d. Ky. (See DAR Lineage Books). She nee Fricker or Freiker. This is the only one in this section for whom there may be no pension file. (Recd. too late to check).

  BOWERS, JOHN D. & REBECCA (MURPHY)   Floyd
He d. Ohio. Married in Warren Co., O. Pens. W.1216 N.J.

  BOWLING, THOMAS & SARAH   Harrison
He d. 1-7-1810, prob. Spotsylvania Co., Va. She in Harrison Co., Ind., 1829. Pens. R.1078.

BOYD, JAMES & LYDIA
He d. Columbiana Co;O., post 1840. Pens. W.9362. She liv. in
Ind. & then tr. to Ohio, Sept. 1864.

BRACKET, HAWKINS & SALLY Johnson
He d. summer 1821, Rutherford Co., N.C. Pens. R.1121 N.C.

CANFIELD, DANIEL & ELIZABETH Jennings
He. d. 10-31-1832, Louis (Lewis?) Co., Va. Pens. W.9768 N.Y.

CARR, JAMES & JULIANA Fountain
He d. Jan. 1807, Ohio. She m.(2) Henry Clark who d. Mar. 1821,
Ohio. Pens. R.1721 N.J. (He is not the "Roster", p.87).

CASTERLINE, LOAMMI & CHARLOTTE (FAIRCHILDS) Blackford
He d. 12-14-1835, Steuben Co., N.Y. (See Shinn--"Blackford &
Grant Cos., Ind., 1914, pp. 152-153). Pens. R.1796 N.J.

CAVENDAR, JOHN & MARGARET Franklin &
He d. 1837, Hamilton Co., O. (See "Ohio Rev. Ripley
Sold.", v.1, & Natl. Gen. Soc. Quart., Dec. 1944, p. 106). She
liv. Ripley Co., Ind., first. Pens. W.9776.

CHAMBERS, DAVID & ISABEL Montgomery
He d 4-1-1809, Rockbridge Co., Va. Pens. W.6657 Va.

CHANDLEY, WILLIAM & SARAH Crawford
He d. 9-22-1829, Sevier Co., Tenn. She m.(2) 4-8-1834, John
Lovell of Crawford Co., Ind. Pens. W.5027 Va.

CHRISTIE, JAMES & SARAH Ripley
He d. 3-8-1837, Shelby Co., Ky. Pens. 9782 Va.

CONINE, ANDREW & LYDIA Switzerland
He d. 6-11-1836, Henry Co., Ky. Pens. W.9809 Va.

CONNELLY, PATRICK & MARGARET Henry
He d. 3-15-1827, Warren Co., O. Pens. W.9815 Pa.

CONNOR, WILLIAM & ROSANNA Warren
He d. 3-14-1827, Scioto Co., O. Pens. W.22817 Va., ½ Pay.

CORWINE, GEORGE & RUTH (CORWINE Henry
He d. Hunterdon Co., N.J. She was a distant cousin. She m.(2)
Luther Calvin & was d. by 1843. Pens. R.1607 N.J

COUGHREN, JOSEPH & PRUDENCE Hamilton
He d. 3-19-1845, Vermilion Co., Ill. Pens. W.1712 Va.

COVALT, ABRAHAM & LOISA Fountain
He d. 3-31-1791, Covalt's Station on Little Miami River, Ohio.
She m.(2) Mr. Davis. Pens. R.2742 Pa.

COY, CHRISTOPHER & ELIZABETH Parke
He d.10-12-1839,Lawrence Co.,Ill.(having liv.prev.Madison Co,Ky.&
tr.to Ind.,Harrison Co.3-11-1828. R.9798Md.See Ill.Rev.Sold.,68.

CRAIN, SAMUEL & JANE (BONNEL) Fountain
He d. 12-1-1821, Preston Co., Va. Pens. W.9822 N.J.

DOWD, CONNER & HANNAH
She tr. from Cincinnati, O., to Ind., 4-10-1854; tr. back to Cincinnati, O., 2-19-1859. Pens.

DUNN, ABNER M. & PRISCILLA Clark
He d. 1796-1797, Cincinnati, O. Pens. W.9842 Cont. (Pa.).

ENDECOTT, THOMAS & WELLMETT Posey
He d. 4-24-1834, Harrison Co., Ky. She (as wid. of Joseph Endecott, relationship not stated) m. Thomas Apr. 1834, 1 mo. ante he d. His pens. appl. rejected. She came to Ind. 1834; Montgomery Co for 3 yr.; then Posey Co. (See Burns--"Abstr. of Pens., Sold of Rev.....Blue Grass Region of Ky.", pp.13-14.)

ERWIN, DAVID & LYDIA (HUTCHINSON) Morgan &
He d 11-20-1843, Daviess Co., Ky. Pens, Hendricks

FIFIELD, BENJAMIN & SUSANNA Porter
He d. New Hampshire. Pens. W.1742 N.H.

FINLEY, SAMUEL & MARY (BROWN) St. Joseph
He d. 4-2-1829, Chillicothe, Ross Co., O. Pens. W.10026 Va.

FISK, ROBERT & ELIZABETH Ripley
He d. 4-19-1824, Ill. Pens. W.9438 Mass.

FOSTER, JOHN & ANNA Jefferson
He d. 11-16-1816, N.H. Pens. W.10034 Mass.

GALBREATH, WILLIAM & PHEBE (FOREMAN) Scott
He d. 5-3-1839, Coles Co., Ill. Pens. W.23093 Pa. & Va.

GODDARD, JOSEPH & FRANCES Switzerland
He d. 6-28-1844, Fleming Co., Ky. Pens. R.4078 Va.

GREEN, CHAFFEY & DIANA Lagrange
He d. New York. She tr. back to Albany, N.Y., Agy., 9-7-1857.
Pens. W.2611 Mass. & R.I.

HALTOM, JOSEPH & MARY Owen.
He d. 1825, Montgomery Co., N.C. Pens. W.27582 N.C.

HAMMONS, JOSEPH & MARTHA Monroe
He d. Apr. 19 (year missing), Surry Co., N.C. Pens. R.4544 Va.

HANDY, THOMAS & SARAH Fountain
He d 1-4-1824, Clark Co., Ill. Pens. R 4561 Pa

HANNA, ADAM & NANCY Putnam
He d. 9-24-1824, Shelby Co., Ky. Pens. R.4575.

HARRIS, RICHMOND & POLLY
She tr. from Ky. to Ind., 3-3-1856. Pens.

HARRIS, THOMAS & NANCY (WOOLEN) Marion
He d. 1843, prob. Campbell Co., Ky. (I see no proof in pens.
file that her residence in Ind. was in Marion Co).

HARVEY, JOHN & COMFORT Montgomery
He d. Greene Co., Tenn., while on visit from his home in Blount
Co., Tenn. She tr. back to Tenn., 11-10-1849. Pens. W.249 N.C.

HICKEY, DANIEL & JANE Jefferson
He d. Fayette Co., Ky. Her 3rd husb. Pens. W.7744 Pa

HILL, CLEMENT & MARY ANN (DOUGLASS) Lawrence
He d. 7-2-1836, Barren Co., Ky. Pens. W.10106 Va.

HOWE, JOHN & RACHEL (PINDELL) Harrison
He d. 5-16-1830, Hardin Co., Ky. Pens. W.10113 Cont. Va.

HOWE, SELAH & ELIZABETH
He d. 3-17-1840, N.Y. She tr. from Albany, N.Y., Agy.,9-15-1846.

HUMPHREY, GEORGE & MARY (ROSE) Gibson
He d. 4-10-1840, Edwards Co., Ill. She m.(2) (Felix?) Hall.
Pens. W.761 Cont. (Va.).

IRELAND, JAMES & NANCY St. Joseph
He d. 1826, Preble Co., O. Pens. R.5494 N.C.

JACKSON, MATTHEW & JANE Shelby
He d. 7-14-1823, Hamilton Co., O. She liv. Noble Twp., Shelby
Co., Ind., & d. ante 9-11-1855. Pens. W.10142 Cont., Mass.

JACKSON, SETH & ELIZABETH Jennings
He d. 4-21-1800, Albany Co. or Seneca Co., N.Y. She m (2)
Joseph Hunter & was d. on 7-29-1855. Pens.

JENNINGS, SOLOMON & POLLY Switzerland
He d. 11-30-1820, Owen Co., Ky. Pens. W.10147 N.Y.

JORDAN, THOMAS & REBECCA (STARBUCK) Brown
He d. 4-15-1850, Belmont Co., O. Pens. Ind. Agy. Rolls say
Elizabeth (by error) instead of Rebecca.

KEATH, WILLIAM & MARY Putnam
He d. 10-19-1838, Wayne Co., Ky. She m.(2) Mr. McInlin.
Pens. W.26150 Va.

KNOX, JOHN & ELIZABETH Owen, Monroe
He d. 12-24-1818, Pulaski Co., Ky. She d. 1-16-1851; last liv.
in Ill. Pens.

KNOX, ROBERT & MILLY   Switzerland
He d. 10-3-1836, Gallatin Co., Ky., but had liv. in Switzerland
Co., Ind. She later retd. to Gallatin Co., Ky. Pens. W.26190
S.C. (Switzerland Co. Probate Bk. A, p.69).

LITTERAL, RICHARD & JANE (CHAMPS)   Wayne
He d. 9-4-1840, Botetourt Co., Va. She tr. from Tenn., 7-10-
1861. Pens. W.26220 Cont; (Va.).

LITTLE, JAMES & ROSETTA (ALLEN)   St. Joseph
He d. 3-24-1843, Morristown, Vt. Pens.

LYON, NATHANIEL & MARCY   Marion
He d. 9-2-1833, Montgomery Co., O. Pens.

McCULLOUGH, JOSEPH & SARAH   Monroe
Had pens. but I couldn't identify from pens. files. N.J. serv.

McILRATH, ANDREW & ALICE   Elkhart
He d. 2-25-1836, Eucl., Cuyahoga Co., O. Pens.

McLEAN, DANIEL & NANCY   Lawrence
He d. 6-6-1821, Scott Co., Ky. Pens. W.9183 Pa. (McClain).

MADDEN, WILLIAM & JANE
She tr. from Ill. to Ind., 8-12-1856. Pens.

MARSH, WILLIAM & ELIZABETH   Harrison
Not the one in "Roster", p.245. She had pens.

MARTIN, ROBERT & NANCY   Fountain
He d. 11-13 or 11-30-1836, Pickaway Co., O. Pens.

MASSEY, JACOB & CATHARINE   Decatur &
He d. 5-14-1796 or ca. 1797, Montgomery Co., Ky.   Johnson
She d. 1844, Decatur Co., Ind. Susp. Pens. List (1852), p.419,
gives her of Johnson Co., Ind.; she prob. liv. there earlier
with son Abraham when she appl. for pens., 2-24-1844. Pens.
R.7006 N.C.

MATHEWS, AMOS V. & DELILA   Ripley &
He d. 8-4-1844, Carroll Co., Ky., but had liv. in   Spencer
Ripley Co., Ind., 1835. She liv. Rockport, Spencer Co., Ind.,
1857, ae. 64. Pens.

MAXWELL, DAVID & ABIGAIL   Ripley
He d. 2-21-1814, Augusta, Maine. Pens.

MEDLOCK, RICHARD & MARY   Jackson
He d. Hawkins Co., Tenn. She also liv. Brown & Bartholomew Cos.,
Indiana. Pens.

MEFFORD, JACOB & ELEANOR   Lawrence
He d 12-14-1844, Campbell Co., Ky. Pens.

MILES, JOHN & POLLY (DUVALL)   Montgomery
He d. 10-9-1828, Henry Co., Ky. She d. 6-30-1855. Pens.

MILLER, WILLIAM & REBECCA   Parke
He d. 1826, Preble Co., O. She m.(2) Hugh Marshall. Pens.

MINTURN, JOHN & REBECCA   Putnam
He d. 7-7-1826, Warren Co., O. She tr. from Ill., 7-22-1846. Pens. W.9203 N.J.

MOSER, JACOB & ELIZABETH   Martin
He d. 7-2-1813, prob. Tenn., as she m.(2) Sept. 1814, Campbell Co., Tenn., Mr. Williams. Pens. W.9164 Cont. (Md.).

NETHERTON, JOHN & REBECCA   Johnson
He d. 10-18-1833, Oldham Co., Ky. He also liv. Shelby Co., Ky., & m. in Jefferson Co., Ky.. Rebecca, wid. of John Frazier. Pens.

NEWTON, BASIL & MARY   Monroe
He d. 11-7-1786, poss. Md. She m.(2) 12-7-1790, William Hall, who d. 11-10-1803. Pens. W.10074 Md. (See Charles Massy in text)

NOLAND, JAMES & BARBARA   La Porte
He d. 12-26-1833, Estill Co., Ky. She tr. from Ky., 11-13-1844. Pens. W.9202 N.C. & Va. (Not the man in the text).

OSBORN, WILLIAM & ELIZABETH   Fountain
She tr. from Mo. to Ind., 5-1-1858. Pens.

PECK, GAD & MARY   Posey
He d. 6-3-1853, New Haven, Conn. Pens.

PETERSON, CONRAD & MARY   Wabash
He d. 1847, Knox Co., O. She is on Susp. Pens. List (1852),p. 419. Later had Pens. W.10226 Va. She d. by 1853.

PIERCE, JAMES & ANN   Tippecanoe
He d. 9-17-1830, Coshocton Co., O. Pens.

PITMAN, JONATHAN & JANE   Decatur
He d. Hamilton Co., O. She m.(2) Mr. Hunt. Pens. W.11353 N.J.

PORTER, JOSIAH & RACHEL   Vigo
He d. 12-17-1814, Davidson Co., Tenn. Pens. R.8351 S.C.

RANDOLPH, HENRY & NANCY (BENNETT)   Vigo
He d. 6-15-1836, Spencer Co., Ky. In 1819 he liv. Shelby Co., Ky. She in Vigo Co., Ind., by Dec. 1841; had chn. in Clark Co., Illinois. Pens.

RANKINS, DANIEL & ELEANOR (TONG)   Montgomery &
He d.4-30-1833,Brown Co.,O. She nee Tong or Tongue,m.(2) George Washburn who d. 3-9-1850,Montgomery Co.,Ind.(See text). She also liv. Tippecanoe Co., Ind. Pens.   Tippecanoe

REED, JOHN & MIRIAM   Howard
He d. 8-27-1844, Darke Co.. O. Pens. R.8667 Md.

ROBERTS, JOHN & SARAH (HAWLEY)   Switzerland
He d. ca. 1820, Henry Co., Ky. Susp. Pens. List,   or Putnam
(1852) p.419, gives her of Putnam Co., Ind.; so she may have mov.
there later. Pens. R.8877 Va. (Not "Roster", p.315)

ROSE, BENJAMIN B. & SUSANNAH (RUTHERFORD)   Johnson
He d. 12-9-1838, Mercer Co., Ky. Pens.

ROSS, WILLIAM & RACHEL   Monroe
He d. 8-30-1825, Wythe Co., Va. Pens. R.9024 N.C.

SACREY, ISAAC & ELIZABETH (GEORGE)   Hendricks
He d. 1807, Franklin Co., Ky. Pens. W.10247 Va.

SANDERS, JOHN & PHEBE   Jay
He d. 5-11-1838, Greene Co., O. Pens.

SCOTT, SAMUEL & MARTHA   Montgomery
He d 1820, Jessamine Co., Ky. Wid. liv. Montgomery Co., Ind.,
1854; she may have liv. Parke Co., Ind., earlier. Sold. may have
liv. Parke Co., Ind., before he d. See "Roster" p.405, and full
discussion in this Suppl. under section of soldiers who moved
away from Indiana to other states. Pens. files.

SIMPSON, ALEXANDER & ELIZABETH (LYNCH)   Wayne
He d. 3-20-1834, Dayton, Montgomery Co., O. Pens.

SMITH, MICHAEL & NANCY   Rush
He d. Harrison Co., Ky. She d. 12-28-1850, Rush Co., Ind. Chn.
given in Pens. W.6088 Md. & Pa.

SMITH, THADEUS & ANNE   Franklin
He d. 4-12-1839, prob. Meigs Co., O. Pens.

STEPHENSON, JAMES & ELIZABETH   Boone
He d. 8-15-1810, prob. Westmoreland Co., Pa. Pens. W.9677 Pa.

STEWART, ARCHIBALD & CATHARINE   Jay & Grant
He d. 5-5-1849, Fayette Co., Pa. She also liv. Grant Co., Ind.
Had pens.

SWORDS, WILLIAM & MARY   Marion (?)
He d. 2-17-1813 in either Ohio or Ky., poss. Scott Co., Ky. Pens.
file papers show wid. liv. in Marion Co., Ind.; but Susp. Pens.
List (1852) p.419 (for proof of identity with the soldier of
Capt. Kinsbury's Comp. of artillery attached to the N.C. Line)
gives her of Rush Co., Ind. He may be the man in the 1820 Cens.,
v.6, p.4, of Fayette Co., Ind. Pens. R.10367 S.C.

TANNER, JOSIAH & MARTHA   Johnson
He d Oct.-Nov.1807, Jefferson Co,Ky.She m.(2)Abraham Lemasters,d.
11-3-1837, Johnson Co., Ind. Pens. W.9503 S.C.

TAYLOR, ARCHIBALD & RACHEL (CHINALT)　　　Hendricks
He d. 5-27-1813 or 1814, Surry Co., N.C.　Pens.

THATCHER, AMOS & JEMIMA　　　Clinton
He d. 6-25-1834, Preble Co., O.　Pens.

THOMPSON, ALEXANDER & SARAH (SCROGGS)　　　Vermillion
He d. 9-25-1840, Whiteside Co., Ill. She liv. Jackson Co., Iowa, in 1855. Pens.

TOWNSEND, JOHN & ELIZABETH　　　Shelby
He d. 8-4-1834, Adair Co., Ky.　Pens. W.9861 Va. (He is not the one in the "Roster", p. 357).

TROUT, CHRISTIAN & ELIZABETH (GEARHART)　　　Greene
He d. 6-16-1847, Pike Co., Ky.　Pens.

TULL, JESSE & REBECCA　　　Wayne
He d. 9-23-1812, Sussex Co., Dela.　Pens.

TURNER, SOLOMON & CASSANDRA (HARVEY)　　　Porter
He d. 4-14-1820, prob. Hardin Co., Ky. She m.(2) Wright Taylor, who d. 5-27-1836. Pens. W.9847 Md.

VANDEVENDER, BARNABAS & ELIZABETH　　　Grant
She tr. from Ohio (poss. Preble Co.) to Ind., 9-4-1864. See "Ohio Rev. Sold.", v.2, p. 349. Pens.

WALKER, BENJAMIN & MARY
She tr. from Ind. to Ohio, 2-10-1860; from Ill. to Ind., 6-21-1865. (See husb. in section of solds. who moved from Ind.). Pens.

WARDWELL, WILLIAM & CATHARINE　　　Marion
He d. 2-12-1848, Oxford, Ohio.　Pens.

WATKINS, OLIVER & LUCY (LOOMER)　　　Lake
He d. 2-11-1833, Oswego, N.Y. She was 2nd wife. Pens.

WATSON, WILLIAM & SARAH　　　Jefferson
He d. 9-11-1827, Pittsfield, prob. Monmouth Co., N.H. Pens. 22537 N.H. (Not the man in the text).

WEIGHTMAN, SAMUEL & SARAH　　　Union
He d. 2-8-1816. Had liv. & mar. in York Co., Pa. Wid. in Union Co., Ind., 1838. Pens. R.11284 Pa.

WILKINSON, BENJAMIN & EVA　　　Marion
He d 3-1-1840, Jefferson Co., Ky.　Pens.

WILKINSON, JOHN & MARGARET　　　Montgomery
He d: 8-29-1841, Butler Co., O.　Pens. W.9890 Pa.

WILLIAMS, GABRIEL & MARGARET　　　Henry
He d. 1827, Monongalia Co., (W.) Va.　Pens.

WILSON, BENJAMIN & HANNAH   Hendricks
He d 7-12-1825. Nicholas Co., Ky. Pens.

      WILSON THOMAS & MARY   Sullivan
He d. 6-25-1811 or 1812, Woodford Co., Ky. Pens. W.27589 Va.

      WOOD, JAMES & JEMIMA   Jay
He d. 1-3-1839, Darke Co., O. She tr. from Ind. to Ohio, 6-19-
1845. See "Ohio Rev. Sold.", v.2, p. 374. Pens.

      WOODCOCK, SAMUEL & RHODA   Fayette
He d. 10-21-1833, Litchfield, Conn. She tr. from N.Y., 11-9-
1838 & d. 7-31-1846. Pens.

INDIANA COUNTIES IN WHICH THESE WIDOWS LIVED

INDIANA
Boyd, Lydia-w. James
Dowd, Hannah-w.Conner
Harris, Polly-w.Richmond
Howe, Elizabeth-w.Selah
Madden, Jane-w.William
Walker, Mary-w.Benjamin
BLACKFORD
Casterline, Charlotte-w.Loammi
BOONE
Stephenson, Elizabeth-w.James
BROWN
Jordan, Rebecca-w.Thomas
CASS
Argenbright, Christina-w.George
CLARK
Bottorff, Sophia-w.Henry
Dunn, Priscilla-w.Abner M.
CLINTON
Thatcher, Jemima-w.Amos
CRAWFORD
Chandley, Sarah-w.William &
  Lovell, John
DECATUR
Massy, Catharine-w.Jacob
Pitman, Jane-w.Jonathan &
  Mr. Hunt
ELKHART
McIlrath, Alice-w.Andrew
FAYETTE
Woodcock, Rhoda-w.Samuel
FLOYD
Bowers, Rebecca-w.John D.

FOUNTAIN
Carr, Juliana-w.James &
  Clark, Henry
Covalt, Loisa-w.Abraham &
  Mr. Davis
Crain, Jane-w.Samuel
Handy, Sarah-w.Thomas
Martin, Nancy-w.Robert
Osborn, Elizabeth-w.William
FRANKLIN
Cavendar, Margaret-w.John
Smith, Anna-w.Thadeus
GIBSON
Humphrey, Mary-w.George
GRANT
Vandevender, Elizabeth-w.Barnabas
GREENE
Trout, Elizabeth-w.Christian
HAMILTON
Coughren, Prudence-w.Joseph
HARRISON
Bowling, Sarah-w.Thomas
Howe, Rachel-w.John
Marsh, Elizabeth-w.William
HENDRICKS
Erwin, Lydia-w.David
Sacrey, Elizabeth-w.Isaac
Taylor, Rachel-w.Archibald
Wilson, Hannah-w.Benjamin
HENRY
Connelly, Margaret-w.Patrick
Corwine, Ruth-w.George
Williams, Margaret-w.Gabriel
HOWARD
Reed, Miriam-w.John

JACKSON
Medlock, Mary-w.Richard
JAY
Sanders, Phebe-w.John
*Stewart, Catharine-w.Archibald
JEFFERSON
Foster, Anna-w.John
Hickey, Jane-w.Daniel
Watson, Sarah-w.William
JENNINGS
Canfield, Elizabeth-w.Daniel
Jackson, Elizabeth-w.Seth
JOHNSON
Adams, Sarah-w.Aaron
Bracket, Sally-w.Hawkins
Massy, Catharine-w.Jacob
Netherton, Rebecca-w.John
Rose, Susannah-w.Benjamin B
Tanner, Martha-w.Josiah &
  Lemasters, Abraham
LAGRANGE
Green, Diana-w.Chaffey
LAKE
Watkins, Lucy-w.Oliver
LA PORTE
Noland, Barbara-w.James
LAWRENCE
Hill, Mary Ann-w.Clement
McLean, Nancy-w.Daniel
Mefford, Eleanor-w.Jacob
MARION
Harris, Nancy-w.Thomas
Lyon, Marcy-w.Nathaniel
Swords, Mary-w.William
Wardwell, Catharine-w.William
Wilkinson, Eva-w.Benjamin
MARTIN
Moser, Elizabeth-w.Jacob &
  Mr. Williams
MONROE
Hammons, Martha-w.Joseph
Knox, Elizabeth-w.John
McCullough, Sarah-w.Joseph
Newton, Mary-w.Basil &
  Hall, William
Ross, Rachel-w.William
MONTGOMERY
Chambers, Isabel-w.David
Endecott, Wellmett-w.Thomas
Harvey, Comfort-w.John
Miles, Polly-w.John
Scott, Martha-w.Samuel
Wilkinson, Margaret-w.John

*Wood, Jemima-w.James

MORGAN
Blackborn, Elizabeth-w.John
Erwin, Lydia-w.David
OWEN
Haltom, Mary-w.Joseph
Knox, Elizabeth-w.John
PARKE
Coy, Elizabeth-w.Christopher
Miller, Rebecca-w.William &
  Marshall, Hugh
PORTER
Fifield, Susanna-w.Benjamin
Turner, Cassandra-w.Solomon &
  Taylor, Wright
POSEY
Endecott, Wellmett-w.Thomas
Peck, Mary-w.Gad
PUTNAM
Hanna, Nancy-w.Adam
Keath, Mary-w.William &
  Mr. McInlin
Minturn, Rebecca-w.John
RIPLEY
Cavendar, Margaret-w.John
Christie, Sarah-w.James
Fisk, Elizabeth-w.Robert
Mathews, Delila-w.Amos V.
Maxwell, Abigail-w.David
RUSH
Blackmer, Mary-w.Ephraim &
  Collins, Samuel
Smith, Nancy-w.Michael
SCOTT
Berry, Hannah-w.William
Galbreath, Phebe-w.William
SHELBY
Jackson, Jane-w.Matthew
Townsend, Elizabeth-w.John
SPENCER
Mathews, Delila-w.Amos V.
ST. JOSEPH
Bivins, Hannah-w.Abner
Finley, Mary-w.Samuel
Ireland, Nancy-w.James
Little, Rosetta-w.James
SULLIVAN
Wilson, Mary-w.Thomas
SWITZERLAND
Blades, Sarah-w.John Levy &
  Lancaster, William
Conine, Lydia-w.Andrew
Goddard, Frances-w.Joseph
Jennings, Polly-w.Solomon
Knox, Milly-w.Robert
Roberts, Sarah-w.John

TIPPECANOE
Pierce, Ann-w.James
Rankins, Eleanor-w.Daniel &
Washburn, George
UNION
Weightman, Sarah-w.Samuel
VIGO
Porter, Rachel-w.Josiah
Randolph, Nancy-w.Henry

VERMILLION
Thompson, Sarah-w.Alexander
WABASH
Peterson, Mary-w.Conrad
WARREN
Connor, Rosanna-w.William
WAYNE
Litteral, Jane-w.Richard
Simpson, Elizabeth-w.Alexander
Tull, Rebecca-w.Jesse

SOLDIERS WHO DIED IN OTHER STATES (HUSBANDS OF ABOVE WIDOWS)

CONNECTICUT
Peck, Gad
Woodcock, Samuel
DELAWARE
Tull, Jesse
ILLINOIS
Coughren, Joseph
Coy, Christopher
Fisk, Robert
Galbreath, William
Handy, Thomas
Humphrey, George
Thompson, Alexander
Walker, Benjamin
KENTUCKY
Blackborn, John
Bottorff, Henry
Christie, James
Conine, Andrew
Endecott, Thomas
Erwin, David
Goddard, Joseph
Hanna, Adam
Harris, Thomas
Hickey, Daniel
Hill, Clement
Howe, John
Jennings, Solomon
Keath, William
*Knox, John
McLean, Daniel
Massy, Jacob
Mathews, Amos V.
Mefford, Jacob
Miles, John
Netherton, John
Noland, James
Randolph, Henry
Roberts, John
Rose, Benjamin
*Knox, Robert

Sacrey, Isaac
Scott, Samuel
Smith, Michael
Tanner, Josiah
Townsend, John
Trout, Christian
Turner, Solomon
Wilkinson, Benjamin
Wilson, Benjamin
Wilson, Thomas
MAINE
Maxwell, David
MARYLAND
Blades, John Levy
NEW HAMPSHIRE
Fifield, Benjamin
Foster, John
Watson, William
NEW JERSEY
Corwine, George
NEW YORK
Bivins, Abner
Casterline, Loammi
Green, Chaffey
Howe, Selah
Jackson, Seth
Watkins, Oliver
NORTH CAROLINA
Bracket, Hawkins
Haltom, Joseph
Hammons, Joseph
Taylor, Archibald
OHIO
Berry, William
Bowers, John D.
Boyd, James
Carr, James
Cavender, John
Connelly, Patrick
Connor, William
Covalt, Abraham

Dunn, Abner M.
Finley, Samuel
Ireland, James
*Jackson, Matthew
Lyon, Nathaniel
McIlrath, Andrew
Martin, Robert
Miller, William
Minturn, John
Peterson, Conrad
Pierce, James
Pitman, Jonathan
Rankins, Daniel
Reed, John
Sanders, John
Simpson, Alexander
Smith, Thadeus
Thatcher, Amos
Wardwell, William
Wilkinson, John
Wood, James
PENNSYLVANIA
Stewart, Archibald
TENNESSEE
Chandley, William
Harvey, John
Medlock, Richard
Porter, Josiah
VERMONT
Little, James
VIRGINIA
Argenbright, George
Bowling, Thomas
Canfield, Daniel
Chambers, David
Crain, Samuel
Litteral, Richard
Ross, William
WEST VIRGINIA
Williams, Gabriel
*Jordan, Thomas

In 1949 I published my "Revolutionary Soldiers Buried in Indiana". It contained 300 names not given in the D.A.R. "Roster", published in 1938. In some cases, additional study has made it possible to make corrections or additions to some of the 300 names. Page numbers below refer to the 1949 book,

ADDINGTON, JOHN - p. 3
b. Eng.; d. Chester, Ind.; son of Henry & Sarah Addington; m.(1) ca. 1769, Mary -----, a Quaker of Bush River M.M., Newberry Co., S.C., who d. 4-25-1774; chn.: William b. 4-14-1770; Alice b. 3-8-1773, m. Mr. Garrett; disowned 1790 by Cane Creek M.M., Union Co., S.C. John Addington m.(2) 5-3-1775, Bush River M.M., Elizabeth Heaton, d. Chester, Ind.; dau. of Joseph & Leada Heaton; chn.: Joseph b. 7-21-1776, d. 1836-1837, m.(1) 1799, Cane Creek M.M., Rachel Randel; m.(2) 12-22-1808 (lic. iss. Preble Co., O., but he liv. Wayne Co., Ind.) Celia Townsend, b. 2-22-1785, d. ca. 1853, dau. of John Townsend; John b. 10-13-1777; Thomas b. 12-1-1778, d. 3-8-1839, m. 10-11-1807, Mary or Tamar Smith, b. 1-18-1786, d. 4-25-1845; Mary b. 11-2-1780, d. 3-12-1866, m. 1803, Thomas Roberds; Sarah b. 9-12-1783, d. 8-26-1814, m. 1808 Phineas Roberts; Elizabeth m. 1809 James Martindale; James m. 6-15-1809 (Preble Co., O., but he liv. Wayne Co., Ind.) Nancy Lewellyn. REF: Mr. Willard Heiss, Indianapolis, Ind.

ANGEVIN, JAMES - p. 3
Delete   Error for John Angevin. See Sec. I, this Supplement.

BARLOW, JOSEPH - p. 3
See notes on John Barlow, Sec. I, this Supplement.

BARNES, JAMES - p. 4
Delete. Despite the definite grave location given by the American Legion Veterans Graves Registration, I believe he died in Tenn. His Ind. Agy. Roll record says trans. to East Tenn., 11-7-1838. He may have d. there shortly after. (He could, of course have been brought back here for burial; but I should think this extremely unlikely for those days.)

BENNETT, TIMOTHY - p. 5
No pens. file can be found & he is not on Ind. Agy. Rolls. The reference shows that he was ae. 73 in 1827 and enl. in N.Y. It is possible that the orig. pens. appl. went astray & that he died shortly thereafter.

BRYANT, WILLIAM G. - p. 6
Delete. Prob. died in Tenn. early in 1840.

BUCKNER, DANIEL - p. 7
Delete. In "Roster", p.113, as Buckner Daniel; in 1840 Pens. List, p. 185, as Buckner Daniels, ae. 79, Monroe Twp., Washington Co., Ind. Daniel or Daniels is the surname.

BURLINGAME, CLARK - p. 7
bur. Kingston Cem., Washington Twp.; m. 12-1-1777, Patience Soper.
Son Abel, b. 1-19-1783, m. Polly Burlingame (sic). REF: I.S.L.
Service: 8 days in Col. Herrick's Regt. in Oct. 1780. (Note: ISL keeps loose-leaf notebook into which such Revolutionary data contributed by patrons is kept. Someone sent in this material.)

BURCH, WILLIAM - p. 7
Finally found under Berch. b. 5-10-1764, on Haw River, N.C.; d. 9-17-1848; son of William & Mary Burch; m.(1); m.(2) 4-2-1812, Surry Co., N.C., Elizabeth Ritter, b. ca. 1787; chn.; 7 sons by 1st wife (all liv. 1853); by 2nd wife (from Bible rec. enclosed): Mary b 2-4-1813; George b. 2-7-1815; Nancy b. 5-27-1817; Lazarus b. 6-6-1819; Sally b. 6-2-1821; Levi b. 9-18-1824; Henry b. 10-18-1826. (Bible also has bros. & sis. of sold., but almost completely illegible. William Burch, son of William & Mary, b. 5-10-1764; Elizabeth, dau. of William & Mary, b. Apr. 1766). Pens. appl. 11-3-1843, ae. 80 next May 10. Decatur Co., Ind. Has copy of his birth rec. copied by "one Thomas Barnes, an Irishman". After War, liv. Fish River, Surry Co., N.C.; Stokes Co., N.C.; Monroe Co., Ind. Affid. 2-26-1844, Monroe Co., Ind., of Delila Edwards, ae. 75, wife of William Edwards of Greene Co., Ind.; she a sis. of sold.; that she knew sold. left home & went to War; that her father liv. Wilks Co., N.C., when her bro. enl. Wid.'s pens. appl. 6-7-1853, ae. 66; Greene Co., Ind.; that husb. decd.; she, nee Ritter, his 2nd wife; she & husb. & chn. left Surry Co., N.C., fall 1823 & arr. in Monroe Co., Ind., in Dec.; 7 chn., all sons, all liv., by his 1st wife. Affid. 2-25-1853, Greene Co., Ind., of Henry Berch, ae. 26; that mother was his father's 2nd wife. Service: enl. Feb., while res. of 20 mi. from Rockford, Surry Co., N.C.; Capt. Jesse Franklin; Capt. Underwood. REF: Pens. R.788 N.C.; Susp. Pens. List (1852) p.411--for proof from the N.C. records.

BURNHAM, JOHN - p. 7
Delete. He trans. to Hamilton Co., O. Prob. died there. REF: I.A.R.; "Ohio Rev. Sold.", v.2, p. 77.

BURTON, GEORGE - p. 7
Delete. "Roster", p. 405, says Indian War. Pens. for War of 1812 was finally found at National Archives.

BUSH, JAPHET - p. 7
Pens. R.1532 Mass.;-1831 Rej. Pens. List, p.48--"Served in a regt. not on continental establishment" d. 6-29-1829, Honey Creek Prairie, Vigo Co., Ind.

CASEBOLT, ROBERT - p. 7
Finally found under Casbold. b. ca. 1753-1754; d. 4-9-1840; m. 8-10-1792, Nashville, Tenn., Mary ("Polly") Todd, b. 6-28 (or 6-8)-1778; no chn. surv. the sold. Pens. appl. 11-22-1828, Xenia Greene Co., O.; again 10-17-1831, ae. 77. Affid. of Naomi Burney (sis. of sold.) & her hush., Thomas Burney. By 12-10-1837, sold. had mov. to Gibson Co., Ind., & asked for pens. tr.,1-20-

1838. On 9-28-1793 had liv. for at least 3 yr. in Mars (sp?) Dist., Davisson Co. (prob. Tenn.). Wid.'s pens. appl. 3-25-1844, Jefferson Co., Ind., ae. 66 on 6-28-1844. Affid. 3-25-1844, Jefferson Co., Ind., of John B. Todd, ae. 60, bro. of Polly Casbolt. Affid. 6-22-1849, Monmouth, Warren Co., Ill., in which wid. says she has now liv. there for 1 wk. & had prev. liv. in Ind. & Iowa. Affid. 10-15-1849, Monroe Co., Iowa, of wid., ae. 71, that she wants pens. paid in Ind. Her pens. was pd. from Springfield, Ill., Agy. from ca. 1854-1857 & then she asked for tr. to Iowa on 4-27-1857. Letter 10-19-1852 says Polly formerly liv. in Ill. but now has liv. in Panora, Guthrie Co. Iowa, for last 3 yr. She evid. retd. to Panora in 1857. RE: sold. dying in Ind. or Ohio-- the Ind. Agy. Rolls list him as transferring from Ohio on 2-16-1838; there is no record of a trans. back to Ohio. This conflicts with "Rev. Sold. Bur. in Ohio", v.1, p.100 which lists Robert Cusbott in Greene Co., O., but has no data, and with "Rev. Sold. Who Lived in Ohio", v.2, p.395, which says he left Greene Co., O., in 1840 and went to Sidney, Shelby Co., O. Service: enl. 4-7-1777; Capt. Claypool, 11th Regt., Pa. Line. REF: Pens. W.8575 Cont., Pa.; BLW 31,440; "Pa. Arch.", v.3, p.653. (Note: for what it is worth, the following man may be a relative altho not a son. Robert Casebott, d. 3-28-1847, Liberty Mills, Wabash Co., Ind.; left wife & 5 sons. REF: obit. in Meth. "Western Christian Advocate", v.14, p.16, 5-7-1847).

CHAMBERS, BENJAMIN - p. 8
Named as one of ten persons selected by the first House of Representatives on 7-29-1805, first Territorial General Assembly, from whom the President would select five of the ten for members of the Legislative Council---Benjamin Chambers of Dearborn Co.(Ohio Co., Ind., formed from Dearborn Co. in 1844). Benjamin Chambers, b. Chambersburg, Pa.; a Revolutionary soldier; second proprietor of Lawrenceburg, Ind. Appt. & commn. Judge of the Court of Common Pleas, Dearborn Co., 3-7-1803; same day, commn Lieut.-Col. Commandant of Militia; again on 12-14-1805, commn. Judge of Common Pleas. REF: "Exec. Journ. of Ind. Terr., 1800-1816", pp.72, 116,117,130; "Hist. of Dearborn Co., Ind." pp.101,200,241,445; Dunn---"Indiana" p.326 & index.

COLTRAN, JOHN - p. 8
Delete. "Roster" p.405, says War of 1812. Unless father John Coltran lived with son John Coltran, I believe this is merely a simple case of confusion.

COVERT, PETER - p. 9
b. N.J. Was commn. Lieut. 3-21-1809, Clark Co. Ind. Terr. Mil. REF: "Exec. Journ. of Ind. Terr., 1800-1816" p.154, 154 n; "Hist. of the Ohio Falls Counties", v.2, pp.374, 550.

CRAWFORD, WILLIAM - p. 9
Delete. I think DAR reference is wrong. A descendant says that, to her knowledge, there is only one William Crawford bur. in the Bryant's Chapel Cem. ("Roster" p.400; b. 1745, d. 1826) and that his stone confirms the dates. The William Crawford of the DAR

reference, b. 1768, d. 1834, could be the son William named in the "Roster". The 1831 list of rejected pensions (under 1818 & 1820 laws) lists a William Crawford "of Indiana"; he is prob. the R.2467 N.J. in the "Natl. Gen. Soc. Quart." index of pens. I have not had a chance to read this file to see if it refers to the father above, to his problematical son, or to a still-unidentified William Crawford of some other Indiana county. I am inclined to think it is the father ("Roster" p.400) since R.2467 N.J. gives widow Martha---altho Ind. Pion. Soc. lineage says he came to Wayne Co., Ind., from Virginia. There is only one William Crawford in the 1820 Cens. of Wayne Co., Ind. REF: Mrs. Floyd Hines, Connersville, Ind.; Mrs. Forrest Kempton. Centerville, Ind.

CUMMINGS, THOMAS - p. 10
He m. Sarah Henry, sis. of Patrick Henry. REF: Mr. Wallace Weatherholt, Tell City & Indianapolis, Ind.

CUNNINGHAM, ELIZABETH - p 10
Delete. She had no Rev. service of her own. Was wid. of Nathaniel Cunningham, "Roster" p.111, Pens. W.9821. Some enumerators in 1840 Cens. included widows receiving pensions; others did not.

CURRANT, JAMES - p. 10
No pens. file found in 1949. Have just learned that file is under Currin, Pems. S.34724 Md.; BLW 2-100; 5-5-1803. (Am informed by Miss Thelma Murphy, Indianapolis, Ind., that he previously liv. in Ky. before Ind.). REF: "Rev. Pens. of 1813", Southern Book Co. (1953) p.35, No.19; pvt.-$40.00.

DAILY, EPHRAIM - p. 10
bur. Big Branch Pioneer Cem., Orangeville Twp., on old Samuel Wilson farm, later owned by William Shirley who in 1925 had massive marker erected on cem. site with inscription: "Two Soldiers of the American Revolution, Samuel Moffett; Ephraim Daily, About 20 Unknown Pioneer Dead were buried here from 1820 to 1840". REF: "Orange Co., Ind., Cem. Rec."--Lost River Chap., DAR, Paoli, Ind. (1947) p. 134.

DAVIS, JOSEPH - p. 10
Delete. "Roster" p.406 says War of 1812.

DEAVER, WILLIAM - p. 10
Had gr-dau., Rose M. Rosener, liv. Indianapolis, Ind., 1890. REF: "Md. Sold. of Rev. War, War of 1812, or Indian Wars Who Drew Pens. While Res. in Ky." (Burns?), p. 64.

DICKENSON, WAITSELL - p. 11
Delete. Pensioned as Waitstill Dickenson; in 1835 Pens. List, Ontario Co., N.Y. Tr. 5-30-1836 from Albany, N.Y., Agy. Roll to Ind. Agy Roll; tr. from Ind. to Pa. Agy. Roll, 9-25-1839. Prob. d. there soon after.

DOANE, JACOB - p. 11
bur. Honey Creek; loc. there 1809; 1st permanent settler there. REF: Stevens-"Hist. of Washington Co., Ind." (1916) p. 633.

DUTTERO, JACOB - p. 12
"Died---At his residence in Utica, Ind., on the night of the 24th Nov. in the 63rd year of his age, Jacob Duttero, a Revolutionary Soldier. He was a kind neighbor and an affectionate parent, a brave soldier, a stanch republican, and an honest man. He served a tour of three years service in the Revolutionary War, and was found again in the defence of his country at the taking of Fort Niagara, where he was taken by the enemy to Montreal, where he was confined till the peace. He was interred with the Honors of War, in obedience to his repeated injunctions --- which ceremony was conducted by Major Coldren of this place, in a menner which does him honor. The procession was large and orderly conducted by George Ross, esq. The manner in which the request of this (now fallen) veteran was fulfilled, is a convincing proof that the Indianaians know how to appreciate patriotism, and that they have tears to shed on the earth that covers the heart in which it glowed, when that heart has ceased to beat forever." REF: "The Charlestown Intelligencer", 12-4-1824, p.3, c.4.

FELLOWS, WILLIS - p. 13
Delete. Seems reasonable to assume he prob. d. in Ill. as Ind. Agy. Rolls have no record of trans. back to Ind. Roll.

FERBY, E. E. - p. 13
Delete. "Roster", p.406, says War of 1812.

FINLEY, DAVID - p. 14
Was commn. 2nd Lieut. in 3rd Regt., Ind. Terr. Mil.. (Note: this is surely not the David Findley of "Roster", p.404, who trans. 3-6-1830 to Ill. from Clark Co., Ind., Ind. Agy. Roll #14,930). REF: "Exec. Journ. of Ind. Terr., 1800-1816", p. 236; "Hist. of Orange Co., Ind.", p. 607. Additional data just found: b. 6-1-1754; d. 4-19-1848, ae. 93-10-18; bur. Finley Cem., Orleans Twp., Orange Co., Ind.; m. Elizabeth -----, d. 1-9-1835, ae. 72 yr., 5 da.; chn. (at least): Jefferson, b 5-16-1805, d. 11-19-1829, m. Miriam -----, d. 12-12-1848, ae. 45-1-8 (she m. 2nd, Mr. A. Tegarden). David Finley said to have been a Rev. sold. REF: "Orange Co., Ind., Cem. Rec."--Lost River Chap., DAR Paoli, Ind. (1947), p. 224.

GILLILAND, JOHN - p. 14
Was commn. County Surveyor for Switzerland Co., 11-8-1814; commn. J.P. for Switzerland Co., 8-5-1815; a Commissioner to locate Indianapolis. REF: "Exec. Journ. of Ind. Terr.", 1800-1816, pp. 225, 225 n, 233; "Hist. of Dearborn, Ohio, & Switzerland Cos., Ind.", pp. 1018, 1032; Woollen's "Sketches", p. 189.

GRIFFITH, JOSEPH - p. 15
Son Abraham, b. 11-30-1774, Chester Co., Pa.; d. 6-19-1829, Crawfordsville, Ind.; m. 10-12-1798, Joanna John, d. 8-12-1815, Frederick Co., Md. (chn.: Lydia T.; Hannah; Thornton; Townsend; Barton, d 1834; Clifford. Abraham Griffith & sons Townsend & Barton and bro. Amos came West son after death of wife, along with 2 grown daus., Lydia & Hannah, ca. 1822-1823; settled in Covington, Ind. Additional data on Abraham in ref. REF: contributed by a library patron.

-146-

GRIFFITH, SAMUEL - p. 15
Pens. file gives middle initial as J.

GULLION, JACKSON - p. 16
Delete. Additional research shows beyond reasonable doubt that this is the John Gullion or John O. Gullion of "Roster", p. 167.

HANDLIN, MATTHIAS - p. 16
Re-check of my pens. notes gives death as 11-7-1840.

HAWLEY, SAMUEL - p. 18
Delete. Pens. S.34916 Mass.; appl. 5-31-1826; tr. 5-7-1828 from Ind. Agy. Roll to Miss. Seems reasonable that he prob. d. there.

HENRY, MOSES - p. 18
Incorrectly given on p. 25 as Moses, Henry. Surname is Henry.

HIGGS, SAMUEL - p. 19
Pens. S.44199 N.Y.; 1831 Rej. Pens. List, p. 48--"did not serve 9 mos. in continental army".

JEBINE, ----- - p. 20
"Old father Jebine, a revolutionary soldier, hung himself upon a sapling in the woods that hardly cleared his knees from the ground." REF: "Cotton's Keepsake" --- by Rev. Judge A. J. Cotton (1858), p. 422, Wright's Corner. (Cotton was Co. Judge & a Methodist preacher.)

JOHNSON, W. (Gen.) - p. 20
Delete. General (forename) Washington Johnson, b. 11-10-1776, from his own Bible (now in possession of Masonic Lodge, Vincennes Ind. REF: "Bible Records of Knox Co., Ind.", Francis Vigo Chap., DAR, Vincennes, Ind.; "Ind. Mag. of Hist.", v.20, p. 123.

JONES, GEORGE - p. 20
Data re 2nd wife's 1st husb. Isaac Dawson, b. 10-25-1773, South Branch of Potomac River, Hampshire Co., Va., short distance above Harper's Ferry; d. Oct. 1824; m. 9-4-1792, Hampshire Co., Va., Sicha -----, b. 5-9-1776, same place as Isaac. She was Irish & was rel. to Burke & Williams fams. To Bourbon Co., Ky.; to Ohio on Scioto River below Chillicothe, on High Bank Prairie; Colerain Twp., Ross Co., O. In War of 1812, took a Comp. of Rangers; after general call for soldiers, he went as Col. of Ross Co., O., Regt. To Vigo Co., Ind., Feb. 1824 & d. following Oct. Chn.(2 sons & 4 daus. surv. the father): Virginia; Elizabeth, b. Va., Hampshire Co., 2-16-1794; Nancy, b. 3-14-1796, Va.; Thomas, b. 3-10-1798, Bourbon Co., Ky.; David, b. 12-9-1799, Ky.; Isaac Milton, b. 8-1-1806; Eleanor, b. 3-31-1802, High Bank, O.; Sarah, b. 4-4-1804, Ross Co., O.; Mary, b. 11-5-1808; Malinda b. 1-28-1811; Benjamin Franklin, b. 4-5-1813; Sicha, b. 11-20-1815; Abigal, b. 8-8-1818.

KENNEY; DANIEL - p. 20
Addn. ref: "Pa. Arch.", 2nd Ser., v.10, p.585; 3rd Ser.,v.23,p595.

KYLE, JOHN - p. 21
(Note: this is not the John Kiles of Lagrange Co., Ind., in War of 1812, "Roster", p.406). b. 1755-1756; d. 8-31-1845, ae. 89; bur. in Wright's Corner Cem.; mar.; chn. (at least): Thomas, b. 3-24-1785, near Winchester, Va.; d. 1-6-1861, ae. 75-10-12; m.(1) 1815, Elizabeth Kerney of Ky.; d. 10-14-1858; m.(2) 2 yr. later, Mrs. Mary Burkdoll. (More in ref. abt. Thomas' chn.). Sold. & fam. came West in 1809 via Pittsburgh, Cincinnati, to Vincennes, Ind. Because of Indian trouble, Gen. Harrison sent them back to Ky. with 75 armed men to protect them. Son Thomas joined Harrison & was in Batt. of Tippecanoe, 11-7-1811. Fam. mov. from Ky. to Dearborn Co., Ind., 1812. Altho John Kyle listed himself as a Rev. pensr., ae. 84, with census enumerator of 1840 Cens., no pens. file for him can be found. Service: "He served under Gen. Washington, assisted in storming the British redoubts at Yorktown, and witnessed the surrender of Gen. Cornwallis." REF: "Hist. of Dearborn, Ohio, & Switzerland Cos., Ind." (1885),800-803.

LASHBROOKS, JOHN or WILLIAM - p. 21
bur. Jackson Twp. Full quote: Near the N boundary line of Jackson Twp., on the farm where the Lashbrooks fam. sett. when they came to Orange Co. & which yet belongs to Lashbrooks descendants, is a lone grave with sandstone marker with date 1820 cut on it, no other inscription. According to fam. trad., John Lashbrooks & a bro. were Hessian solds. who left the Brit. army & joined the Continentals, were mustered out in Va., went to Ky., & John eventually came to Ind. However, both a William & a John are named as early settlers, & probate records show that in Sept. 1820, James Rodin returned a list of appraisement of property of William Lashbrooks, decd. His name may have been John William. John, son of the supposed sold., was b. 12-25-1794 & d. 1884; he is bur. at Moore's Ridge Cem. His mother had d. after the fam. came to Ind. but before they arrived in Orange Co. REF: "Orange Co.,Ind. Cem. Rec." --Lost River Chap., DAR, Paoli, Ind. (1947), p.361.

LASSELLE, HYACINTH - p. 21
Delete He was b 1777 at Kekionga, Indian village at site of Ft. Wayne, Ind. Service was in Ind. Terr. Mil. & Ind. Mil. REF: "Exec Journ. of Ind. Terr., 1800-1816", pp.185, 232; "Ind. Exec. Proceedings, 1816-1836", p.83; Dunn--"Indiana", p.436 & index.

LOWE, WILLIAM - p. 22
A William Lowe was elected to the Constitutional Convention, meeting at Corydon, Ind. (the first state capitol) 6-10-1816, as representative from Washington Co., Ind. (Monroe Co. was formed 1818 from Orange Co., which was formed 1815 from Washington Co.; but Orange Co. was not mentioned in the Enabling Act & was treated as part of Washington Co. in the enumeration of the inhabitants.) William Lowe was commn. Associate Judge for Washington Co., 1-6-1816. REF: "Exec. Journ. of Ind. Terr., 1800-1816",pp.87,88,239.

McARTHUR, JAMES - p. 22
bur. in Old Town Cem., Crawfordsville, Ind. REF: "Rev. Sold. Bur. in Montgomery Co., Ind."--Amer. Legion (1952 ed.), p. 18.

McKINNEY, ROBERT - p. 23
Delete. "Roster", p.406, says Wayne's Campaign, 1791.

McNULTY, JOHN - p. 23
Since I found no Rev. pens., this may be War of 1812 or Indian Wars. The 1840 Pens. List, p.184, has a John McCully of Montgomery TOWNSHIP, Owen Co., Ind. Possible confusion between McCully--McNulty and Montgomery Twp.---Montgomery Co.

MARTIN, JOHN - p. 24
Ind. Agy. Roll says d. 12-12-1842. See Elijah Stinson in the "Roster", p. 345.

MILLER, WILLIAM - p. 24
Ind. Agy. Roll says trans. here 3-27-1835 from Ky.

MITCHELL, JOSEPH - p. 24
1831 Rej. Pens. List, p.49; reason:"served in a vessel not on continental establishment; mariner."

MODERELL, ANDREW - p. 24
Delete. After re-reading pens. file, it is now clear that the father, George Moderell, was the soldier.

MOFFETT, SAMUEL - p. 25
bur. Big Branch Pioneer Cem., Orangeville Twp., on old Samuel Wilson, later owned by William Shirley who in 1925 had massive marker erected on cem. site with inscription: "Two Soldiers of the American Revolution, Samuel Moffett, Ephraim Daily, About 20 Unknown Pioneer Dead were buried here from 1820 to 1840". REF: "Orange Co., Ind., Cem. Rec."--Lost River Chap., DAR, Paoli, Ind. (1947), p. 134.

MOORE, JOSEPH - p. 25
Will written 3-3-1827; proved 4-10-1827; wife Peninnah; sons: John, Samuel, Alfred, William; daus.: Mary, Eliza, Jane. REF: Washington Co., Ind., Will Rec. 1, pp. 150-152

MOSES, HENRY - p. 25
Incorrectly listed. Surname was Henry.

NEWELL, SAMUEL - p. 25
Delete. Is in "Roster", p. 278.

NORRIS, JOSEPH - p. 25
b. Harford Co., Md.; d. 8-19-1849. Emigr. to Mason Co., Ky., 1796. REF: abstr. of "Madison, Ind., Daily Courier" by Miss Mary Hill, Madison, Ind.; obit pub. 9-3-1849.

OGDEN, STEPHEN - p. 25
Delete. He d. in Ill. See "Ill. Rev. Sold.", p.34. Is in 1831 Rej. Pens. List (of Indiana), p.49--served in a regiment not on continental establishment.

POTONGER, ROBERT - p. 27
Additional ref.:"List of Soldier Dead of Montgomery Co., Ind."--
1941 ed., p. 17.

REECE, JEHU - p. 27
Also Reese. b. 1740, Wales; bur. Posey Cem., Madison Twp., Sec. 13, Twp. 1, Range 2; first man bur. there; m.(2) in Tenn., Elizabeth Elsbury. Sett. in Delaware; then to Tenn. for a no. of yrs. after serving in Rev. War. REF: Stevens--"Hist. of Washington Co., Ind." (1916), p. 632.

RHOADS, DANIEL - p. 27
1831 Rej. Pens. List, p.49--did not serve 9 mo. in cont. army.

NEWELL, SAMUEL - p. 28
Delete. Is in "Roster", p. 278.

ROBERTS, WILLIAM - p. 29
1831 Rej. Pens. List, p.49--served in a regiment not on continental establishment.

ROSE, WILLIAM - p. 29
Delete. Ind. Agy. Roll says trans. 5-7-1827 to Mo.; 1835 Pens. List, v.3, p.7, Clay Co., Mo., ae. 82. Seems reasonable that he died in Missouri.

RUSSELL, DAVID - p. 29
Son of John Russell, b. Ire.; d. 1786, Shenandoah Co., Va. David Russell m. 2-4-1790, Jane Slater of Va.; she d. 1845, Vermillion Co., Ind.; chn. (b. Shenandoah Co., Va.): Elizabeth b. 1791; William b. 1797; John b. 1799; Jane b. 1800; Annie b. 1802; David b. 1806; Mary Baughzel b. 1808; Richard Slater b. 1812. REF: DAR Mag., v.66, p.365; Miss Thelma Murphy, Indianapolis, Ind.

RUST, DAVID - p. 30
1831 Rej. Pens. List, p.49--served in a regiment not on continental establishment.

SCOTT, SAMUEL - p. 30
Delete. War of 1812.

SHAVER, JACOB - p. 31
Wife d. 9-17-1853. REF: Ind. Agy. Roll.

SHAW, JAMES - p. 31
Delete. Papers in the pens. files of several James Shaws were mixed up and mis-files, resulting in a confusion with Gallatin Co., Ky.; Campbell Co., Ky., and Indiana counties of Carroll, Tippecanoe, and Parke. I think it likely that there was only one Ind. James Shaw ("Roster" p.328, Parke Co.) who was in Carroll Co. 1835 Pens. List & in Tippecanoe Co. 1840 Pens. List, ae. 82. He may have d. in Tippecanoe Co. instead of Parke Co.

SHAW, JOHN - p. 31
"This day John Shaw, a Revolutionary soldier came personally into court the same being a court of record for Clark County in the State of Indiana, being a resident of said county aged seventy five years. He took oath that he John Shaw enlisted in the service of the United States for the term of five years or during the war on or about the tenth day of June in the year 1775 in the State of New York in a company commanded (this applicant thinks) by Capt. Nabb, in the regiment commanded by Col. Marshall in the Line of the State of New York on Continental Establishment, and he continued to serve in said corps until the close of the War when he was discharged from service at Valley Forge, in the State of Pennsylvania, that he was in the Battles of Bunker Hill, White Plains, Germantown, and Stony Point where he was wounded in the leg and was at the capture of Cornwallis, shortly after which he was discharged.---the worth of his property is estimated at $58.50---by occupation a farmer---wife Sarah Shaw who like myself is very feeble and far in the decline of life being seventy years of age." Sworn to in open court before me, the presiding Judge to the Circuit Court for the County of Clark in the State of Indiana this the 21st day of June, 1825. Judge John F. Ross.
REF: Clark Co., Ind., Civil Order Bk. 1, pp. 354-356; copied for me by Mary Osterman, Seymour, Ind. No identifiable pens. file could be found. It is possible that the orig. appl. went astray & that the sold. died shortly after.

SKEETS, JAMES - p. 32
This name is variously spelled Scates, Skatts, Skaats, Skaits, Scaats, Scuitts. I firmly believe that he died in Dearborn Co., Ind. Note this: "Old Father Skaats, a Revolutionary soldier, was buried here (Yorktown, Dearborn Co., Ind.) with military honors." REF: "Cotton's Keepsake", p. 429. This was written (pub. in 1858) by the Rev. Judge A. J. Cotton. He was a Methodist minister & a Judge of Dearborn Co. Obviously contemporary with the soldier, who prob. died not long after 1840, Rev. Cotton's words can surely be trusted despite the evidence below which indicates that the soldier might have died in Hamilton Co., O. The soldier was b. 1756; d. ca. 1840 plus; bur. Yorktown, Ind.; m. Harriet -----, b. 1756; chn.: several; at least a son liv. Cincinnati, O.; poss. a dau. or two in Dearborn Co., Ind. (Possible sons-in-law might be William Row & Daniel T. Craig). First pens. appl. 3-31-1818, ae. nearly 61, New York City; next appl. 9-18-1820, ae. 64, Dearborn Co., Ind.; wife ae. 84.(64?). Pens. tr. from N.Y. Agy. to Ind. Agy., 12-28-1826; tr. from Ind. Agy. to Ohio Agy., 1-22-1830, to take effect 9-4-1829. On 12-30-1829, from Cincinnati, O., he writes that he now has mov. to Ohio to live with his son in Cincinnati & asks for pens. tr. He is in the 1835 Pens. List, v.3, p.65, Hamilton Co., O., ae. 77. On 9-9-1837, from Cincinnati, he writes that he lost his pens. certificate at or near the house of Daniel T. Craig in Logan Twp. in Ind. (this would be Dearborn Co., Ind.) & wants a new certificate. He is in the 1840 Pens. List, ae. 84, Kelso Twp., Dearborn Co., Ind., liv. with William Row, and is also in the 1840 Pens. List, ae. 87, 6th Ward, Cincinnati, Hamilton Co., O. I believe this

proves how much he lived back and forth between Ohio & Indiana during these years as in 1840 he was enumerated at two different times in two different places. (We can hardly assume that there were two men of the same name in such nearby places). While I concede that he may have died in Cincinnati, I believe that he is definitely buried in Indiana, according to Cotton's words. Service: Corp. in Capt. John Francis Hamtranck's Comp. of Light Inf. in 2nd Inf. Regt., Col. Philip VanCortland, N.Y. Line. REF: Pens. S.36752 N.Y.; 1840 Pens. List, Ind., p.182; 1840 Pens. List, Ohio, p.172; Cotton--"Cotton's Keepsake" (1858), p.429; "N.Y. in the Rev.", p.37.   Addn. info just found: James Skaats, b. Holland; came with father when very young to Hudson River & settled among the Knickerbockers; was a Lieut. in Rev. War.; served till close; to Dearborn Co., Ind., 1817; d. 1843, ae. 88, in Dearborn Co., Ind.. Son, James, liv. Tanner's Creek, Dearborn Co., Ind.; 7 mi. from Lawrenceburg, Ind.; in 1823 to Cincinnati, O.; d.1860. REF: Ford--"Hist. of Cincinnati, O." (1881), p. 458.

STEELE, NINIAN - p. 32
Ref. below says b. 6-14-1763, Thunder Hill, Chester Co., Pa. (son of Samuel Steele, also a Rev. sold.); m. 3-5-1784, Jane Armstrong b. 1763; d. 1826; chn.: James Armstrong b. 12-11-1784; d. 12-29-1855;   Mary Ann b. 10-31-1788; d. 11-28-1830;   Samuel b.11-16-1790;   Elizabeth b. 2-8-1793;   Jesse b. 2-7-1795; d. 1845; Margaret b.4-6-1798; d. 10-24-1847;   Nancy b. 7-6-1800; Joseph Howe b. 4-6-1802; d. 4-26-1863;   Ninian, Jr., b. 10-21-1804;   Robert b. 12-6-1806; d. 1851. REF: N.C. Commn.; Dr. Walter O. Shriner, Ind. State Tchr. Coll., Terre Haute, Ind.

TACKETT, LEWIS - p. 33
Was commn. Capt. in 4th Regt., Ind. Terr. Mil., 8-7-1813. REF: "Exec. Journ. of Ind., Terr., 1800-1816", p. 200.

TAYLOR, SILAS - p. 33
1831 Rej. Pens. List, p.49--served in a regiment not on continental establishment.

TILFORD, JAMES - p. 34
He & wife were among 14 families who were first members of the Presbyterian Church in Charlestown, the society being organized in 1812. Obit: "Departed this life on the 10th instant, James Tilford, aged sixty-one years, who was active in the grand revolutionary conflict, which gave liberty to the present sons of freedom; who was a believer of the doctrines of christianity, and died exulting in the hopes of complete salvation, through him who was, who is, and who is to come." REF: "Charlestown Intelligencer", 5-24-1821, p.3, c.2; Miss Dorothy Riker, Indpls., Ind.

TILLINGHAST, JOHN - p. 34
Delete. Prob. no service except Wayne's Indian Wars.

TOOTHMAN, JACOB - p. 34
Delete. "Roster", p.407, says War of 1812.

WESTFALL, ABEL - p. 36
b. Hampshire Co., Va.; d. 1814 (will wr. 7-10; pr. 8-10); (son of John & Sarah Westfall; bro. of Isaac; Jacob, "Roster", p.378; Cornelius, "Roster", p.377; Abraham, & John (both in this Suppl.); mar.; chn.: Newton Edwards (oldest son); Sally Edwards (oldest dau.); Juliet m. Mr. Giles; Jenny m. Daniel Whitmore; Indiana m. George Ruble; John Wesley m. Eliza Foster. Abel Westfall was appt. Justice of the Court of General Quarter Sessions of the peace for Knox Co., Ind., & Justice of the Court of Common Pleas for same on 1-4-1800, the day the Government of the Indiana Territory commenced; same again on 2-3-1801; on 1-7-1814 was commn. 2nd Judge of the Circuit Court for Knox Co., Ind. Terr. Service: Capt. in Hampshire Co., Va., Mil. REF: Eckenrode (1912), p.465 & (1913), pp. 319-320; Gwathmey--"Va. in the Rev.", p.818; Pens. S.36842 (of bro. Cornelius); father's will in Judy--"Hist. of Grant & Hardy Cos., W. Va. (1951), p.303; Mrs. Eva B. Davenport, Vincennes, Ind.; "Exec. Journ. of Ind. Terr., 1800-1816", pp. 91, 96,206; "Hist. of Knox Co., Ind." (1886) pp. 173,204; Haymond--"Hist. of Harrison Co., W. Va." (1910), p.277; Carter--"Territorial Papers", v.7, p.502.

WRIGHT, PHILBURD - p. 37
Philburd Wright, Junior, was the son of Philburd Wright, Sr., who was b. Baltimore Co., Md.; went in 1762 to Orange Co., N.C. (part later called Randolph Co.) with his (Sr.'s) bro., Richard Wright, Sr. (Richard Wright, Sr., also b. Baltimore Co., Md.; d. 1786, Rowan Co., N.C.; had a son, Philburd Wright, b. 1768, who mov. to Cumberland Co., Ky.; then to Washington Co., Ind., where he made affid. for pens. appl. 1832 of his bro., William Wright, "Roster" p.391). Philburd Wright, Jr.'s chn.: Joshua (disappeared 1815, New Orleans); Caroline Delilah m. John Summey; Sarah m. John Fontz; Mary m. John Beard; Noah b. 8-30-1784, Randolph Co., N.C.; d. 7-11-1863, Perry Twp., Marion Co., Ind.; m. 7-28-1814, Washington Co., Ind., Susannah Parr, d. 10-9-1842 (dau. of Arthur & Mary (Morgan) Parr, natives of Rowan Co., N.C.); Levi b. 6-12-1790, N.C.; d. near Salem, Washington Co., Ind.; m. Sarah Wright, b. 8-31-1797, d. 8-19-1834 (cousin; dau. of William & Elizabeth (Morgan) Wright; William a Rev. sold.; "Roster" p.391); Joel b. 2-5-1795, Randolph Co., N.C. (or born 2-5-1793, Stokes Co., N.C.); d. 4-9-1828; m. 9-10-1812, N.C., Sarah Birely, b. 4-30-1789, d. ae. 76; Jesse m. Mary Brown; Elizabeth m. James Rains; Aaron m. Ruhama Sellers; Eli (liv. Wayne Co., Ind., 1893; mar., & a son). Noah Wright to Jeffersonville, Ind., 1808; back to N.C. a yr.; to Washington Co., Ind., 1810; in 1831 to Marion Co., Ind., & sett. in Perry Twp. Levi Wright to Ind. 1810 & sett. near Salem, Ind. Joel Wright to Ind. Terr. 1813 with parents; in Nov. 1815, Joel sett. on W fork of Whitewater in (now) Wayne Co., Ind.; to Washington Twp., Marion Co., Ind., Dec. 1821. REF: "Ind. Mag. of Hist.", v.36, pp. 160-161; "Pict. & Biog. Mem. of Indpls. & Marion Co." (1893) pp. 243-244; Sulgrove--"Hist. of Indpls. & Marion Co., Ind." (1884), p. 628.

WYATT, JEREMIAH - p. 37
Vanderburgh Co., Ind., seems indicated instead of Gibson Co.,Ind.
b. Feb. 1762 (see later discrepancies), Mechlinburg, N.C.; still
liv. 12-7-1852; mar.; chn.(at least): his only son, Edmund, killed
at Batt. of Buena Vista, Mex. Pens. appl. 8-17-1847, ae. 86,
Vanderburgh Co., Ind. After War, liv. Mechlinburg, Lincoln, &
Rutherford Cos., N.C., till 1808; to Wilson Co., Tenn., ca. 6 yr.;
to Vanderburgh Co., Ind., fall of year before Batt. of New Orleans. Bailie Taylor (see Sec. I, this Suppl.) living in Vanderburgh Co., Ind., knew him in service. From 1850 Cens.: Jeremiah Wyatt, 90, b. N.C., farmer; Margarette, 84, N.C.; Sally, 38,
Tenn.; Margarette, 15, Ind.; Elizabeth, 10, Ind.; James, 8, Ind.
Service: enl. as subst., 6-1-1780, Mechlinburg, N.C.; Capt. John
Hamright, Col. Thomas Taylor; was a subst. for James Parks; gave
his discharge to a Board of Officers in Lincoln Co., N.C., 4-5-
years after War; names Bailie Taylor of this region who appl. for
pens. several yrs. ago for pens. on service as a subst. & was rejected. REF: Pens. R.11916, N.C.; "Susp. Pens. List." (1852), p.
414--"for further proof"; 1850 Cens., Armstrong Twp., Vanderburgh Co., Ind., p.869, fam. 90, taken 9-24-1850.

YOUNG, JAMES - p. 37
If this is the same man, he did not die in 1822. James Young,
will wr. 3-20-1829; pr. 4-14-1829; wife Elizabeth; sons: Miles
King Young, James Turner Young; daus.: Jane Matilda, Elizabeth
Clarissa, Martha Tabitha; other heirs (rel. not stated): Alexander Young, Jacob Banta, Joseph Young, Samuel Wharton Young,
Thomas Davidson Young, Robert McCoskey, Jancinantillo Young.
A James Young, b. N.C., was appt. J.P., 10-21-1809 for Harrison
Co., Ind. Terr.(part of which was formed into Washington Co.,
Ind. Terr., 1814); on 1-20-1814, appt. J.P. for Washington Co.;
on 7-7-1814, commn. Judge of Circuit Court, Washington Co. REF:
Washington Co., Ind., Will Rec. 1, pp. 246-247; "Exec. Journ. of
Ind. Terr., 1800-1816", pp. 157, 208, 215.

DELETE

page 39
ALLEN-Lasselle, Hyacinth
CARROLL-Shaw, James
DEARBORN-Angevin, James
    Toothman, Jacob
FLOYD-Burnham, John
    Hawley, Samuel
    Ogden, Stephen
    Rose, William
GREENE-Bryant, William G.
    Fellows, Willis
HOWARD-Gullion, Jackson
JACKSON, Buckner, Daniel
page 40
JEFFERSON-Burton, George
JOHNSON-Davidson, Isaac
KNOX-Johnson, W.

KNOX-Moses, Henry (change to
    Henry, Moses
LAGRANGE-Dickenson, Waitsell
MONTGOMERY-Newell, Samuel
OWEN-Moderell, Andrew
    Newell, Samuel
POSEY-Scott, Samuel
PUTNAM-Cunningham, Elizabeth
RANDOLPH-Davis, Joseph
    Ferby, E. E.
page 41
VERMILLION-Tillinghast, John
VIGO-Barnes, James
    Coltran, John
WASHINGTON-McKinney, Robert
WAYNE-Crawford, William

INDEX

Names indexed: wives (if maiden name is known); husbands and wives of children; miscellaneous names; names of soldiers in Sections IV through X.

Names not indexed: soldiers in Sections I through III; their children; their wives; their officers; places.

ABERNATHY Elizabeth 97-98 James 98;Susannah 33; William 33
ACRED Christopher 16;Mary 16
ACRES Austin 46;Valentine 46
ADAIR John 97;Susannah 97
ADAMS Bartholomew 51;Charlotte 131;George 45;Jennie 45;Margaret 26;Nancy 45;Simon 69
ADDINGTON Henry 142;John 142; Sarah 142
AGIN Benjamin 91
ALBRIGHT Sarah 26
ALEANDORF Catharine 29
ALEXANDER George 6;Jane 6-71; Thomas 71-105;William 6-9
ALLAN family 30
ALLEN John 36;Martha 7;Polly 36;Rosetta 135;Samuel 7
ALSTOTT Mr. 66;John 66;Margaret 66;Sarah 66
ANDERSON Martha 5;Patsy 5; Rhoda 16;William 16
ANGEVIN James 142;John 142
ANTHONY Peter 60
APPLEGATE family 29;Irwin 9; Vincent 9
ARBUCKLE Sallie 92
ARD George W. 17;John 17; Susan 17
ARMSTRONG Jane 152
ARNOLD Presley 22;Sally 22; Ziba 42
AUDUBON John 44
AUSTIN Lucy 116
AVERY Alpheus 111;Rachel 111

BACON Almoda Fellers 10;Elijah 10;Susan 18
BADOLLET John 83
BAILEY see Bayly
BAKER Miss 113;George 57;Jane 113;Leannah 57;Lewis J. 10
BANTA Antie 10;Henry 10;Jacob 154

BARGER family 59
BARLOW John 142;Joseph 11-142
BARNES David 64;James 142; Thomas 143
BARNETT Adam 17;Barbara 17;Spencer 46
BARR Mary 5
BARRACKMAN Mr. 97;Susannah 97
BARTON Delilah 75
BASS Winney 96
BASSETT Amy 106;Hannah 106;John 106;Jonathan 106
BATES Reuben 110
BAYLY Eliza P. 70;Elizabeth 70; James 70
BEAL Campbell 21
BEALL see Bell;Ninian 37
BEARD Mary 153;John 153
BEASLEY Mary 10
BEAVER Robert 107
BECKES Parmenas 119
BEDELL Mary 108
BELL see Beall;John 76;Mary Ann 76;Nathaniel 12
BELLAMY Samuel 64
BENEFIEL America 43;Helen 43; Jesse J. 43;Virginia 43
BENNETT Nancy 136;Timothy 142
BERCH see Burch;William 143
BERRY Mary E. 65
BETTS Flora 18
BICKERSTAFF Mary 29
BILES Charles 65
BIRD Mr. 75;Mary 75;William 75
BIRELY Sarah 153
BIRNEY see Burney
BLACK Margaret 116
BLACKMON Mary 9
BLAINE Elizabeth 96;James 13; Robert 13
BLAIR Mr. 56;Aris 56;Delilah 56; Jane 115
BLAKE John 28
BLANKENSHIP Mr. 16;Joseph 16; Louisa 16;Nancy 16

BLEVINS James 31
BLIZZARD Jane 54;Ruth 54
BLOYD Hannah 97;Jacob 97
BLUE Jacob 14;John 14;Uriah 14
BLYTHE Andrew 115;Polly 115
BOESEA Joseph 118
BOLDEN Elizabeth 111;Hugh 111;
 Sarah 111
BOMINGON Rachel 52
BONER Mary 100
BONNEL Jane 133
BOREN Chane 115
BOSS Catharine 113;Molly 113;
 Peggy 113;Philip 113
BOWEN Margaret 40
BOWER Joseph 88
BOWERMAN Elizabeth 15
BOWLER Elizabeth 58
BOWMAN Mr. 58;John 15;Mary 58
BOYD Fanny 40;John 107
BRANAN Thomas 95
BRASHEAR Mr. 52;Sally 52
BRAY Susanna 62
BRECK Daniel 104
BREICH Sophia 43
BRENT William 82
BRENTON Mr. 18;Catharine 18
BRIDGES Agnes 111
BROCK Elizabeth 18;Evan 18
BRODIE Ann 26;James 26;Samuel
 26;Sarah 26
BROOKHART Barbara 58;Charles
 58;Elizabeth 58;Jacob 58;
 Julia 58;Lewis 58
BROOKS Susan 113;William 113
BROWN James 66;Mary 66-133-153;
 Thomas 17
BROWNING Sarah 11
BRUNER 78;Henry 100;Julia Ann
 17;Martha 100;Michael 78
BRYANT William G. 142
BUCKNER Daniel 142
BUDD Daniel 106;Rebecca 106
BUFFINGTON Mrs. 22;John 22
BURCH Delila 143;Elizabeth 143;
 John 19;Mary 143;William 143
BURKDOLL Mary 148
BURKE family 147;Nancy 15
BURLINGAME Clark 143;Polly 143
BURNEY Naomi 143;Thomas 143
BURNHAM John 143
BURTON George 143;Sarah 49
BUSH Japhet 143;William 105
BUSKIRK see VanBuskirk;John 20

Mary 22;Michael 22;Thomas 22
BUTLER Thomas 31

CALVIN Luther 132;Rachel 104;
 Ruth 132;Vincent 104
CALWELL see Oolwell; Mr. 111
CAMPBELL Ann 82;Catharine 32;
 Enos 64;Polly 18;William 18-103
CANTER George A. 42
CARNES Catharine 113
CARNINE Catharine 92
CARRENTON George 61
CART Catharine 96
CARTER Travis 79
CARTWRIGHT Julia A. 43;Sarah 63;
 William 63
CASBOLD see Casebolt
CASE Rebecca 40;William 40
CASEBOLT Naomi 143;Robert 143;
 Robert 144
CASSA Robert 6;Sarah 6
CASSELL Abraham 66;Catharine 66
CATT Mary 37;Philip 38-97
CHAMBERS Benjamin 144
CHAMPS Jane 135
CHARLEY George 36;Peter 36
CHASE William 57
CHASTAIN Absalom 87;Polly 87
CHEEK Francis 85;Nicholas 22;
 Page 22;Tavner 22
CHENAULT see Chinalt
CHENOWETH Richard 22
CHINALT Rachel 138
CLARK Judge 11-119;Eliza 11;
 Elizabeth 48-119;Henry 132;
 Juliana 132;Mary 56;Will 11-119
CLARKSON Drury 57;Elizabeth 57;
 Joseph 57;Mary 57;Thomas 57;
 William 57
CLAYCOMB Frederick 59
CLEMENTS David 93;William 93
CLIFFEN Joshua 51
CLINE Eleanor 53;William G. 53
COBB John 83
CODY David 44
COFFMAN see Coughman
COLDREN Major 146
COLLETT see Cullett
COLLINS Mary 23-131;Samuel 131
COLTRAN John 144
COLWELL see Calwell;John 26-30-
 34-71
COMBS Hannah 40;Nelson 40
COMINGORE see Bomingon

CONNELLY family 29
CONRAD George B. 62
COOK Jeremiah H. 24
COOKSEY Margaret 68
COONS John, Sr. 5
CORWINE Ruth 132
CORYA Stephen 10
COUCH Jane 25;John 25;Lois 25;
  Prudence 25
COUGHMAN Mary Ann 16
COVERT Peter 144
CRAIG Daniel T. 151;Sarah 62
CRAWFORD Martha 145;William
  144-145
CRIDER John 27;Rebecca 27
CROAKS John 6;Naomi 6
CROSS Letitia 24
CRUM John 8;Rachel 8
CRUSE Alison 30-71
CULLETT John 99
CULLY Elizabeth 48
CULVER Aaron 52;Casander 52
CUMMINGS Thomas 145
CUNNINGHAM Elizabeth 145;
  Nathaniel 145;Pelina 51
CURRANT James 145
CURRIN James 145
CURRY William 26
CURTISS Arthur 38
CUSBOTT see Casbolt
CUTSHAW Samuel 79

DAILY Eleanor 9;Ephraim 145-149
DANIEL Buckner 142
DAVIS Catharine 107;Ebenezer
  27;Elizabeth 72;Forrest 41;
  James 107;John 27-34-50-51;
  Joseph 145;Lodowick 41;Loisa
  132;Luther M.,Sr. 7;Margaret
  107;Peter 107
DAVISON James 28
DAWDEN see Dowden; Mr. 46;
  Sarah 46
DAWSON Isaac 147;Sicha 147
DEAN Joshua 77;Susan 77
DEAVER William 145
DECKER Luke 11;Moses 11
DEMAREST Antie 10;Catharine
  92;Rachel 92
DEMOSS Andrew 28;Catharine 101;
  Reuben 13
DENBO Joseph 28;Robert 28
DENNIS Lucina 24

DICKENSON Waitsell 145
DICKERSON John 29
DIXON George 29;John 29;Peter 29
DOANE Jacob 145
DORSEY James 7
DOUGHMAN Elizabeth 23;Jacob 23;
  Mary A. 23
DOUGLAS Edward 35;Mary Ann 134;
  Thomas 24
DOW Henry 64
DOWDEN see Dawden;John 54;Mary
  54;Rebecca 54-82
DOWNEY Mr. 43;Katherine 43
DRAIN Mr. 75;Fanny 75
DUBOIS Rebecca 33
DUNAGAN Thomas 30
DUNCAN Charles 50;Robert 50
DUNGAN see Duncan
DUNN George G. 52;James 104;
  Susan 104
DURFEY James 7
DURHAM Ann 30;William 26-30-71
DURIE Mary Magdalena 10;Samuel 10
DURSEY James 7
DUTTERO Jacob,146
DUVALL Polly 136

EAGELTON Alexander 30-71
EARLY Esther 111
EATON Christina 131
ECSTINE Leonard 58;Margaret 58
EDWARDS Delila 143;Elizabeth 32;
  William 143
ELKINS Shadrack 119
ELLIOTT Isabella 43
ELROD Elizabeth 113;Stephen 113
ELSBURY Elizabeth 150
EMERSON Miss 77
ENDECOTT Joseph 133
ENGLISH William H. 75
ETCHINSON James 42
EULE John 69
EULEZ John 69
EVANS John 32;Rosa 115
EWEN Julius 32

FAGAN Mr. 104
FANCHER William 118
FARR Nicholas 74
FARRISS Thomas 32
FEAMSTER Margaret 116:William 116
FELLOWS Willis 146
FERBY E.E. 146
FERGUSON Andrew 95;Catharine 95;

FERGUSON Elizabeth 65; John 65; Kinard 95;Martha E.65; Rebecca 108;Sarah E. 65
FENNER Juliana 70
FERRIS,SEE Farriss;John 97; Susannah 97
FINDLEY David 146
FINLEY David 146;Miriam 146
FINN Juliana 33
FISLAR John 80;Sophia 80
FITTS Henry 17;Jacob 17; Susan 17
FITZGERALD Daniel 35
FLOWERS Prudence 108
FLOYD Emeraine 65;Mary 65
FOGELSONG George 78;John 78; Mary 78
FONTINE Leah 92
FONTZ John 153;Sarah 153
FOOTE George 91;Newton 36; William 36
FORBES Jane 77
FORD Elizabeth 64;Warner 64
FOREMAN Phebe 133
FOSTER Eliza 153
FRAVEL Mr. 43;Sophia 43
FRAZEE Jonas 10
FRAZIER John 136;Rebecca 136
FRICKER Sophia 131
FRIEND Sarah 111
FROMAN Christina 25
FULTON Robert 58

GADDIS Priscilla 40;Thomas 40
GAITHER Rachel 54-82
GALLAMORE John 49
GALLEMORE Richard 6
GALLION see Gullion;Thomas 38
GALLOWAY Jonathan N. 38
GALYEAN see Gallion
GARNER Thomas 49
GARRETT see Garriott; Mr. 76-142;Alice 142;Nancy 48;Polly 48;Robert 70;Sarah V. 76
GASAWAY Elizabeth 86;Margaret 86;Nicholas 86;Thomas 86
GEARHART Elizabeth 138
GEORGE Elizabeth 89-137;John 40
GIBSON Elizabeth 78
GIFT William 33
GILBERT Michael 28
GILES Mr. 153;Juliet 153; Polly 15
GILL Nancy 63;William 95

GILLILAND John 146
GILMORE Lucinda 54
GILSTRAP Effee 27;John 27
GOARE see Gore
GOE Elizabeth R. 115;Hezekiah M. 115;William 115
GOLD see Gould
GOLDSMITH family 29
GOODING see Goodwin
GOODWIN John 53;Mary 53
GOOLD see Gould
GORE Mary 54;Sally 22
GOTH Catharine 92
GRAHAM Elizabeth 23
GRANT Phoebe 104;Smith 41; William 41-104
GRAY Job 95
GRAYBILL John 59;Margaret 59
GREEN Malinda 40
GREGG Johnson 21
GREGORY Abram 95
GRIFFIN Mr. 18;Nancy 18
GRIFFITH Amos 146;Joseph 146; Samuel J. 147
GRIMES James 67;John 67
GROSS William 24
GROVES David 59;Mary Jane 59
GUFFY James 98
GULLION see Gallion;Jackson 147; John 111-147

HAAS Ezra 43;John 43
HADDON David 43;Esther 43
HAGAN John C. 58;Rosanna 58
HAGGERTY Henderson 76;Temperance 76
HAINES Eliza P. 70;Job 70
HAIRSTON Peggy 78
HALEY Hugh 48
HALL Judge 100;Benajah 119;Benjamin 119;Elizabeth 52;Felix 134;George W. 119;John 44-52; Lewis 119;Margaret 119;Mary 72-134-136;Raynier 47;Simon 119; William 52-136
HALTOM Joseph 84;Mary 84; Wm. 84
HAMBLEN Job 57
HAMER James 44
HAMES James 44
HAMILTON Hannah 48
HAMMOND Thomas 74
HAMPSON Mary Catharine 115
HANDLIN Matthias 147
HANNEGAN E.A. 50

HARBIN Elizabeth 108;Joshua 108;Massey 108;Sarah 11
HARD Sarah 131
HARDEN Mr. 90;Elizabeth 54; Margaret 90;Mason 90
HARDING see Harden
HARLIN Jane 97
HARNER see Hamer
HARNES see Haines
HARNESS Sarah 108
HARNEY Elizabeth 119;Sarah 27; Shelby 27
HARPER Catharine 101;Eliza Ann 43;Henry 43;James 26;Margaret 26;Mary 101;Samuel 101
HARRIS see Harrison
HARROD Mary 86;Samuel 86
HARROLD Mary 25
HARTLEY David 47;Hugh 47
HARVEY*Caleb;Cassandra 138; Elizabeth 119;Sarah 6*
HASS*Azuba; see Haas;James 104*
HATTON Mr. 44;Amy 44
HAWLEY Samuel 147;Sarah 137
HAYMOND John 47
HEATH Lucy 116;Samuel 116; Sarah Elizabeth 116
HEATON Elizabeth 142;Leada 142
HEDELSTON see Huddleston
HENDRICKS Sarah 15
HENDRIX Irena 27;John 27
HENLEY Thomas 65
HENNING Angelo E. 14;Barbara Ellen 14
HENRY Hannah 48;John 48;Moses 48-147;Patrick 145;Sarah 145
HENSLEY Elizabeth 48;George 48;Jane 38;John 38;Rachel 38; Richardson 38;Samuel 48; Sarah 48;William R. 46
HENSON Jeremiah 49;Jesse 50-119;John 119;Joseph 49;Wm.119
HETRICK Jacob 6;Margaretta 6
HEWARD Lydia 45
HIATT Messick 50;Samuel 50
HICKEY Nancy 85
HIGGS Samuel 147
HILLY Hugh 48
HINCKLEY Genet 50;Seth 50
HINES John 50
HINKLEY W.C. 50
HISER Anna Margaret 78
HOBBS Robert 51
HODGEN Miss 97;Robert 97

HOGG Isabella 26;Polly 26
HOGGATT Moses 51;William 51
HOLIDAY Elizabeth 60;William 60
HOLLENBECK Mary 47
HOLLINGSWORTH Mr. 97;Rebecca 97
HOLLOWAY Levi 21
HOLMAN Catharine 82;Eda 82;Isaac 54-82;Mary 54
HOLMES James 104;Sarah 104
HOLT Mr. 47;Dorcas 47;John 47
HOOVER David 100;Elizabeth 100
HOPKINS Francis 75;Mary 75
HOUGHLAND Henry 92;Rachel 92
HOUSTON Samuel 52
HOWARD Andrew 45;Elizabeth 32; Nancy 45
HOWELL John 36;Nancy 36
HUDELSON John M. 53
HUFF Peter 100
HUGHES Andrew 86;Nancy 86
HUNGERFORD Lemuel 61
HUNT Mr. 136;Jane 136;Joseph 53
HUNTER Elizabeth 134;James 32; Joseph 134;William 32
HUTCHERSON Sarah 48
HUTCHINSON Lydia 133
HYATT see Hiatt

INDIAN Robin 67
INGLE Sarah 26
IRELAND James 79
ISEMINGER Jacob 87;Nancy 87

JACKSON Ebenezer 116
JACOBS Jeremiah 54-82;John 76; Martha 82;Rachel 54;Rebecca 82
JEBINE Mr. 147
JENKINS Catharine 63;David 29; Hannah 29
JENNINGS Jonathan 99
JOB Thomas 42
JOHN Joanna 146
JOHNSON David 27-56;Ebenezer 56; Elizabeth 36;Gen. W. 147;George 14-147;Henry 53;Jane Elizabeth 53;Nancy 96;Sally 116
JOHNSTON Constant 14;Dorothy 14; Elizabeth 119;General W. 119-147;Joseph 13;Mehitable 13;Seth 14;Thankful 13
JONES Ann 19;Betsy 57;Cad 57; David 57;Godfrey 57;Griffin 57; James 19;John 57;Joseph 57;Lewis 57;Mary 131;Otis 83;Sarah 45;
                Susannah 86

JORDAN Frank 115;Hester Ann 115;Margaret 11
JOY James 64

KARNES see Carnes
KEEN William C. 44
KEESUCKER William 59
KELLER Catharine 58;Charles 58
KENDALL Mr. 68;Barbara 68
KENNEY Daniel 147
KERNEY Elizabeth 148
KEYSACKER Aaron 59;Mary 59
KILES John 148
KINDER Peter 15;Sally 15
KING Arra 60;Mary 74;Sally 5
KIRBY Richard 17
KIRKHAM Sarah 40
KIRKPATRICK John 53;Sarah 53
KISLER Philip 52
KITCHEN Elizabeth 25
KLEPINGER Mary Jane 59
KNOWLES Nathan 115;Temperance 115
KRIDER see Crider
KURTZ Sarah 43
KYLE John 148

LACKEY Mary E. 76
LAMB Hannah 38;James 61;Mahulda 38;Thomas 38
LAMPKIN Edward 10;Lucy 10
LANCASTER Sarah 131
LANCASTER William 131
LANE Joseph 15
LARGENT Catharine 62;Randall 62;Samuel 62;William 62
LASHBROOKS John 148;William 148
LASSELLE Hyacinth 148
LAWRENCE see Lorance;Mr. 23; Elizabeth 23;George 23;Polly 23;Sarah 101
LAWSON James 16
LAY Abraham 9;Mary 9
LAYCOCK Rachel 104
LEACH Eliza 113
LEATCH Mr. 10;Susan 10
LEDGERWOOD James 119;Rebecca 63;William 63
LEE Charles G. 54;Eleanor 64; John 64;Joseph 64;Margaret 64; Maria 54;William 8
LEFEVERS Abraham 17;Molly 17
LEHBERG see LeMountain
LELL Mary 102
LEMAN Nancy 63; see Lemon

LEMASTERS Abraham 137;Martha 137
LEMON see Leman;Mr. 43;see Lemmon
LEMMON Alexander 111;Christina 43;Elias 65;Martha 65
LeMOUNTAIN John 95
LEONARD Charlotte 78
LEVI Isaac 74
LEVINSTON George 79;Jane 79
LEWELLYN Nancy 142
LEWIS George 12;Hannah 38
LINDSEY John 14
LINGENFELTER Catharine 66
LISMAN James 63;Margaret 63
LITTLETON Charles 17;Mark 17; Savage 17
LLOYD see Loyd
LOCKWOOD Thomas 66
LONG Samuel 66
LONGWELL Ruth 78
LOOKEY James 103;Thomas 103
LOOMER Lucy 138
LORANCE William 61
LORE Andrew 46;Henry 46
LOVELL John 132;Sarah 132
LOW Matilda 75;Nelus 67;Woodbeck 75
LOWE William 148
LOWDERBACK Andrew 104;Nancy 104
LUCAS Abram 40;Elizabeth 40, William H. 45
LUCKY see Lookey
LUTHER Jacob 65
LYNCH David 98;Elizabeth 137; Hannah 98
LYNN Craven 36;Judge 36;Martha 36

McABEE Mr. 81;Margaret 81
McAFEE Miss 26
McALISTER Jane 70-71
McANNELLY Peter 95
McARTHUR James 148
McBRIDE Ezekiel 44;Mary 44
McCARROLL Lettice 87
McCARTHY Mr. 62;Nancy 62
McCARTNEY John 103
McCLAY Catharine 70;Eleanor 70; Jane 70;John 70;Samuel 70
McCLURE Eliza Ann 43;Jane 26; John 26;John Alexander 43;Mary 26;Samuel 26
McCOSKEY Robert 154
McCOUN Elizabeth 63;James 63; Margaret 63
McCRARY Polly 115
McCRAY Alexander 97;Drusilla 97

McCULLY John 149
McCUTCHEON Alexander 7
McDANIELS Nancy 104
McGAHEY William 41
McGILL William 69
McINLIN Mary 134
McKAY Mr. 62;Abisha 62-85;
  Mary 62;Milley 62;Rebecca 85;
  Sarah 62;Zachariah 62
McKINLEY Samuel 73
McKINNEY family 29;Robert 149
McKNIGHT Catharine 71;Charles
  M. 71;David 71;Eleanor 71;
  John,Sr. 70;William 71
McMAHAN Peter 107
McNEELEY Isaac 27;John 27;
  Levi 27;Nancy 27
McNULTY John 149
McNUTT John 48;Mahala 48
McROBERTS Andrew 23
McWHORTER Jane 6;Robert 6;
  William 71

Maclay see McClay
MACON Joseph 30-71
MADDEN see Maden;William 99
MADEN Nancy 13;Polly 13
MALLINCOAT Elizabeth 66;John 66
MALONE Francis 5;Leslie 5
MANCHESTER Avis 29;Benjamin 29;
  Nancy 29
MANN Ormon 71
MANSFIELD James 8;Mary 8
MARS Alexander 42
MARSHALL Hugh 136;Rebecca 136
MARTIN Jesse 15;John 149
MARTINDALE Elizabeth 142;
  James 142
MASON Daniel 6;Debby 6
MASSEY Thomas 72
MATTHEWS Jessie 92
MATNEY Thomas 51
MATTS Isaac 118
MAYS James 60
MEADOWS Mary 116;Sarah 116;
  William 116
MEADS William 42-43
MECK Mr. 43;Lydia 43
MEREDITH Lucy 87;Samuel 29
MERRICLE Mary 29
MERRY Charlotte 131;Ebenezer 131
MILES Evan 83;Hannah 83;Isaac
  83;Margaret 108

MILHOLLAND Margaret 76
MILLER Barney 59-73;Daniel 27;
  Jacob 102;James 73;Mary 59-102;
  Nicholas 73;William 149
MITCHELL Joseph 149
MIZNER Demarquis 47
MODERELL Andrew 149;George 149
MOFFETT Samuel 145-149
MONTFORT Susan 8
MONTGOMERY Julia Ann 76
MOODY Rebecca 63
MOORE Joseph 149;Rosannah 102;
  Susan R. 93
MORGAN Elizabeth 48-153;Mary
  153;Nancy 42
MORRIS Bethuel F. 79
MORRISON Flora 18;James 94
MOSES Henry 147-149
MOUNTS Thomas 64
MUNDAY Elizabeth 56
MUNDEN P.T. 56
MURPHY Rebecca 131;Robert 33

NANN Lucretia 36
NASH America 43;Virginia 43
NEAL Campbell 21
NEWELL Samuel 149
NEWKIRK Agnes Anna 76;Henry 76
NEWLAND Peter 45;Susan 45
NEWTON Basil 72;Mary 72;Mary P.77
NICEWANDER see Nighswonger
NICHOLLS Lucy 46;Thomas 46
NICHOLSON Benjamin 20(2);David
  D. 20;Henry W. 20;Peter J. 20;
  William M. 20
NIGHSWONGER Jemima 117;Solomon 117
NIGHTEVER Abraham 17;Caty 17;
  Elizabeth 17;Frederick 17;Sarah
  17;Susan 17
NORRIS Joseph 149

OARD see Ord; Mr. 18;Susan 18
OGDEN Stephen 149
OLDWEILER Elizabeth 54
ORD see Oard;Sarah 18
OSBORN Pamelia 76
OWEN Edward 47;Eleanor 47
OWENS Charles 78;John 78

PARKER Abigail 77;Edmund 16
PARKS James 154
PARR Arthur 153;Mary 153;Susannah 153
PATRICK Mary 54;William 54

PATTERSON Mary 43;William M.43
PAUL George 59-73
PAYNE James 80
PAYTON see Peyton;Valentine 82
PEA Elizabeth F. 11
PECK Eleanor 74
PENQUITE Agnes 101
PERKINS Dicy 39
PERRY John 66;Nancy 66;Saml.66
PETERS Elizabeth 62
PETRE Mary 45
PEYTON see Payton;Mr. 10;Elizabeth 10
PHELPS Epaheras 66;Susanna 66
PHILIPS Mr. 52;Susan 52
PIERCE Richard 43;Virginia 43
PIETY Elizabeth 43
PINCHBACK Miss 54
PINDELL Rachel 134
PITTMAN Benjamin 81
POINDEXTER Robert 64
POLLARD William 94
POPE Elijah 57
PORTER Nicholas 82;Polly 38; Rhoda Jane 97
POSEY Thomas 99
POTONGER Robert 150
PRATHER Basil 54-82;Martha 54; Walter 54
PREBLE James 99-100
PRICE Stephen 64
PRIDDY Ann 48
PRIDMORE Jonathan 82
PRIEST Mr. 62;Lucy 62
PROTZMAN Flora 18;Polly 18; William 18
PURDY John 16
PURKHEISER Dawson 57
PURSELL William 10

RAINEY James 84;John 84; Joseph 84; see Raney
RAINS Anthony 50;Elizabeth 153; James 153
RAMEY Frederick 58;Martha 58
RANDEL Rachel 142
RANEY see Rainey;Jeremich 84
RANKINS Daniel 104;Eleanor 104
RAZOR Mr. 87;Nancy 87
REAUGH David 97;Mary 97
REDMON Nancy 82
REDWINE Mr. 81;Ellender 81
REECE Jehu 150
REED Ruth 40;William 40;Henry 37

REEDER Jesse 70;Mary 70
REEL Henry 85
REESE Jehu 150
REMY see Ramey
REES Esther 58;Joel 58
REISTER Elizabeth 106;John 106
RENO Presley 119
REUBLE family 29
REUTER Mr. 43;Harriet 43
REYNOLDS Rachael 51
RHOADS Daniel 150
RICHARDSON Sarah 48
RIGGS Isaac 81;Moses 81
RISINGER Sally 58
RISK Mary Ann 97
RITCHEY Rachel 27;Solomon 27
RITTER Elizabeth 143
ROBERDS see Roberts 142;Mary 142; Thomas 142
ROBERTS see Roberds;Harriet 9; Henly 86;Hezekiah 22;Mary 39; Moses Perry 85;Nehemiah 85-86; Phineas 142;Sarah 142;Will. 150
ROBERTSON see Robinson;Chloe 82; Chlorinda 82;Lucy 51;Robert 86
ROBESON see Robinson
ROBIN Indian 67
ROBINS Azuba 104;Rachel 92;William 92
ROBINSON see Robertson;Agnes 85; Elizabeth 40;Martha 31;Stephen 31
RODGERS Alexander 7;Elizabeth 7
RODIN James 148
ROGERS see Rodgers;David 87; Nelson 45
ROSE Mary 134;William 150
ROSEBERRY Mary 116
ROSENER Rose M. 145
ROSS George 146
ROUSE Mary 111
ROW William 151
RUBISON John S. 87;Jonah L. 87; Rice M. 87;Thomas J. 87
RUBLE Indiana 153
RUMINER Daniel 88
RUMINGHER John 88
RUNION William 103
RUSSELL Anna 23;Elijah 103;Elizabeth 102;John 23-150;Samuel 102
RUST David 150
RUTHERFORD Susannah 137
RUTLEDGE Daniel 54; E.B. 54
RYKER Gerardus 92; Leah 92

SACREY Elizabeth 89;Isaac 89
SADLER Mr. 62;Chloe 62
SALYERS Sallie 92
SANGSTER Thomas 95;George 95
SAUNDER Jacob 52
SCAATS see Skeets 151
SCATES see Skeets 151
SCHRUM John L. 1-2
SCHULTHEIS Mrs. Leo 2
SCOTT Elizabeth 46;John 93; Rebecca 43;Sally 108;Samuel 150;Thomas 43;William 46-108
SCROGGS Sarah 138
SCUITTS see Skeets 151
SEARS Molly 114
SEATON Lucy 96
SEBURN Catharine 92;Cornelius 92;John V. 92;Mary 92
SEELY Elizabeth 5
SELBY Ann Wilson 74;Richard 74
SELLERS Ruhama 153
SHANNON George 90
SHAVER Jacob 150
SHAW James 150;John 151;Sarah 151
SHAWHAN Elizabeth 86
SHEARER Mary 48
SHELDON Ichabod 90;Isaac 90
SHEPHERD Elizabeth 6;Patsey 85; Solomon 6
SHINGLEDECKER Isaac 18;Jemima 18
SHIPMAN Benjamin 58;Margaret 58
SHIRLEY Catharine 113;Henry 113 William 145-149
SHUCK Agnes 10;Mary Magda. 10
SHUE Israel 24;Letitia 24
SHY Levi 27;Susannah 27
SILVERS Julia 43
SIMMINS Eliza 82
SIMONTON Margaret 102
SINGLETON W.G. 15
SKAATS see Skeets 151
SKAITS see Skeets 151
SKATTS see Skeets 151
SKEETS Harriet 151;James 151-152
SLATER Jane 150
SMALL Mr. 78;Mary 78;Nancy 78
SMARTWOOD see Swartwood
SMITH Mr. 113;Andrew 45-76;John 36;Margaret 45-113;Mary 142; Olner H.79;Robert 87;Sarah V. 76;Tamar 142;Thomas 61
SMOCK Ann 92;John 92;Leah 92

SOPER Patience 143
SOURWINE Jacob.60
SPAHR John 29;Sabra 29
SPEAKS family 86;Eleanor 86; Elizabeth 86;Hezekiah 86
SPEAR Mr. 10;Anna 10
SPERRY Rachel 104;Samuel G. 104
SPICKLEMORE Abram 89
SPILLERS Elizabeth 74;Philip 74; Thomas 74-75
SPIVEY Mr. 102;Margaret 102
SPRINGER Polly 108
St. CLAIR General 101
STANSBURY John 104;Rebecca 104
STARBUCK Elizabeth 134;Rebecca 134
STARNES Joseph 32
STARR Barbara 58;Jane 27;Jeremiah 58;Jesse 33;Samuel 27; Zervian 58
STARRS Richard 51
STEAN John 113
STEELE Ninian 152;Samuel 152
STEPHEN see Stiffey
STEPHENS Mr. 10;Catharine 22; Eliza 10;John 50;Robert 50; William 22
STEVENSON see Stinson;Miss 65
STIFFEY Isaac 46;Peter 46
STILWELL Jacob L. 42
STINNETT Mary A. 96
STINSON Elijah 149;Isaac 94;John 94;William 94
STIPE Frederick 88
STOCKSLAGER Alexander 58;Esther 58
STOKEY see Stuckey
STONE Delilah 62;Eva 62;Jane 9; Nimrod H.62;Sarah 62;William 9
STOUT Sally 87
STRATTON Persia 71
STROTHER Daniel 65
STUART Isabella 15
STUCKEY Catharine 84;Martin 84; Samuel 85
STURGEON Susan 78;Susannah 78; William 78
SULLIVAN Drusilla 97;William 97
SUMMEY Caroline Delila 153;John 153
SWAN John 55
SWARTWOOD John 101
SWARTZ Elizabeth 54;John 54
SWINDELL Willis 95
SWINGLE Mr. 81;Susannah 81
SWOPE Joseph 29

TACKETT Lewis 152
TAFF James 47
TAYLOR Mr. 51;Bailie 154;Cassandra 138;Daniel 96;David 51;Esther 33;James Loudon 33; Julia Anna 76;Mary 33;Sarah 51;Silas 152;Wright 138
TEGARDEN Mr. A. 146;Miriam 146
TELL Mary 102
TEMPLETON Jane 68
THACHER family 29
THARP see Thorp;Lois 24
THOMAS Mr. 75;Ann Wilson 74; David 108;Eleanor 74;Elizabeth 74;Mahala 75
THOMPSON Elijah 15;Elizabeth 23;Jesse W.99;John 33-39-98; Robert 99;William 98
THOMSON Archibald 57;Margaret 57
THORN Cassandra 46;Michael 38-46-108;Zenion 99
THORNTON Mr. 23;Nancy 23
THORP Lois 23
THRASHER Mary 100
THURSTON Lucretia 76
TILFORD James 152
TILLINGHAST John 152
TINDALL Elizabeth 17;John 17; Samuel 17
TODD John B. 144;Mary 143; Nancy 45
TONG Eleanor 104-136
TOOTHMAN Jacob 152
TOWNSEND Celia 142;John 142
TRANTER Elizabeth 100
TRINE Margaret 107;Peter 107
TRIPLETT Daniel 36;Hedgman 22, Polly 22
TUCKER Alexander 86;Cassandra 86;Edward 86;Eleanor 86; Elizabeth 86;Nancy 86;Sarah 86
TURNER Jane S.70;Juliana 70; Ralph 70
TURPEN Mary 39
TYLER see Taylor

UMBARGER Anna 66;John 66

VANARSDALL Cornelius 100
Van BLARICUM Mary 71-72
Van BUSKIRK see Buskirk;Isaac 20
VANCE Agnes 101;David 101;Samuel 101;Samuel Colville 101
Van NISE Nancy 10
VAUGHN Nancy 39;Rebecca 39
VEAL Campbell 21
VINNEDGE Adam 73;Margaret 102; Mary 73;William 102
VOSS Tarquina 45

WALKER Mr. 14;Hannah 14;Margaret 63;Sally 40
WALTERS Rachel 29;William 29
WARD Katie-Prince 1-2;Rebecca 104
WARREN James 38;Sophia 38;Tabitha 38
WARRENTON Alexander 21
WASHBURN George 136;Eleanor 136
WATERS Mary Ann 101
WATSON John 105;Sarah 11-26; William 11-105
WATTERHOUSE Hannah 131
WAUGH John 113
WAYMAN Charles L.6;Edmond 6
WEBB Abel 106;Joseph 106;Mary 11
WEIDNER Isabella 43;John 43
WEIR family 29
WELCH James 64
WELLER Elizabeth 76;John 76;Margaret 58
WEST James 115;Ruth 115
WESTBROOK Samuel 101
WESTFALL Abel 108-153;Abraham 46-153;Cornelius 108-153;Isaac 108-153;Jacob 108-153;John 108-153;Massa 46;Sarah 108-153
WHEELER Thankful M. 10
WHITACRE John 109
WHITE Agnes Anna 76;Alb. T. 12; Isaac 10;John 13;Olive 10
WHITMORE Daniel 153;Jenny 153
WHITTAKER John 109
WILCOX Catharine 82
WILHOIT Jesse 39;Margaret 39
WILLIAMS family 147;Mr. 136; Elizabeth 136
WILLYARD John 111
WILMETH William 107
WILSON Charles 81-102; Elizabeth 111;Frances 111;Isabel 111; James 111;John 111;Noah 111; Robert F.111;Samuel 111-145-149; William 111;William J.111
WINCHELL Elizabeth Ann 45;Mary 111;Peter 45;Stephen 111
WINGATE Cassandra 118;John 118
WITHERO Mrs. 62

WITT Elizabeth 33; John Daniel 33
WITTERS David 78;Elizabeth 78
WOOD Agnes 33;Ebenezer 29; George W. 33
WOODFON Sarah 47
WOODRUFF Phebe 93
WOODSON Sarah 47
WOODWORTH Dyer 76;Keturah 76; Riley 76
WOOLCOTT Augustus 112;Charles 112;Joseph 119;Norman 112
WOOLEN Nancy 134
WRIGHT Elizabeth 153;Evans 50; Mollie 29-114;Philburd 114-153;Richard 153;Sarah 114-153;William 49-64-153
WYATT Jeremiah 154
WYMAN Anna 113;Henry 113; Jane 113;Lewis 113;Noah 113; Samuel 113

YARBERRY Mr. 13
YOAST Malinda 76;Zeala 76
YORK Aquilla 113;Jerry 50; Shubel 50
YOST see Yoast
YOUNG James 154;Jane 44; John G. 79;John L. 64
YOUNGS Benjamin Seth 118(2)

ZUMBRUM Hetty 78

www.ingramcontent.com/pod-product-compliance
Lightning Source LLC
Chambersburg PA
CBHW070401240426
43661CB00056B/2488